Supply Chain Risk Management

Yacob Khojasteh
Editor

Supply Chain Risk Management

Advanced Tools, Models, and Developments

Springer

Editor
Yacob Khojasteh
Graduate Program in Business and
Development Studies
Sophia University
Tokyo
Japan

ISBN 978-981-10-4105-1 ISBN 978-981-10-4106-8 (eBook)
DOI 10.1007/978-981-10-4106-8

Library of Congress Control Number: 2017933853

Printed on acid-free paper

This Springer imprint is published by Springer Nature
The registered company is Springer Nature Singapore Pte Ltd.
The registered company address is: 152 Beach Road, #21-01/04 Gateway East, Singapore 189721, Singapore

Preface

Supply chains today are vulnerable to disruptions with a significant impact on firms' business and performance. The aim of supply chain risk management is to identify the potential sources of risks and implement appropriate actions in order to mitigate supply chain disruptions.

This book presents a set of models, frameworks, strategies, and analyses that are essential for managing supply chain risks. It contributes by combining theoretical findings and research results with a practical and contemporary view on how companies can manage the supply chain risks and disruptions, as well as how to create a resilience supply chain. The book provides the state-of-the-art developments in managing supply chain risks from various perspectives. It can be used as an essential source for students and scholars who are interested in pursuing research or teaching courses in the rapidly growing area of supply chain risk management. It also provides an interesting and informative read for managers and practitioners who need to deepen their knowledge on effective supply chain risk management.

Structured in a modular fashion, each chapter in this book introduces and analyzes a specific topic on supply chain risk management, allowing readers to identify the chapters that relate to their interests. More specifically, the book is presented in three sections: (1) supply chain risk management, (2) supply chain vulnerability and disruptions management, and (3) toward a resilient supply chain.

The first two sections of the book focus on risk and disruption management in supply chains that provide related concepts, tools, and newly developed models, while the third section focuses on resiliency in supply chains and a firm's ability to return to its original state after a disruption occurs.

In Chap. 1, Zohreh Khojasteh-Ghamari and Takashi Irohara present a comprehensive review on supply chain risk management, and investigate recent research developments in the field. They summarize previous review papers in the field of supply chain risk management, followed by reviewing the recently published related works. Also, they develop a framework to categorize those papers, and present the observed pattern of the research in supply chain risk management. In Chap. 2, Abroon Qazi, John Quigley and Alex Dickson address the decision problem of ranking supply chain risk mitigation strategies and introduce a new method for prioritizing those strategies based on associated cost and effectiveness. They develop a framework using Bayesian Belief Networks and demonstrate its application via numerical experiments. The proposed framework can help managers and practitioners select a best combination of strategies considering the efforts involved in implementing and managing such strategies. In Chap. 3, Kristian Rotaru and Mehrdokht Pournader develop a model for risk emergence and propagation in buyer–supplier–customer relationships and identify and formalize the structural and relational patterns. They categorize the identified generic patterns reflecting the emergence and propagation of potential adverse events and behaviors within buyer–supplier–customer service triads into a comprehensive typology. By an example, they illustrate how the methodological approach underlying the proposed typology facilitates risk assessment in service triads and service networks.

Chapters 4 and 5 focus on managing specific types of risks in supply chains that have not been addressed widely in the literature. In Chap. 4, Fred Lemke and Henry Petersen address reputational risks in supply chains. They discuss the nature of reputation and the related risks involved in a supply chain setting from a practical point of view by pointing out that the understanding, identifying, and mitigating reputational risks are considered as a key management task. They emphasize on corporate social responsibility as a mitigation strategy for reputational risks. In Chap. 5, Barbara Gaudenzi and Giorgia Siciliano focus on information technology and cyber risks in supply chains. They describe the potential impact of information technology and cyber risks on the continuity and vulnerabilities of a supply chain. They propose a theoretical framework that may guide managers to perceive, control, assess, and manage those risks within the supply chain. The proposed framework explores how systematic information technology and cyber risk management may enhance the ability to share information and better manage supply chain processes.

Chapter 6 presents an overview of supply chain risk management by focusing on Japanese companies. In this chapter, I first describe the different types of potential risks in supply chains, and then provide some examples of disruptions in Japanese supply chains caused by the Great East Japan earthquake in 2011. I also outline some strategies and developments on how to mitigate supply chain disruptions in case of a natural disaster. Finally, I introduce a supply chain risk management software developed by Fujitsu.

The second section of the book continues on managing supply chain risks by focusing on vulnerability and disruption management. Jyri Vilko and Lauri Lättilä begin the section with a chapter that analyzes supply chain vulnerability through simulation. They present a conceptual framework to examine the feasibility of using simulation methods for analyzing supply chain vulnerability. They develop and test a discrete event simulation model to reduce the overall vulnerability, and show how it can be used to gain a more holistic view of supply chain vulnerability. In the next chapter (Chap. 8) Amit Sonar and Cameron MacKenzie use a dynamic model to measure the supply chain disruptions preparedness. They analyze different disruption scenarios by considering the impacts of disruptions at a supplier, the firm's production facility, and a firm's warehouse. They use Wagner–Whitin model to solve the optimal ordering strategy for each type of disruption. Chapter 9 analyzes market response when a disruption occurs in the supply chain. In this chapter, Arun Vinayak and Cameron MacKenzie develop a quantitative model that represents the way the customer or marketplace reacts to a supply chain disruption. They analytically interpret the impact of different customer behaviors in such conditions on the firm's post-disruption performance.

In Chap. 10, Artur Swierczek develops a framework for risk management in supply chains that aims at mitigating negative consequences of the transmission and amplification of disruptions. The framework includes identification of potential and actual disruptions, estimation of disruptions, evaluation of the most appropriate approach to deal with those disruptions, and the application of the mitigating strategy. In Chap. 11, Prasanna Venkatesan and Mark Goh address strategic sourcing issue under supply disruption risk. They present a mixed integer linear programming model for supplier selection and order quantity allocation for the suppliers. By applying the particle swarm optimization technique, the model minimizes the expected total cost which includes supplier management cost, raw material purchase cost, and expected supplier loss. In Chap. 12 the last chapter of this section, Yasutaka Kainuma presents a model that considers disruption risk in designing and evaluating global supply chains. He addresses an important issue in supply chain risk management since disruptions caused by natural disasters have become a serious problem in global supply chains. A mathematical model is developed with the objective function of maximizing total profit, and several key factors are considered and discussed.

The last section in the book focuses on supply chain resiliency which represents the ability of a firm to return to its original state, within an acceptable period of time, after a disruption occurs. The first chapter of the section provides a broad overview of the field of supply chain resiliency. In this chapter, Srinivasan Radhakrishnan, Benjamin Harris, and Sagar Kamarthi discuss different components that contribute to the resiliency of a supply chain. The chapter also outlines processes that are used for building resilient supply chains, and provides a unifying exploration of the various aspects and perspectives on supply chain engineering, including how they can be utilized for developing and measuring the resiliency of a supply chain. In Chap. 14, Anirban Ganguly, Debdeep Chatterjee, and Harish Rao discuss the critical phases and attributes of a resilient supply chain along with discussing important supply chain resiliency strategies. They highlight the advantages of a resilient supply chain through insightful examples from a range of industries, and discuss how firms can react effectively to negative effects of disruptions.

In Chap. 15, Sigurd Pettersen, Bjørn Asbjørnslett, and Stein Erikstad present a methodology for designing resilient service supply chains by combining system design methods with methods from risk assessment. The proposed methodology provides decision supports by reducing the vulnerabilities of the service supply chains through design actions that can increase overall supply chain resilience. In Chap. 16, Arash Azadegan and Jayanth Jayaram develop a conceptual model for resilience in supply chains using systems theory and the family resilience model.

They identify a series of organizational characteristics that combine to form supply chain resilience. Their developed model shows the inter-relationship among the building blocks of supply chain resilience as well as how they can enhance response and recovery in the case of supply chain disruptions.

In Chap. 17, Michael Braunscheidel and Nallan Suresh focus on the cultivation of supply chain agility as a risk management initiative that enables a firm to anticipate and respond rapidly to marketplace changes and disruptions in the supply chain. They propose a set of supply chain initiatives as antecedents for cultivation of agility, and identify drivers for cultivating agility in the supply chain. By conducting an empirical study, they provide a set of managerial practices as a guideline to address the cultivation of agility for both mitigation and response. In the last chapter of the book, Paolo Trucco, Boris Petrenj, and Seyoum Eshetu Birkie address resilience improvement in key resources supply chains by focusing on assessing the impact of critical infrastructure disruptions on the supply chain, the economic losses caused, and the potential effectiveness of different strategies. They use a multilevel modeling approach by combining discrete event simulation and system dynamics, and assess the economic loss impact of disruptions in critical infrastructure systems and the potential effectiveness of different strategies to improve resilience in the supply chain.

I would like to thank all the authors who have contributed to this book. Also, I would like to express my gratitude to Mr. Yutaka Hirachi and Misao Taguchi of Springer Japan for their help and support on this project.

I would also like to thank my wife Miya and sons Nima and Yuma for allowing me to devote the time necessary to complete this book. I dedicate this book to them.

Tokyo, Japan
July 2017

Yacob Khojasteh

Contents

About the Editor

Dr. Yacob Khojasteh is an Associate Professor of Operations Management at the Graduate Program in Business and Development Studies, Sophia University, Tokyo, Japan. He received his Ph.D. in Engineering from the University of Tsukuba, Japan. He also received his M.Sc. in Policy and Planning Sciences, and in Industrial Engineering from the University of Tsukuba, and Tarbiat Modares University, respectively. He has several years of professional experience in industry and consulting. His first book entitled "Production Control Systems: A Guide to Enhance Performance of Pull Systems" was published in 2016 by Springer. His research interests include production and operations management, supply chain management, systems modeling and optimization, and lean production systems.

Part I
Supply Chain Risk Management

Chapter 1
Supply Chain Risk Management: A Comprehensive Review

Zohreh Khojasteh-Ghamari and Takashi Irohara

Abstract The purpose of this chapter is to investigate recent research developments in supply chain risk management (SCRM) and to provide a comprehensive outline for researchers and practitioners who are trying to identify the existing state of research in the SCRM area. The importance of a literature review is to enhance the understanding of researchers by cataloging previous research in an area and clarifying the strengths and weaknesses of existing studies and what they might mean. Since the number of studies on SCRM has increased dramatically, several review papers of existing papers have been published. By finding significant number of review papers in the area, we convinced about the necessity of including summary of review papers. Therefore, we first summarize previous SCRM review papers. Second, we review recent papers that have not been mentioned in these review papers. Third, we develop a framework by which to categorize these papers. We conclude by presenting the observed pattern of SCRM research.

1.1 Introduction

Recently, managing risk has become a crucial challenge for supply chain managers owing to several factors, such as growing global competition, rising cost pressures, increasing customer expectations, and ever-increasing complexity (Daultani et al. 2015). Due to the increasing complexity and interrelation of modern supply chains, the type and nature of uncertain developments and the impact of an action have become difficult, or even impossible, to predict (Helbing et al. 2006). Risks and uncertainties frequently interrupt the operational efficiency of the supply chain and hence adversely impact a firm's profits (Kumar et al. 2010). A literature survey is an attempt to clarify important issues and challenges in a given field, including the

Z. Khojasteh-Ghamari (✉) · T. Irohara
Graduate School of Science and Engineering, Sophia University, Tokyo, Japan
e-mail: khojaste.z@gmail.com

Y. Khojasteh (ed.), *Supply Chain Risk Management*,
DOI 10.1007/978-981-10-4106-8_1

current status and theory development in that field (Tang and Musa 2011). Initially, we found that most recent review papers (Ho et al. 2015; Heckmann et al. 2015; Fahimnia et al. 2015) considered only supply chain risk management (SCRM) papers published prior to 2014. As such, we herein consider papers published between 2014 and 2016 and categorize them from different points of view.

Behnezhad et al. (2013) pointed out the trend towards globalization has intensified the exposure to risk and consequently enhanced the likelihood of disruption in the supply chain. Singhal et al. (2011) mentioned that SCRM is an exponentially growing area of research, the exploration of literature from a 'nature of the study' perspective identifies how the study contributes to the literature and indicates whether the study describes risk issues and proposes solutions with due analysis or, as in some cases, whether researchers prescribe solutions based on their experience and expertise. Lastly, Trkman and McCormack (2009) indicated that the literature in the field of SCRM is chaotic and disorganized.

From 2000 to 2005, although there was an increase in the number of research papers on proactively managing risk, the literature consisted of descriptive and conceptual models rather than quantitative models (Tang and Musa 2011). Sodhi et al. (2012) declared that, since SCRM is just beginning to exist, the scope of research in this field has not yet been clearly defined. Paulsson (2004) mentioned that, while only one paper dealt with SCRM in 1995, that number increased to 23 by 2002. According to Tang and Musa (2011) and Ghadge et al. (2012), a sudden increase in the number of papers published in SCRM occurred in 2004. Kamalahmadi and Parast (2015) indicated that the research for papers published in 2004 had been started in 2002 and 2003, after the September 11, 2001 attacks, which disrupted numerous supply chains around the globe. Finally, any approach to SCRM must attempt to clarify and reduce vulnerabilities to the supply chain as a whole, rather than at a focal firm level (Rao and Goldsby 2009). The remainder of this chapter is organized as follows. Section 1.2 summarizes the existing survey papers. Section 1.3 provides an explanation of the SCRM concept. Sections 1.4 reviews quantitative approaches to managing risk and categorizes papers from different point of views. Section 1.5 concludes the chapter.

1.2 Literature Review

In the following, we present a summary of key and important review papers on SCRM. Tang (2006) reviewed more than 200 papers published between 1964 and 2005 that applied quantitative models for managing supply chain risks. He classified these papers based on the supply chain management unit that was considered in dealing with risk (supply, demand, product, or information management). This review paper is the most cited review paper, with 628 citations by review papers in the field of SCRM. To the best of our knowledge, no other review paper has this many citations. In fact, it is the most cited paper over all (by both normal and review papers), among review papers. Ritchie and Brindley (2007) presented a new framework that helps to integrate the dimensions of risk and performance in supply chains and provides categorization of risk drivers. Their paper consolidates the work in an emerging strand of supply chain management. Two key challenges facing the research community are addressed: the ability to prescribe strategies to address particular risk drivers, and the interaction of risk management and performance. Rao and Goldsby (2009) reviewed 55 papers on SCRM published between 1998 and 2008. They identified a gap in terms of research dealing with the identification of risk resources within supply chains. Subsequently, they developed a typology of risk so as to enable the identification of vulnerabilities within supply chains. Narasimhan and Talluri (2009) summarized some key papers on SCRM in order to highlight it as an important area for investigation in operations and supply chain management and to present a compendium of articles that break new ground in addressing methodological and theoretical issues in dealing with SCRM. Tang and Musa (2011) conducted a literature survey analysis on 138 papers published between 1995 and 2008 and identified and classified potential risks regarding material flow, financial flow, and information flow. Sodhi et al. (2012) explored the characterization of the diversity of risk and identified three gaps: a definition gap, a process gap, and a methodology gap. In order to analyze the introduction of supply chain management in the construction industry and the investigation of risk factors affecting the implementation of supply chain management principles, Aloini et al. (2012) conducted a literature survey involving the selection and classification of approximately 140 papers. The results of their work identified a lack of construction supply chain risk management literature, which is mainly conceptual and descriptive and is focused especially on the risk assessment phase. Colicchia and Strozzi (2012) conducted a focused literature survey, investigating the process of knowledge creation, transfer, and development from a dynamic perspective within the context of SCRM. They combined a systematic literature review approach to identify the most relevant articles and citation network analysis to clarify the dynamics of the field under study. Then they applied their method to 55 papers published from 1994 to 2010. Singhal et al. (2011) provided a review that classified literature according to research approaches and key issues in SCRM. In order to investigate the fine-grained elements of diversified risks within supply chain, they presented a multi-layered top-down classification scheme. In the first layer, they considered the research approach and exploration of risk issues. In the second layer, they examined the nature of the study, research methods, orientation of risk definitions, structural elements, and the level of implementation. Finally, in the third layer, the key discriminating elements of each factor were considered and were further categorized into detailed attributes. In addition, they used a logical codification scheme employing an alphanumeric code, which can be helpful in quantitative and qualitative analysis. They further explored the literature from two very important and practical standpoints: coordination and decision making in an uncertain business environment, and implementation of SCRM for various sectors. The outcomes of these analyses have been presented in the form of propositions. In addition to describing the contributions of these studies, they also provided new insights for practical aspects of SCRM. In summary, they studied the pool of

SCRM literature focusing on coordination, decision making, and sector-wise SCRM implementation issues and derived relevant propositions. Behnezhad et al. (2013) conducted a comprehensive literature search in SCRM. Although there are a variety of risks in the supply chain, they focused on uncontrollable risks, which they categorized as (1) environmental, (2) political, and (3) economic risks. Kamalahmadi et al. (2015) investigated studies in supply chain resilience and undertook a literature survey to review literature on enterprise and supply chain resilience. They reviewed 100 publications, including journal papers, conference proceedings, and books from 2000 to 2014. They summarized their findings in several categories, including enterprise and supply chain resilience definitions, supply chain resilience principles, and supply chain resilience strategies. Based on their assessment, they presented a framework for the principles of supply chain resilience that can be used as a basis for understanding supply chain resilience. Fahimnia et al. (2015) presented a systematic review of the quantitative and analytical models (i.e., mathematical programming, optimization, and simulation modeling efforts) for managing supply chain risks. They used bibliometric and network analysis tools to generate insights that were not revealed by previous reviews on the subject. In particular, they presented a systemic mapping of the literature that identified key research clusters/topics, interrelationships, and generative research areas that have provided the field with foundational knowledge, concepts, theories, tools, and techniques. Heckmann et al. (2015) reviewed existing approaches to quantitative SCRM by focusing on the definition of supply chain risk and related concepts. As risk considerations are already deeply embedded in other fields and are partly applied in supply chain management, they conducted a wide literature analysis of risk concepts in general, and of conceptual as well as mathematical supply chain risk approaches in particular. Based on their literature review, they identified core characteristics used to define, quantify, and model risk, which can also define supply chain risk. They concluded that the modeling and quantification of supply chain risk remains a real challenge in the field of SCRM. Ho et al. (2015) reviewed 224 international journal articles on SCRM published between 2003 and 2013. They categorized all these articles according to definitions, types, factors, and SCRM methods. They proposed five common risks arising across various types of supply chains, including macro risk, demand risk, manufacturing risk, supply risk, and infrastructural risk (information risk, transportation risk, and financial risk). Another significant study by Chopra and Sodhi (2004) on SCRM was published as a book chapter that has been cited more than 1,200 times. Similar content was presented by Sodhi and Tang (2012). They stated that understanding various threats, alone and collectively, is the starting point of practical SCRM. They also mentioned the necessity of stress testing of the supply chain and tailoring reserves to improve the bottom line while confronting numerous types of supply chain risk. Upon reviewing these papers, we determined that the majority of papers published in the last decade have applied quantitative methods. As a result, we decided to concentrate on papers that employed quantitative methods.

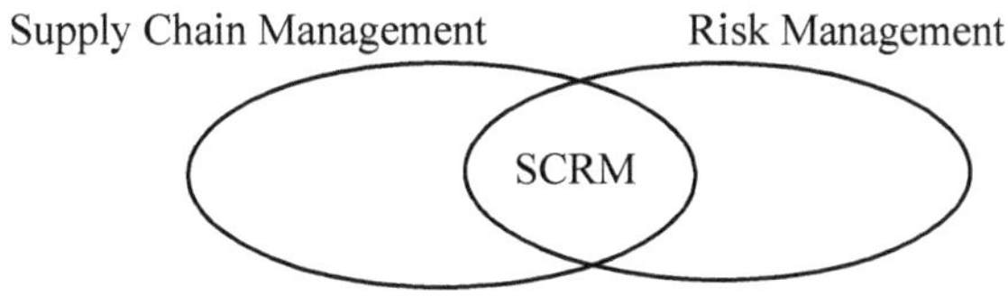

Fig. 1.1 Conceptual description of SCRM (Paulsson 2004)

1.3 Supply Chain Risk Management (SCRM)

Although numerous discussions and studies have considered the definition of SCRM, there is still no consensus on the definitions of 'supply chain risk' and 'SCRM' (Sodhi et al. 2012; Diehl and Spinler 2013). SCRM can be described as the intersection of supply chain management and risk management (Fig. 1.1).

1.3.1 Supply Chain Management

The term "supply chain management" is relatively new in the literature, first appearing in 1982 (Oliver and Weber 1982) and used to describe connecting logistics with other functions. The term was also used by Houlihan (1985, 1988) to describe the connections between logistics and internal functions and external organizations (Ellram and Cooper 2014).

A supply chain consists of all activities associated with the flow and transformation of goods from raw materials to end users. According to Ganeshan and Harrison (1995), a supply chain is a network of facilities and distribution options that performs the function of procurement of materials, transformation of these materials into intermediate and finished products, and the distribution of these finished products to customers.

1.3.2 Risk Management

Ritchie and Brindley (2007) pointed out three dimensions of risk as follows:

1. Likelihood/probability of the occurrence of particular events/outcomes;
2. Consequences/severity of the occurrence of particular events;
3. Causal pathways leading to these events (detection).

$$\text{Risk} = \text{Likelihood} \times \text{Severity} \times \text{Detection}$$

In practice, the amount of risk is usually categorized into a small number of levels because neither the probability nor the impact of the risk can typically be

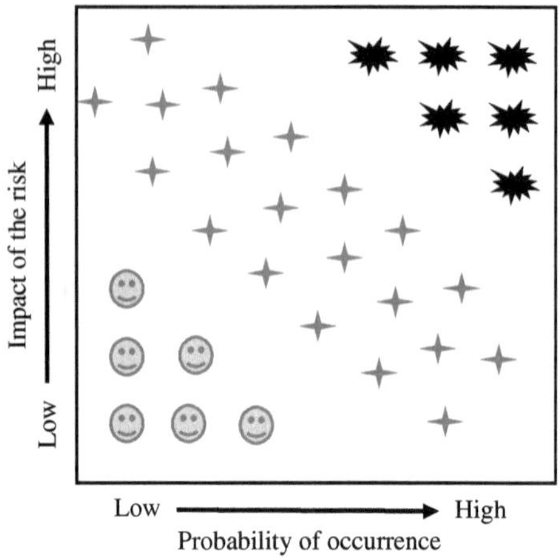

Fig. 1.2 Probability-impact matrix

estimated with accuracy and precision. A risk matrix defines the various levels of risk, considering both risk probability and risk impact. This is a simple mechanism to increase the visibility of risks and assist management decision making (Kester 2013). A risk matrix can be used for both qualitative and quantitative risk analyses of a supply chain, where probabilities and impacts are considered as subjective values and objective values, respectively (Norman and Lindroth 2004).

The two main elements, which are probability of occurrence and impact of risk, are critical to determining the necessity of an action to combat a risk in a supply chain. In general, there are three risk levels. The safest condition for a supply chain is when either the probability of occurrence or the impact of risk (or both) are very low. This level is referred to as the low level risk and usually does not require any effort with respect to risk management. In contrast, when both the probability of occurrence and the impact of risk are high, immediate action is required. The third level is defined such that the probability of occurrence or the impact of risk, or both, are moderate or high. This level, although requiring careful management, the risk is not as critical (Fig. 1.2).

1.3.3 Definition of Supply Chain Risk Management

SCRM has been defined in a number of ways. For example, Tang (2006) described SCRM as the management of supply chain risk through coordination or collaboration among supply chain partners so as to ensure profitability and continuity. Thun and Hoenig (2011) reported that a characteristic specific to SCRM, as opposed to traditional risk management, is that SCRM is characterized by cross-company orientation with the goal of identifying and reducing risk, not only at the company level, but with a focus on entire supply chains. Ho et al. (2015) defined SCRM as "the implementation of strategies to manage both everyday and exceptional risks along the supply chain based on continuous risk assessment with the objective of reducing vulnerability and ensuring continuity".

1.4 Research Methodology and Findings

In this section, we categorize papers published within the last three years, from 2014 to 2016. In the first stage, for collecting this set of papers we primarily used the science direct database with "supply chain risk management", "supply chain risk", and "supply chain under uncertainty" as keywords. The terms "risk" and "uncertainty" are frequently used interchangeably. In this initial search, we found more than 200 papers. We also tracked the references of these papers in order to find any related recent publications. Next, we carefully read the titles and keywords of studies. At this stage, we selected approximately 100 papers. In order to achieve a higher level of relevance, we read the abstracts and conclusions of published studies in order to ensure that the papers were related to SCRM. Moreover, a brief examination of the content of the papers led to the removal of more than half of the papers due to lack of relevance. We eventually selected 29 papers. Based on the content of these papers, we created tables and categorized the papers. Among the collection of 29 papers, which were carefully read and analyzed, 21 used mathematical programming methods and two applied game theory in order to deal with the SCRM issues. Moreover, six papers used statistical methods (Cantor et al. 2014; Wiengarten et al. 2016; Giannakis and Papadopoulos 2016; Yang et al. 2015; Li et al. 2015; Bot et al. 2015) to analyze empirical test results and observations. However, in the present study, we focus on analyzing the mathematical programming and game theory papers. We categorize these papers according to the model used to present the problem in SCRM and the proposed solutions. In addition, in order to categorize the models according to modeling approaches and analytical methods, the papers that applied the optimization methods, we designated as single- or multi-objective. We also added details about the most common objective function/constraint considered in all of the papers. In addition, we investigated the types of risks with which these papers deal and the risk assessment location in the mathematical models, in the other words, in which section of the mathematical programming the risk is considered. The consideration of features such as cost and other related parameters was ubiquitous in these papers.

1.4.1 Mathematical Programming and Game Theory Methods

After studying the problem formulation in the papers with mathematical programming and game theory approaches, we found that the majority of these studies used pure mathematical modeling to formulate the problem. For example, all of the papers that applied unconstrained and constrained mathematical programming, linear and nonlinear programming, integer nonlinear programming, stochastic linear programming, stochastic integer linear programming, mixed integer linear programming, multi-objective mixed integer linear programming, or multi-stage stochastic programming were categorized as belonging to the pure mathematical programming group. Only two papers used game theory to formulate the SCRM problem. Fang and Shou (2015) used game theory to study the competition between two supply chains that are subject to supply uncertainty. Moreover, Fallah et al. (2015) used game theory to study the competition between two closed-loop supply chains that include manufacturers, retailers, and recyclers in an uncertain environment. Game theory is used when the objective is competition between two supply chain plans. There were also two papers that simultaneously applied both mathematical (optimization) and simulation approaches (Govindan and Fattahi 2017; Aqlan and Lam 2016). In these studies, optimization is applied considering the deterministic feature of the supply chain, and simulation is applied considering the stochastic feature of the supply chain.

1.4.2 Modeling Approach

Researchers have investigated a number of ways to consider uncertainty within the framework of mathematical programming. Two main approaches are stochastic and deterministic. In the deterministic approach, the output of the model is fully determined by the parameter values and the initial conditions. However, the stochastic approach has inherent randomness and is a general method for finding optimal decisions prior to learning some of the random variables (Lee 2014). A stochastic approach for managing risk in global supply chains was developed by Goh et al. (2007). The present study shows that the majority of the papers that applied mathematical modeling used the stochastic approach (papers 1–7, 9–19, 21 and 22 in Table 1.1). In the stochastic approach, uncertainty is described by considering a set of scenarios. The reason for this is the existing uncertainty and risk in the problem modeling.

1.4.3 Risk Quantification

In real-world situations, we face uncertain conditions due to lack of data and the absence of knowledge about most of the parameters (Fallah et al. 2015). Liu and Iwamura (1998) considered the uncertainty in terms of probability and possibility. In probabilistic cases, the distribution function can be found through experiments, where stochastic programming approaches are used to cope with the randomness of parameters. Possibility theory is used to measure subjective parameters related to

Table 1.1 Classification of mathematical and game theory studied papers

Paper number	Authors	Modelling approach		Methodology			Objective		Case study (location)
		Stochastic	Deterministic	Mathematical	Game theory	Simulation	Single	Multi	
1	Yolmeh and Salehi (2015)	✓		✓			✓		–
2	Nooraie and Parast (2015)	✓		✓				✓	–
3	Nooraie and Parast (2016)	✓		✓				✓	–
4	Aqlan and Lam (2016)	✓	✓	✓		✓		✓	High-end server (USA)
5	Sharifzade et al. (2015)	✓	✓	✓			✓		Biofuel (UK)
6	Subulan et al. (2015)	✓		✓				✓	Acid (Turkey)
7	Govindan and Fattahi (2017)	✓		✓		✓		✓	Glass supply chain (Iran)
8	Fallah et al. (2015)				✓				Battery (Iran)
9	Nunes et al. (2015)	✓		✓			✓		Hydrogen (UK)
10	Lee (2014)	✓		✓			✓		Energy (US)
11	Sahling and Kayser (2016)	✓		✓			✓		–
12	Jabbarzadeh et al. (2017)	✓		✓				✓	SLA –Chair (Australia)
13	Rodriguez et al. (2014)	✓	✓	✓			✓		Electric motors (Sweden)
14	Yang et al. (2015)	✓		✓				✓	Dairy (China)
15	Yu and Goh (2014)	✓		✓				✓	Toyota motors (Japan)
16	Shabani et al. (2014)	✓		✓				✓	Biomass (Canada)
17	Pishvaee et al. (2014)	✓		✓				✓	Medical (Iran)
18	Marufuzzaman et al. (2014)	✓		✓			✓		Biomass (USA)
19	Sawik (2014)	✓		✓			✓	✓	–
20	Aqlan and Lam (2015)	✓		✓			✓		High end server (USA)
21	Shabani and Sowlati (2016)	✓		✓				✓	Biomass power (Canada)
22	Daultani et al. (2015)	✓		✓				✓	–
23	Fang and Shou (2015)				✓				–

fuzzy set arguments. It is used in cases involving some type of ill-known parameters (Fallah et al. 2015). Zadeh (1978) first introduced possibility theory as an extension of his theory of fuzzy sets and fuzzy logic. Most existing risk measures are based on probability theory. The majority of papers can be interpreted as having treated a set of risks that are measurable with known parameters.

Heckman et al. (2015) explained that, in a stochastic optimization problem, in order to make decisions that restrict the extent of risk, it is often required to quantify the risk. For the purpose of assessing and comparing different solutions to limiting the extent of risk, decision-makers need to quantify the imprecise parameters (risk and uncertainty). Standard deviation, mean-variance approaches, value-at-risk, conditional-value-at-risk, and premiums are risk measures that attempt to describe the interaction of uncertainty and the extent of its related harm or benefit. Owing to the lack of quantitative measures that capture the more complex realities of supply chains, these measures, which were developed in finance and insurance contexts, are also applied to supply chain risk. Based on these concepts, supply chain risk is also measured by the likelihood and the severity of adverse effects or the extent of loss (Fishburn 1984; Morgan et al. 1992; Haimes et al. 2002).

Among the 23 papers considered herein, some assumed uncertainty to be probabilistic and to have originated from different scenarios, such as forecasting, benchmarking, and market analysis data (Nooraie and Parast 2015), and some used scenario-based modeling, which has been widely used in stochastic programming problems. In this case, the total probability, which is equal to one, is distributed between all of the scenarios (Yolmeh and Salehi 2015). Some other papers used deviation-based measures, such as variance, standard deviation, and expected or absolute values of deviation (papers 7, 9–12, and 23 in Table 1.1). Variance or standard deviation is widely used as a measure of supply chain risk. In financial engineering and financial risk management, positive and negative deviations are referred to as upside and downside risks, respectively, where downside risk reflects the risk associated with undesirable outcomes, i.e., losses (Heckman et al. 2015). Two papers considered only downside risks (papers 6 and 17 in Table 1.1). The use of downside risk is primarily due to decreasing the size of the problem. In general, according to You et al. (2009), the most commonly used risk measures applied for managing are variance, variability, probabilistic financial risk, and finally downside risk.

In rare cases, lack of knowledge about the real value of input parameters mostly originates from the dynamic nature of the supply chain and the unavailability or incompleteness of data required for a high degree of uncertainty in such a problem. For example, in a case study by Pishvaee et al. (2014), there were no historical data on the quantity of return products, and only partial data on customer demand were available. Even when historical data are available, the behavior of parameters may not necessarily follow with their historical pattern in the future, due to the dynamic nature and strategic horizon of the supply chain network design problem (see Pishvaee et al. 2011). Occasionally, the use of probability distributions is impossible in some case studies due to the lack of required historical data and the impreciseness of the available data. Therefore, as an appropriate alternative, possibility distributions (fuzzy theory, Zadeh 1978) are used in these cases to formulate the imprecise parameters by relying on both available objective (but not sufficient) data and expert subjective opinions.

1.4.4 Economic Evaluation Placement

In financial mathematics, a risk measure is used to determine the amount of an asset or set of assets (traditionally currency) which is to be kept in reserve (Adam 2008). This explains why money is involved whenever there is discussion of risk, and, in all of the papers we reviewed, economic evaluation was the most important element to be considered, although it sometimes appeared through concepts such as budget, profit, cost, or net present value. In all 23 of these papers, economic evaluation is definitely present in the concepts of profit/cost/budget/net present value (NPV). The distribution of these concepts is depicted in Fig. 1.3. Economic evaluation can be interpreted as the most often considered feature in SCRM. Note that all mathematical programming papers considered economic evaluation as the objective function. In contrast with economic evaluation, risk evaluation was placed in the constraints (Table 1.2). The comparison of the placement of economic evaluation versus the placement of risk evaluation is depicted in Fig. 1.5.

1.4.5 Risk Placement

Supply chain risk has been categorized in different ways. However, we categorize it exclusively into three components:

1. ***Supply risk***: any risk that may occur on the supply side with regard to the input material, e.g., disruptions and delays in supply, inventory, and schedules, or delays in inbound logistics.
2. ***Demand risk***: any risk that may occur on the customer side, e.g., variations in demand.
3. ***Process risk***: any risk that may occur during manufacturing and warehousing, e.g., machine breakdowns, human resource errors, operations failures, and financial problems. The last component exists between supply and demand risks.

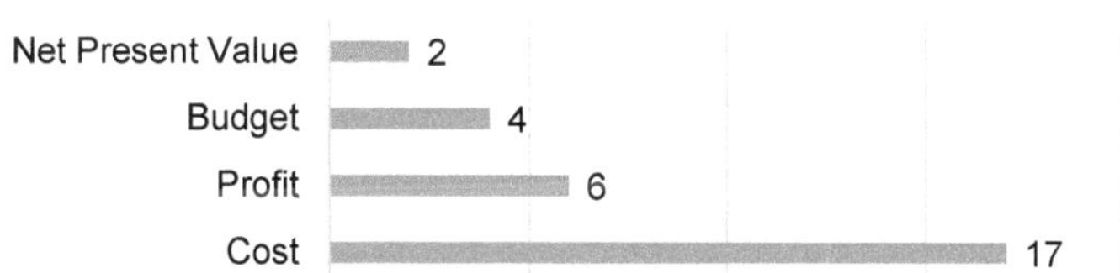

Fig. 1.3 Classification of economic evaluation in papers published between 2014 and 2016

Table 1.2 Classification of economic evaluation placement and risk placement in the studied papers

Paper number	Economic evaluation placement							Risk placement						
	Objective function				Constraint			Objective function				Constraint		
	Profit	Cost	Budget	NPV	Profit	Cost	Budget	NPV	Supply	Demand	Process	Supply	Demand	Process
1		✓					✓						✓	
2		✓				✓	✓		✓	✓				
3		✓										✓	✓	
4	✓					✓						✓	✓	✓
5				✓								✓		
6		✓										✓		✓
7		✓											✓	
8	✓												✓	
9		✓											✓	
10		✓												✓
11				✓									✓	
12		✓										✓	✓	
13		✓											✓	
14		✓											✓	✓
15		✓					✓		✓			✓		
16	✓											✓		
17		✓							✓					
18		✓												✓
19		✓										✓		
20		✓					✓		✓	✓	✓	✓	✓	✓
21	✓											✓		
22	✓								✓	✓				
23	✓					✓						✓	✓	✓

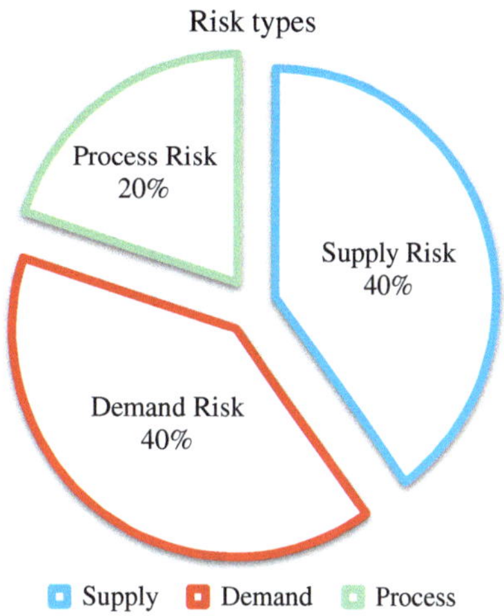

Fig. 1.4 Distribution of journal papers from 2014 to 2016

The majority of the papers formulated the SCRM problem under the risk/uncertainty of demand and supply (Fig. 1.4). However, the tendency of the papers from 2003 to 2013 was slightly different, where the most widely studied risk type was supply risk, 70 papers in 10 years, followed by demand risk in 39 papers, and process risk in only 13 papers (Ho et al. 2015). The present study shows that, from 2013 to 2016, the number of papers investigating supply risk was the same as the number of papers investigating demand risk, namely, 14 papers each. This can be interpreted as a recent increase in addressing demand risk. Moreover, the number of papers investigating process risk was approximately half of the number of papers investigating supply risk or demand risk (Fig. 1.4).

In our categorization, macro risks, such as natural disasters, terrorist attacks, financial crises, and other such events that have enormous consequence, can be placed into any of the abovementioned categories depending on whether the macro risk affects the supply, demand, or process. Note that few papers considered macro risks, primarily because the probability of their occurrence is low compared to the supply, demand, and process risks, even though the impact of macro risks is enormous. For example, although the impact of the 2011 earthquake off the Pacific coast of Tohoku in Japan was high, the probability of a reoccurrence of that disaster is very low. Therefore, industries do not invest huge amount of money in order to protect the supply chain from such macro risks with a low probability of occurrence. However, since macro risks drastically disrupt the supply chain, the history of SCRM papers reveals that the number of papers that consider such global macro risks increases after such an event (for example, the terrorist attack on September 11, 2001 in New York city).

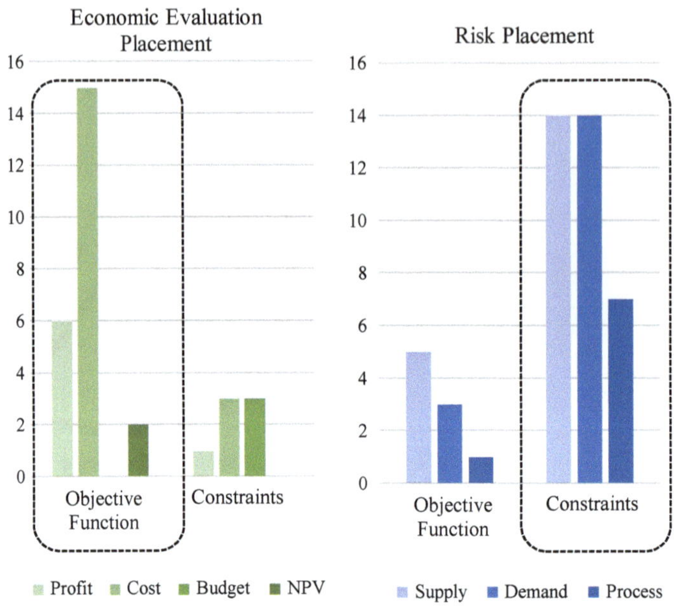

Fig. 1.5 Placement of economic evaluation and risk

In contrast with the economic evaluation placement, in optimization approaches, risk assessment is primarily considered in constraints, rather than appearing in an objective function (Fig. 1.5).

1.4.6 Decision Variables

As shown in Fig. 1.6, the majority of the reviewed papers used facility location (papers 2, 5, 12, 14–16, 19, 21, and 22 listed in Table 1.1) and supplier selection (papers 3, 5–11, 17, and 18 in Table 1.1) as decision variables. Supplier selection is the optimal selection of material providers based on cost and quality. In contrast, facility location is the optimal placement of facilities to minimize transportation costs, while considering factors such as safety and distance from competitors' facilities. The rest of the papers used other decision variables such as assembly line management, mitigation strategy selection, warehouse management, and stakeholder management.

We found that the supplier selection problem is involved in considering supply risk. Moreover, papers (papers 20 and 23 in Table 1.1) that considered all risk types (supply, demand, and process), the decision variables were mitigation strategy selection (refer to Table 1.3).

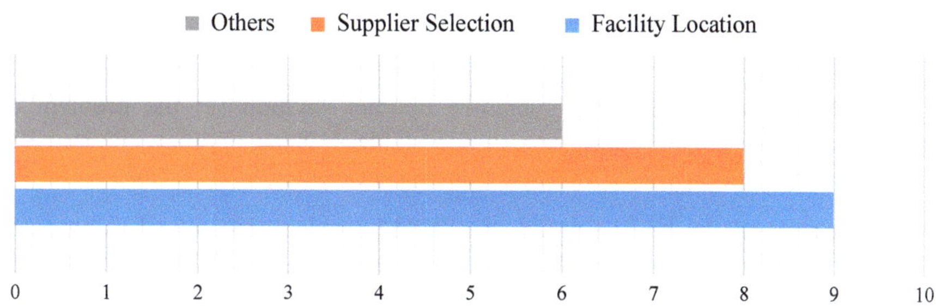

Fig. 1.6 Number of papers based on their decision variables

Table 1.3 Relation between decision variables and risk types

Papers number	Decision variable	Risk type		
		Supply	Demand	Process
1	Assembly line management		✓	
2	Supplier selection	✓	✓	
3	Facility location	✓	✓	
4	Mitigation strategy selection	✓	✓	✓
5	Facility location-supplier selection	✓		
6	Facility location	✓		✓
7	Facility location		✓	
8	Facility location		✓	
9	Investment in plants and warehouses		✓	
10	Facility location			✓
11	Facility location		✓	
12	Supplier selection	✓	✓	
13	Warehouse (inventory) management		✓	
14	Transportation Management		✓	✓
15	Supplier selection	✓		
16	Supplier selection	✓		
17	Facility location	✓		
18	Facility location			✓
19	Supplier selection	✓		
20	Mitigation strategy selection	✓	✓	✓
21	Supplier selection	✓		
22	Stakeholder management	✓	✓	
23	Supplier selection	✓	✓	✓

1.4.7 Solution Method

Unlike the exact methods that guarantee optimal solutions to the problem of interest, a heuristic method provide an acceptable, but not optimal solution. We categorize the papers into two groups with respect to their solution methods:

1. **Exact method**: In the first group, the SCRM problem was solved using exact methods, which always provide an optimal solution (papers 8, 10–12, 20, and 21 in Table 1.1). As an example, Jabbarzadeh et al. (2017) (paper number 12 in Table 1.1) solved their problem by the elastic p-robustness approach using minimax cost and minimax regret algorithms and compared their performances.
2. **Heuristic algorithm**: Most of the reviewed papers used heuristic algorithms to solve the SCR problem (papers 2, 3, 13–15, 17, 18, and 22 in Table 1.1). Note that, when supply and demand risks are considered simultaneously, the solution method is a heuristic algorithm. The primary reason for this is that the size of the problem increases by considering both the supply and demand risks. In such a situation, exact methods may not be used on available hardware or in a reasonable time length. The most commonly used heuristic method was Benders decomposition (papers 17 and 18 in Table 1.1), which is a technique in mathematical programming that allows the solution of very large linear programming problems that have a special block structure. This block structure often occurs in applications such as stochastic programming, because the uncertainty is usually represented through scenarios (Benders 1962).

1.4.8 Case Studies

There are two methods by which the applicability of a solution is determined. One method is to use simulated data as input data in order to obtain a result. A number of papers used this method (papers 1–3, 11, 19, and 22 in Table 1.1). The other papers considered herein used the data of real case studies. Most of the reviewed papers (approximately 75%) investigated real-life cases in industry, and the remainder of the papers (25%) simply used simulated data to prove the effectiveness and efficiency of their proposed methods. We observed that a significant number of case studies used in SCRM research examined the biomass energy industry (papers 5, 16, 18, and 21 in Table 1.1). The reason for this is that the U.S. biofuel industry is expanding rapidly. The U.S. Energy Information Administration reported that the production of bio-ethanol in the U.S. has increased dramatically (10-fold) from 2000 to 2011 and is projected to increase further (US Energy Information Administration, 2013). Moreover, the primary risk involved in the biofuel industry is supply risk, since the supply is dependent on nature, which is unstable because of environmental instabilities (atmospheric temperature, global warming, etc.). This is why a significant number of SCRM papers that considered supply risk used this industry as case studies.

1.5 Conclusions

In this chapter, we reviewed the SCRM papers published within the last three years. The review results revealed that the tendency of the studies was still the same as that of previous decades, with more quantitative and analytical studies than qualitative conceptual ones. A closer examination of existing mathematical programming papers revealed that features such as economic evaluation were considered in all of the papers on managing supply chain risk. In the other words, companies are attempting to manage supply chain risk while minimizing cost and maximizing profit as well as net present value. Risk is either in supply side, or in demand side, or in process side. We observed that stochastic approaches to modeling are common in supply chain management when risk and uncertainty are involved, which is in conflict with the previous research tendency in which deterministic approaches were more common than stochastic approaches. We believe that applying a stochastic approach to SCRM is becoming more popular over time. As a matter of fact, a larger span of data will help to clarify the tendency in SCRM research. As such, in the future, by considering older papers on SCRM, we hope to further clarify the evolution and tendencies of SCRM research from various points of view.

References

Adam, A. (2008). *Handbook of asset and liability management: From models to optimal return strategies* (p. 10). New York: Wiley.

Aloini, D., Dulmin, R., Mininno, V., & Ponticelli, S. (2012). Supply chain management: A review of implementation risks in the construction industry. *Business Process Management Journal, 18*(5), 735–761.

Aqlan, F., & Lam, S. S. (2015). Supply chain risk modelling and mitigation. *International Journal of Production Research, 53*(18), 5640–5656.

Aqlan, F., & Lam, S. S. (2016). Supply chain optimization under risk and uncertainty: A case study for high-end server manufacturing. *Computers & Industrial Engineering, 93,* 78–87.

Behnezhad, A., Connett, B. I., & Nair, M. (2013). The evolution of supply chain risk management. *Journal of Supply Chain and Operations Management, 11*(1), 77–89.

Benders, J. F. (1962). Partitioning procedures for solving mixed-variables programming problems. *Numerische Mathematik, 4*(1), 238–252.

Bot, P., van Donk, D. P., Pennink, B., & Simatupang, T. M. (2015). Uncertainties in the bidirectional biodiesel supply chain. *Journal of Cleaner Production, 95,* 174–183.

Cantor, D. E., Blackhurst, J. V., & Cortes, J. D. (2014). The clock is ticking: The role of uncertainty, regulatory focus, and level of risk on supply chain disruption decision making behavior. *Transportation Research Part E: Logistics and Transportation Review, 72,* 159–172.

Chopra, S., & Sodhi, M. S. (2004). Managing risk to avoid supply-chain breakdown. *MIT Sloan management review, 46*(1), 53.

Colicchia, C., & Strozzi, F. (2012). Supply chain risk management: A new methodology for a systematic literature review. *Supply Chain Management: An International Journal, 17*(4), 403–418.

Daultani, Y., Kumar, S., Vaidya, O. S., & Tiwari, M. K. (2015). A supply chain network equilibrium model for operational and opportunism risk mitigation. *International Journal of Production Research, 53*(18), 5685–5715.

Diehl, D., & Spinler, S. (2013). Defining a common ground for supply chain risk management—A case study in the fast-moving consumer goods industry. *International Journal of Logistics Research and Applications, 16*(4), 311–327.

Ellram, L. M., & Cooper, M. C. (2014). Supply chain management: It's all about the journey, not the destination. *Journal of Supply Chain Management, 50*(1), 8–20.

Fahimnia, B., Tang, C. S., Davarzani, H., & Sarkis, J. (2015). Quantitative models for managing supply chain risks: A review. *European Journal of Operational Research, 247*(1), 1–15.

Fallah, H., Eskandari, H., & Pishvaee, M. S. (2015). Competitive closed-loop supply chain network design under uncertainty. *Journal of Manufacturing Systems, 37,* 649–661.

Fang, Y., & Shou, B. (2015). Managing supply uncertainty under supply chain Cournot competition. *European Journal of Operational Research, 243*(1), 156–176.

Fishburn, P. C. (1984). Foundations of risk measurement. I. Risk as probable loss. *Management Science, 30*(4), 396–406.

Ganeshan, R., & Harrison, T. P. (1995). *An introduction to supply chain management.* Technical Report; Department of Management Science and Information Systems, The Pennsylvania State University.

Ghadge, A., Dani, S., & Kalawsky, R. (2012). Supply chain risk management: Present and future scope. *The International Journal of Logistics Management, 23*(3), 313–339.

Giannakis, M., & Papadopoulos, T. (2016). Supply chain sustainability: A risk management approach. *International Journal of Production Economics, 171,* 455–470.

Goh, M., Lim, J. Y., & Meng, F. (2007). A stochastic model for risk management in global supply chain networks. *European Journal of Operational Research, 182*(1), 164–173.

Govindan, K., & Fattahi, M. (2017). Investigating risk and robustness measures for supply chain network design under demand uncertainty: A case study of glass supply chain. *International Journal of Production Economics, 183,* 680–699.

Haimes, Y. Y., Kaplan, S., & Lambert, J. H. (2002). Risk filtering, ranking, and management framework using hierarchical holographic modeling. *Risk Analysis, 22*(2), 383–397.

Heckmann, I., Comes, T., & Nickel, S. (2015). A critical review on supply chain risk—Definition, measure and modeling. *Omega, 52,* 119–132.

Helbing, D., Ammoser, H., & Kühnert, C. (2006). Disasters as extreme events and the importance of network interactions for disaster response management. In *Extreme events in nature and society* (pp. 319–348). Berlin: Springer.

Ho, W., Zheng, T., Yildiz, H., & Talluri, S. (2015). Supply chain risk management: A literature review. *International Journal of Production Research, 53*(16), 5031–5069.

Houlihan, J. B. (1985). International supply chain management. *International Journal of Physical Distribution and Materials Management, 15,* 22–39.

Houlihan, J. B. (1988). International supply chains: A new approach. *Management Decision, 26* (3), 13–19.

Jabbarzadeh, A., Fahimnia, B., & Sheu, J.-B. (2017). An enhanced robustness approach for managing supply and demand uncertainties. *International Journal of Production Economics, 183,* 620–631.

Kamalahmadi, M., & Parast, M. M. (2015). A review of the literature on the principles of enterprise and supply chain resilience: Major findings and directions for future research. *International Journal of Production Economics, 171,* 116–133.

Kester, Q. A. (2013). Application of formal concept analysis to visualization of the evaluation of risks matrix in software engineering projects. *International Journal of Science, Engineering and Technology Research, 2*(1), 220–225.

Kumar, S. K., Tiwari, M. K., & Babiceanu, R. F. (2010). Minimisation of supply chain cost with embedded risk using computational intelligence approaches. *International Journal of Production Research, 48*(13), 3717–3739.

Lee, J. H. (2014). Energy supply planning and supply chain optimization under uncertainty. *Journal of Process Control, 24*(2), 323–331.

Li, G., Fan, H., Lee, P. K., & Cheng, T. C. E. (2015). Joint supply chain risk management: An agency and collaboration perspective. *International Journal of Production Economics, 164,* 83–94.

Liu, B., & Iwamura, K. (1998). Chance constrained programming with fuzzy parameters. *Fuzzy Set Syst, 94,* 227–237.

Marufuzzaman, M., Eksioglu, S. D., Li, X., & Wang, J. (2014). Analyzing the impact of intermodal-related risk to the design and management of biofuel supply chain. *Transportation Research Part E: Logistics and Transportation Review, 69,* 122–145.

Morgan, M. G., Henrion, M., & Small, M. (1992). *Uncertainty: A guide to dealing with uncertainty in quantitative risk and policy analysis* (p. 155). Cambridge: Cambridge University Press.

Narasimhan, R., & Talluri, S. (2009). Perspectives on risk management in supply chains. *Journal of Operations Management, 27*(2), 114–118.

Nooraie, S. V., & Parast, M. M. (2015). A multi-objective approach to supply chain risk management: Integrating visibility with supply and demand risk. *International Journal of Production Economics, 161,* 192–200.

Nooraie, S. V., & Parast, M. M. (2016). Mitigating supply chain disruptions through the assessment of trade-offs among risks, costs and investments in capabilities. *International Journal of Production Economics, 171,* 8–21.

Norrman, A., & Lindroth, R. (2004). Categorization of supply chain risk and risk management. In: *Supply chain risk* (pp. 14–27). Farnham: Ashgate.

Nunes, P., Oliveira, F., Hamacher, S., & Almansoori, A. (2015). Design of a hydrogen supply chain with uncertainty. *International Journal of Hydrogen Energy, 40*(46), 16408–16418.

Oliver, R. K., & Weber, M. D. (1982). Supply-chain management: Logistics catches up with strategy. In M. L. Christopher (Ed.), *Logistics: The strategic issues* (pp. 63–75). London: Chapman & Hall.

Paulsson, U. (2004). Supply chain risk management. In C. Brindley (Ed.), *Supply chain risk: A reader* (pp. 79–96), Farnham: Ashgate.

Pishvaee, M. S., Rabbani, M., & Torabi, S. A. (2011). A robust optimization approach to closed-loop supply chain network design under uncertainty. *Applied Mathematical Modelling, 35*(2), 637–649.

Pishvaee, M. S., Razmi, J., & Torabi, S. A. (2014). An accelerated Benders decomposition algorithm for sustainable supply chain network design under uncertainty: A case study of medical needle and syringe supply chain. *Transportation Research Part E: Logistics and Transportation Review, 67,* 14–38.

Rao, S., & Goldsby, T. J. (2009). Supply chain risks: A review and typology. *The International Journal of Logistics Management, 20*(1), 97–123.

Ritchie, B., & Brindley, C. (2007). Supply chain risk management and performance: A guiding framework for future development. *International Journal of Operations & Production Management, 27*(3), 303–322.

Rodriguez, M. A., Vecchietti, A. R., Harjunkoski, I., & Grossmann, I. E. (2014). Optimal supply chain design and management over a multi-period horizon under demand uncertainty. Part I: MINLP and MILP models. *Computers & Chemical Engineering, 62,* 194–210.

Sahling, F., & Kayser, A. (2016). Strategic supply network planning with vendor selection under consideration of risk and demand uncertainty. *Omega, 59,* 201–214.

Sawik, T. (2014). Optimization of cost and service level in the presence of supply chain disruption risks: Single vs. multiple sourcing. *Computers & Operations Research, 51,* 11–20.

Shabani, N., & Sowlati, T. (2016). A hybrid multi-stage stochastic programming-robust optimization model for maximizing the supply chain of a forest-based biomass power plant considering uncertainties. *Journal of Cleaner Production, 112,* 3285–3293.

Shabani, N., Sowlati, T., Ouhimmou, M., & Rönnqvist, M. (2014). Tactical supply chain planning for a forest biomass power plant under supply uncertainty. *Energy, 78,* 346–355.

Sharifzadeh, M., Garcia, M. C., & Shah, N. (2015). Supply chain network design and operation: Systematic decision-making for centralized, distributed, and mobile biofuel production using mixed integer linear programming (MILP) under uncertainty. *Biomass and Bioenergy, 81,* 401–414.

Singhal, P., Agarwal, G., & Mittal, M. L. (2011). Supply chain risk management: Review, classification and future research directions. *International Journal of Business Science and Applied Management, 6*(3), 15–42.

Sodhi, M. S., Son, B. G., & Tang, C. S. (2012). Researchers' perspectives on supply chain risk management. *Production and Operations Management, 21*(1), 1–13.

Sodhi, M. S., & Tang, C. S. (2012). Mitigating risks; Managing supply chain risk (Vol. 172, p. 301). Berlin: Springer Science & Business Media.

Subulan, K., Baykasoğlu, A., Özsoydan, F. B., Taşan, A. S., & Selim, H. (2015). A case-oriented approach to a lead/acid battery closed-loop supply chain network design under risk and uncertainty. *Journal of Manufacturing Systems, 37,* 340–361.

Tang, C. S. (2006). Perspectives in supply chain risk management. *International Journal of Production Economics, 103*(2), 451–488.

Tang, O., & Musa, S. N. (2011). Identifying risk issues and research advancements in supply chain risk management. *International Journal of Production Economics, 133*(1), 25–34.

Thun, J. H., & Hoenig, D. (2011). An empirical analysis of supply chain risk management in the German automotive industry. *International Journal of Production Economics, 131*(1), 242–249.

Trkman, P., & McCormack, K. (2009). Supply chain risk in turbulent environments—A conceptual model for managing supply chain network risk. *International Journal of Production Economics, 119*(2), 247–258.

US Energy Information Administration. (2013). *International energy statistics*. Available on March 2016 at http://www.eia.gov/cfapps/ipdbproject/iedindex3.cfm?tid=79&pid=80&aid=1&cid=regions&syid=2000&eyid=2011&unit=TBPD

Wiengarten, F., Humphreys, P., Gimenez, C., & McIvor, R. (2016). Risk, risk management practices, and the success of supply chain integration. *International Journal of Production Economics, 171,* 361–370.

Yang, G. Q., Liu, Y. K., & Yang, K. (2015). Multi-objective biogeography-based optimization for supply chain network design under uncertainty. *Computers & Industrial Engineering, 85,* 145–156.

Yolmeh, A., & Salehi, N. (2015). An outer approximation method for an integration of supply chain network designing and assembly line balancing under uncertainty. *Computers & Industrial Engineering, 83,* 297–306.

You, F., Wassick, J. M., & Grossmann, I. E. (2009). Risk management for a global supply chain planning under uncertainty: Models and algorithms. *AIChE Journal, 55*(4), 931–946.

Yu, M. C., & Goh, M. (2014). A multi-objective approach to supply chain visibility and risk. *European Journal of Operational Research, 233*(1), 125–130.

Zadeh, L. A. (1978). Fuzzy sets as a basis for a theory of possibility. *Fuzzy Sets and Systems, 1,* 3–28.

Chapter 2
Cost-Effectiveness and Manageability Based Prioritisation of Supply Chain Risk Mitigation Strategies

Abroon Qazi, John Quigley and Alex Dickson

Abstract Risk treatment is an important stage of the risk management process involving selection of appropriate strategies for mitigating critical risks. Limited studies have considered evaluating such strategies within a setting of interdependent supply chain risks and risk mitigation strategies. However, the selection of strategies has not been explored from the perspective of manageability-the ease of implementing and managing a strategy. We introduce a new method of prioritising strategies on the basis of associated cost, effectiveness and manageability within a theoretically grounded framework of Bayesian Belief Networks and demonstrate its application through a simulation study. The proposed approach can help managers select an optimal combination of strategies taking into account the effort involved in implementing and managing such strategies. The results clearly reveal the importance of considering manageability in addition to cost-effectiveness within a decision problem of ranking supply chain risk mitigation strategies.

2.1 Introduction

Risk management involves important stages of risk identification, risk analysis, risk evaluation, risk treatment and risk monitoring (SA 2009). Supply chain risk management (SCRM) is gaining an increasing interest both from the researchers and practitioners (Sodhi et al. 2012). Complex interactions between supply chain risks ranging across the entire spectrum of a supply network make it a challenging task to identify, assess and manage key risks. Limited studies have focused on exploring causal interactions between supply chain risks (Badurdeen et al. 2014; Garvey et al. 2015)

A. Qazi (✉) · J. Quigley
Department of Management Science, University of Strathclyde Business School, Glasgow, UK
e-mail: abroon.qazi@strath.ac.uk

A. Dickson
Department of Economics, University of Strathclyde Business School, Glasgow, UK

Y. Khojasteh (ed.), *Supply Chain Risk Management*,
DOI 10.1007/978-981-10-4106-8_2

and integrating the impact of risk mitigation strategies on associated risks within the modelling framework (Aqlan and Lam 2015). However, to the best of our knowledge, no attempt has been made to capture the manageability associated with implementing a mitigation strategy within the modelling framework. Manageability relates to the concept of ease involved in managing a strategy. Besides capturing the manageability of risks (effectiveness of strategies) representing the potential for reducing the risk (Aven et al. 2007), we propose integrating the cost and manageability of mitigation strategies within a theoretically grounded framework of Bayesian Belief Networks (BBNs) encompassing complex interactions between risks and strategies.

BBN is a directed acyclic graph comprising nodes representing uncertain variables and arcs indicating causal relationships between variables whereas the strength of dependency is represented by the conditional probability values. BBNs offer a unique feature of modelling risks combining both the statistical data and subjective judgment in case of non-availability of data (Qazi et al. 2014). In the last years, BBNs have also started gaining the interest of researchers in modelling supply chain risks (Badurdeen et al. 2014).

In this chapter, we aim to address the decision problem of prioritising risk mitigation strategies considering the cost, effectiveness and manageability of such strategies within an interconnected network of interacting supply chain risks and strategies. The proposed method is deemed as contribution to the literature on Risk Management in general and SCRM in particular. Existing models focusing on cost-effectiveness of strategies assume the same level of manageability for all strategies.

The remainder of the chapter is organised as follows: A brief review of the relevant literature is presented in Sect. 2.2. The modelling approach of prioritising risk mitigation strategies is described in Sect. 2.3 and demonstrated through a simulation study in Sect. 2.4. Results and managerial implications are also described in Sect. 2.4. Finally, key findings and future research agenda are presented in Sect. 2.5.

2.2 Literature Review

SCRM is gaining interest of researchers and practitioners because of the occurrence of major supply chain disruptions (Sodhi et al. 2012). Global sourcing and lean operations are the main drivers of supply chain disruptions (Son and Orchard 2013). The likelihood of the occurrence of an (undesirable) event, and the negative implications of the event are the two common measures of risk (Bogataj and Bogataj 2007). Risk mitigation strategies are implemented in order to reduce the likelihood of occurrence and/or negative impact of risks (Tang and Tomlin 2008). Robust strategies must be developed in order to help firms reduce cost and/or improve customer satisfaction under normal conditions and to enable firms sustain operations during and after a disruption (Tang 2006).

According to Johnson (2001), capacity risks can be reduced by outsourcing and building a flexible web of partners whereas operational hedging can help in reducing currency and political risks. Christopher and Lee (2004) proposed a number of strategies including information accuracy, visibility, accessibility and responsive corrective actions. Zsidisin et al. (2004) recommended implementation of supplier improvement programs and mitigation of supply disruptions through creating business interruption plans, developing demand forecasts and modelling supply processes.

Using the interpretive structural modelling, Faisal et al. (2006) introduced an approach of understanding dynamics between different enablers of risk mitigation. A similar concept of establishing cause and effect relationships between the enablers of risk mitigation was explored in the Electronic supply chain in order to determine the main drivers (Rajesh and Ravi 2015). Using a multi-method approach, Speier et al. (2011) introduced a framework to examine the threat of potential disruptions on supply chain processes and identified suitable potential mitigation strategies under different conditions. Christopher et al. (2011) used a multiple case study approach in several industries to understand how managers assess and mitigate global sourcing risks across the entire supply chain. They proposed four generic strategies including network re-engineering, collaboration, agility and risk management culture for managing global sourcing risk. Son and Orchard (2013) developed an analytical model for examining the effectiveness of two inventory based policies for mitigating the impact of supply-side disruptions in a supply chain.

The main limitation of existing studies is their limited focus on capturing interdependency between supply chain risks and mitigation strategies. Keeping in view the significance of modelling systemic risks and capturing non-linear complex interactions (Ackermann et al. 2014), researchers have started modelling interdependency between supply chain risks (Badurdeen et al. 2014; Garvey et al. 2015). However, to the best of our knowledge, interdependency between risks and risk mitigation strategies has not been explored within a probabilistic network setting including cost, effectiveness and manageability of strategies. Qazi et al. (2015b) introduced a model for prioritising strategies within a probabilistic network of interacting risks and strategies. In order to capture the risk appetite of a decision maker, Qazi et al. (2015c) proposed an expected utility based method to select optimal strategies. In this chapter, we integrate cost, effectiveness and manageability of strategies within a single model and focus on a different problem where the main purpose is to prioritise specific number of strategies instead of optimising a portfolio of strategies subject to a budget constraint.

BBNs present a useful technique for capturing interaction between risk events and performance measures (Badurdeen et al. 2014). Another advantage of using BBNs for modelling supply chain risks is their ability of back propagation that helps in determining the probability of an event that may not be observed directly. BBNs also provide a clear graphical structure that most people find intuitive to understand. Besides, it becomes possible to conduct flexible inference based on partial observations, which allows for reasoning (Onisko 2008). Another important feature of using BBNs is to conduct what-if scenarios (Blodgett and Anderson 2000). There are certain problems associated with the use of BBNs: along with the increase in number of nodes representing supply chain risks, a considerable amount of data is required in populating the network with (conditional) probability values; similarly, there are also computational challenges associated with the increase in number of nodes.

2.3 Proposed Modelling Approach

Based on the efficacy of BBNs in capturing interdependencies between risks, we consider BBN based modelling of a supply network as an effective approach. Such a modelling technique can help managers visualise interaction between supply chain risks and take effective mitigation strategies (Qazi et al. 2014, 2015a). BBNs have already been explored in the literature on SCRM, however, the proposed approach is unique in terms of integrating the cost, effectiveness and manageability of risk mitigation strategies within the network setting of interacting supply chain risks and strategies.

2.3.1 BBNs

BBN is a graphical framework for modelling uncertainty. BBNs have their background in statistics and artificial intelligence and were first introduced in the 1980s for dealing with uncertainty in knowledge-based systems (Sigurdsson et al. 2001). BBNs have been successfully used in addressing problems related to a number of diverse specialties including reliability modelling, medical diagnosis, geographical information systems, and aviation safety management among others. For understanding the mechanics and modelling of BBNs, interested readers may consult Charniak (1991), Sigurdsson et al. (2001), Nadkarni and Shenoy (2001), Nadkarni and Shenoy (2004), Jensen and Nielsen (2007), and Kjaerulff and Anders (2008). A BBN consists of following elements:

- A set of variables (each having a finite set of mutually exclusive events) and a set of directed edges between variables forming a directed acyclic graph; a directed graph is acyclic if there is no directed path $A_1 \to \cdots \to A_n$ so that $A_1 = A_n$, furthermore, the directed edges represent statistical relations if the BBN is constructed from the data whereas they represent causal relations if they have been gathered from experts' opinion,
- A conditional probability table $P(X|Y_1, \ldots, Y_n)$ attached to each variable X with parents $Y_1, \ldots, Y_n$.

2.3.1.1 Chain Rule for BBNs

Let a Bayesian Network be specified over $A = \{A_1, \ldots, A_n\}$, the chain rule of probability theory allows factoring joint probabilities resulting in the calculations made under certain probability states. The structure of a BBN implies that the value of a particular node is conditional only on the values of its parent nodes. Therefore, the unique joint probability distribution $P(A)$ representing the product of all conditional probability tables is given as follows:

$$P(A) = \prod_{i=1}^{n} P(A_i | pa(A_i)), \tag{2.1}$$

where $pa(A_i)$ are the parents of A_i.

2.3.2 *Assumptions*

Our model is based on following assumptions:

1. Supply chain risks and corresponding sources are known and these can be modelled as a directed acyclic graph.
2. All random variables and risk mitigation strategies are represented by binary states.
3. Conditional probability values for the risks and associated losses can be elicited from stakeholders and the resulting network represents close approximation to the actual perceived risks and associated interdependency.
4. Cost and manageability associated with each potential risk mitigation strategy are known.
5. All stakeholders within the supply chain are willing to share information about key risks, loss values and effort involved in implementing potential strategies.

2.3.3 *Supply Chain Risk Network*

A discrete supply chain risk network $RN = (X, G, P, L, U, C, C_m)$ is a seven-tuple consisting of [adapted from Kjaerulff and Anders (2008)]:

- a directed acyclic graph (DAG),$G = (V, E)$, with nodes (V) representing discrete risks and risk sources (X_R), discrete risk mitigation strategies (X_S), loss functions (L), utility functions (U), cost functions (C), manageability weighted cost functions (C_m) and directed links (E) encoding dependence relations,
- a set of conditional probability distributions (P) containing a distribution, $P(X_{R_i} | X_{pa(R_i)})$, for each risk and risk source (X_{R_i}),

- a set of loss functions (L) containing one loss function, $l(X_{pa(V)})$, for each node v in the subset $V_l \in V$ of loss nodes,
- a set of utility functions (U) containing one utility function, $u(X_{pa(V)})$, for each node v in the subset $V_u \in V$ of utility nodes,
- a set of cost functions (C) containing one cost function, $c(X_{pa(V)})$, for each node v in the subset $V_c \in V$ of cost nodes,
- a set of manageability weighted cost functions (C_m) containing one manageability weighted cost function, $c_m(X_{pa(V)})$, for each node v in the subset $V_{c_m} \in V$ of manageability weighted cost nodes.

Risk network expected loss, $RNEL(X)$, is given as follows (Qazi et al. 2015b):

$$RNEL(X) = \prod_{X_v \in X_R} P(X_v | X_{pa(v)}) \sum_{w \in V_L} l(X_{pa(w)}) \tag{2.2}$$

Risk network expected utility for loss, $RNEU(X)$, is given as follows (Qazi et al. 2015c):

$$RNEU(X) = \prod_{X_v \in X_R} P(X_v | X_{pa(v)}) \sum_{w \in V_L} u(X_{pa(w)}) \tag{2.3}$$

2.3.3.1 An Illustrative Example of a Simple BBN

We present a very simple BBN comprising three risks; R1, R2 and R3 as shown in Fig. 2.1. Each risk is assumed to have two states: True (T) or False (F). R3 is the parent node influencing two child nodes 'R1' and 'R2' which are the leaf nodes. The (conditional) probability values of the risks are given in Table 2.1. The updated probability value of R1 and R2 can be calculated using Eq. (2.4). One of the benefits of BBNs relates to the revision of beliefs once any evidence is propagated across a variable or set of variables. The posterior belief about R3 can be calculated using Eq. (2.5) once the evidence is instantiated at R1 or R2. The updated probabilities of R1 and R2 are 0.44 and 0.544, respectively as shown in Eqs. (2.6) and (2.7). Similarly, the posterior probabilities of R3 are 0.82 and 0.99 corresponding to the realisation of R1 and R2, respectively as shown in Eqs. (2.8) and (2.9).

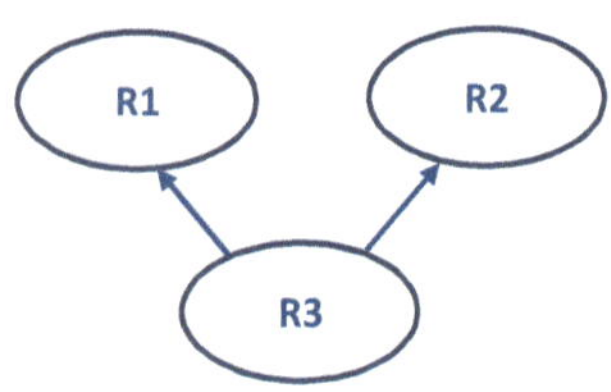

Fig. 2.1 A BBN comprising three variables

Table 2.1 (Conditional) probability values for the three nodes

Parent	*P(Risk|Parent)*			
	R1		R2	
R3	T	F	T	F
T (0.6)	0.6	0.4	0.9	0.1
F (0.4)	0.2	0.8	0.01	0.99

$$P(Ri = T) = P(Ri = T|R3 = T) * P(R3 = T) + P(Ri = T|R3 = F) * P(R3 = F) \tag{2.4}$$

$$P(R3 = T|Ri = T) = \frac{P(R3 = T, Ri = T)}{P(Ri = T)} = \frac{P(Ri = T|R3 = T) * P(R3 = T)}{P(Ri = T)} \tag{2.5}$$

$$P(R1 = T) = (0.6 * 0.6) + (0.2 * 0.4) = 0.44 \tag{2.6}$$

$$P(R2 = T) = (0.9 * 0.6) + (0.01 * 0.4) = 0.544 \tag{2.7}$$

$$P(R3 = T|R1 = T) = \frac{0.6 * 0.6}{0.44} = 0.82 \tag{2.8}$$

$$P(R3 = T|R2 = T) = \frac{0.9 * 0.6}{0.544} = 0.99 \tag{2.9}$$

In order to calculate $RNEL(X)$ and $RNEU(X)$, we assume the loss and utility values corresponding to different states of risks as shown in Table 2.2 where utility function is considered as $u(loss) = -(loss * loss)$. Using Eqs. (2.10) and (2.11), the expected loss and expected utility values are calculated as 537 and -461428, respectively.

$$\begin{aligned} RNEL(X) = {} & P(R1 = T, R2 = T, R3 = T) * l(R1 = T, R2 = T, R3 = T) \\ & + P(R1 = T, R2 = F, R3 = T) * l(R1 = T, R2 = F, R3 = T) \\ & + P(R1 = T, R2 = T, R3 = F) * l(R1 = T, R2 = T, R3 = F) \\ & + P(R1 = T, R2 = F, R3 = F) * l(R1 = T, R2 = F, R3 = F) \\ & + P(R1 = F, R2 = T, R3 = F) * l(R1 = F, R2 = T, R3 = F) \\ & + P(R1 = F, R2 = T, R3 = T) * l(R1 = F, R2 = T, R3 = T) \\ & + P(R1 = F, R2 = F, R3 = T) * l(R1 = F, R2 = F, R3 = T) \\ & + P(R1 = F, R2 = F, R3 = F) * l(R1 = F, R2 = F, R3 = F) \\ = {} & 537 \end{aligned} \tag{2.10}$$

Table 2.2 Loss and utility values for different states of risks

Risk			Loss (l) (monetary units)	Utility (u) (10^3)
R1	R2	R3		
State				
T	T	T	1000	−1000
T	F	T	750	−562.5
T	T	F	550	−302.5
T	F	F	300	−90
F	T	F	200	−40
F	T	T	700	−490
F	F	T	400	−160
F	F	F	0	0

$$\begin{aligned} RNEU(X) = {} & P(R1 = T, R2 = T, R3 = T) * u(R1 = T, R2 = T, R3 = T) \\ & + P(R1 = T, R2 = F, R3 = T) * u(R1 = T, R2 = F, R3 = T) \\ & + P(R1 = T, R2 = T, R3 = F) * u(R1 = T, R2 = T, R3 = F) \\ & + P(R1 = T, R2 = F, R3 = F) * u(R1 = T, R2 = F, R3 = F) \\ & + P(R1 = F, R2 = T, R3 = F) * u(R1 = F, R2 = T, R3 = F) \\ & + P(R1 = F, R2 = T, R3 = T) * u(R1 = F, R2 = T, R3 = T) \\ & + P(R1 = F, R2 = F, R3 = T) * u(R1 = F, R2 = F, R3 = T) \\ & + P(R1 = F, R2 = F, R3 = F) * u(R1 = F, R2 = F, R3 = F) \\ & = -461428 \end{aligned} \tag{2.11}$$

2.3.4 Problem Statement

Given different options of implementing risk mitigation strategies within a probabilistic network of interconnected supply chain risks and strategies, how do we prioritise these strategies keeping in view the cost, effectiveness and manageability of strategies?

2.3.5 Objective Function

In this chapter, we aim to prioritise risk mitigation strategies yielding maximum weighted summation of normalised expected utility for loss and normalised utility for manageability weighted mitigation cost.

$$\max_{\gamma_{x_s} \in \gamma_{X_S}} w * \overline{RNEU}(X_{\gamma_{x_s}}) + (1 - w) * \overline{U}(C_{m_{\gamma_{x_s}}}), \quad s.t. \; 0 < n \leq N \tag{2.12}$$

where

γ_{X_S} is a set of all possible orderings of different states of n mitigation strategies $(x_{s_1} \times x_{s_2} \times \ldots \times x_{s_n})$,
$\overline{RNEU}(X)$ is the normalised expected utility for loss,
w is the relative importance weighting of normalised expected utility for loss,
$\overline{U}(C_{m_{\gamma_{x_s}}})$ is the normalised utility for manageability weighted cost of implementing γ_{x_s} combination of mitigation strategies,
n is the number of strategies considered for implementation,
N is the maximum number of potential strategies.

In the case of a risk-neutral decision maker (assumed in the simulation study), the objective function transforms as follows:

$$\max_{\gamma_{x_s} \in \gamma_{X_S}} w * \overline{U}(RNEL(X_{\gamma_{x_s}})) + (1 - w) * \overline{U}(C_{m_{\gamma_{x_s}}}), \quad s.t. \; 0 < n \leq N \tag{2.13}$$

where $\overline{U}(RNEL(X))$ is the normalised utility for risk network expected loss.

In order to assign manageability score to the strategies, we propose using the ordinal scale (1–10) shown in Table 2.3.

2.3.6 Modelling Process

The following steps must be followed in developing the proposed network of interacting supply chain risks and mitigation strategies:

1. Define the boundaries of the supply network and identify stakeholders.
2. Identify key risks and potential risk mitigation strategies on the basis of input received from each stakeholder through interviews and/or focus group sessions.
3. Refine the qualitative structure of the resulting network involving all stakeholders.

Table 2.3 Manageability scale for ranking of risk mitigation strategies

Manageability scale	Ease of managing risk mitigation strategy
1–2	Very easy
3–4	Easy
5–6	Neither easy nor difficult
7–8	Difficult
9–10	Very difficult

4. Determine (conditional) probability values, loss values resulting from risks and cost and manageability score associated with implementing each potential mitigation strategy and populate the BBN with all parameters.
5. Run the model for each combination of strategies and determine the expected utility (loss) value.
6. Analyse the results and prioritise risk mitigation strategies on the basis of relative importance of normalised expected utility for loss and normalised utility for manageability weighted cost of strategies.
7. Validate the model output involving stakeholders.

2.4 Simulation Study

We demonstrate the application of our proposed approach through a simple supply network (Garvey et al. 2015) as shown in Fig. 2.2. The model was developed in GeNIe 2.0 (2015). The supply network comprises a raw material source (RM), two manufacturers (M1 and M2), a warehouse (W) and a retailer (R). We also consider a transportation link between the warehouse and retailer (W-R). Risks are represented by nodes comprising bar charts whereas resulting losses and mitigation strategies are represented by diamond and rectangular shaped nodes, respectively. Though each domain of the supply network may comprise a number of risks and corresponding sources, we consider limited risks for the sake of simplicity. Although the presented model represents the process flow of the supply chain, the

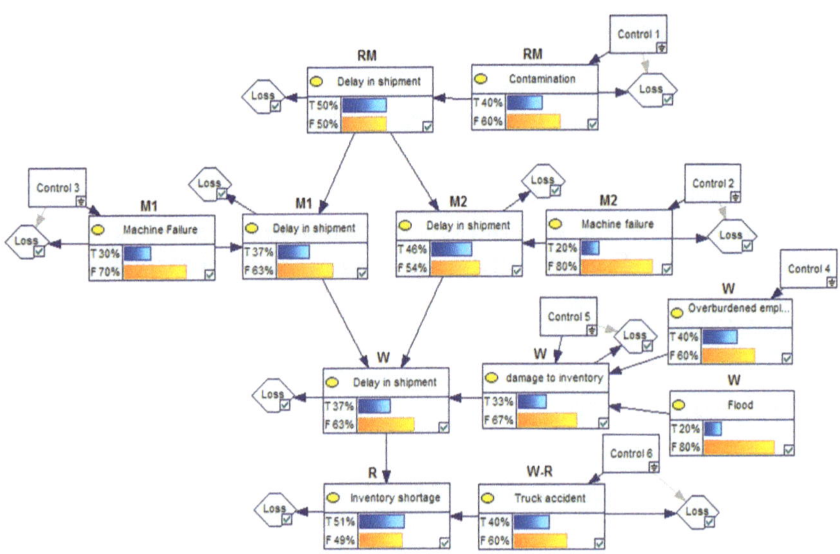

Fig. 2.2 Bayesian network based model of a supply network developed in GeNIe 2.0 (2015) (adapted from Garvey et al. (2015))

Table 2.4 Loss values for different risks

Supply chain element	Risk	Loss (monetary units)
Raw material source	Contamination (R1)	200
	Delay in shipment (R2)	400
Manufacturer-I	Machine failure (R4)	200
	Delay in shipment (R5)	400
Manufacturer-II	Machine failure (R3)	200
	Delay in shipment (R6)	400
Warehouse	Overburdened employee (R7)	–
	Damage to inventory (R8)	500
	Delay in shipment (R9)	600
	Flood (R12)	–
Warehouse to retailer	Truck accident (R10)	500
Retailer	Inventory shortage (R11)	800

proposed approach is not strictly limited to capturing the network configuration of a supply chain as it might not be feasible to model a huge supply network. Therefore, we focus on modelling the risk network instead of mapping the entire supply network.

Each risk and mitigation strategy is represented by binary states of 'True (T)' or 'False (F)' and 'Yes' or 'No', respectively. Assumed loss values associated with the risks are shown in Table 2.4. The strength of interdependency between risks and the impact of strategies on related risks are represented by (conditional) probability values as shown in Table 2.5. As R1 does not have a parent node, its probability value is not contingent on any node. The italicised value represents the reduced probability of a risk after implementation of the related strategy. The conditional probability value of R2 (being True) is 0.8 given that its parent node 'R1' is in 'True' state. Implementation of each mitigation strategy is assumed to incur a cost of 100 units. The assumed manageability scores are shown in Table 2.6. All parameters specific to a real case study can be elicited from experts through interviews and focus group sessions.

2.4.1 *Results and Analysis*

After populating the model with assumed parameters, it was updated and the array of values corresponding to different combinations of mitigation strategies was exported to a Microsoft Excel worksheet. We evaluated the potential strategies with respect to the cost-effectiveness based ranking scheme followed by the prioritisation of strategies considering both manageability and cost-effectiveness. The results provided an important insight into realising the significance of incorporating manageability aspect into the model and prioritising strategies through the proposed approach.

Table 2.5 (Conditional) probability values $[P(risk = F|parents) = 1 - P(risk = T|parents)]$

Parents				P(risk = T|parents)					
*R*1	*R*2	*R*3	*R*4	*R*1	*R*2	*R*3	*R*4	*R*5	*R*6
				0.4					
				0.1					
T					0.8				
F					0.3				
						0.2			
						0.1			
							0.3		
							0.2		
	T		T					0.7	
	T		F					0.4	
	F		T					0.6	
	F		F					0.1	
	T	T							0.9
	T	F							0.6
	F	T							0.5
	F	F							0.2

Parents							P(risk = T|parents)					
*R*5	*R*6	*R*7	*R*8	*R*9	*R*10	*R*12	*R*7	*R*8	*R*9	*R*10	*R*11	*R*12
							0.4					
							0.3					
		T				T		0.8				
								0.5				
		T				F		0.3				
								0.15				
		F				T		0.6				
								0.4				
		F				F		0.2				
								0.15				
T	T		T						0.9			
T	T		F						0.5			
T	F		T						0.6			
T	F		F						0.3			
F	T		T						0.4			
F	T		F						0.3			
F	F		T						0.3			
F	F		F						0.2			
										0.4		
										0.15		
				T	T						0.9	

(continued)

Table 2.5 (continued)

Parents							$P(\text{risk} = \text{T}\vert\text{parents})$					
*R*5	*R*6	*R*7	*R*8	*R*9	*R*10	*R*12	*R*7	*R*8	*R*9	*R*10	*R*11	*R*12
				T	F						0.7	
				F	T						0.6	
				F	F						0.2	
												0.2

Table 2.6 Manageability scores assigned to the risk mitigation strategies

Risk mitigation strategy (control) ID	Strategy	Impact on risk	Manageability score
1	Quality assurance program	R1	10
2	Scheduled maintenance program	R3	1
3	Scheduled maintenance program	R4	2
4	Scheduling software and monitoring program	R7	6
5	Early warning system	R8	5
6	Training on simulator	R10	9

2.4.1.1 Cost-Effectiveness Based Prioritisation of Strategies

We evaluated the cost-effectiveness of strategies and prioritised these through the lens of risk network expected loss as shown in Fig. 2.3. Each point represents one of the 64 different combinations of six mitigation strategies whereas the corresponding value was calculated using Eq. (2.2) for the specific combination of strategies applied to the risk network shown in Fig. 2.2. As each strategy was assumed to incur 100 units of mitigation cost, the strategies represented by the lowest points corresponding to each number of strategies are also the cost-effective strategies. Considering the cost-benefit analysis, strategies resulting in maximum improvement in the risk network expected loss (less mitigation cost) must be selected. Such strategies are represented by the peak points appearing in Fig. 2.4.

It is interesting to note that there is only one cost-effective combination of 5 strategies, however, implementation of all 6 strategies does not result in achieving the net gain. Moreover, the value of net improvement increases up to 2 strategies and declines beyond that point. Optimal strategies are shown in Table 2.7. Strategy 4 is not a feasible strategy except once all the potential strategies need to be implemented.

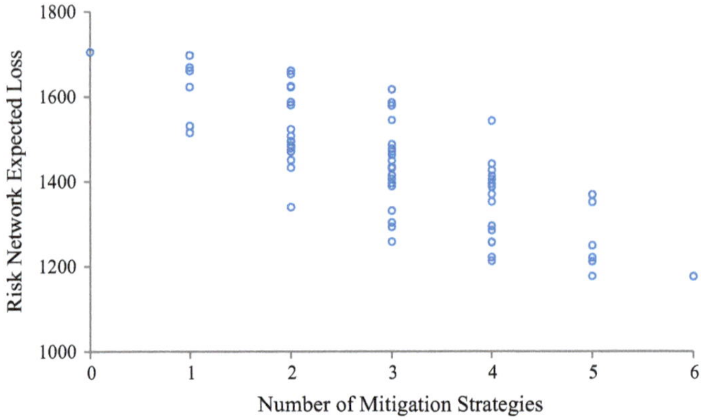

Fig. 2.3 Variation of risk network expected loss with respect to the number of strategies

Fig. 2.4 Variation of cost-effectiveness of risk mitigation strategies with respect to the number of strategies

This is mainly because of the fact that the strategy is linked to R7 with no loss value associated with the risk (Table 2.4). Furthermore, R7 does not appear to be a major source of disruption across the entire risk network and even if all 6 strategies are implemented (including Strategy 4), the risk network expected loss is not reduced substantially (Fig. 2.3). That is why, when all 6 strategies are selected, the total cost outweighs the associated benefit.

Table 2.7 Cost-effectiveness based prioritisation of strategies

Number of risk mitigation strategies	Prioritised strategies
1	6
2	1 and 6
3	1, 5 and 6
4	1, 3, 5 and 6
5	All except 4
6	All

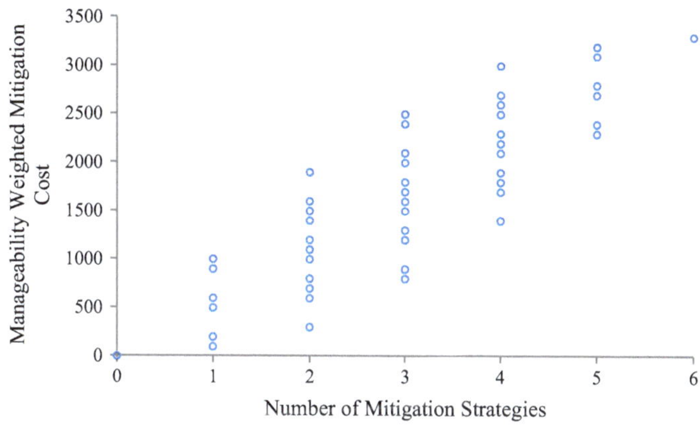

Fig. 2.5 Variation of manageability weighted mitigation cost with respect to the number of strategies

2.4.1.2 Manageability and Cost-Effectiveness Based Prioritisation of Strategies

We prioritised the strategies on the basis of associated manageability, cost and effectiveness. Values of manageability weighted cost corresponding to different combinations of strategies are depicted in Fig. 2.5. As each strategy was assumed to incur a cost of 100 units, the manageability weighted cost directly reflects the manageability score assigned to each strategy. The lowest points corresponding to the number of strategies are the optimal combinations keeping in view the factors of cost and manageability; however, these may not necessarily achieve the maximum improvement in the risk network expected loss.

As we assumed the decision maker as risk-neutral, the utility for risk network expected loss could be substituted for the expected utility for loss. Utility for manageability weighted mitigation cost was assumed as a decreasing linear function. Variation of both the normalised utility functions considering maximum values with the number of strategies is shown in Fig. 2.6. Normalised utility for the manageability weighted cost attains the maximum value once no strategy is selected and reduces to the minimum value in case of selecting all 6 strategies and vice versa

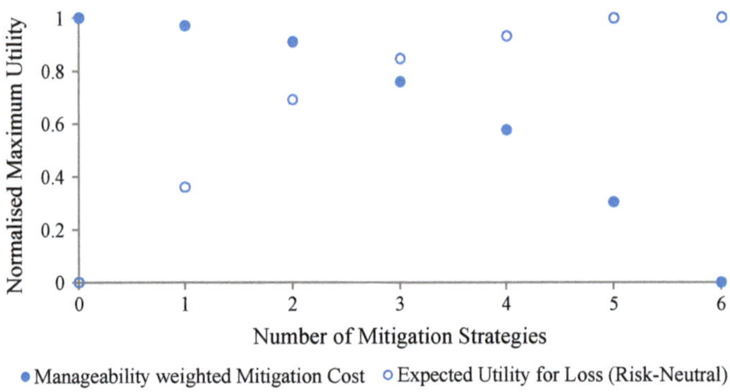

Fig. 2.6 Variation of utility values with respect to the number of strategies

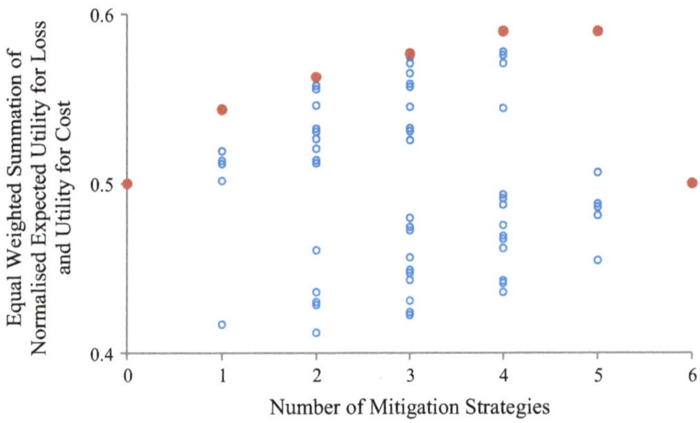

Fig. 2.7 Variation of equal weighted summation of normalised utility values with respect to the number of strategies

in case of normalised expected utility for loss. The two points corresponding to each number of strategies represent optimal combinations of strategies with respect to the two utility functions that might comprise different strategies. It is also important to realise the non-linear trend of utility functions.

Considering equal weights assigned to the two normalised utility functions, we analysed the behavior of the resulting function as shown in Fig. 2.7. It can clearly be observed that a risk-neutral decision maker will prefer implementing 4 strategies. Implementing all 6 strategies yields the minimum utility to the decision maker. Points appearing in red colour are the optimal combinations of strategies corresponding to the specific number of strategies.

We also conducted the sensitivity analysis through varying the weightings for normalised utility functions as shown in Fig. 2.8. Optimal strategies considering critical factors of cost, effectiveness, manageability and importance weighting of each normalised utility function are given in Table 2.8. The optimal strategies vary

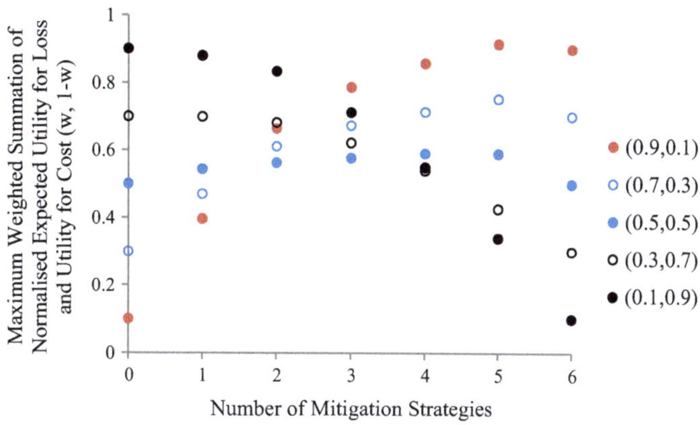

Fig. 2.8 Variation of maximum weighted summation of normalised utility values with respect to different weighting schemes and number of strategies

Table 2.8 Cost-effectiveness and manageability based prioritisation of strategies

Number of risk mitigation strategies	Prioritised strategies based on different weighting schemes [risk network expected loss (w), manageability weighted cost $(1-w)$]				
	(0.9, 0.1)	(0.7, 0.3)	(0.5, 0.5)	(0.3, 0.7)	(0.1, 0.9)
1	6	6	6	2	2
2	1 and 6	1 and 6	2 and 6	2 and 3	2 and 3
3	1, 5 and 6	1, 5 and 6	1, 2 and 6	2, 3 and 5	2, 3 and 5
4	1, 3, 5 and 6	1, 3, 5 and 6	1, 2, 3 and 6	2, 3, 5 and 6	2, 3, 4 and 5
5	All except 4	All except 4	All except 4	All except 4	All except 1

in relation to different weighting schemes. Strategy 4 appears to be the least important strategy in all weighting schemes except the one in which minimum importance is given to normalised expected utility for loss ($w = 0.1$). For the weighting schemes considering relative importance of normalised expected utility for loss as $w = 0.9, 0.7, 0.5$, it is always optimal to implement the same combination of 5 strategies. The sensitivity analysis also helped in verifying the validity of our simulation model. Weighting schemes assigning substantial importance to the normalised utility for manageability weighted cost ($w = 01, 0.3$) result in implementing no strategy.

Evaluation of risk mitigation strategies through the proposed approach results in prioritisation of strategies considering holistic interaction of supply chain risks and strategies, and integrating important factors of cost, effectiveness and manageability of strategies within the modelling framework. As the approach is grounded in the theoretical framework of BBNs the resulting solution can be considered as viable.

However, it is assumed that all stakeholders would be willing to share their information and furthermore, elicited values would truly reflect the real-time risk scenario. Furthermore, modelling the risk attitude of a decision maker and assigning the relative importance weights to each utility function are challenging tasks.

2.4.2 *Managerial Implications*

The proposed modelling approach can help supply chain managers prioritise risk mitigation strategies taking into account the cost, effectiveness and manageability of strategies. Based on the risk attitude of a decision maker, optimal strategies can easily be prioritised. The approach is equally beneficial for managers dealing with complex supply chains as the development of a risk network does not necessarily follow the process flow of a supply chain. Causal mapping (qualitative modelling of BBNs) is beneficial to managers in identifying important risks and understanding dynamics between these risks.

2.5 Conclusions

SCRM is an active area of research focusing on effective management of risks ranging across the entire supply network. A number of models have been proposed to identify and assess risks. Similarly, researchers have also proposed appropriate strategies to mitigate specific risks. Limited studies have considered evaluating supply chain risk mitigation strategies within an interdependent setting of interacting supply chain risks and strategies. However, the evaluation of such strategies within a probabilistic network model capturing cost, effectiveness and manageability of potential strategies has not been addressed in the literature. Besides considering cost of implementing a strategy, it is also important to model the associated manageability-ease of implementing and managing a strategy.

In this chapter, we have proposed a modelling process of prioritising risk mitigation strategies on the basis of relative cost, effectiveness and manageability within a theoretically grounded framework of BBNs and demonstrated its application through a simulation study. Although we have assumed the decision maker as risk-neutral in the study, the proposed modelling process can be adapted to capture specific risk appetite of a decision maker which is represented by the unique utility function for loss and the relative importance of cost for implementing strategies.

In models ignoring manageability of strategies, it is assumed that all strategies are equally manageable. However, strategies differ in terms of manageability and such an assumption undermines the efficacy of models in evaluating strategies. The proposed process helps in determining optimal strategies for a given number of potential strategies. As the optimal strategies are different for cost-effectiveness and cost-effectiveness cum manageability based prioritisation schemes, we consider it important to model the manageability of strategies without which a decision maker would select and implement sub-optimal strategies.

We have represented risks and mitigation strategies by binary states. In future, risks can be modelled as continuous variables whereas strategies can be represented by a continuum of control levels. The proposed method is a first step towards modelling manageability of strategies within a framework of interdependent risks and strategies. It is important to consider the practical implications of adopting such an approach within a real case study. Another interesting and related theme is to model the adaptability of strategies and to explore the control levels of existing strategies yielding maximum net improvement in the expected loss less cost. Furthermore, less labour intensive elicitation methods may be developed and evaluated to help practitioners implement the process.

References

Ackermann, F., Howick, S., Quigley, J., Walls, L., & Houghton, T. (2014). Systemic risk elicitation: Using causal maps to engage stakeholders and build a comprehensive view of risks. *European Journal of Operational Research, 238*(1), 290–299.

Aqlan, F., & Lam, S. S. (2015). Supply chain risk modelling and mitigation. *International Journal of Production Research, 53*(18), 5640–5656.

Aven, T., Vinnem, J. E., & Wiencke, H. S. (2007). A decision framework for risk management, with application to the offshore oil and gas industry. *Reliability Engineering & System Safety, 92*(4), 433–448.

Badurdeen, F., Shuaib, M., Wijekoon, K., Brown, A., Faulkner, W., Amundson, J., et al. (2014). Quantitative modeling and analysis of supply chain risks using bayesian theory. *Journal of Manufacturing Technology Management, 25*(5), 631–654.

Blodgett, J. G., & Anderson, R. D. (2000). A bayesian network model of the consumer complaint process. *Journal of Service Research, 2*(4), 321–338.

Bogataj, D., & Bogataj, M. (2007). Measuring the supply chain risk and vulnerability in frequency space. *International Journal of Production Economics, 108*(1–2), 291–301.

Charniak, E. (1991). Bayesian networks without tears: Making bayesian networks more accessible to the probabilistically unsophisticated. *AI Magazine, 12*(4), 50–63.

Christopher, M., & Lee, H. (2004). Mitigating supply chain risk through improved confidence. *International Journal of Physical Distribution & Logistics Management, 34*(5), 388–396.

Christopher, M., Mena, C., Khan, O., & Yurt, O. (2011). Approaches to managing global sourcing risk. *Supply Chain Management: An International Journal, 16*(2), 67–81.

Faisal, M. N., Banwet, D. K., & Shankar, R. (2006). Supply chain risk mitigation: Modeling the enablers. *Business Process Management Journal, 12*(4), 535–552.

Garvey, M. D., Carnovale, S., & Yeniyurt, S. (2015). An analytical framework for supply network risk propagation: A bayesian network approach. *European Journal of Operational Research, 243*(2), 618–627.

Genie 2.0. (2015). *The decision systems laboratory, genie and smile* [Online]. Available: http://genie.sis.pitt.edu/about.html. Accessed 5 June, 2014.

Jensen, F. V., & Nielsen, T. D. (2007). *Bayesian networks and decision graphs*. New York: Springer.

Johnson, M. E. (2001). Learning from toys: Lessons in managing supply chain risk from the toy industry. *California Management Review, 43*(3), 106–124.

Kjaerulff, U. B., & Anders, L. M. (2008). *Bayesian networks and influence diagrams: A guide to construction and analysis*. New York: Springer.

Nadkarni, S., & Shenoy, P. P. (2001). A bayesian network approach to making inferences in causal maps. *European Journal of Operational Research, 128*(3), 479–498.

Nadkarni, S., & Shenoy, P. P. (2004). A causal mapping approach to constructing bayesian networks. *Decision Support Systems, 38*(2), 259–281.

Onisko, A. (2008). Medical diagnosis. In O. Pourret, P. Naïm, & B. Marcot (Eds.), *Bayesian networks: A practical guide to applications.* West Sussex: Wiley.

Qazi, A., Quigley, J., & Dickson, A. (2014). *A novel framework for quantification of supply chain risks*. In 4th Student Conference on Operational Research, University of Nottingham, UK.

Qazi, A., Quigley, J., & Dickson, A. (2015a). *Supply chain risk management: Systematic literature review and a conceptual framework for capturing interdependencies between risks* (pp. 1–13). In 5th International Conference on Industrial Engineering and Operations Management, Dubai, UAE.

Qazi, A., Quigley, J., Dickson, A., & Gaudenzi, B. (2015b). A new modelling approach of evaluating preventive and reactive strategies for mitigating supply chain risks. In F. Corman, S. Voß, & R. Negenborn (Eds.), *Computational logistics.* Berlin: Springer International Publishing.

Qazi, A., Quigley, J., Dickson, A., Gaudenzi, B., & Ekici, S. O. (2015c). *Evaluation of control strategies for managing supply chain risks using Bayesian belief networks* (pp. 1146–1154). In International Conference on Industrial Engineering and Systems Management.

Rajesh, R., & Ravi, V. (2015). Modeling enablers of supply chain risk mitigation in electronic supply chains: A grey-dematel approach. *Computers & Industrial Engineering, 87,* 126–139.

SA. (2009). *Risk management: Principles and guidelines (as/nzs iso 31000: 2009).* Sydney: Standards Australia.

Sigurdsson, J. H., Walls, L. A., & Quigley, J. L. (2001). Bayesian belief nets for managing expert judgement and modelling reliability. *Quality and Reliability Engineering International, 17*(3), 181–190.

Sodhi, M. S., Son, B.-G., & Tang, C. S. (2012). Researchers' perspectives on supply chain risk management. *Production and Operations Management, 21*(1), 1–13.

Son, J. Y., & Orchard, R. K. (2013). Effectiveness of policies for mitigating supply disruptions. *International Journal of Physical Distribution and Logistics Management, 43*(8), 684–706.

Speier, C., Whipple, J. M., Closs, D. J., & Voss, M. D. (2011). Global supply chain design considerations: Mitigating product safety and security risks. *Journal of Operations Management, 29*(7–8), 721–736.

Tang, C., & Tomlin, B. (2008). The power of flexibility for mitigating supply chain risks. *International Journal of Production Economics, 116*(1), 12–27.

Tang, C. S. (2006). Robust strategies for mitigating supply chain disruptions. *International Journal of Logistics Research and Applications, 9*(1), 33–45.

Zsidisin, G. A., Ellram, L. M., Carter, J. R., & Cavinato, J. L. (2004). An analysis of supply risk assessment techniques. *International Journal of Physical Distribution & Logistics Management, 34*(5), 397–413.

Chapter 3
Modeling Risk Emergence and Propagation in Buyer-Supplier-Customer Relationships

Kristian Rotaru and Mehrdokht Pournader

Abstract The present study aims to identify and formalize the structural and relational patterns, which account for risk emergence and propagation in buyer-supplier-customer service triads. Following the guidelines of the design science research approach and based on the existing literature, buyer-supplier-customer service triads are categorized into a coherent typology according to the role that each supply chain dyad plays in the emergence and propagation of risk within the triad it forms. In the context of this study, such triads are referred to as Risk-aware Service Triads (RaSTs). To explore all the feasible forms of RaSTs, including the ones that have not yet been addressed in the literature, this study adopts the formalism of weighted directed graphs. As a result, a typology based on thirty different types of RaSTs is suggested. This typology allows: (i) to systematize and formally represent a variety of hypothetical scenarios when each of the dyadic structures within buyer-supplier-customer service triads acts as risk trigger, risk taker or risk neutral component of the respective RaST; and (ii) to calculate the maximal and minimal risk index specific to each of the identified type of RaST, thereby facilitating the identification and assessment of risk exposures associated with buyer-supplier-customer service triads. An illustrative example of how the methodological approach underlying the suggested RaST typology facilitates risk assessment in service triads and service networks is presented.

K. Rotaru (✉)
Monash Business School, Monash University, Melbourne, VIC, Australia
e-mail: kristian.rotaru@monash.edu

M. Pournader
Macquarie Graduate School of Management, Macquarie University, Sydney, NSW, Australia

Y. Khojasteh (ed.), *Supply Chain Risk Management*,
DOI 10.1007/978-981-10-4106-8_3

3.1 Introduction

Globalization and the recent technological advancements coupled with the need to cut costs and gain competitive advantage in an increasingly volatile global marketplace have resulted in a dramatic increase in outsourcing levels by servicing companies, looking for further means of cost reduction and efficiency improvement (Gunasekaran and Kobu 2007). In view of the growing complexity of modern, highly diversified supply chains, the inherent linearity underlying the traditional focus on the dyadic relationships between the members of a supply chain does not allow to capture the nature of the properties, emerging within more complex supply chain networks (Choi et al. 2002; Wu et al. 2010). To provide a more realistic account of the network structure and inherent characteristics of the modern supply chains, a number of studies suggested shifting the focus towards the elementary form of the supply chain network: a supply chain triad (Finne and Holmström 2013). This was followed by a call for further investigation into the structural and relational characteristics of service triads (Holma 2012), including the study of risks causing failure in outsourcing practices (Choi and Wu 2009; Bastl et al. 2013).

Since the earlier articles introducing triadic relationships in the context of supply chain management (e.g., Choi et al. 2002), the literature has reported on the following common types of supply chain triads including: *buyer-supplier-customer* (e.g., Rossetti and Choi 2005; Niranjan and Metri 2008), *buyer-supplier-supplier* (Wu et al. 2010), and *buyer-buyer-supplier* (e.g., Choi and Kim 2008). Notably, most of these studies investigate the supply chain triads operating in manufacturing rather than services domain. Hence, the focus of this study is on a relatively less investigated form of supply chain triads, the ones supporting the service outsourcing processes (Niranjan and Metri 2008; Li and Choi 2009).

To date, the literature exploring the patterns of risk emergence and propagation in the context of buyer-supplier-customer service triads has been limited but growing (Wynstra et al. 2015). Despite a number of attempts to represent the underlying factors that account for adverse behaviors by triad members (e.g., Choi and Wu 2009; Bastl et al. 2013), the literature on supply chain triads still lacks a systematic approach that would categorize risks according to where within supply chain triads these risks emerge and what are the possible pathways for their propagation between the member organizations of the supply chain triads. To the best of our knowledge, no research study has attempted to develop a generic typology outlining the core relational properties in buyer-supplier-customer service triads service triads and, using this information, to attribute corresponding generic risk profiles to the types of supply chain triads being analyzed. In this regard, a number of studies could be outlined as conducting the assessment of relational properties in supply chain service triads with the view to better understand the performance drivers in the triadic relationships. Peng et al. (2010) used social networks to study cooperative performance of service triads, while Holma (2012) borrowed from social capital theory to investigate interpersonal interactions and their effects on service triads. Depending on the initiating party, Wynstra et al. (2015)

identified three types of service triads, i.e. 'buyer-initiated', 'customer-initiated', and 'supplier-initiated', and outline a number of characteristics for each of these types, including: initiating party, focal service provider, service user (beneficiary), as well as who are the providers of inputs for the focal service. While the suggested typology serves as a generic framework to consider some of the properties of the service triads, it does not provide any formal mechanism of informing the user about either the performance drivers or the risk profile of the service triads being investigated through the prism of the suggested typology.

To address this research gap, the present study seeks ways to categorize the identified generic patterns reflecting the emergence and propagation of potential adverse events and behaviors within buyer-supplier-customer service triads into a comprehensive typology. Specifically, the concept of risk-aware service triads (RaSTs) is introduced to outline and categorize relational and structural properties of buyer-supplier-customer interactions that account for the increased levels of risk exposure within a given buyer-supplier-customer service triad. It is also expected that a greater clarity around the risk patterns delineated by RaSTs would facilitate the evaluation of the risk levels according to the identified types of RaSTs. Accordingly, the aim of this study is threefold: (i) to identify and formalize the structural and relational patterns which account for risk emergence and propagation in buyer-supplier-customer service triads; (ii) to design a coherent typology for classification of the modeled RaSTs according to the nature of their implicit mechanisms of risk emergence and propagation within the triads; and (iii) based on the suggested RaST typology, to suggest an approach for evaluation of the inherent risks associated with each RaST type.

Using guiding principles of design science research approach (van Aken 2004; Holmström et al. 2009) and the modeling apparatus of graph theory in supply chains (Borgatti and Li 2009; Kim et al. 2015), thirty types of RaST models are developed and categorized within a coherent RaST typology. Each RaST model has been ranked according to its implicit Risk Index (RI), which represents a quantitative measure of risk associated with the structural relationships among the members of a given RaST. Therefore, the taxonomy of RaST models, as well as the underlying approach for categorizing supply chain service triads according to their inherent risk profile, provide a comprehensive tool for risk assessment of triadic relationships that match specific RaST types outlined in the RaST taxonomy. We apply the suggested RaST taxonomy to review recent articles on buyer-supplier-customer service triads, and specifically to categorize the relational properties and risks categorized in these articles. This allows us to identify the types of RaSTs that have been overlooked in this emerging body of literature but still impose risks that threaten the objectives of supply chain partners operating within service triads, as well as service triads seen as complex adaptive systems. With the view to justifying the relevance of the proposed RaST typology, we use an illustrative example of the application RaSTs to assess risks in service triads and subsequently in service supply networks.

The remainder of this chapter is organized as follows. In the next section we provide a brief background by discussing the properties of service triads, specifically focusing on the phenomenon of risk emergence in the context of service triads. We then outline the research method built upon the design science, adopted as a research approach that guides the process of building RaST typology, and graph theory adopted as a modeling methodology. Subsequently, in line with the principles of design science and using the toolset of graph theory, a range of RaSTs types are suggested and categorized into three groups based on the nature of the risk and emergence mechanisms reflected in each RaST types. The identification of groupings and types of RaSTs is supported by a detailed review of the literature on buyer-supplier-customer service triads. Based on the properties of the directed graphs associated with each individual RaST type, a risk index is calculated following a formal procedure reported in operations and supply chain management. Next, the relevance of the suggested RaST typology is justified by showing how the proposed RaSTs can facilitate risk assessment in service triads and more complex service networks. Finally, the chapter is concluded by outlining a number of research limitations and discussing the core future research directions triggered by this study.

3.2 Background

The enhanced ability to respond to changes in demand and to the opportunities that may emerge, often goes hand in hand with the increasing dependency on quantum of work outsourced by servicing companies to their suppliers leading to an extension of the supply chains in both size and complexity (Ellram et al. 2008; Tate et al. 2009). Along with the increasing profit margins and other performance improvement outcomes achieved through the growing complexity and dynamism of the modern supply chains, comes the issue of the increased vulnerability of the supply chains and their individual members (Wagner and Bode 2008).

Having in mind the purpose of a desirable level of services delivered, service providing companies seek to establish proper relationships with members participating in the outsourcing practices considering such relationships as the key for achieving this purpose (Bastl et al. 2012). As a result, the companies today are urged to establish additional forms of risk response strategies and control procedures as part of their profiles to avoid the emergence of new sets of risks including adversarial buyer-supplier relations or winning customers over by suppliers, to name a few (Choi and Kim 2008). A considerable amount of risks threatening supply chains, including service supply chains and their individual service triads, are context-specific, i.e. their probability and magnitude largely depend on the structural characteristics of the operational context where they emerge (Neiger et al. 2009). Both emergence and propagation of these risks across organizational boundaries largely depend on the structural characteristics of the supply chain network and the nature of the relationships of its members (van de Valk and van Weele 2011; Bellamy and Basole 2013). To understand better these characteristics some general properties of the service triads are discussed below.

A service triad is commonly regarded as an independent elementary form of a service supply chain network that shares certain structural and behavioral characteristics of the network (Niranjan and Metri 2008). The term 'possible tie(s)' used in (Wasserman and Faust 1994) the definition of triads by Wasserman and Faust (1994), implies up to six different types of triads built on a continuum of inter-organizational relationships from less to more connected members (see Peng et al. 2010). While such view could be applicable to the study of manufacturing triads, in the context of service triads, where there is an ongoing interaction taking place between the members of the triad (Li and Choi 2009; Li 2011), such diversity of relationships is unlikely. It thus becomes of an utmost importance to take into consideration all three bidirectional relationships of service triad members in order to determine the possible risk propagation within the triad as well as the triad's degree of risk exposure. This concern has been addressed in the following sections that address the development of the RaST typology.

Service triad as an elementary form of supply chain network possesses the characteristics of a complex adaptive system whose behavior is determined by the activity of agents that are part of this system. Thus, a service triad exhibits unique characteristics or emergent properties, which are not properties of its distinct components but the whole network (Bastl et al. 2013). This view implies inherent qualitative and quantitative differences in risk profile of a service triad when compared to the sum of the risk profiles of the individual members of the triad, even if the dyadic relationships of each individual member is taken into account when conducting such risk assessment. Thus, in the context of buyer-supplier-customer service triads, new risk types emerge which are neither inherent properties of the distinct members of these types of triads nor their dyadic relationships but refer to the relationships between all the members within the network.

The need to account for the interactions among all members of service triads when assessing their risk exposures precludes researchers and practitioners to directly adopt the heuristics and more formal methods of risk assessment applicable in the context of risk analysis of single organizations or their dyadic relationships. At the same time, the literature investigating the issues of risk modeling/assessment in the context of service triads is still scarce. One of the examples is the study by Li and Choi (2009) who adopted the social network theory lens to highlight an emerging condition implying that in time and upon building some confidence, a customer may find it more comfortable working directly with the supplier without the buyer being involved. This phenomenon deprives buyer of the benefits of being the sole intermediary between customer and supplier (Rossetti and Choi 2005; Peng et al. 2010) and delegate the associated competitive advantages (i.e. information benefit and control benefit) to the supplier. These transitions in the triadic relations of buyer-supplier-customer are referred to as 'bridge decay' and 'bridge transfer' conditions. Another example is the study by Niranjan and Metri (2008) who identified the underlying premises of the ties in 'client-vendor-consumer' triad addressing issues that arise from insufficient and unsatisfying levels in the quality of the services provided.

Despite the first steps that have been made in the literature to explain and document a number of mechanisms associated with risk emergence and propagation within service triads, and specifically buyer-supplier-customer service triads, to the best of authors' knowledge no comprehensive approaches have been suggested to widen the scope of such investigation beyond the boundaries of the single case studies. Specifically, no theoretically grounded approaches have been suggested to support reasoning about the potential risk scenarios associated with service triads, considering the nature of potential vulnerabilities in the relationships between the members of these triads. Thus, a comprehensive typology, which would allow to formally represent and categorize such scenarios based on a variety of factors involved, as well as on the risk ratings assigned to each individual scenario, is introduced further as a viable solution to address this research gap. Below we present the research method supporting the design of such typology.

3.3 Research Method

In this study, the design science research approach is adopted to guide the identification and categorization of the structural and relational patterns underlying risk emergence and propagation in buyer-supplier-customer service triads, whereas graph theory is used as a modeling methodology that supports the development of the RaST typology.

3.3.1 Design Science Research Approach

Design science has a long history as a set of pragmatic principles underlying the invention of novel artifacts based on a previously acquired technological knowledge, and as such, it is not t a discipline-specific approach to knowledge building. It has been widely adopted in the fields of information systems and computer science where it was reported to assist in understanding, explaining and frequently improving the behavior of existing systems by creating innovative and unique artifacts in a well-defined manner or by analyzing the use and performance of the designed artifacts. The design science approach has also been adopted in organizations science (van Aken 2004), operations and supply chain management (Holmström et al. 2009), and specifically supply chain service triads (Finne and Holmström 2013). Applied to operations and supply chain management, design science is introduced as an approach aiming primarily at discovery and problem solving, and emphasizing the novelty of the knowledge generated as a product of the design process (Holmström et al. 2009). In doing so, design science provides a utility-oriented methodology for addressing business needs through a purposeful design of an artifact or intervention (van Aken 2004, p. 226). These needs can be represented in terms of desirable properties that give a purposeful dimension to the process of artifact building.

In the context of this study, the design science research approach is used to support the formulation of our novel artifact, the RaST typology, which so far has not been suggested in the research literature or practice. Thus, we see the end product of the design process as a set of technological rules, each formalizing a unique configuration of a RaST model according to the innate characteristics of risk emergence and propagation associated with each individual type of a buyer-supplier-customer service triad. To guide the design of the RaST typology we conduct a literature review on service triads, their reported typology and the nature of the dyadic relationships they are composed of. We then adopt graph theory as a modeling method that supports the development of a set of technological rules suggested to formulate the desirable artifact. We formalize the relational properties between supply chain dyads, which form part of the triadic structures and account for the emergence and propagation of risks within buyer-supplier-customer service triads. Then, as part of our design process which follows Holmström and Romme (2012), the risk trigger, risk taker or risk neutral roles of the pairwise inter-organizational relationships between the members of buyer-supplier-customer service triads are formulated. This allows for the formal definition and categorization of the relational factors, or technological rules, introduced in this study that increase the probability of risk events in these triads (Figs. 3.1, 3.2 and 3.3). Next, RaSTs, which have been identified and categorized into RaST typology are justified by demonstrating the relevance of the specific RaST models matching them with the evidence reported in the research literature (Table 3.1).

3.3.2 *Graph Theory: A Modeling Methodology for Designing RaSTs*

The versatility of graphs in modeling the relationships between members of networks has made them widely applicable in social, technological, informational and biological networks (Wasserman and Faust 1994; Borgatti and Li 2009). In their recent review of the studies adopting network analysis approaches in the context of supply chain management, Borgatti and Li (2009) and Bellamy and Basole (2013) distinguish a number of promising research directions among which is the application of the graph theoretical approach to model the network structure and relevant properties of supply chains. The applicability of graph theory to modeling supply chain risks has been recently confirmed in the literature (Wagner and Neshat 2010).

The simplest mode of a graph is comprised of a set of vertices linked by edges. In more complex graphs, the vertices could each represent a particular feature,

Group 1 (1 Risk Trigger /1 Risk Taker/ 1 Risk Neutral) of RaSTs *(Buyer=B, Supplier=S, Customer=C)*

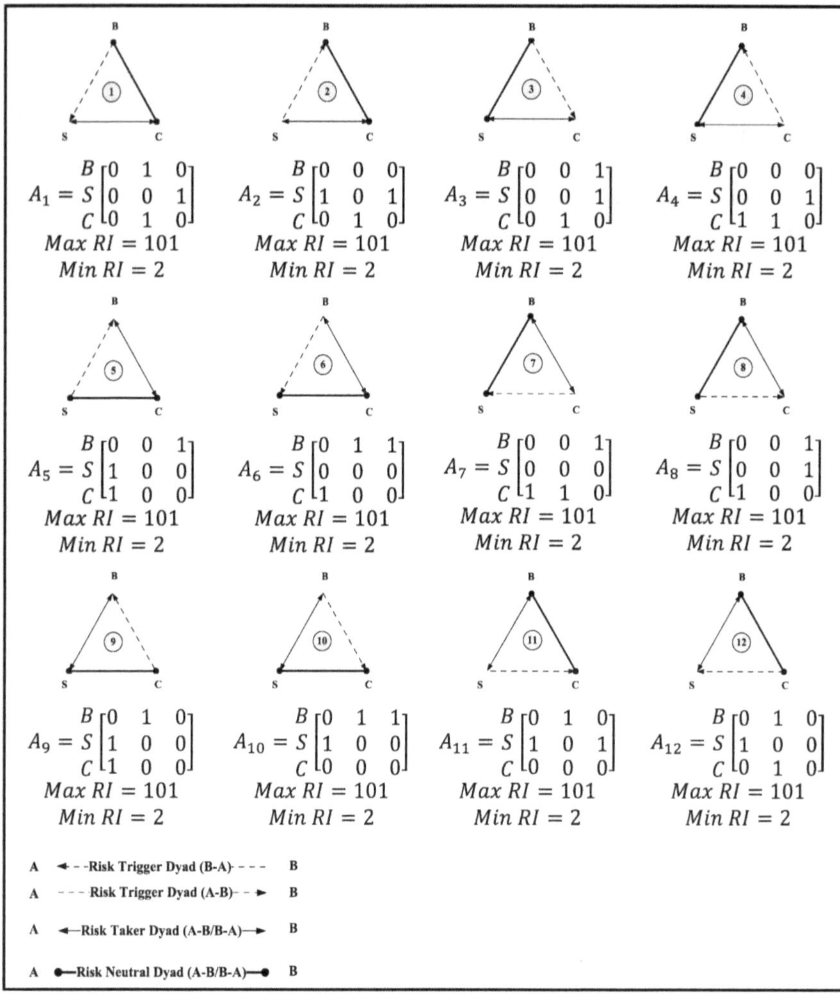

Fig. 3.1 Group 1 (1 Risk Trigger/1 Risk Taker/ 1 Risk Neutral) of RaSTs (*B* Buyer, *S* Supplier, *C* Customer)

identity or entity (West 2001). Similarly the edges could also be directed and/or have weights. The graph theory is adopted in this study to assist in modeling of a range of risks that stem from the bidirectional relationships between the members of a supply chain triad. The risks under consideration include those that are triggered

Group 2 (2 Risk Triggers/1 Risk Taker) of RaSTs (*Buyer=B, Supplier=S, Customer=C*)

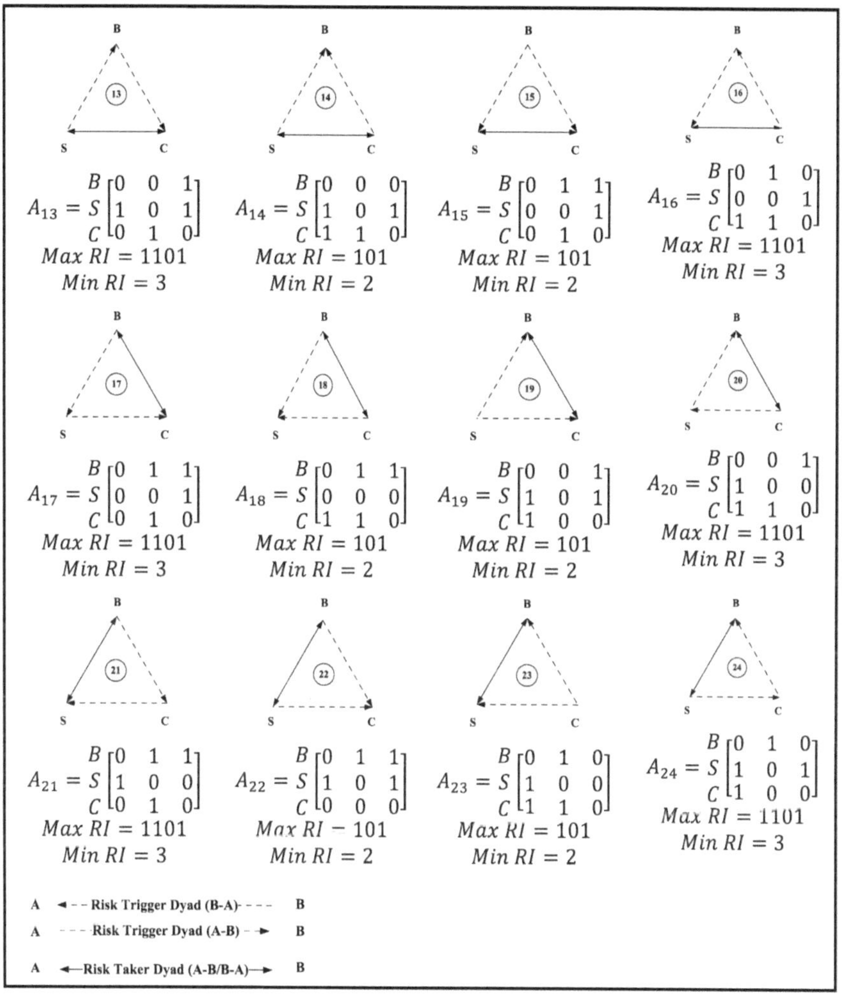

Fig. 3.2 Group 2 (2 Risk Triggers/1 Risk Taker) of RaSTs (*B* Buyer, *S* Supplier, *C* Customer)

by an external event pertaining to dyadic cross-organizational process(es) within the service triad and then propagate further, affecting other dyadic relational aspects within the triad. Hence, in line with the graph theory, it is suggested that the RaSTs can be modeled as weighted directed graphs in which the vertices represent either buyer, supplier or customer and the directed edges illustrate the risk transferred from one vertex to the other.

Group 3 (1 Risk Trigger/ 2 Risk Takers) of RaSTs (Buyer=*B*, *Supplier=S*, *Customer=C*)

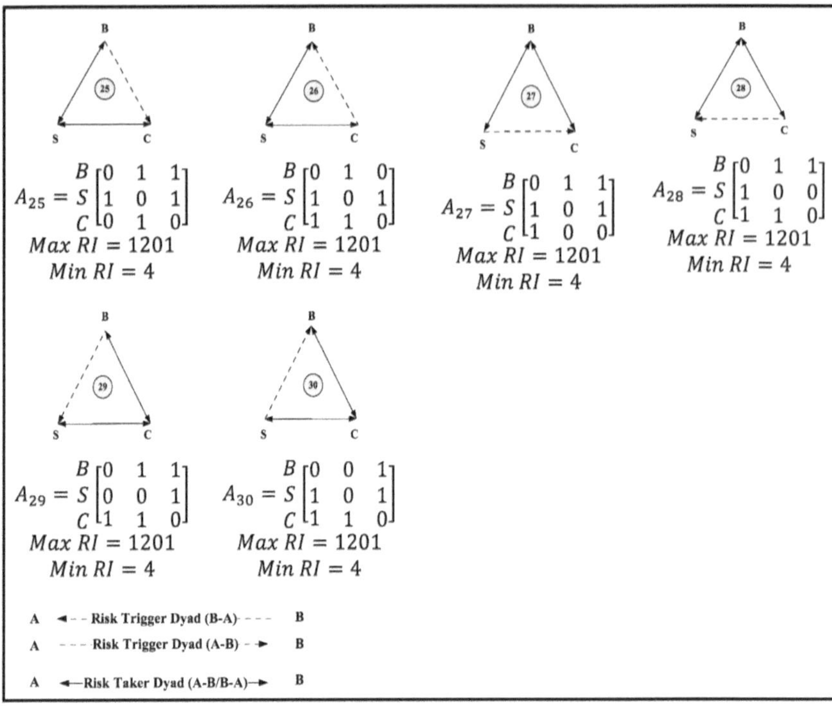

Fig. 3.3 Group 3 (1 Risk Trigger/2 Risk Takers) of RaSTs (*B* Buyer, *S* Supplier, *C* Customer)

3.4 RaST Typology: Groupings and Types of RaSTs and their Risk Ratings

In line with the graph theoretical approach, the pairwise relationships between the distinct members in buyer-supplier-customer service triads are categorized as follows:

1. *Risk trigger dyad*: the dyadic relationship among two vertices (i.e. buyer-supplier, or supplier-customer, or buyer-customer), which transfers risk to another dyad.
2. *Risk taker dyad*: the dyadic relationship among two vertices, which is exposed to risk by a risk trigger dyad.
3. *Risk neutral dyad*: the risk neutral dyad is not affected by risks that emerge in the risk trigger dyad and propagate within the risk taker dyad.

The risk trigger, risk taker and risk neutral dyads in Figs. 3.1, 3.2 and 3.3 are illustrated by a dotted unidirectional arrow, non-dotted bidirectional arrow, and a continuous line respectively. The direction of the arrow in the risk trigger dyad

Table 3.1 Review of recent articles on buyer-supplier-customer service triads through the prism of RaST typology

RaST type	Risk neutral	Risk taker(s) (Dyad)	Risk trigger(s) (Dyad)	Article
Type 3	*Buyer-supplier*	Lack of harmony between customer expectations and the received services by buyer *(supplier-customer/customer-supplier)*	Service quality gap between client and customer *(buyer-customer)*	Niranjan and Metri (2008)
Type 7	*Buyer-supplier*	Customer dissatisfaction *(buyer-customer/customer-buyer)*	Customer influence negatively affecting buyer's performance *(customer-supplier)*	
Type 5 Type 6	*Customer-supplier*	Customer dissatisfaction *(buyer-customer/customer-buyer)*	Legal/operational/relational risks between client and buyer *(supplier-buyer or buyer-supplier)*	
Type 8	*Buyer-supplier*	Deteriorating relationship between buyer and customer *(buyer-customer/ customer-buyer)*	Solidification of bridge position by supplier *(supplier-customer)*	Li and Choi (2009), Li (2011)
Type 17	–	Deteriorating relationship between buyer and customer *(buyer-customer/customer-buyer)*	(1) Adversarial buyer-supplier relationship *(buyer-supplier)* (2) Solidification of bridge position by supplier *(supplier-customer)*	
Type 9	*Supplier-customer*	Having the advantage of critical information by supplier *(supplier-buyer/buyer-supplier)*	Deteriorating relationship between customer and buyer and bridge transfer *(customer-buyer)*	
Type 8	*Buyer-supplier*	Customer dissatisfaction *(buyer-customer customer-buyer)*	Reduction in the quality of services *(supplier-customer)*	
Type 5	*Supplier-customer*	Deteriorating relationship between customer and buyer and bridge transfer *(buyer-customer/customer-buyer)*	Supplier's appropriation behavior *(supplier-buyer)*	

(continued)

Table 3.1 (continued)

RaST type	Risk neutral	Risk taker(s) (Dyad)	Risk trigger(s) (Dyad)	Article
Type 8	*Buyer-supplier*	Customer dissatisfaction *(buyer-customer/ customer-buyer)*	Inappropriate behavior of suppliers towards customers *(supplier-customer)*	van der Valk and van Iwaarden (2011) and van Iwaarden and van der Valk (2013)
Type 18	–	Customer dissatisfaction *(buyer-customer/ customer-buyer)*	Conflicting objectives between: *(1) Buyer-supplier* *(2) Customer-supplier*	
Type 17	–	Customer dissatisfaction *(buyer-customer/customer-buyer)*	(1) Too much monitoring of supplier by customer *(buyer-supplier)* (2) Negative reaction of supplier on customer *(supplier-customer)*	
Type 8	*Buyer-supplier*	Increased downtime and higher maintenance costs of the customers *(buyer-customer/customer-buyer)*	Suppliers lacking expertise in maintaining buyer's products for the customers *(supplier-customer)*	Finne and Holmström (2013)
Type 5 Type 6	*Customer-supplier*	Supplier increasing costs or decreasing the quality of services to maximize returns, resulting into customer dissatisfaction of buyer's brand *(buyer-customer/customer-buyer)*	Conflicting goals between buyer and supplier (buyer pursuing brand equity while supplier aims at maximizing returns) *(supplier-buyer or buyer-supplier)*	Zhang et al. (2015)
Type 8	*Buyer-supplier*	Developing an unfavorable perception of buyer and possibly terminating relationships with the buyer *(buyer-customer/customer-buyer)*	Customers dissatisfied by the quality of services provided by the supplier *(supplier-customer)*	Wuyts et al. (2015) and Modi et al. (2015)

depicts the adverse effect(s) of risk(s) imposed from one member of the dyad to another. A bidirectional arrow of the risk taker dyad indicates that both members in a particular type of dyadic relationship are exposed to risks by a risk trigger dyad.

All three groups of RaSTs discussed next should comprise at least one risk trigger and one risk taker dyad. This condition assures the presence of at least one inter-organizational risk affecting the service triad under investigation.

3.4.1 Group 1 (1 Risk Trigger/1 Risk Taker/1 Risk Neutral) of Buyer-Supplier-Customer RaSTs

The first group of the RaSTs encompasses all three different types of the above-mentioned dyadic relationships (Fig. 3.1). Triads in this group have a unique feature characterized by a risk neutral dyad. This indicates that regardless of the presence of mutual risk(s) between two members of the triad, the relationship between the third member and either one of the first two members sharing the risk remains unaffected.

$A_i, (1 = 1, \ldots, n)$ in Fig. 3.1 represents the adjacency matrix of the bilateral relations in service triads. Also *RI* reprents the Risk Index in service triads. Further information on *RI* and how it is calculated is provided below and after introducing the types of RaSTs. An example of this kind of relationship is RaST Type 8 indicating the bridge decay and bridge transfer case (Li and Choi 2009), where the supplier tries to solidify its bridge position by making stronger ties with the customer ('risk trigger' dyad). This type of risk is then imposed on the buyer-customer relationship ('risk taker' dyad) but does not have a negative impact on the buyer-supplier relationship ('risk neutral' dyad) (See Table 3.1). Figure 3.1 illustrates the twelve possible types of RaSTs in Group 1 along with their adjacency matrices and RIs which are going to be discussed in more detail after the introduction of all three groups of buyer-supplier-customer RaSTs.

3.4.2 Group 2 (2 Risk Triggers/1 Risk Taker) of Buyer-Supplier-Customer RaSTs

Group 2 (Fig. 3.2) contains two risk trigger dyads that impose risk(s) to the remaining dyad. There is no risk neutral dyad present in Groups 2 and 3. An instance of this group, RaST Type 18, is discussed by van der Valk and van Iwaarden (2011) and includes conflicting objectives in the buyer-supplier and supplier-customer relations (risk triggers), leading to negative impacts on buyer-customer relationship ('risk taker' dyad, further referred to as risk taker) (Table 3.1). Figure 3.2 illustrates the twelve possible types of RaSTs in Group 2 along with their adjacency matrices and RIs.

For instance for A_{13} in Fig. 3.2, the RI is calculated using the formula in the Appendix A as below:

$$RI = 1 \times 1 \times 1 + 1 \times 1 \times 1 + 1 \times 1 \times 0 + 1 \times 0 \times 1 + 0 \times 1 \times 0 + 1 \times 1 \times 1 = 3$$

For all the RIs, we consider the main diagonal to be 1[1]. Also if we consider that the remainder of non-zero arrays having their highest values of 10 (according to the Likert Scale of 1-10), the max number obtained for RI is calculated as follows:

$$RI = 1 \times 1 \times 1 + 1 \times 10 \times 10 + 1 \times 10 \times 0 + 1 \times 0 \times 10 + 0 \times 10 \times 0 + 10 \times 10 \times 10 = 1101$$

3.4.3 *Group 3 (1 Risk Trigger/2 Risk Takers) of Buyer-Supplier-Customer RaSTs*

Another possible configuration according to predefined conditions of buyer-supplier-customer RaSTs encompasses risk trigger dyadic relationships between two vertices that impose risk(s) to the remaining two dyads (risk takers). Figure 3.3 illustrates the remaining six possible types of RaSTs in Group 3 along with their adjacency matrices and RIs.

Carson et al. (1997) argue that given the presence of a risk trigger dyad in a supply chain triad (Group 1), if not neutralized, it will soon affect the other dyadic relationships within this triad. According to this statement, RaSTs of Group 1 may potentially transform into RaSTs of Group 3 characterized by a higher level of hazard.

---

[1]For the matrices shown in the Figs. 3.1, 3.2 and 3.3, the values for all diagonals equal to 0 as the RaST models presented in these figures do not account for risks/vulnerabilities inherent in the processes of each node (i.e. each member of the supply chain triad). This assumption is dictated by the fact that the focus of the RaSTs depicted in these figures is on network risks (risks imposed by one RaST member to another). However, for the purpose of calculating the RIs, it is assumed that all the diagonals are equal to 1. Indeed, if the diagonal values are considered as being equal to 0, this would result in 0 permanent for all RaSTs, thereby making problematic the calculation of the corresponding RIs. On the other hand, assuming the diagonal values equal to 1 allows to acquire meaningful (non-zero) values for RIs and thus to compare the risk levels of different RaSTs.

3.4.4 Further Instructions on the Application of the RaSTs

The graph models (RaSTs) specified in Figs. 3.1, 3.2 and 3.3 exhibit a number of properties facilitating understanding, formalization, and quantification of the inherent risks:

1. The *Nodal-in degree* or *Nodal-out degree* of vertices represent the extents to which a vertex is subjected to risk(s) or imposes risk(s). These characteristics can be easily extracted by summation of the columns and rows of the adjacency matrix. According to the suggested typology of the triads, it is apparent that in the adjacency matrix comprised of arrays with the highest value of 1, the maximum *Nodal-in degree* or *Nodal-out degree* of each vertex could be 2. Thus, considering RaSTs in Group 1, and for instance RaST Type 1, if the supplier's vertex value has the *Nodal-in degree* = 2, it indicates that it has the highest exposure to risk(s). This concept is critical especially when there exists a complex network of suppliers, buyers and customers to be investigated (Bezuidenhout et al. 2011).
2. According to Wagner and Neshat (2012) the risk index (RI) of graphs or weighted graphs could be calculated using *matrix permanent*. The similar approach has been adopted in the literature that uses matrix permanent as an indicator of cost effectiveness (Sabharwal and Garg 2013), effectiveness of risk mitigation strategies (Rajesh et al. 2014), or for ranking agility enablers in a manufacturing environment (Aravind Raj et al. 2013). The calculation of matrix permanent represents a four-step procedure and includes the following: (i) identifying the vertices, which in case of RaSTs represent buyer, supplier, and customer; (ii) defining the directions and weights of the edges, which in case of RaSTs reflect the types of the dyadic relationships between buyers, suppliers and customers in a service triad; (iii) calculating the adjacency matrix permanent and the RIs associated with the specific types of RaSTs (see Appendix A for more details on calculating matrix permanent); and (iv) comparing the calculated indices for ranking purposes.[2]
3. When defining the RaSTs, we posit that no vertex contains internal risk(s) that constitutes a *self-loop*. Therefore, the diagonal of the adjacency matrices for the RaSTs in all three groups should constitute an array of 0s. Nevertheless, in order to avoid 0 values for RIs, especially for Group 1 of RaSTs where: $\forall i \in I = \{1, \ldots, 12\}$, $per(A_i) = 0$ (see Appendix A), we posit that the gradient of matrix for all weighted graphs extracted subsequently in our empirical study is 1 instead of 0. Accordingly, if we define a value range of 1–10 for all the other arrays of RaSTs according to their adjacency matrices, the maximum RIs for the triads in Groups 1, 2, and 3 are going to be 101, 1101, and 1201 respectively. These values for RIs indicate the extent to which a triad is exposed to risk.

[2]For additional information we suggest to refer to the extant literature on measuring matrix permanent for matrices with unlimited number of nodes, e.g.(Glynn 2010)

3.4.5 Justification of RaST Typology and an Illustrative Example of its Use

To date, there have been no attempts in the literature to view and categorize the relational properties of the supply chain service triads from the point of view of their contribution towards the risk profile of the supply chain triad, seen as a system of interrelated supply chain partners. Below we adopt our RaST typology to categories the knowledge on the emerging risks within different types of supply chain service triads.

In Table 3.1, we categorize the buyer-supplier-customer RaSTs explored in the research literature according to the proposed typology of RaSTs. In some cases (e.g., Niranjan and Metri 2008), despite the fact that the service triads and their associated risks represent the core unit of analysis, only dyadic risks have been identified and no further investigation was conducted to analyze their impact on the adjacent dyads. In such cases, we used logical deduction to identify the adverse effects of these risks and to assign them to a particular RaST.

Though the number of studies investigating the buyer-supplier-customer triadic relationships is still limited, it can be concluded from the main groupings of Table 3.1 that certain types of triads in the proposed groups of RaSTs have attracted more interest from researchers than others. In particular, this relates to the first two groups, and especially RaST Type 8. This RaST type mainly deals with risks imposed by supplier on customer by the quality of the services provided and leading to the deterioration of the level of customer satisfaction (e.g., Niranjan and Metri 2008; Finne and Holmström 2013). Such negative effect may potentially propagate into the relationship between the customer and the buyer who acts as an intermediary party. In some cases, similar to the bridge solidification scenario (Li and Choi 2009; Li 2011), the strengthening of the ties in the supplier-customer dyad has detrimental impact on buyer-customer relations overtime. It is also posited that the aforementioned risks do not affect buyer-supplier relations or else they would be categorized in Group 3 and more specifically Type 27.

In summary, the result of the mapping reported in Table 3.1 reveals that the classification properties of the proposed RaST typology are sufficient to depict the examples of buyer-supplier-customer service triads and their associated risks reported in the literature. Moreover, the outcomes presented in Table 3.1 clearly indicate that a significant number of types of RaSTs specified in the reported typology (e.g., Group 3) have not yet been addressed in the research literature.

We illustrate the proposed typology of buyer-supplier-customer RaSTs by using it in the context of a service network comprised of a buyer, two customers and a supplier. It should be noted that the proposed approach based on RaST typology can be adopted in of more complex supply networks, which include more than three actors. An example is the quadratic risk-aware relationships in a buyer-supplier-customer 1-customer 2 network presented in Fig. 3.4.

Figure 3.4 is illustrative of any simple service supply network in which the buyer has outsourced certain services to a supplier that simultaneously provides

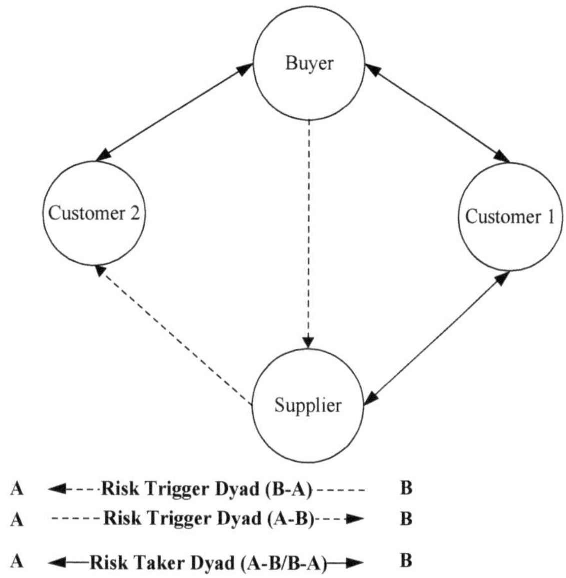

Fig. 3.4 Quadratic risk-aware structure of buyer-supplier-customer relationships

services to multiple customers. While fundamentally the nature of the two triads is the same (buyer-supplier-customer triad), it is only logical to assume that the risks and the severity of the disruptions that might occur in different triads of this network (i.e. buyer-supplier-customer 1 and buyer-supplier-customer 2) could differ. The two triads forming the quadratic network in Fig. 3.4 have unique RIs and Nodal-in degree/Nodal-out degree values. In the first triad, on the right, one risk trigger dyad (i.e., buyer-supplier) and two risk taker dyads (i.e., buyer-customer 1 and supplier-customer 1) are presented, matching RaST type 29 in Fig. 3.3. Depending on the values for risk trigger and risk taker dyads and using the formula in Appendix A and the adjacency matrix for this type of RaST in Fig. 3.3, the permanent of this matrix could be calculated as the RI of this specific triad. The second triad on the left shows two risk trigger dyads (i.e., buyer-supplier, supplier-customer 2), and a risk taker dyad (i.e., customer 2-buyuer), which matches RaST type 17 in Fig. 3.2. Similar to the other triad in this network, RI of this triad could be calculated by assigning values to the risk exposures and possible disruptions occurring in the risk trigger and risk taker dyads. Next, by comparing the RIs, the triad characterized by a higher exposure to risk (i.e. a higher RI score) could receive a higher priority as part of the risk response and mitigation phase of the risk management process. As per the earlier comment, the suggested RaST-based approach to risk assessment is generalizable to more complex supply networks than the one described for illustrative purposes in this section.

3.5 Conclusions and Future Research

This study proposes and justifies a novel typology of the risk-aware buyer-supplier-customer service triads. The development of the typology has been guided by the design science research approach and the graph theory used as a modeling methodology formalizing the structural and relational properties of different types of Risk-aware Service Triads (RaSTs). Each individual RaST model forming the suggested typology is built on a unique set of characteristics (technological rules) outlining the mechanism of risk emergence and propagation among dyadic structures within each buyer-supplier-customer service triad. Specifically, the dyadic components of the service triads were classified according to their active, passive or neutral role in risk emergence and propagation within RaSTs. The categorization of these components and their formal representation using the graph theoretical approach resulted in thirty distinct types of RaST models, categorized in three groups.

The application of the graph theory allowed calculating the Risk Index (RI) as an implicit quantitative measure of risk, in line with the structural and relational properties of the underlying dyadic structures informed by the RaST typology. The suggested approach provides a quick and intuitive tool for risk assessment and ranking of RaSTs in line with their type and group within the RaST typology. It should be noted though that the application of this approach should not be regarded as the end point in the assessment of risks in service supply networks, but rather as a means to identify the critical areas (triads) and to timely allocate resources needed to address high risk exposures. Hence, based on the problem context, the risk assessment approach formulated in this study still requires to further conduct more context-specific analyses into the risk factors and vulnerabilities that shape risk exposures of the supply network (or its individual components) under consideration.

By presenting the RaST typology, the study focuses explicitly on risks triggered by the link-level properties (Bellamy and Basole 2013) of the service triads. However, the vertex-specific risks triggered by the distinct members of the triads as well as the risks external to the service triads, that may affect the dyadic relations and the triad as a whole, have not been included in the proposed RaST typology. In the real-world situations, such assumption does not hold and the vertices, in addition to edges, could play a major role as risk triggers within a service triad. Having said this, the arrays of the gradient would have distinct numerical values other than non-zero values that are posited in the calculation phase. Furthermore, in conducting of real-world evaluations of risk exposures in service triads and to achieve more accurate scores of the resulting RIs, we recommend triangulating the managerial judgments about the severity of the risk exposures associated with the given processes from different sources including observations, historical loss data and semi-structured interviews (Barratt et al. 2011).

The output of this study calls for a wider application of graph theory for the analysis of risks in the context of cross-organizational collaborative relationships, including the buyer-supplier-supplier triads (e.g. Choi et al. 2002) and/or buyer-buyer-supplier triads (e.g. Choi and Kim 2008). To further progress the ideas discussed in this chapter, our future research directions include an empirical evaluation of the proposed RaST typology via a series of case studies.

Appendix A

Permanent Calculation Formula of the RaST Adjacency Matrix

$$A = \begin{bmatrix} r_{11} & r_{12} & r_{13} \\ r_{21} & r_{22} & r_{23} \\ r_{31} & r_{32} & r_{33} \end{bmatrix}$$

$$\boldsymbol{Per}(\boldsymbol{A}) = r_{11}r_{22}r_{33} + r_{11}r_{23}r_{32} + r_{22}r_{13}r_{31} + r_{33}r_{12}r_{21} + r_{12}r_{23}r_{31} + r_{13}r_{21}r_{32}$$

References

Aravind Raj, S., Sudheer, A., Vinodh, S., & Anand, G. (2013). A mathematical model to evaluate the role of agility enablers and criteria in a manufacturing environment. *International journal of production research, 51*(19), 5971–5984. doi: 10.1080/00207543.2013.825381

Barratt, M., Choi, T. Y., & Li, M. (2011). Qualitative case studies in operations management: Trends, research outcomes, and future research implications. *Journal of Operations Management, 29*(4), 329–342. doi:10.1016/j.jom.2010.06.002

Bastl, M., Johnson, M., & Choi, T. Y. (2013). Who's seeking whom? Coalition behavior of a weaker player in buyer–supplier relationships. *Journal of Supply Chain Management, 49*(1), 8–28. doi:10.1111/j.1745-493x.2012.03274.x

Bastl, M., Johnson, M., Lightfoot, H., & Evans, S. (2012). Buyer-supplier relationships in a servitized environment: An examination with Cannon and Perreault's framework. *International Journal of Operations & Production Management, 32*(6), 650–675.

Bellamy, M. A., & Basole, R. C. (2013). Network analysis of supply chain systems: A systematic review and future research. *Systems Engineering, 16*(2), 235–249. doi:10.1002/sys.21238

Bezuidenhout, C. N., Bodhanya, S., Sanjika, T., Sibomana, M., & Boote, G. L. N. (2011). Network-analysis approaches to deal with causal complexity in a supply network. *International Journal of Production Research, 50*(7), 1840–1849. doi:10.1080/00207543.2011.575088

Borgatti, S. P., & Li, X. U. N. (2009). On social network analysis in a supply chain context. *Journal of Supply Chain Management, 45*(2), 5–22. doi:10.1111/j.1745-493X.2009.03166.x

Carson, P., Carson, K., Knouse, S., & Roe, C. W. (1997). Balance theory applied to service quality: A focus on the organization, provider, and consumer triad. *Journal of Business and Psychology, 12*(2), 99–120.

Choi, T. Y., & Kim, Y. (2008). Structural embeddedness and supplier management: A network perspective. *Journal of Supply Chain Management, 44*(4), 5–13. doi:10.1111/j.1745-493X.2008.00069.x

Choi, T. Y., & Wu, Z. (2009). Triads in supply networks: Theorizing buyer–supplier–supplier relationships. *Journal of Supply Chain Management, 45*(1), 8-25. doi:10.1111/j.1745-493X.2009.03151.x

Choi, T. Y., Zhaohui, W., Ellram, L., & Koka, B. R. (2002). Supplier-supplier relationships and their implications for buyer-supplier relationships. *Engineering Management, IEEE Transactions on, 49*(2), 119–130. doi:10.1109/TEM.2002.1010880

Ellram, L. M., Tate, W. L., & Billington, C. (2008). Offshore outsourcing of professional services: A transaction cost economics perspective. *Journal of Operations Management, 26*(2), 148–163.

Finne, M., & Holmström, J. (2013). A manufacturer moving upstream: Triadic collaboration for service delivery. *Supply Chain Management: An International Journal, 18*(1), 21–33. doi:10.1108/13598541311293159

Glynn, D. G. (2010). The permanent of a square matrix. *European Journal of Combinatorics, 31* (7), 1887–1891.

Gunasekaran, A., & Kobu, B. (2007). Performance measures and metrics in logistics and supply chain management: A review of recent literature (1995–2004) for research and applications. *International journal of production research, 45*(12), 2819–2840. doi:10.1080/00207540600806513

Holma, A. M. (2012). Interpersonal interaction in business triads—case studies in corporate travel purchasing. *Journal of Purchasing and Supply Management, 18*(2), 101–112. doi:10.1016/j.pursup.2012.04.002

Holmström, J., Ketokivi, M., & Hameri, A.-P. (2009). Bridging practice and theory: A design science approach. *Decision Sciences, 40*(1), 65–87. doi:10.1111/j.1540-5915.2008.00221.x

Holmström, J., & Romme, G. (2012). Exploring the future of operations management: Toward an innovation mindset among practitioners and researchers. *Journal of Operations Management: Operations & Supply Management Forum,* Vol. Essay 15, No. pp.

Kim, Y., Chen, Y.-S., & Linderman, K. (2015). Supply network disruption and resilience: A network structural perspective. *Journal of Operations Management, 33–34,* 43–59. doi:10.1016/j.jom.2014.10.006

Li, M. E. I. (2011). *The impacts of bridge transfer on service outsourcing: A social network perspective.* (Doctoral Dissertation), Arizona State University.

Li, M. E. I., & Choi, T. Y. (2009). Triads in services outsourcing: Bridge, bridge decay and bridge transfer. *Journal of Supply Chain Management, 45*(3), 27–39.

Modi, S. B., Wiles, M. A., & Mishra, S. (2015). Shareholder value implications of service failures in triads: The case of customer information security breaches. *Journal of Operations Management, 35,* 21–39. doi:10.1016/j.jom.2014.10.003

Neiger, D., Rotaru, K., & Churilov, L. (2009). Supply chain risk identification with value-focused process engineering. *Journal of Operations Management, 27*(2), 154–168. doi:10.1016/j.jom.2007.11.003

Niranjan, T. T., & Metri, B. A. (2008). Client-vendor-end user triad: A service quality model for is/ites outsourcing. *Journal of Services Research, 8*(1), 123–138.

Peng, T.-J. A., Lin, N.-J., Martinez, V., & Yu, C.-M. J. (2010). Managing triads in a military avionics service maintenance network in Taiwan. *International Journal of Operations & Production Management, 30*(4), 398–422.

Rajesh, R., Ravi, V., & Venkata Rao, R. (2014). Selection of risk mitigation strategy in electronic supply chains using grey theory and digraph-matrix approaches. *International Journal of Production Research, 53*(1), 238–257. doi:10.1080/00207543.2014.948579

Rossetti, C. L., & Choi, T. Y. (2005). On the dark side of strategic sourcing: Experiences from the aerospace industry. *The Academy of Management Executive, 19*(1), 46–60.

Sabharwal, S., & Garg, S. (2013). Determining cost effectiveness index of remanufacturing: A graph theoretic approach. *International Journal of Production Economics, 144*(2), 521–532. doi:10.1016/j.ijpe.2013.04.003

Tate, W. L., Ellram, L. M., & Brown, S. W. (2009). Offshore outsourcing of services: A stakeholder perspective. *Journal of Service Research, 12*(1), 56–72.

van Aken, J. E. (2004). Management research based on the paradigm of the design sciences: The quest for field-tested and grounded technological rules. *Journal of Management Studies, 41*(2), 219–246. doi: 10.1111/j.1467-6486.2004.00430.x van de Valk, W., & van Weele, A. (2011). *Business service triads: A new area for service research.* Paper presented at the IPSERA 2011 Conference Proceedings, Maastricht, Netherlands

van der Valk, W., & van Iwaarden, J. (2011). Monitoring in service triads consisting of buyers, subcontractors and end customers. *Journal of Purchasing and Supply Management, 17*(3), 198–206.

van Iwaarden, J., & van der Valk, W. (2013). Controlling outsourced service delivery: Managing service quality in business service triads. *Total Quality Management & Business Excellence, 24* (9–10), 1046–1061. doi:10.1080/14783363.2013.776766

Wagner, S. M., & Bode, C. (2008). An empirical examination of supply chain performance along several dimensions of risk. *Journal of Business Logistics, 29*(1), 307–325. doi:10.1002/j.2158-1592.2008.tb00081.x

Wagner, S. M., & Neshat, N. (2010). Assessing the vulnerability of supply chains using graph theory. *International Journal of Production Economics, 126*(1), 121–129.

Wagner, S. M., & Neshat, N. (2012). A comparison of supply chain vulnerability indices for different categories of firms. *International Journal of Production Research, 50*(11), 2877–2891. doi:10.1080/00207543.2011.561540

Wasserman, S., & Faust, K. (1994). *Social network analysis: Methods and applications* (Vol. 8). Cambridge, UK: Cambridge University Press.

West, D. B. (2001). *Introduction to graph theory* (Vol. 2). Upper Saddle River, NJ: Prentice hall Upper Saddle River.

Wu, Z., Choi, T. Y., & Rungtusanatham, M. J. (2010). Supplier–supplier relationships in buyer–supplier–supplier triads: Implications for supplier performance. *Journal of Operations Management, 28*(2), 115–123. doi:http://dx.doi.org/10.1016/j.jom.2009.09.002

Wuyts, S., Rindfleisch, A., & Citrin, A. (2015). Outsourcing customer support: The role of provider customer focus. *Journal of Operations Management, 35,* 40–55. doi:10.1016/j.jom.2014.10.004

Wynstra, F., Spring, M., & Schoenherr, T. (2015). Service triads: A research agenda for buyer–supplier–customer triads in business services. *Journal of Operations Management, 35,* 1–20. doi:10.1016/j.jom.2014.10.002

Zhang, J. J., Lawrence, B., & Anderson, C. K. (2015). An agency perspective on service triads: Linking operational and financial performance. *Journal of Operations Management, 35,* 56–66. doi:10.1016/j.jom.2014.10.005

Chapter 4
Managing Reputational Risks in Supply Chains

Fred Lemke and Henry L. Petersen

Abstract In the face of ever expanding global markets, supply chain risks have become increasingly important. Most professionals are fully aware of the risks that have the potential to disrupt supplies such as minor design problems or even natural disasters. However, there is one kind of risk that has been often overlooked in supply chain management but is now becoming a threat: reputational risk. This chapter will explain the theoretical underpinnings of this vital management area and how to mitigate reputational risks in a practical supply chain setting.

4.1 Introduction

In this chapter, we begin by explaining the concept of reputation and how important it is to a corporation. This will lead us to the reputational triggers and the dimensions that carry an inherent risk to partnering organisations. These characteristics are particularly relevant in the supply chain context and the nature of spillover and the reputational ripple effect will bring 'reputational owners' and 'reputational borrowers' in the supply chain to the fore. Within this setting, corporations can use this effect to their advantage as it helps them to identify the zones of risk and to address these with mitigating strategies early on. Corporate social responsibility (CSR) serves as a contemporary measure to manage reputational risks – a critical aspect that we will further elaborate on in the discussion and conclusion of this chapter.

F. Lemke (✉)
Vlerick Business School, Avenue du Boulevard—Bolwerklaan 21, 1210 Brussels, Belgium
e-mail: fred.lemke@vlerick.com; fredlemke@googlemail.com

H.L. Petersen
Department of Management, University of Wisconsin-La Crosse, La Crosse, USA

Y. Khojasteh (ed.), *Supply Chain Risk Management*,
DOI 10.1007/978-981-10-4106-8_4

4.2 Corporate Reputation

Reputation is a dynamic and valuable asset that has been shown to mitigate the negative outcomes stemming from a crisis (Vanhamme and Grobben 2009), and serves as a fundamental source of competitive advantage (Dierickx and Cool 1989). The significance for managing the organization's reputation cannot be over stated – particularly in the supply chain context.

Fombrun (1996) identified three foundational elements in the development of a reputation: First, it is based upon perceptions. Second, it is the aggregated perceptions of all stakeholder groups; and third, it is comparative. Individuals form an impression of who and what an organization represents by their individual experiences with the firm (Lemke et al. 2011) and by the way the firm manages its assets (Reese and Kossovsky 2011). In the former, the impression is shaped by the consumer's experience with the firm regarding its *actions* (including how the firm interacts with the local community), the *offering* (including products and services), and lastly the firm's *communications* (including official standards and third-party certifications). These three triggers convey an impression, and when considered collectively with other stakeholders, result in a reputation. These are thus considered 'reputational triggers'. Take for instance McWane Inc., a U.S. manufacturer of pipe used in municipal utilities. Its reputation for being a dangerous company is due in large part by its actions associated to the health and safety of its employees. Over the years, a significant number of employees have been injured or killed while working at the facilities (Mokhiber and Weissman 2004). Apple Inc. (the U.S. technology company) has the reputation of being an innovator. This is a result of their product offerings, sporting state of the art design, and cutting edge technology. Lastly, whether we read it on social media platforms, on the firm's own website, or hear it from other stakeholders, we may decide that the BMW may not be the vehicle of our choice. It is a decision based upon a series of communications that influenced our perception. Others may have a completely different opinion. We, as consumers, pay attention to information that we deem relevant, which in turn impacts our views and resulting reputation.

The three general triggers, actions, offering and communications are made up of individual dimensions that form the basis of a reputation. Before proceeding to look at these more closely, it is important to recognise that we often associate a firm's reputation with the end-consumer market. But if we were to broaden our focus beyond the consumer, even past the retailer, multiple stakeholder groups would come under consideration. In this larger context, we then see that reputation is relevant in both the business-to-consumer (B2C) and the business-to-business (B2B) setting. In order to capture the various impressions, we draw upon the relevant academic work (Fombrun 1996; Worcester 2009; Lemke and Petersen 2013, Petersen and Lemke 2015) to form the integrative model that uses reputational triggers as a starting point to highlight the various stakeholder views.

Figure 4.1 details the three triggers of reputation. Each trigger has specific dimensions that are relevant for all stakeholder groups. Given that end-consumers' perceptions play a dominant role for today's market-oriented companies, an asterisk highlights the dimensions that are particularly relevant for this stakeholder group.

With respect to the first trigger, the firm's actions, this entails the quality of management, how management treats its employees, how the firm's resources are being utilized, what long-term investments are made, their corporate social responsibility efforts, the image that is casted and lastly, the firm's culture. Activities in any one or a collective of these activities can influence a reputation. Regarding the firm's offerings, the second trigger, this captures the products and services, innovativeness, its origin, the brand, the class image of the offering, the experience consumers have with the offer, and lastly, the image of the brand users. With respect to the last trigger, communications, the financial performance, corporate design, industry standards and third-party certifications are influential, as well as the classic marketing communication tools such as advertising, promotions, direct marketing, and public relations.

These triggers serve as a set of variables for the formation and development of a reputation, which reflects a multi-stakeholder acuity whether it is in a B2C or B2B setting. Within each of the three triggers, we can see how corporate reputation can be developed or in particular easily damaged (Dowling 2004; Hamilton 1995), especially when it is not developed, managed, and protected in a timely and appropriate fashion (Casado-Díaz et al. 2009). Wasting resources and taking a short-term horizon in investments may signal negligence. Employee complaints of mistreatment and superior financial performance may signal that an organization is greedy. That may be reinforced by insufficient activities in CSR and the destruction of the natural environment. In short, the reputation of any corporation is at risk and needs to be closely and regularly monitored.

4.3 Reputational Risks

Reputational risks are defined as the cumulative likelihood that events resulting from exogenous or endogenous sources can occur and negatively impact the stakeholder's perception of the firm's behaviour and performance (Roehrich et al. 2014). They may be based upon an economic, societal, or environmental event that involves the firm directly or they may arise indirectly via the activities of another organization in the supply chain (Hoejmose et al. 2014). An organization's reputation may be placed at risk if a member organization conducts itself in such a manner that the behavioural outcomes spread beyond its organizational boundaries. It is not surprising that this type of risk, if not realized, goes unnoticed. On the one hand, reputational risks rarely result in the disruption of resources and they hardly impact the quality and quantity of a supply—two major risks that tend to receive the most attention. On the other, it is generally problematic to assess their associated costs, if realized, making mitigation difficult to justify. Lastly, estimating the probability of an event occurring and the impact the event will have on a reputation

Action Trigger	Managerial Quality	Employee Management	Resource Use	Long-term Investments	Corporate Social Responsibility	Corporate Image*	Corporate Culture/ Personality*
Offering Trigger	Products and Services	Innovation	Image of Country of Origin*	Brand*	Product/Service Class Image*	Experience*	Brand Users Image*
Commun-ication Trigger	Financial Performance	Corporate Design*	Industry Standards and Third-Party Certifications*	Promotion*	Advertising*	Personal Selling and Direct Marketing*	Public Relations*

*Note:
The reputational dimensions are relevant for all stakeholders. An asterisk sign indicates that this dimension is most relevant for the end-consumer stakeholder group.

Fig. 4.1 Reputational triggers and dimensions in a multi-stakeholder environment

(and to what extent) is very difficult. This means that assessing the costs and benefits of managing such risks are highly unpredictable. In order to mitigate the potential risks that threaten a firm's reputation, we must first understand its function in the supply chain context. Lets look at the theoretical underpinnings before proceeding with some of the practical steps.

4.4 Reputation, Spillover and the Ripple Effect in the Supply Chain

We will start with describing reputation in a supply chain setting, before moving on to how the variables of reputation can 'travel' via the reputational ripple effect. After the theoretical foundation is established, we will outline the management tool that helps in detecting and capturing reputational spillovers.

4.4.1 Supply Chain Reputation

The reputational triggers and dimensions discussed thus far are particularly suitable for capturing the perspectives of all stakeholders associated with the processes and outcomes of a supply chain. Figure 4.2 represents a simplified view of such a chain. We only consider one raw material producer (tier-2 supplier), system supplier (tier-1), manufacturer, and a distributor for practical purposes but in reality, there may be many more with multiple tiers. Yet, the underlying principle applies just the same: along the chain, each firm forms their own reputation based upon the perceptions of stakeholders with respect to the firm's behaviours and competences for each of the three triggers.

The reputation derived from any one or more dimensions (i.e., within the respective trigger) has the probability of being transferred from one party to another

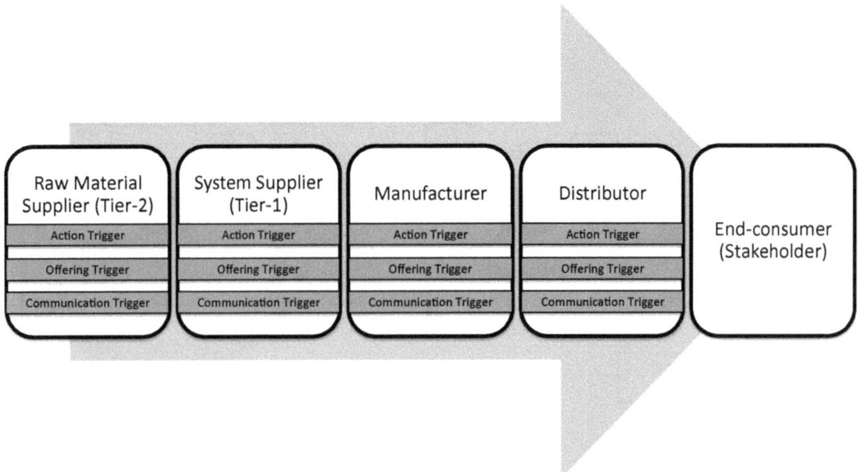

Fig. 4.2 Diagrammatic representation of a supply chain and member reputational triggers

(Fiol et al. 2001; Lemke and Petersen 2013). This is another way of saying that the three reputational triggers have the potential to traverse the supply chain, i.e., moving up- and down-stream the chain irrespective of organisational boundaries. For instance, a raw material supplier that causes a significant amount of damage to the natural environment will develop a reputation that formed primarily from the CSR dimension. There is now a high probability that partnering firms will experience a spillover effect in which they may also be associated with the misdeed, being guilty by association, and therefore, placing their reputation at risk. Importantly, reputational dimensions are transferrable in both the negative and the positive. A mere partnership with an innovative company may result in a positive spillover whereby the associated company may also be perceived as being innovative.

4.4.2 *The Mechanics of Reputational Spillover and the Ripple Effect*

Even though a corporation will develop a reputation along the chain (Eltantawy et al. 2009) this is not in isolation. In fact, there is an associated chain where 'reputational owners' and 'reputational borrowers' co-exist (see Lemke and Petersen 2013). Knowing which dimensions remain with the party that essentially earned it and which dimensions have a probability of spillover is the key to understanding when or where risks should be mitigated. Figure 4.3 provides a snapshot of the underlying mechanics:

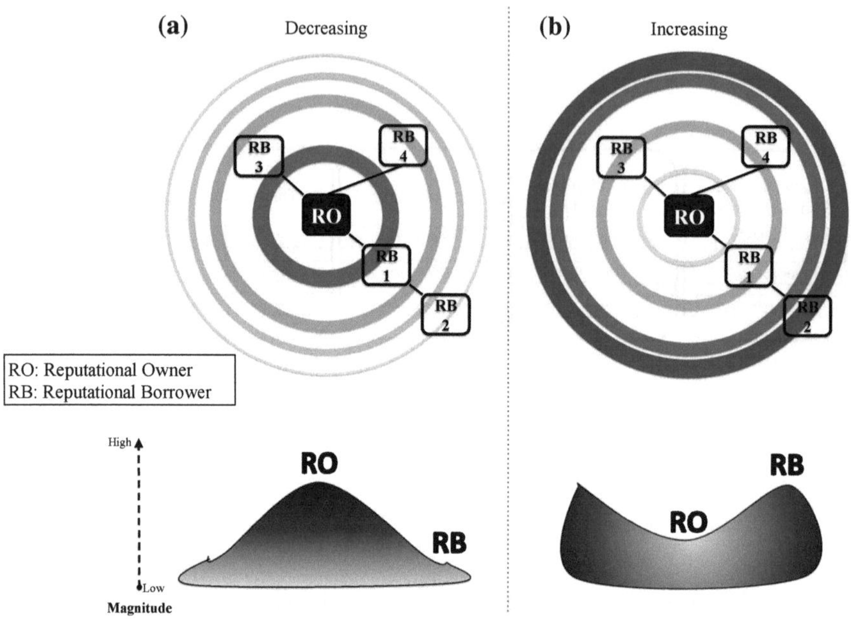

Fig. 4.3 Reputational spillover and the ripple effect

The *reputational owner* (RO in the figure) forms a reputation through the varying triggers associated with its market offering, communications, and actions. The *reputational borrower* (RB) will passively or indirectly be impacted by the reputation from the owner merely by association. This association could be embedded in a contractual frame (e.g., business partnership), industry setting (e.g., electronics), geographical region (e.g., South America), and others. *Transferring reputation* from the owner to the borrower is what we consider the *spillover effect.* The spillover could be direct (RO to RB1, RB3, and RB4) or indirect (RO to RB2) via multiple partners.

Although a full treatment of wider network considerations is beyond the scope of this chapter, it is important to understand that whoever is in the associative network of the reputational owner could be affected by it. This is because any reputational spillover is largely a matter of perception and thus, there are no physical boundaries. If we consider the temporal aspects of how reputation spreads outwards in incremental steps (i.e., away from the RO), this forms a ripple effect in which the transfer of reputation varies in length, direction, time, and magnitude. In nature, the magnitude of the ripples may weaken as they spread out and thus, the strength of the impact will be greatest at the core and begin to fade with every progressive wave (section 'A' in figure, on the left). In the business context, we see this happening with organizations that extract natural resources. The raw resource will eventually make its way along the supply chain to become any number of products that are eventually offered by retailers. Oil is a good example. Extraction methods in the North of Canada have been questioned with respect to the impact on human health. Regionally, stakeholder perceptions will impact the reputation of the organization (Jamasmie 2014). However, downstream, after the oil is transported, refined and transported yet again to become products in local gas retail outlets, the associated reputation with being a hazard to the North Canadian community is all but non-existent.

By contrast, the ripple effect could be like a tsunami that will erupt at some breaking point and reach its greatest impact at the outer-layer. In this case, we see that the magnitude of the effect increases or becomes amplified ('B', on the right) and a small – almost unnoticeable – action may turn into an enormous reputational effect. Take the 2014 UK poultry dilemma as an example (Lawrence and Wasley 2014). Clearly, customers enjoyed the lower prices. That is until they learned that unhealthy poultry, travelling across a number of countries, avoided safety standards, ending up on the shelves for an unreasonably low price. The issue grew to a point in which the reputations of several end of the chain retailers of various supply chains were threatened. Therefore, such a ripple effect can be seen to extend beyond the supply chain.

No matter whether the ripple effect becomes reduced or amplified, corrective actions should be taken to first address the effect and somewhat insulate or minimize the organization from the spillover and then second, take the appropriate measures to eliminate the risk right at the core of the effect. As shown in Fig. 4.4, certain reputational triggers will have a multi-dimensional effect and spill over from one chain to another.

We draw attention to four different reputational spillover states (R1 to R4 in Fig. 4.4) to explain variations in the supply chain context:

- Stemming from the reputational borrower, R1 is a direct downstream spillover. Note that 'down' refers to the supply chain, meaning that the reputation transfers from one supply chain actor to another that is positioned closer to the target market. For instance, a manufacturing firm that has a significant reputation for being fashionable, like Superdry (the UK clothing company), may have a spillover effect and thereby enhances the reputation for being fashionable to a partnering firm. Put another way, the retailer borrows the reputation for being fashionable from the manufacturer.
- R2 describes an interesting spillover that first directly transfers undetected to a downstream partnering firm (R2a) and re-spills detected to the next downstream organisation. This is an indirect down spill from the reputational owner to a reputational borrower without any direct relationship (R2b). For example, the reputation of a manufacturer for following fair trade principles may not be important for a global distributor of food. Given that this is neither relevant for the distributor nor for its stakeholders, there is a hidden fair trade reputational effect. The distributor could borrow the reputation, but does not look for it, does not detect it, and does not publicise it. Stakeholders also do not deem this important and are, thus, not concerned with this. Next, the retailer buys a range of products from the distributor and will then offer these to the end-consumer

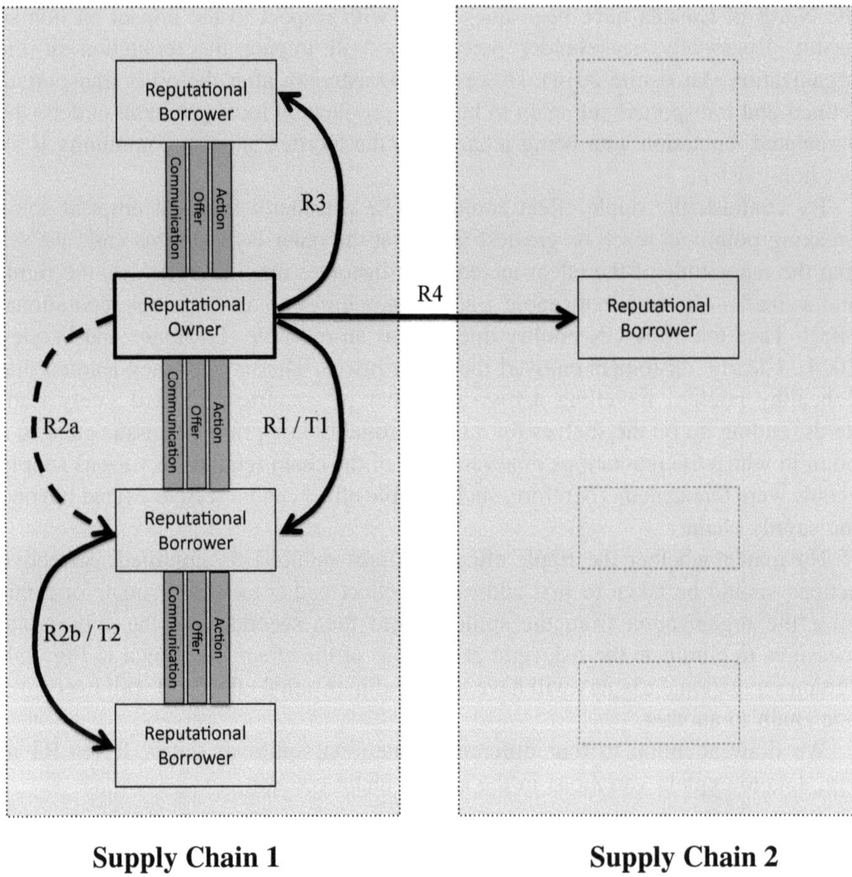

R1: Detected Direct Down Spill Over
R2a: Undetected Direct Down Spill Over
R2b: Detected Re-spill of R2
R3: Detected Direct Up Spill Over
R4: Detected Horizontal Spill Over
T1: Immediate Spill Over
T2: Delayed Spill Over

Fig. 4.4 Reputational spillover, length, and time

market. If end-consumers, as a stakeholder group, are looking for fair trade products, the manufacturer's fair trade reputation becomes relevant and re-spills, via the distributor, to the retailer who will borrow it for attracting end-consumers. In this scenario, we see that spillovers can vary in length, sometimes transferring reputation to both upstream and downstream companies that are more than one tier away. It is all about sequencing, which is another way of saying that the reputational ripple effect underlines the supply chain system and extends beyond it. A re-spill creates the next wave that, in this particular case, increases in magnitude (variation 'B' in Fig. 4.3). Following this thought, R1 could be further transferred, providing that the reputation (for being fashionable, to stay with the example above) becomes relevant for organisations and stakeholders further downstream the supply chain.

- R3 describes an upstream spill of reputation. A supplier that works with Apple Inc. could borrow Apple's reputation for being innovative and could "use the high-tech reputation to present itself as a highly capable and innovative supplier to new potential customers", as Smals and Smits (2012, p. 161) explain. In this example, we see that reputational spillovers can be multi-directional.
- R4 is an example that goes beyond the realm of a single supply chain. Thus far, R1 to R3 described vertical spillovers that stay within a given chain. R4 demonstrates that an organisation outside that chain can borrow the reputation from the owner. For instance, the reputation of Volkswagen (the German automotive manufacturer) for being environmentally responsible was tarnished with the diesel emissions scandal (Farrell and Ruddick 2015). As soon as it became public that the French police raided some of the manufacturing sites of Renault (the French automotive manufacturer), stock prices fell by 20% because investors were worried that Renault would be pulled into the Volkswagen emissions scandal as well (Topham and Kollewe 2016). Even the reassurances of the French government that Renault is not involved in any fraud, did not help to recover the losses. In this example, we see that the reputation of one company can spill horizontally to another organisation, even though these are embedded in two different supply chains.

The figure also draws attention to two time lapses (T1 and T2):

- T1 shows that reputation could spill over with an immediate effect. For instance, the reputation of a company manufacturing real fur coats spills over to partner organisations (e.g., retailers) as soon as 'wearing real fur products' becomes unfashionable, unethical, unsustainable, etc. The negative or positive reputation of the manufacturer has the potential to spillover directly and immediately to others.
- T2 highlights that reputation could remain latent and stay with the owner for some time and may spill over later to another party as soon as the reputational trigger becomes relevant and active in a given situation. For example, a clothing company sourcing products from countries where child labour is the norm has no reputational damage, as long as 'child labour' is not perceived as being wrong. Retailers will not experience any spillover, given that its immediate stakeholders do not deem this important. As soon as child labour becomes a topic of debate and stakeholders (such as end-consumers) perceive this as being negative, the reputation of the clothing company will spill over to the retailer, regardless of whether the retailer offers products from the clothing company at present. Given that the manufacturer-retailer association has already been established, activities and market offerings of the past could result in a latent reputational spillover at a later point in time.

4.4.3 The Tool to Detect and Capture Reputational Spillover

Regardless of time and the reach of a reputational spillover within the ripple zone, it is important to understand what reputational dimensions typically stay with the reputational owner and what dimensions have the propensity to transfer to borrowers. When seen from a distant, reputation in a supply chain becomes an unknown entity making it difficult to tease out the processes that lie behind it. The conceptual model presented next captures this by arranging the dimensions in the supply chain context.

Figure 4.5 is a template that illustrates the individual firm-specific triggers for reputation, which have the potential to surface in the supply chain as a holistic and multi-source construct that then poses a risk to all chain members. The figure outlines a simplified supply chain at the top; a matrix, cross-tabulating the dimensions for each of the supply chain parties, is given underneath, extending to the right, depending on chain length. Populating the matrix with ROs and RBs is contextual and thus, it is helpful to objectify and note the risk zones that are largely subjective in a given situation. For instance, managerial quality is a dimension that applies to every single firm and can spill over from any one member to another, depending on the specific setting of relationships. Hence, as an example, the manufacturer Foxconn engaged in questionable activities that generated a reputation for employee mismanagement, human rights abuses and negligence (Chan et al. 2013). The directionality of the spillover will be dependent upon the organization and its stakeholders. Spilling forward, Apple was a recipient and thus, the reputational borrower (RB) as shown in Fig. 4.5. Foxconn, the tier-1 supplier, is the reputational owner (RO) associated with the events and as seen in the figure, demonstrates this via the triggers. They are the RO for employee management, CSR, and corporate image. The RO-RB setup of other triggers would normally be included in Fig. 4.5, but they are not for illustrative purposes. The reputation on these dimensions is negative, and Apple has reluctantly become a recipient.

Other firms may experience a spillover as well, e.g., Amazon.com Inc. (the U.S. online distributor) and this could also happen via a different category or different supply chain. By the same token, the spillover could also occur upstream. But regarding the Foxconn-Apple example, this has not been reported in the media. This may be a result of tier-2 suppliers being in the same country of origin as Foxconn (tier-1); thereby perhaps the events are considered business as usual and therefore not a risk. The figure notes 'contextual', as a firm can be a reputational owner or reputational borrower. In this light, mitigation begins with analysing how the dimensions of reputation are developed and transferred and then assessing options for buffering or risk removal. This aspect draws the attention to reputational risk management and will be discussed next.

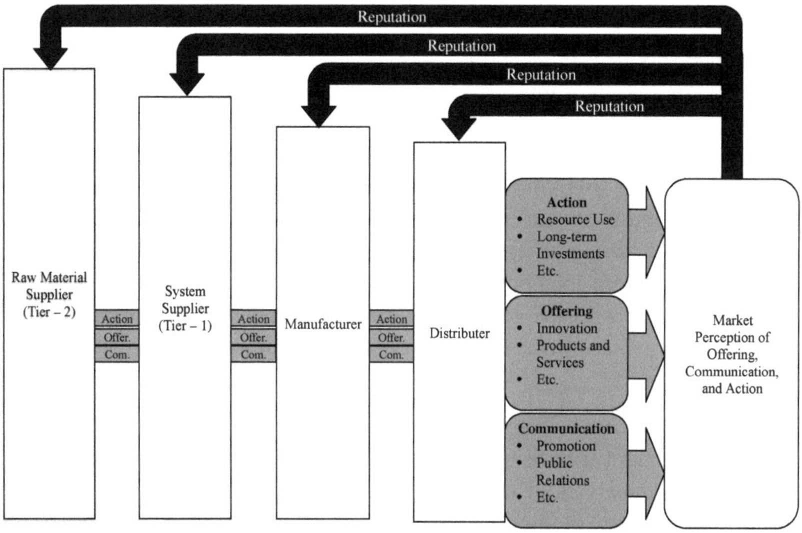

Reputational Trigger	Reputational Dimension	Raw Material Supplier (2nd Tier)	System Supplier (1st Tier)	Manu-facturer	Distributor
Action	Managerial Quality	*contextual*	RO	RB	*contextual*
	Employee Management	*contextual*	RO	RB	*contextual*
	Resource Use				
	Long-term Investments				
	Corporate Social Responsibility	*contextual*	RO	RB	*contextual*
	Corporate Image*	*contextual*	RO	RB	*contextual*
	Corporate Culture / Personality*				
Offering (Offer.)	Products and Services				
	Innovation				
	Image of Country of Origin*				
	Brand*				
	Product / Service Class Image*				
	Experience*				
	Brand Users Image*				
Communication (Com.)	Financial Performance				
	Industry Standards & 3rd-Party Certifications*				
	Corporate Design*				
	Promotion*				
	Advertising*				
	Personal Selling and Direct Marketing*				
	Public Relations*				

*Note: The reputational dimensions are relevant for all stakeholders. An asterisk sign indicates that this dimension is most relevant for the end-consumer.
RB = Reputational Borrower
RO = Reputational Owner
contextual = it depends on the specific setting and the member could be either a RB or a RO

Fig. 4.5 Supply chain reputation: the market, generators, and borrowers. *Source* Based on Lemke and Petersen (2013)

4.5 Reputational Risk Management

Integrating CSR into the supply chain serves to guide members with incentives and tools to enhance performance, a strategy that builds on the notion of 'greening' the supply chain (Björklund et al. 2012). We have found that this approach is structurally sounder than invoking rules, having to monitor member performance or using surveys. Figure 4.6 outlines the relevant management steps.

Assessing and managing for reputational risks entails a coordinated effort to assess all supply chain members' commitment, actions, and surrounding policies. The emphasis is to target the governance of partnering firms. Figure 4.6 shows the seven-step management process that the environment initiates—one has to take these in stated order:

1. *Member Orientation*—The process begins with the gathering of information from supply chain members. This entails their responsibility and sustainability statements, an analysis of their policies and procedures, corresponding performance, the quality of their metrics, and their connections to other business parties. This procedure would make the supply chain transparent (Doorey 2011) and creates a platform where knowledge-sharing, learning, developing a sense of shared meaning and values, etc. is encouraged (cf. Hernández-Espallardo et al. 2010). Other efforts, such as conducting a lifecycle analyses on the products (Lemke and Luzio 2014), would assist in identifying opportunities to mitigating environmental issues, human rights problems or disruptions to supplies. Scanning the environment for issues associated to the specific activities an organization engages in (i.e., regulatory matters, public policy issues, and societal trends) helps to identify and navigate through potential risks. This also includes regulatory non-compliance and/or awards. Ensuring that interested and affected parties are taken into consideration, identifying risks early on will assist in addressing and mitigating stakeholder issues at a later date.
2. *Risk Analysis*—Assessment begins with the characterization of the risks. Probability, impacts, social burden and cost to the organization are conducted here. Prioritization should occur to determine which risks should receive immediate attention as per stakeholder preferences and their input. Nevertheless, capturing and detailing the risks, based on accurate and relevant information, will lead to better decision-making. For instance, the lifecycle analysis will identify whether any supply chain member uses conflict materials in the production process or perhaps detail the carbon footprint of their product or service. It will also indicate the risk type perceived by each stakeholder group.
3. *Risk Ranking*—Risks should be prioritized and then categorically assessed for how the organization should manage them. This step could be based on the costs, resources, capabilities, impact, etc. involved in addressing the risk or on the consequences resulting from it.
4. *CSR Mitigating Strategies*—CSR is shaped by the activities of the firm, the environmental situation, and the perceptions of respective stakeholders. The result of the previous step, risk ranking, provides a process of prioritization that

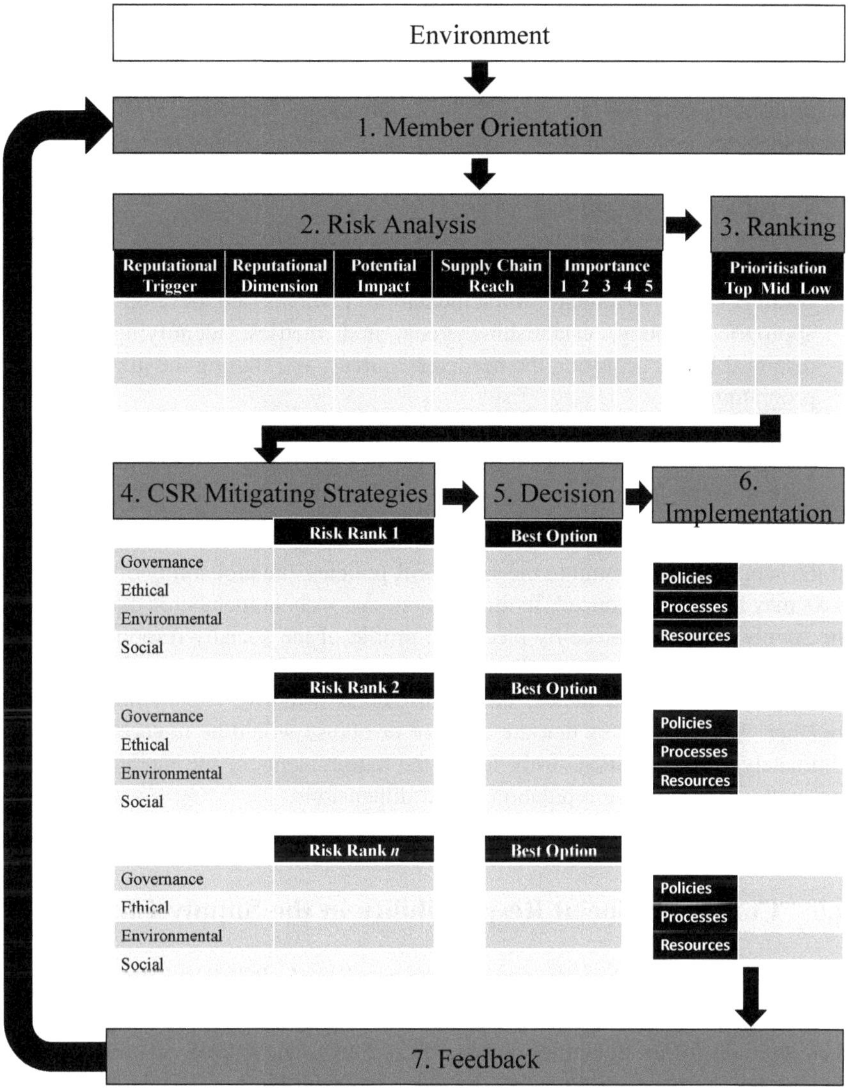

Fig. 4.6 Assessing and managing reputational risk in supply chains

is captured within a CSR framework, and would then provide options for mitigation. Given the complexity, CSR allows the formulation of counter-strategies specifically in light of governance, ethical, environmental, and social aspects of the business, which shall be discussed later.

5. *Decision*—Selection of the best option should lead to reducing or eliminating the risk in the most cost effective manner. Management's approach must be collaborative. Reducing or eliminating the risk is in the best interests of all

supply chain members, but more so with those that have more to lose. By developing the managerial competencies of all parties in the analysis, recognition and decision-making process, the chain becomes stronger and has the probability of providing a competitive advantage. Selection of the mitigating options are contingent upon ensuring that there is a collaborative approach that considers the resources required by the decision, the intensity of the effort, and the parties that are affected.

6. *Implementation*—Collecting and assessing the performance data for effectiveness ensures that management practices are measured. This then will allow for continuous improvement. Implementation involves the development of the appropriate policy, establishing goals and metrics, identifying roles and responsibilities, acquiring the needed resources, and starting the implementation programme.
7. *Feedback*—After the data is collected, procedures implemented, and performance evaluated, the loop must be closed. Performance evaluation data is fed back in at the front of the loop and the risk analysis process begins once again.

Assessing and managing reputational risks is an iterative process. If all members of the supply chain commit to the same CSR policies, the probability of reputational risks may be greatly reduced. In this fashion, every chain member is contributing to the supply chain and piece-by-piece, the profile of the socially responsible supply chain (SRSC) is taking shape. This idea furnishes a different perspective on supply chain performance and hence, this is an added incentive for members to work together. Those members that are inactive or obtuse would be replaced over time. Ultimately, only the SRSC truly fulfils the requirements of the modern consumer and will earn a positive reputation on all dimensions.

4.6 Corporate Social Responsibility in the Supply Chain

From a traditional stakeholder vantage point, one of the primary roles or responsibilities of business is wealth generation (Friedman 1970) which guides them on their duties as for-profit entities (Davis 1973). This is an extreme view, and one held by very few business people today. Included in the building up of monetary wealth, business now must also strive to assume CSR, which entails responsibilities surrounding economic, societal and environmental issues (Jo and Harjoto 2012; Petersen and Vredenburg 2009a; Orlitzky et al. 2003). Although it is a topical business practice with a pedigree of academic writing, the CSR concept is still somewhat ill-defined (Freeman and Hasnaoui 2011). This is due, in part, to varying stakeholder expectations (Franz and Petersen 2012) and what one would consider to be a CSR-related action (cf. Alessandri et al. 2011).

Our conceptualisation is based on the works that have defined and identified stakeholder expectations (Epstein and Roy 2001; Carroll 1991), and four distinctive

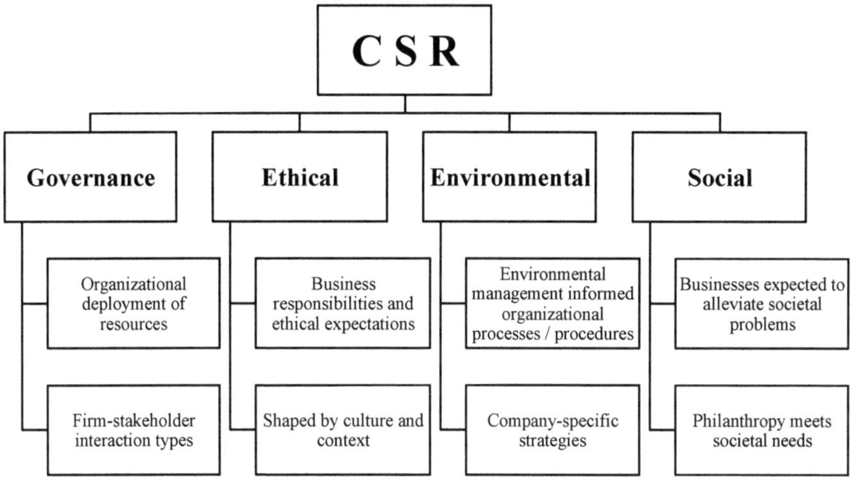

Fig. 4.7 Four spheres of corporate social responsibility. *Source* Based on Lemke and Petersen (2013), Petersen and Lemke (2015)

spheres shoulder our operational approach: governance, ethics, environment and social (see Fig. 4.7).

The first CSR sphere, *governance,* views a corporation as being embedded in existing social structures and international business networks. This sphere encapsulates how organizational resources are being deployed and the type of interaction the organization has with its stakeholders (Daily et al. 2003). Responsible firms have better organizational performance, good risk management practices, support from institutional investors, satisfied employees, and loyal customers (cf. Petersen and Vredenburg 2009b; Becker-Olsen et al. 2006; Peloza and Shang 2011; Du et al. 2007; Hansen et al. 2011). Compliance and organizational responsiveness among chain members should be observed at the level of governance. Here, we could point to the very charter[1] of member partners and a commitment of upper management that is transparent and observable.

The second sphere is *ethics* which captures the expectations of stakeholders and also the corporation's willingness to assume its ethical responsibility (Perrini 2006). In general, ethical behaviour has a direct impact on shareholder value (Johnson 2003) and in the supply chain, organizations are serving a more diverse and global market and thus, have to cooperate with multiple and sometimes international suppliers and buyers. Ethics covers the materials and working processes employed

[1]In a number of economies, a company charter is a legal document filed with the regulatory body to describe a company as to why it exists including its objectives, operations and so forth. In other countries, this may be considered a company constitution, article of incorporation or certificate of incorporation.

at each link of the supply chain that may start in one country, and cross national boundaries, cultural zones, legal systems, and individual viewpoints. On this journey, the interpretation of ethics can and does change and what appeared to be ethical at one stage – even with the best intentions at any given time – may look neutral or unethical in the next (cf. Adebanjo et al. 2013). Although many stakeholders of a supply chain are important, in the end, it is the consumer that fuels the production process and, therefore, the final ethical verdict would come from the end-consumer. This highlights the necessity that the ethical interpretation of all supply chain members becomes united and reflects one and the same ethical approach.

The *environment* represents the third sphere and it captures the responsibilities and actions pertaining to the management of the natural environment. This sphere includes business processes (Brundtland 1987) so that the organization and the environment form a symbiotic relationship in which both entities flourish. In this instance, a future-oriented and pro-active environmental strategy could reap financial rewards for the business (Yu et al. 2014; Luzio and Lemke 2013).

The last CSR sphere is *social* and it involves the public's expectations on business leaders that surpass their fiduciary duties. Just as we would expect of a good citizen to participate in alleviating social ills, businesses are expected to contribute in the same way. Human rights atrocities, racial disparity, the prevention of child labour, creating awareness of alcohol abuse, anti-smoking campaigns—there are many issues needing attention and socially responsible firms get behind those that they believe they can contribute the most.

As you can see, CSR becomes the mainframe for not only the identification and mitigation of reputational risks but also serves as a means for the selection of partnering firms, identifying and managing stakeholders, and so on. It ultimately becomes the lynch pin for keeping on top of many risks in the supply chain context.

4.7 Discussion and Conclusions

In this chapter, we discussed the nature of reputation and the risks involved in a supply chain setting. Understanding, identifying, and mitigating reputational risks becomes a key management task. Our four-lenses CSR perspective enables companies to improve upon the risk identification process (Ennis 2015) and as Peters and Romi (2014) note, may also increase the transparency of members which may mitigate or even eliminate the risks entirely. What this means is that chain members would commit to a common CSR profile. In this fashion, the CSR philosophy serves as a source code that becomes firmly implanted in the DNA of the chain. CSR would, therefore, become SCSR as the philosophy sits within the supply chain, rather than in an isolated corporation. Then, for example, if environmental management is highlighted, it is more likely that a tier-2 supplier will observe its environmental impact with an eye to continual improvement and maybe even the adoption of cradle-to-cradle practices. That the governing body of the firm has made a commitment to this may increase the likelihood that both their immediate stakeholders and their immediate chain members will hold them more accountable.

Another aspect of mitigation is in reference to the spillover and ripple effect. Mitigation begins with minimizing the impact a negative reputation can have as a result of any number of combinations of triggers. As in the case discussed earlier, Apple Inc. may increase their investments in CSR, an actionable trigger, to buffer the risks generated by Foxconn until such a time that they are able to effectively encourage Foxconn to change their practices, or find an alternative manufacture that therefore eliminates the risk entirely. However, influencing Foxconn to alter their practices and commit to a common set of responsibilities may need to be embedded in the fabric of the organization. Committing to a code of conduct may not be as effective of a catalyst as opposed to having an organizational commitment to social responsibility that comes from the Board of Directors.

Our emphasis on promoting the mitigation of reputational risks via CSR stems from what has been considered a substandard approach to supply chain management (Storey et al. 2006), and the management of risks (Fischl et al. 2014). It is for this reason that we see how the adoption of a common CSR policy by associated members may address reputational risks and improve upon the mitigation of any number of supply chain risks with respect to quality and supply disruptions. Perhaps this becomes a supply chain social responsibility (SCSR) 'charter' that details a commitment to a common understanding of governance, ethics, social and environmental responsibilities that in turn guides corporate practices. From a stakeholder's viewpoint, it would be the psychological signature that is shorthand for 'trust'. Analysing the competitive landscape with a social responsibility focus would provide managers with an appreciative vantage point to position their offering more favourably in the B2B market. Hence, collaboration with suitable partners will clearly indicate needle-moving improvement, but can only be done when the set of supplier selection factors are relevant, transparent and as we have described, socially responsible. Pursuing this line of thought further, the same principle applies to partners downstream in the chain. Manufacturers need partners that have the ability to control the reputational risk since they are positioned at the 'supply chain-market interface'. They will also have to assess their individual reputational risks and their own mitigating practices. This will inform the discussion with manufacturers that are looking for suitable partners delivering the SCSR performance created by all members.

References

Adebanjo, D., Ojadi, F., Laosirihongthong, T., & Tickle, M. (2013). A case study of supplier selection in developing economies: A perspective on institutional theory and corporate social responsibility. *Supply Chain Management: An International Journal, 18,* 553–566.

Alessandri, T. M., Black, S. S., & Jackson, W. E. (2011). Black economic empowerment transactions in South Africa: Understanding when corporate social responsibility may create or destroy value. *Long Range Planning, 44,* 229–249.

Becker-Olsen, K. L., Cudmore, B. A., & Hill, R. P. (2006). The impact of perceived corporate social responsibility on consumer behavior. *Journal of Business Research, 59,* 46–53.

Björklund, M., Martinsen, U., & Abrahamsson, M. (2012). Performance measurements in the greening of supply chains. *Supply Chain Management: An International Journal, 17,* 29–39.

Brundtland, G. H. (1987). *Our common future, from one earth to one world.* Oxford: World Commission on the Environment and Development (WCED).

Carroll, A. B. (1991). The pyramid of corporate social responsibility: Toward the moral management of organizational stakeholders. *Business Horizons, 34,* 39–48.

Casado-Díaz, A. B., Mas-Ruiz, F. J., & Sellers-Rubio, R. (2009). Stock market reactions to third-party complaints. *International Journal of Bank Marketing, 27,* 167–183.

Chan, J., Pun, N., & Selden, M. (2013). The politics of global production: Apple, Foxconn and China's new working class. *New Technology, Work and Employment, 28*(2), 100–115.

Daily, C. M., Dalton, D. R., & Cannella, A. A. J. (2003). Corporate governance: Decades of dialogue and data. *The Academy of Management Review, 28,* 371–382.

Davis, K. (1973). The case for and against business assumption of social responsibilities. *Academy of Management Journal, 16,* 312–322.

Dierickx, I., & Cool, K. (1989). Asset stock accumulation and sustainability of competitive advantage. *Management Science, 35,* 1504–1511.

Doorey, D. J. (2011). The transparent supply chain: From resistance to implementation at Nike and Levi-Strauss. *Journal of Business Ethics, 103,* 587–603.

Dowling, G. R. (2004). Corporate reputations: Should you compete on yours? *California Management Review, 46,* 19–36.

Du, S., Bhattacharya, C. B., & Sen, S. (2007). Reaping relational rewards from corporate social responsibility: The role of competitive positioning. *International Journal of Research in Marketing, 24,* 224–241.

Eltantawy, R. A., Fox, G. L., & Giunipero, L. (2009). Supply management ethical responsibility: Reputation and performance impacts. *Supply Chain Management: An International Journal, 14,* 99–108.

Ennis, T. (2015). Risk management: Reputation is key. *Professional Safety, 60,* 8.

Epstein, M. J., & Roy, M.-J. (2001). Sustainability in action: Identifying and measuring the key performance drivers. *Long Range Planning, 34,* 585–604.

Farrell, S., & Ruddick, G. (2015). *Volkswagen CEO Martin Winterkorn quits over diesel emissions scandal* [Online]. http://www.theguardian.com/business/2015/sep/23/volkswagen-ceo-martin-winterkorn-quits-over-diesel-emissions-scandal. Accessed January 23, 2016.

Fiol, C. M., O'Connor, E. J., & Aguinis, H. (2001). All for one and one for all? The development and transfer of power across organizational levels. *The Academy of Management Review, 26,* 224–242.

Fischl, M. C., Scherrer-Rathje, M., Friedli, T., Wagner, B., & Wagner, B. (2014). Digging deeper into supply risk: A systematic literature review on price risks. *Supply Chain Management: An International Journal,* 19, null.

Fombrun, C. J. (1996). *Reputation: realizing value from the corporate image.* Boston: Harvard Business School Press.

Franz, R. S., & Petersen, H. L. (2012). Role of business: A portfolio model of corporate social responsibility. *Journal of Global Responsibility, 3,* 83–110.

Freeman, I., & Hasnaoui, A. (2011). The meaning of corporate social responsibility: The vision of four nations. *Journal of Business Ethics, 100,* 419–443.

Friedman, M. (1970). The social responsibility of business is to increase its profits. *New York Times Magazine, 13*(09), 1970.

Hamilton, J. T. (1995). Pollution as news: Media and Stock market reactions to the toxics release inventory data. *Journal of Environmental Economics and Management, 28,* 98–113.

Hansen, S. D., Dunford, B. B., Boss, A. D., Boss, R. W., & Angermeier, I. (2011). Corporate social responsibility and the benefits of employee trust: A cross-disciplinary perspective. *Journal of Business Ethics, 102,* 29–45.

Hernández-Espallardo, M., Rodríguez-Orejuela, A., & Sánchez-Pérez, M. (2010). Inter-organizational governance, learning and performance in supply chains. *Supply Chain Management: An International Journal, 15,* 101–114.
Hoejmose, S. U., Roehrich, J. K., & Grosvold, J. (2014). Is doing more doing better? The relationship between responsible supply chain management and corporate reputation. *Industrial Marketing Management, 43,* 77–90.
Jamasmie, C. (2014). Oil sands producer settles lawsuit by buying four farms.
Jo, H., & Harjoto, M. (2012). The causal effect of corporate governance on corporate social responsibility. *Journal of Business Ethics, 106,* 53–72.
Johnson, H. H. (2003). Does it pay to be good? Social responsibility and financial performance. *Business Horizons, 46,* 34–40.
Lawrence, F., & Wasley, A. (2014). *Chicken factories inspected by FSA as Tesco reveals surprise spot check* [Online]. The Guardian. Available: http://www.theguardian.com/business/2014/jul/25/chicken-factories-inspected-fsa-tesco-reveals-surprise-spot-check. Accessed July 25, 2014.
Lemke, F., Clark, M., & Wilson, H. (2011). Customer experience quality: An exploration in business and consumer contexts using repertory grid technique. *Journal of the Academy of Marketing Science, 39,* 846–869.
Lemke, F., & Luzio, J. P. P. (2014). Exploring green consumers' mind-set towards green product design and life cycle assessment: The case of sceptical Brazilian and Portuguese green consumers. *Journal of Industrial Ecology, 18,* 619–630.
Lemke, F., & Petersen, H. L. (2013). Teaching reputational risk management in the supply chain. *Supply Chain Management: An International Journal, 18,* 413–428.
Luzio, J. P. P., & Lemke, F. (2013). Exploring green consumers' product demands and consumption processes: The case of Portuguese green consumers. *European Business Review, 25,* 281–300.
Mokhiber, R., & Weissman, R. (2004). The ten worst corporations of 2004. *Multinational Monitor, 25,* 8–21.
Orlitzky, M., Schmidt, F. L., & Rynes, S. L. (2003). Corporate social and financial performance: A meta-analysis. *Organization Studies, 24,* 403–441.
Peloza, J., & Shang, J. (2011). How can corporate social responsibility activities create value for stakeholders? A systematic review. *Journal of the Academy of Marketing Science, 39,* 117–135.
Perrini, F. (2006). SMEs and CSR theory: Evidence and implications from an Italian perspective. *Journal of Business Ethics, 67,* 305–316.
Peters, G. F., & Romi, A. M. (2014). Does the voluntary adoption of corporate governance mechanisms improve environmental risk disclosures? Evidence from greenhouse gas emission accounting. *Journal of Business Ethics, 125,* 637–666.
Petersen, H. L., & Lemke, F. (2015). Mitigating reputational risks in supply chains. *Supply Chain Management: An International Journal, 20,* 495–510.
Petersen, H. L., & Vredenburg, H. (2009a). Corporate governance, social responsibility and capital markets: Exploring the institutional investor mental model. *Corporate Governance, 9,* 610–622.
Petersen, H. L., & Vredenburg, H. (2009b). Morals or economics? Institutional investor preferences for corporate social responsibility. *Journal of Business Ethics, 90,* 1–14.
Reese, C. L., & Kossovsky, N. (2011). Intangibles and the new reality: Risk, reputation, and value creation. *Corporate Finance Review, 16,* 20–32.
Roehrich, J. K., Grosvold, J., & Hoejmose, S. U. (2014). Reputational risks and sustainable supply chain management: Decision making under bounded rationality. *International Journal of Operations & Production Management, 34,* 695–719.
Smals, R. G. M., & Smits, A. A. J. (2012). Value for value—The dynamics of supplier value in collaborative new product development. *Industrial Marketing Management, 41,* 156–165.
Storey, J., Emberson, C., Godsell, J., & Harrison, A. (2006). Supply chain management: theory, practice and future challenges. *International Journal of Operations & Production Management, 26,* 754–774.

Topham, G., & kollewe, J. (2016). *French government reassures Renault investors there is 'no emissions fraud'* [Online]. http://www.theguardian.com/business/2016/jan/14/renault-shares-plunge-police-raid-linked-vw-crisis: Guardian News and Media Limited. Accessed January 23, 2016.

Vanhamme, J., & Grobben, B. (2009). "Too good to be true!" The effectiveness of csr history in countering negative publicity. *Journal of Business Ethics, 85,* 273–283.

Worcester, R. (2009). Reflections on corporate reputations. *Management Decision, 47,* 573–589.

Yu, W., Chavez, R., Feng, M., & Wiengarten, F. (2014). Integrated green supply chain management and operational performance. *Supply Chain Management: An International Journal, 19,* 683–696.

Chapter 5
Managing IT and Cyber Risks in Supply Chains

Barbara Gaudenzi and Giorgia Siciliano

Abstract This chapter describes the potential impact of Information Technology (IT) and cyber risks on the continuity and vulnerabilities of the supply chain. We propose a theoretical framework and direction to help organizations to manage these risks. The evidence gleaned from an empirical investigation will illustrate how organizations actually perceive, control, and manage IT and cyber risks within the supply chains. The findings will underline that managers tend to invest in few mitigation strategies; hence, they take risks that are much higher than their declared risk appetites. In addition, managers denounce a general lack of awareness regarding the effects that IT and cyber risks may have on supply operations and relationships.

5.1 IT Risks and Cyber Risks: Real Threats for All Supply Chains

Global trends, such as digitalization and servitization, have caused an evolution in all conventional supply chains whose structures have switched from a "web of disconnected islands" to a network of interconnected processes, which are strongly oriented toward flexibility, efficiency, and resilience.

In this context, Internet platforms assure operational benefits, such as cost reduction, inventory pooling, postponement, a reduction of the bullwhip effect, and shorter lead times, to allow for faster information sharing across different organizations. For example, supply chain leaders such as Wal-Mart, Warnier-Lambert, Procter and Gamble, and Levi Strauss, have achieved great benefits from their investments in Information Technology (IT) tools such as the Enterprise Resource

B. Gaudenzi (✉) · G. Siciliano
Department of Business Administration, University of Verona, Verona, Italy
e-mail: barbara.gaudenzi@univr.it

Y. Khojasteh (ed.), *Supply Chain Risk Management*,
DOI 10.1007/978-981-10-4106-8_5

Planning (ERP). In particular, these companies have improved their performances in demand planning and scheduling production, which have created better coordination with their key suppliers.

However, the use of IT tools and Internet platforms generates new forms of supply chain vulnerability and new risks, which may affect the supply chain's continuity and performance. Managers should recognize these new threats as critical issues that may exacerbate the other supply chain risks throughout interdependencies (Gaudenzi and Borghesi 2006). However, recent reports (PWC Report 2014, 2015a) show that the awareness of these risks is still low: among security incidents across geographic regions, IT and cyber breaches are rising significantly in Europe, which reported a 41% jump over the previous year. Thus, supply chain managers need to focus more attention on the management of all risks that may be generated by IT tools, such as ERP or any vertical software, and external Cyberspace.

5.2 How External Cyberspace and IT Tools Generate Risks

A McKinsey report (Bailey et al. 2014) considers "Cyberattacks" to be events such as fraud, identity or intellectual property theft, and political statements made by hacktivists. A PWC report (2015b) sees IT as a tool and an enabler of seamless and real-time interconnectivity across the entire network. Part of the literature considers the two risks related and even occasionally exchangeable. Both are not easily predictable, and they always imply a violation of three key properties: confidentiality, availability, and integrity.

Some authors consider IT as the foundation of Cyberspace (Melville 2010), while others consider it a mere infrastructure, where hardware, software, and external data represent "Cyber assets" (D'Amico et al. 2010). Cyberspace is typically considered an external environment with low entry barriers, which have an ambiguity characterized by a certain risk exposure.

In practice, IT risks seem strictly technical: they stem from failures of ERP/IT systems and impact only on the flow of information itself. Here, the control of technical features and procedures plays a key role in assuring information security. Cyber risks go beyond mere IT disruptions; they are linked to human Cyberattacks, where hackers intentionally access an organization or a network with the goal of either gaining an economic advantage or causing sabotage. These actions are typically linked to cyber bullying, cyber terrorism, or political issues (Garfinkel 2012; von Solms and van Niekerk 2013).

In 2014, McKinsey found that, while IT and cyber-related breaches are occurring with growing regularity, executives perceive that they are not quickly responding with adequate tools (Bailey et al. 2014). In the Global Risk

Management Report (Aon 2015), "Cyberattacks" were listed in the top 10 threatening risks for organizations and networks.

Despite these perceptions, cyber security and IT security remain the areas of risk management with the largest gap between the level of threat and the amount of resources invested. Several studies (Bandyopadhyay et al. 2010; Kong et al. 2012; Gao and Zhong 2015; Gao et al. 2015; PWC Report 2015a) have revealed that, as these threats become more frequent and severe, investments in security initiatives decrease. Even with this attention on IT and cyber security management, recent literature has mainly focused on managerial perceptions, technical aspects, or legislative perspectives (Ellison and Woody 2010; Ozkan and Karabacak 2010; Huang et al. 2011; Markmann et al. 2013; Brender and Markov 2013; Mukhopadhyay et al. 2013; Yang et al. 2013; Biener et al. 2015). From the supply chain risk management perspective, authors only recently investigated the impacts of IT risks and cyber risks on supply chains (Olson and Wu 2010; Järveläinen 2013; Bartol 2014; Boyson 2014; Khan and Estay 2015; Gaudenzi and Siciliano 2016).

Therefore, supply chain managers should carefully focus on two critical points:

1. Information security should not be considered as a technology investment itself. Instead, decisions should be made that involve all the actors in the supply chain, create an awareness about IT and cyber risks, and define clear procedures to identify these threats to protect the supply chain from these vulnerabilities.
2. Managing IT and cyber risks may increase the overall performance, which will augment the sharing of information and collaboration as well as the efficient management of processes across the supply chain.

5.3 Managing IT and Cyber Risks in Supply Chains: A Practical Framework

We propose a supply chain risk management framework that may guide managers to assess and manage IT and cyber risks in protecting supply chain processes. We addressed key risks, such as IT failures, piracy and thefts, product shortages, safety and security, inventory levels, and supplier dependence, which may significantly affect strategic, financial, and operational performances of all actors in a supply chain. Nonetheless, to the best of our knowledge, there are very few theoretical frameworks (Khan and Estay 2015) that link the supply chain risk management process to IT and cyber risks throughout the entire value chain.

To fill this gap, we adapted a framework based on Fawcett et al. (2011), whose objective was to study the effective deployment of IT by analyzing why some types of investments are more successful than others. We aimed to enlarge the above-mentioned scope by considering how systematic IT and cyber risk management may enhance the ability to share information and better manage supply chain processes. The proposed framework is shown in Fig. 5.1, which represents how the

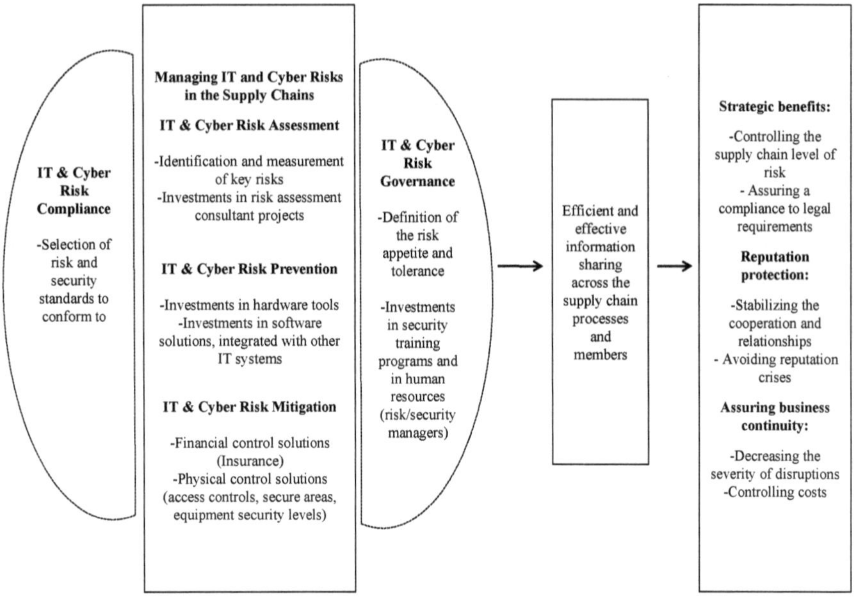

Fig. 5.1 A framework for managing IT and cyber risks in supply chains

key steps of a risk management process (risk assessment, risk treatment, risk governance, and risk compliance) should be adapted to IT and cyber risks.

A robust IT and cyber risk management program may protect the strategic goals of the supply chain, preventing business disruptions and protecting the reputation of all actors involved. Firstly, managing IT and cyber risks would have the strategic benefits of enhancing the firms' capability to guarantee a tolerable level of overall risk for all actors involved and consistently do so within their real risk appetite. Thus, managers should monitor if and how IT and cyber risks may threaten relevant assets and relationships with upstream and downstream supply chain partners.

Secondly, IT failures, piracy, thefts, and Cyberattacks are listed among the major causes of reputation crises and losses of reputation value. Protecting the supply chain against those risks requires stable relationships amongst supply chain members and fostering collaboration.

Thirdly, IT failures and Cyberattacks may cause business interruptions, which in turn may damage suppliers' and customers' operational and financial performances.

The risk management process should therefore start with a careful assessment of the sources of IT and cyber risks amongst all supply chain members. In companies that lack awareness of these risks, the role of the "channel captain" is essential. These supply chain leaders should, for example, lead supply chain risk management projects or include them in their contractual agreements or sourcing strategies' ad hoc requirements regarding investments in IT and cyber risk consultancy projects.

After the assessment (identification, measurement, and evaluation) of these risks, each supply chain member should decide the nature and amount of investments in risk prevention strategies, such as investments in hardware and software, which they plan to implement. Risk mitigation strategies reduce the severity of disruptions, control costs, and assure continuity of supplies. Risk mitigation comprises both financial controls (IT and cyber risk insurance programs) and physical controls (investing in access control, secure areas, equipment security levels).

This framework offers a holistic risk management process, in which the abovementioned strategies, processes, technologies, and human resources should be aligned in coherence with the governance of each organization and of the supply chain as a whole. Several variables will influence the implementation of the risk management process such as the position of the supply chain captain (i.e., a manufacturer or a retailer), strategic priorities (i.e., efficiency vs. responsiveness), the industry/markets (there are different security standards to conform to, such as ISO/IEC 27001:2013, depending on the sector/markets), and organizations' dimensions. The final result should be a supply chain where the actors share more information throughout the whole process, which guarantees strategic benefits, reputation protection, and business continuity.

Notably, empirical studies have demonstrated that IT-enabled information sharing promotes advantages, such as logistics integration and agility, which has a positive impact on operational, strategic, and financial performances (Trkman et al. 2010; Dewan and Ren 2011; Giannakis and Louis 2011; Mithas et al. 2011; Tallon and Pinsonneault 2011; Prajogo and Olhager 2012; PWC Report 2015b). Thus, companies that show a real commitment to safeguarding the entire value chain from IT and cyber risks have greater control over the supply chain's level of risk, build solid reputations, and assure business continuity.

5.4 Practical Evidence from a European Sample of Companies

Recent literature has poorly investigated the perceptions and decision-making processes regarding the management of IT and cyber risks within the supply chain (Benlian and Hess 2011; Yildirim et al. 2011; Pezderka and Sinkovics 2011). This led us to conduct an empirical investigation of European organizations that rely on security and risk management standards in order to choose the drivers of systematic IT and cyber risk management (risk assessment, risk prevention, risk mitigation, risk compliance, and risk governance), as shown in Table 5.1.

To investigate whether or not the perceptions and management of these risks vary, depending on the industry, performance, and globalization choices of organizations, we considered heterogeneity with regard to the industries they operate in, their size, and their level of internationalization (Martin and Eisenhardt 2010). The sample involved several European companies including: one small, local company, with a revenue under €1 million, which had between 10 and 100 employees; seven medium companies, with revenues between €1 million and €500 million, less than

Table 5.1 IT and cyber risk management constructs

Risk management process	Main references
Risk assessment	
• Identification and measurement of key risks such as - Inadvertent breaches - Deliberate attacks - Asset thefts - Equipment failures - Backup failures - Data thefts - Site disasters - Copyright infringements • Presence of a dedicated budget for IT security management • Investments in risk assessment consulting projects	Yildirim et al. (2011) Biener et al. (2015) Järveläinen (2013)
Risk prevention	
- Investments in hardware tools - Investments in software solutions integrated with other IT systems	Ifinedo (2012) Järveläinen (2013) Yildirim et al. (2011) Biener et al. (2015) Boyson (2014) Silva et al. (2014)
Risk mitigation	
- Financial control solutions (insurance) - Physical control solutions (access controls, secure areas, and equipment security levels)	Biener et al. (2015) Silva et al. (2014) Feng et al. (2014) Yildirim et al. (2011)
Risk governance	
- Defining the organization's risk appetite and tolerance - Investments in ad hoc training programs in security - Investments in organizational human resources (risk manager, security manager, etc.)	Järveläinen (2013) Yildirim et al. (2011) Boyson (2014) Ifinedo (2012) Johnston et al. (2010) Biener et al. (2015)
Risk compliance	
- Perception of the organization regarding exposure and vulnerability toward IT and cyber risks - Risk appetite of an organization	Yildirim et al. (2011) Ifinedo (2012) Bulgurcu et al. (2010) Feng et al. (2014) Biener et al. (2015) Boyson (2014)

50 thousand employees, and that represented various interests internationally; and seven large companies, which were evenly distributed throughout their level of internationalization, with revenues exceeding €10 billion and more than 50 thousand employees.

We interviewed more than one key informant, including CEOs, supply managers, risk managers, and/or IT managers, within the same organization to consider whether or not their role might impact the way IT and cyber risks are seen and faced. This process allowed us to reach the point of theoretical saturation with fifteen organizations.

Some evidences from our research are summarized in Table 5.2. The sample revealed that managing IT risks and cyber risks positively influences reputation toward both the upstream and downstream actors of the supply chain. However, the commitment to managing these risks and protecting reputation varied by the dependence of the supply chain under observation: IT and cyber risk management toward the upstream supply chain was almost non-existent, while a higher commitment was seen toward clients and customers. In fact, managers perceived breaches to private and personal information as less tolerable than threats to business-to-business partners.

Strategic and operational advantages related to careful IT and cyber risk management currently lack acknowledgement. Thus, managers usually neither stipulate contractual agreements with key suppliers nor implement systematic plans for disaster recovery, business continuity, or the backup of sensitive data. Moreover, there is a low commitment at the corporate level: risk and security managers show a greater awareness about IT and cyber risks, while top managers do not prioritize their management. The consequence is a scarce effort in building a deeper awareness among employees through systematic training.

Regarding risk assessment, IT and cyber risks were systematically assessed by more than half of the sample, who also had a dedicated budget. However, the identification and measurement of key risks appeared to be far from effective: three out of four of the respondents had faced some IT and cyber breaches in the last 24 months.

Investments in risk assessment consulting projects were low for the majority of larger, multinational organizations, which used consultancy "on demand" for testing protection systems (penetration intrusion test), disaster recovery, and backup systems.

Regarding risk treatment, mitigation strategies were widely used, even if the majority was exclusively dedicated to IT risks. More than half of the sample had a budget solely dedicated to software, hardware, insurance, physical entry controls, secure areas, and equipment security levels. Interestingly, managers appeared genuinely convinced that effective IT and cyber risk management was possible solely through these types of investments. Risk prevention rarely accounted for ad hoc investments by most of the organizations. Thus, they seemed somewhat disoriented by the breaches from which they suffered; a third of the sample admitted that companies tend to be high-risk takers, with a dramatic number of IT and cyber breaches discovered roughly six months after the fact.

Table 5.2 Some evidences from the interviews

IT and cyber risk assessment	C1: *When we analyze risks, what we measure is the reputational damage. We also address the economic damage for the company, but the reputational damage is our priority, as it is knowable to anybody and it takes time to reabsorb* C2: *We assess risks through daily antivirus scanning and we keep ourself updated about the possible IT and cyber risks through specialized journals and blogs* C1: *In the last 24 months we suffered from inadvertent breaches, deliberate attack, asset theft, equipment failure, backup failure, copyright and compliance infringement. We focus our risk assessment on these risks*
IT and cyber risk prevention	C7: *We do not have a dedicated budget for IT and cyber risk prevention. The problem is that there are urgent needs, and we invest only on emergencies. In this way, sometimes we spend more than we would if we were investing in formal prevention plan* C3: *We get there only when it is too late, when the damage has been done. There is little strategy and a lot of tactics, and little prevention* C14: *Only a careful training could improve the efficacy and the efficiency of the IT risk prevention*
IT and cyber risk mitigation	C2: *The back-up procedures (for IT risk) are formal and these are able to reconstruct the history of up to three years. The back-up is on a daily base, business continuity is excellent. The disaster recovery is great and there are two separate sites. However all of this is just for IT risks, not cyber risks* C4: *On average we realize we had an intrusion 180 days later, and between 70 and 80% of internal fraud are discovered only by informers. So our mitigation strategy is not efficient yet*
IT and cyber risk compliance	C8: *We decided not to follow some specific information security standard. We just follow our best practices*
IT and cyber risk governance	C7: *The risk manager is also responsible for IT risk, but he cannot be good in everything! He assigns priorities to the problems to solve* C15: *Top managers consider themselves completely risk adverse. Nonetheless, they do not care sufficiently about IT risks* C2: *We do not have systematic training on IT and cyber risk management. We rely just on our perceptions* C7: *The IT manager is not in the management committee, and his language is too technical to deal with the top management. There is a communication problem*

In general, risks were assessed by only one out of three organizations. Interestingly, the majority of them were medium and small companies, which invested in protection, disaster recovery, and backup consultancy services. The only exception to this trend was represented by multinational operations in the financial and oil industries, which invested significantly in risk assessment consulting projects. However, they often required consultancy services exclusively to assess cyber risks and rarely for IT risks.

Efforts in IT and cyber risk prevention were performed systematically by all the multinational companies and by the small organization, which operates in the software industry. As mentioned earlier, roughly all the sampled companies implemented systematic mitigation strategies. The only striking exceptions were the small organization and all those operating in the healthcare industry.

The majority of the medium and small companies perceived low exposure and vulnerability toward IT and cyber risks, while risk appetite was declared to be very low throughout all companies and industries. Roughly all the companies invested in ad hoc training programs in security, but they were only directed toward the risk and security managers, never to all the employees.

In general, finance and high technology industries showed the most careful and systematic IT and cyber risk management processes, while the healthcare sector implemented only occasional measures.

5.5 Conclusions

The pervasive use of Internet throughout the entire value chain may assure significant advantages to organizations, particularly in terms of resilience. To investigate how companies in practice perceive IT and cyber risks and whether they include them in their decision-making process, we conducted an exploratory survey among different European companies, leaders in their industries. The findings show a lack of awareness at different organizational levels. Employees seem to be unprepared to deal with these risks and with their effects onto processes and operations. From the top management perspective, managers seem to dedicate insufficient efforts and investments particularly in IT and cyber risk mitigation strategies, mainly using reactive approaches instead of proactive ones.

The proposed risk management framework seems to fill an existing gap in the literature, addressing how systematic IT and cyber risk management may enhance the ability to share information and better manage supply chain processes. From a practitioner perspective, the framework addresses those risks—such as IT failures, piracy and thefts, product shortages, safety and security, inventory over-stocks, and supplier dependence—which may significantly affect supply chain performances. In practice, this approach may guide managers to formally assess and manage IT and cyber risks in order to protect supply chain processes. Moreover, the framework promotes a formal mitigation plan to update systematically, in order to respond to IT and cyber risks, considering the time pressure these new threats impose to all the actors of the supply chain. These risk management process should be constantly supported by strong commitment from top management, especially in conforming to the ad hoc security standards and the definition of the real risk appetite and tolerance of the company. Managers should also be engaged in promoting an overall "IT and cyber culture" transversally in the entire supply chain, because IT and cyber risks represent significant threats for both the upstream and downstream supply chain.

References

Aon Risk Solutions. (2015). *Global Risk Management Survey 2015*. Available at: http://www.aon.com/2015GlobalRisk/. Accessed April 04, 2016.

Bailey, T., Miglio, A. D., & Richter, W. (2014). The rising strategic risks of cyberattacks. *McKinsey Quarterly, 2*(2014), 17–22.

Bandyopadhyay, T., Jacob, V., & Raghunathan, S. (2010). Information security in networked supply chains: Impact of network vulnerability and supply chain integration on incentives to invest. *Information Technology and Management, 11*(1), 7–23.

Bartol, N. (2014). Cyber supply chain security practices DNA–filling in the puzzle using a diverse set of disciplines. *Technovation, 34*(7), 354–361.

Benlian, A., & Hess, T. (2011). Opportunities and risks of software-as-a-service: Findings from a survey of IT executives. *Decision Support Systems, 52*(1), 232–246.

Biener, C., Eling, M., & Wirfs, J. H. (2015). Insurability of cyber risk: An empirical analysis. *The Geneva Papers on Risk and Insurance-Issues and Practice, 40*(1), 131–158.

Boyson, S. (2014). Cyber supply chain risk management: Revolutionizing the strategic control of critical IT systems. *Technovation, 34*(7), 342–353.

Brender, N., & Markov, I. (2013). Risk perception and risk management in cloud computing: Results from a case study of Swiss companies. *International Journal of Information Management, 33*(5), 726–733.

Bulgurcu, B., Cavusoglu, H., & Benbasat, I. (2010). Information security policy compliance: An empirical study of rationality-based beliefs and information security awareness. *MIS Quarterly, 34*(3), 523–548.

D'Amico, A., Buchanan, L., Goodall, J., & Walczak, P. (2010, April). Mission impact of cyber events: Scenarios and ontology to express the relationships between cyber assets, missions and users. In *International Conference on Information Warfare and Security* (p. 388). Academic Conferences International Limited.

Dewan, S., & Ren, F. (2011). Information technology and firm boundaries: Impact on firm risk and return performance. *Information Systems Research, 22*(2), 369–388.

Ellison, R. J., & Woody, C. (2010, January). Supply-chain risk management: Incorporating security into software development. In *System Sciences (HICSS), 2010 43rd Hawaii International Conference on* (pp. 1–10). IEEE.

Fawcett, S. E., Wallin, C., Allred, C., Fawcett, A. M., & Magnan, G. M. (2011). Information technology as an enabler of supply chain collaboration: A dynamic-capabilities perspective. *Journal of Supply Chain Management, 47*(1), 38–59.

Feng, N., Wang, H. J., & Li, M. (2014). A security risk analysis model for information systems: Causal relationships of risk factors and vulnerability propagation analysis. *Information Sciences, 256*, 57–73.

Gao, X., & Zhong, W. (2015). Information security investment for competitive firms with hacker behavior and security requirements. *Annals of Operations Research, 235*(1), 277–300.

Gao, X., Zhong, W., & Mei, S. (2015). Security investment and information sharing under an alternative security breach probability function. *Information Systems Frontiers, 17*(2), 423–438.

Garfinkel, S. L. (2012). The cybersecurity risk. *Communications of the ACM, 55*(6), 29–32.

Gaudenzi, B., & Borghesi, A. (2006). Managing risks in the supply chain using the AHP method. *The International Journal of Logistics Management, 17*(1), 114–136.

Gaudenzi, B., & Siciliano, G. (2016). Just do it. Managing IT and cyber risks to create value. In *6th Global Innovation and Knowledge Academy (GIKA) Conference*, March 21–23, 2016, Valencia, Spain.

Giannakis, M., & Louis, M. (2011). A multi-agent based framework for supply chain risk management. *Journal of Purchasing and Supply Management, 17*(1), 23–31.

Huang, S. M., Hung, W. H., Yen, D. C., Chang, I. C., & Jiang, D. (2011). Building the evaluation model of the IT general control for CPAs under enterprise risk management. *Decision Support Systems, 50*(4), 692–701.
Ifinedo, P. (2012). Understanding information systems security policy compliance: An integration of the theory of planned behavior and the protection motivation theory. *Computers & Security, 31*(1), 83–95.
ISO/IEC 27001:2013. *Information technology-security techniques-information security management systems-requirements*. Available at: http://www.iso.org/iso/catalogue_detail?csnumber=54534. Accessed April 04, 2016.
Järveläinen, J. (2013). IT incidents and business impacts: Validating a framework for continuity management in information systems. *International Journal of Information Management, 33*(3), 583–590.
Johnston, A. C., & Warkentin, M. (2010). Fear appeals and information security behaviors: An empirical study. *MIS quarterly,* 549–566.
Khan, O., & Estay, D. A. S. (2015). Supply chain cyber-resilience: Creating an agenda for future research. *Technology Innovation Management Review, 5*(4), 6–12.
Kong, H. K., Kim, T. S., & Kim, J. (2012). An analysis on effects of information security investments: A BSC perspective. *Journal of Intelligent Manufacturing, 23*(4), 941–953.
Markmann, C., Darkow, I. L., & von der Gracht, H. (2013). A Delphi-based risk analysis—identifying and assessing future challenges for supply chain security in a multi-stakeholder environment. *Technological Forecasting and Social Change, 80*(9), 1815–1833.
Martin, J. A., & Eisenhardt, K. M. (2010). Rewiring: Cross-business-unit collaborations in multibusiness organizations. *Academy of Management Journal, 53*(2), 265–301.
Melville, N. P. (2010). Information systems innovation for environmental sustainability. *MIS Quarterly, 34*(1), 1–21.
Mithas, S., Ramasubbu, N., & Sambamurthy, V. (2011). How information management capability influences firm performance. *MIS Quarterly, 35*(1), 237–256.
Mukhopadhyay, A., Chatterjee, S., Saha, D., Mahanti, A., & Sadhukhan, S. K. (2013). Cyber-risk decision models: To insure IT or not? *Decision Support Systems, 56,* 11–26.
Olson, D. L., & Dash Wu, D. (2010). A review of enterprise risk management in supply chain. *Kybernetes*, *39*(5), 694–706.
Ozkan, S., & Karabacak, B. (2010). Collaborative risk method for information security management practices: A case context within Turkey. *International Journal of Information Management, 30*(6), 567–572.
Pezderka, N., & Sinkovics, R. R. (2011). A conceptualization of e-risk perceptions and implications for small firm active online internationalization. *International Business Review, 20* (4), 409–422.
Prajogo, D., & Olhager, J. (2012). Supply chain integration and performance: The effects of long-term relationships, information technology and sharing, and logistics integration. *International Journal of Production Economics, 135*(1), 514–522.
PWC Report (2014). *Information security breaches survey 2014 technical report*. Available at: http://www.pwc.co.uk/services/audit-assurance/insights/2014-information-security-breaches-survey.html. Accessed April 04, 2016.
PWC Report. (2015a). Managing cyber risks in an interconnected world. In *Key findings from The Global State of from The Global State of Information Security® Survey 2015*. Available at: www.pwc.com/gsiss2015. Accessed April 04, 2016.
PWC Report. (2015b). Reinventing information technology in the digital enterprise. In *PwC's New IT Platform: Achieve High Velocity IT in a Digital World*. Available at: http://www.pwc.com/us/en/increasing-it-effectiveness/publications/new-it-platform.html. Accessed April 04, 2016.
Silva, M. M., de Gusmão, A. P. H., Poleto, T., e Silva, L. C., & Costa, A. P. C. S. (2014). A multidimensional approach to information security risk management using FMEA and fuzzy theory. *International Journal of Information Management*, *34*(6), 733–740.

Tallon, P. P., & Pinsonneault, A. (2011). Competing perspectives on the link between strategic information technology alignment and organizational agility: Insights from a mediation model. *MIS Quarterly, 35*(2), 463–486.

Trkman, P., McCormack, K., De Oliveira, M. P. V., & Ladeira, M. B. (2010). The impact of business analytics on supply chain performance. *Decision Support Systems, 49*(3), 318–327.

Von Solms, R., & Van Niekerk, J. (2013). From information security to cyber security. *Computers & Security, 38,* 97–102.

Yang, Y. P. O., Shieh, H. M., & Tzeng, G. H. (2013). A VIKOR technique based on DEMATEL and ANP for information security risk control assessment. *Information Sciences, 232,* 482–500.

Yildirim, E. Y., Akalp, G., Aytac, S., & Bayram, N. (2011). Factors influencing information security management in small-and medium-sized enterprises: A case study from Turkey. *International Journal of Information Management, 31*(4), 360–365.

Chapter 6
Developing Supply Chain Risk Mitigation Strategies

Yacob Khojasteh

Abstract In this chapter, the different types of potential risks in supply chains are described and the specific impacts of natural disasters such as the Great East Japan earthquake and tsunami on Japanese supply chains are outlined. Moreover, some strategies and developments on how to mitigate supply chain disruptions are presented.

6.1 Introduction

Supply chain management is responsible for managing and controlling all material flow within a supply chain. It includes the movement of materials from suppliers to different sections in the firm, and from those sections to distribution centers or end users. The flow of materials would be affected by any unexpected event (a potential risk) that may disrupt the smooth movement. Supply chain vulnerability can also be considered a risk factor, which is defined as *exposure to serious disturbance arising from supply chain risks and affecting the supply chain's ability to effectively serve the end customer market* (Mason-Jones and Towill 1998). Therefore, managing risks or disruptions becomes an essential task in an effective supply chain management. The aim of supply chain risk management (SCRM) is to identify the potential sources of risk and implement appropriate actions in order to avoid supply chain vulnerability (Jüttner et al. 2003).

A firm's business and its financial performance could be affected by supply chain disruptions. Smooth movement of materials or operations in the supply chain might be affected as well. Supply chain disruptions may cause delay in production or deliveries. A late delivery of raw materials might stop production, raise costs by forcing a move to alternative transport, materials, or operations, raise the work-in-process (WIP) inventory, and make partners reconsider their trading relationships (Waters 2007).

Y. Khojasteh (✉)
Graduate Program in Business and Development Studies,
Sophia University, Tokyo, Japan
e-mail: khojast@sophia.ac.jp; khojastey@gmail.com

Y. Khojasteh (ed.), *Supply Chain Risk Management*,
DOI 10.1007/978-981-10-4106-8_6

Accenture conducted a survey and reported in 2006 that 73% of organizations have experienced a significant disruption in the past five years. Of those, nearly 32% required more than one month to recover, and another 36% took between one week and one month. The ability to meet the needs of customers and constituents was compromised in 94% of these situations (Inagaki and Kuroda 2007). Also, according to a survey done by Hendricks and Singhal (2003, 2005), sales typically fall by 7% in the year after a major supply chain disruption, shareholder return falls by 7–8% on the day that a disruption occurs, operating income falls by 42%, and return on assets is down by 35%. This highlights the importance of strategies to be developed by the companies to mitigate the supply chain disruptions and to manage supply chain risks.

The remainder of this chapter is organized as follows: Sect. 6.2 describes different types of supply chain risks. Some examples of disruptions in Japanese supply chains caused by the Great East Japan earthquake are provided in Sect. 6.3. Section 6.4 outlines some strategies to mitigate risk, and Sect. 6.5 introduces a supply chain risk management software.

6.2 Supply Chain Risks

Supply chain risks can be generally categorized into internal risks and external risks.

6.2.1 Internal Risks

Internal risks are originated from sources inside the supply chain and they usually occur in normal operations. They include machine breakdowns, late deliveries, forecast error, supplier failure, supplier quality problems, malfunction of information technology and communication systems, change in customer demand, transportation failure, human error, etc. An effective planning and scheduling is crucial to control most of those risks.

Internal risks can be divided into *internal controllable* and *internal partially controllable risks*. Internal controllable risks originate from sources that are most likely to be controllable by the company. For example, the quality and cost of the products. Internal partially controllable risks originate from sources that are partially controllable by the company; for example, a fire accident in the company (Wu et al. 2006).

6.2.2 External Risks

External risks come from outside the supply chain and managers have little or no control on them. They include natural disasters (earthquake, hurricane, tsunami, etc.), war, oil crises, terrorist attacks, the outbreak of disease, financial irregularities, crime, rising custom duty, etc.

External risks in supply chains can be divided into *external controllable risks*, *external partially controllable risks*, and *external uncontrollable risks*. External controllable risks originate from sources that are mostly controllable by the supplier company. For example, the selection of the next-tier suppliers. External partially controllable risks originate from sources that are partially controllable by the supplier company. For example, customer demand can be partially impacted by company's promotion plan. External uncontrollable risks originate from sources that are uncontrollable by the supplier company. For example, natural disasters such as earthquake and tsunami (Wu et al. 2006).

Internal risks are mostly controlled by Japanese companies via an effective and efficient planning and scheduling system. For instance, they are controlled in Toyota partly by Toyota production system. However, external risks are mostly difficult to control or impossible to prevent. Therefore, they should be taken into account as an important factor in supply chain management.

An example of external uncontrollable risk is the Great East Japan Earthquake that occurred in 2011. It had a serious impact on Japanese supply chains that caused various production and delivery problems. The next section presents some of those problems in supply chains with a focus on Japanese companies.

6.3 Natural Disasters and Supply Chain Disruption

The Great East Japan Earthquake hit the north-eastern parts of Japan (the Tōhoku region) in March 2011, and its scale was the fourth largest in the world since 1900 and the largest in recorded history in Japan. It triggered a destructive Tsunami that reached more than ten kilometers inland. Besides it serious social effects, it had a significant impact on industries as well. It caused significant disruptions in both domestic and global supply chains by halting production at several companies and their part suppliers which resulted in significant delay in delivery of parts.

Japan has been a major producer of parts and products worldwide, and the disruption in its supply chains caused disruptions in supply chain globally. The followings are just few examples of such disruptions (Khojasteh and Abdi, 2016).

Japan provides 60% of the world's silicon which is an important raw material for semiconductor chips. It is also the world's largest supplier of dynamic random-access memory and flash memory which are critical raw materials for liquid-crystal displays (LCD). Right after the disaster, the prices for these components in the world market soared by 20%, showing the world's strong dependence on the Japanese supply chain (Park et al. 2013).

Apple faced shortages of the lithium-polymer batteries used in its iPods. The reason was that a crucial polymer used in those batteries was provided by Kureha, a Japanese chemical company, and the company had to shut its factory down due to serious damages caused by the disaster (Sanchanta 2011). The production cites of Xirallic pigments (paints used to give greater color intensity to automobiles' appearance) were badly damaged. The shortage of these parts caused some operational shutdowns in the plants of world's automakers including GM, Ford, and Chrysler (Park et al. 2013).

Two major Japanese suppliers, Mitsubishi Gas Chemical and Hitachi Chemical, provided more than 85% of the world's BT resin, which is a critical raw material for circuit boards. However, operation of some plants was suspended due to damaged infrastructure after the earthquake (Chiu 2011).

After the disaster, many other Japanese large companies such as Panasonic, Sony and Fujitsu had to close their damaged plants. Panasonic, the Japan's biggest maker of batteries, closed two plants; and Fujitsu, a personal computers and home appliances maker closed 10 plants (Ohnsman et al. 2011). Renesas Electronics, a major global producer of chips to be used in automotive microcontrollers, was badly damaged. Its plant operations stopped for nearly three months, and after restarting production, it operated at only about 10% of capacity (Matsuo 2015).

Toyota, more than its domestic competitors, faced with supply chain disruptions. For two weeks after the disaster, the entire Toyota plants in Japan stopped completely. The problems were lack of parts, or not even knowing which parts would be missing when the plants resumed production. It is reported that it took a week for Toyota to list the 500 parts sourced from 200 locations which would be difficult to secure, and then recover to the normal production level. Although it grasped the availability of parts up to the second tier suppliers, Toyota did not keep track of the suppliers of the third tier or further down in general. This is a period when one-of-a-kind-product companies like Fujikura Rubber Ltd., which had 1333 employees and produced rubber parts that were used in some of Toyota's cars, became well-known to the public (Matsuo 2015).

These disruptions in the supply chains pushed the companies to develop (or to revise) strategies to mitigate risk in their supply chains. Some of those strategies are outlined in the next section.

6.4 Developing Risk Mitigation Strategies

Prior to 2011, risks were not seriously taken into account in the supply chain of many Japanese companies. Many companies developed plans to consider the risk mitigation strategies in the supply chains after the Great East Japan Earthquake and floods in Thailand had a significant impact on their production and delivery of their products. In fact, the concept of risk in the supply chain was extended to include all parties in the supply chain, and external factors as well (Khojasteh and Abdi, 2016).

For instance, Toyota revised the supply chain coordination mechanism of its production system, which considers the followings (Matsuo 2015):

- Monitoring the information on all the suppliers of key parts/materials across the entire supply chain.
- Managing the inventory of key parts/materials across the entire supply chain.
- Ensuring the continuing supply of key parts/materials.
- Increasing the standardization of key parts/materials and their production methods.

The followings are also examples of companies' strategies in order to avoid a significant disruption in their supply chains:

- Companies should request their suppliers to develop disaster plans in order to get prepared for taking a set of actions to minimize the effect of disruption and the recovery period. This strategy could be even considered in service sectors as well. The author experienced developing "backup syllabus" requested by his university located in Tokyo short after the Great East Japan Earthquake in 2011. The backup syllabus contained a detailed plan on how to resume the course when the classes have to be canceled when a similar disaster occurs.
- Having only one supplier for critical parts and materials is too risky. Thus, companies should not fully rely on single source suppliers even though they are the best in terms of cost, quality, and trust. Dual or multi sourcing for critical parts and suppliers would be a good strategy even in small scales. Regarding the dual-sourcing, one plan could be buying the majority of the parts and materials from the primary supplier, and the rest from a secondary one that is possibly located in another region. This can keep the secondary supplier operational and ready to be switched at any time.
- Companies should group the suppliers geographically and identify the suppliers who are located in risky areas. As a result, buying the critical parts and materials from those suppliers should be limited and different alternatives should be planned (Mojonnier 2011). For instance, the area that is currently considered highly risky in Japan is Tōkai area. The probability of a magnitude eight or greater earthquake along the Nankai Trough within the next forty years is about 80%.

6.5 A Supply Chain Risk Management Software

Fujitsu Research Institute introduced a Supply Chain Continuity Assessment system in 2007. It identifies potential supply chain problems arising from contingencies and can evaluate various countermeasures. The system is able to evaluate and analyze a firm's business continuity capabilities in cases of natural disasters and other unexpected situations. The system has the following features (Fujitsu 2007, 2013):

(1) Evaluating and analyzing business continuity capabilities of suppliers

The system enables companies to perform quantitative analyses regarding the resumption of suppliers' operations, the amount of time required for recovery, damage projections, and the status of implemented countermeasures before a disaster occurs.

(2) Using hazard maps to evaluate geographic risks for suppliers

It uses the latest hazard maps with the addresses of suppliers' production facilities and offices, which makes it possible to visually simulate the expected damage that will occur during a natural disaster.

(3) Analyzing the impacts on the firm's own products

Based on an evaluation of suppliers' business continuity capabilities and the results of geographic risk evaluations using hazard maps, the system enables a firm to quantitatively analyze the impact of a disaster on its own products. For example, firms can estimate which products will be affected by production stoppages and calculate when production will resume.

After the Great East Japan Earthquake, Fujitsu added some new feature for its Supply Chain Continuity Assessment system to reduce supply chain disruptions after occurrence of an unexpected event. It developed the *SCRKeeper system* that can provide damage forecasting and assessment for the regions where suppliers are located. The *SCRKeeper system* has the following additional feature (Fujitsu 2013; Japanbullet 2013):

(4) The system visualizes supply chain risk per each production part or production site of a supplier to manage the supplier's damage situation in disaster time. It provides immediate damage status updates on suppliers. When a disaster actually occurs, the system is immediately updated with reports from suppliers about the status of damage and the situation of their operations. This makes it possible for firms to check on the status of their suppliers in real time and overview their damage status, so that they can quickly respond to their suppliers or select alternative suppliers (Fujitsu 2013).

Acknowledgements This work was supported by the Japan Society for the Promotion of Science, Grant-in-Aid for Scientific Research (C), 16K01257.

References

Chiu, Y. T. (2011) How Japan's earthquake is shaking up Taiwan's high-tech sector. IEEE Spectrum. Available at http://spectrum.ieee.org/semiconductors/memory/how-japans-earthquake-is-shaking-up-taiwans-hightech-sector. Last accessed on December 10, 2016.

Fujitsu. (2007). Fujitsu enhances business continuity management in procurement. Available at http://www.fujitsu.com/global/about/resources/news/press-releases/2007/0821-01.html. Last accessed on December 10, 2016.

Fujitsu. (2013). 'SCRKeeper,' Japan's first cloud-based supply chain risk management service. Available at http://jp.fujitsu.com/solutions/cloud/saas/application/scrkeeper/en/. Last accessed on November 2, 2015.

Hendricks, K. B., & Singhal, V. R. (2003). The effect of supply chain glitches on shareholder value. *Journal of Operations Management, 21*(5), 501–522.

Hendricks, K. B., & Singhal, V. R. (2005). An empirical analysis of the effect of supply chain disruptions on long-run stock price performance and risk of the firm. *Production and Operations Management, 14*(1), 35–52.

Inagaki, M., & Kuroda, K. (2007). Supply chain management in Japan. *Supply and Demand Chain Executive, 8*(3), 68.

Japanbullet. (2013). Fujitsu launches Scrkeeper Japan first cloud—Based supply chain risk management service. Available at http://www.japanbullet.com/technology/fujitsu-launches-scrkeeper-japan-first-cloud-based-supply-chain-risk-management-service. Last accessed on December 10, 2016.

Jüttner, U., Peck, H., & Christopher, M. (2003). Supply chain risk management: outlining an agenda for future research. *International Journal of Logistics: Research and Applications, 6*(4), 197–210.

Khojasteh, Y., & Abdi, M. R. (2016). Japanese supply chain management, In P. Haghirian (Ed.), *Routledge handbook of japanese business and management*, UK: Routledge.

Mason-Jones, R., & Towill, D. R. (1998). Shrinking the supply chain uncertainty circle. *Control, 24*(7), 17–22.

Matsuo, H. (2015). Implications of the Tohoku earthquake for Toyota's coordination mechanism: Supply chain disruption of automotive semiconductors. *International Journal of Production Economics, 161*(1), 217–227.

Mojonnier, T. (2011). Reducing risk in the automotive supply chain. *Business Theory.* Available at http://businesstheory.com/reducing-risk-automotive-supply-chain-2/. Accessed on December 15, 2016.

Ohnsman, A., McCombs, D., & Edwards, C. (2011). Toyota, Sony disruptions may last weeks after Japan earthquake. *Bloomberg Business.* http://www.bloomberg.com/news/articles/2011-03-19/toyota-sony-disruptions-may-last-weeks-after-japan-quake-power-shortages (March 20, 2011).

Park, Y. W., Hong, P., & Roh, J. (2013). Supply chain lessons from the 2011 natural disasters in Japan. *Business Horizons, 56*(1), 75–85.

Sanchanta, M. (2011), Chemical reaction: iPod is short key material. *The Wall Street Journal.* Available at https://www.wsj.com/articles/SB100014240527487044719045762283904005 76486. Accessed on December 15, 2016.

Waters, D. (2007). *Supply chain risk management: Vulnerability and resilience in logistics.* London: Kogan Page.

Wu, T., Blackhurst, J., & Chidambaram, V. (2006). A model for inbound supply risk analysis. *Computers in Industry, 57,* 350–365.

Part II
Supply Chain Vulnerability and Disruptions Management

Chapter 7
Analyzing Supply Chain Vulnerability Through Simulation

Jyri Vilko and Lauri Lättilä

Abstract Supply chain vulnerabilities have attracted little research attention despite being recognized as an important issue. To provide further insights into this issue, this chapter uses a simulation approach for analyzing supply chain vulnerability. Specifically, simulations are used to gain additional insights into multi-echelon supply chains and the impact of supply disruptions. This study employs an integrated literature review of supply chain vulnerability and risk management and a discrete-event-simulation. The presented framework and simulation models provide important information about the feasibility of using a simulation for analyzing supply chain vulnerability. The results of this study suggest that supply chain vulnerability depends on both the complexity of the supply chain as well as the disruption risks inherent in it. To gain a more holistic view of an entire supply chain system, it is imperative to use proper tools to analyze vulnerabilities. Simulations can be used to model both the system complexity and the different levels of operation holistically and gain insights into managing supply chain vulnerability. By analyzing supply chain vulnerability, managers can ground their decisions in a more holistic understanding of the issue.

7.1 Introduction

During the last decade, improving efficiency and delivery times has become a key issue in many organizations. Supply chains have become a focal point for improving competitiveness in an increasingly global marketplace. While numerous trends (e.g., development of communications and other technologies, e-business

J. Vilko (✉)
School of Business, Lappeenranta University of Technology, Lappeenranta, Finland
e-mail: jyri.vilko@lut.fi

L. Lättilä
SimAnalytics, Kaisaniemenkatu, Helsinki, Finland

Y. Khojasteh (ed.), *Supply Chain Risk Management*,
DOI 10.1007/978-981-10-4106-8_7

outsourcing, and lean and agile logistics) have made it possible to develop complex international networks of industrial partners, they have also made organizations vulnerable to various risks arising from these networks (Narasimhan and Talluri 2009; Thun and Hoenig 2011; Vilko 2012). Many recent events have highlighted the vulnerability of long and complex service supply chains. A risk realization affecting operations anywhere in the system can directly affect its ability to continue operations, thus endangering customer value creation. A recent study presents a good example of the vulnerability of value provision in supply chains (Hendricks et al. 2009), where companies admitting to major supply chain difficulties lost 10% of their shareholder value on average. These issues have become increasingly relevant as the global financial crisis emphasized the role of supply chain risk management in many companies (Blome and Schoenherr 2011).

In international supply chains, interorganizational dependencies and relationships have become increasingly important, and while the network exposes organizations to various risks, it is difficult to be competitive in the modern world without them (Soosay et al. 2008). Therefore, organizations need to understand and analyze the causalities of network processes to ensure that the goals of the supply chain fit with their own organizational strategy. It is essential for actors to collaborate and share information in their network to avoid interruptions in logistic flows (Edwards et al. 2001; Svensson 2001).

Indeed, supply chain management is undergoing continuous, considerable, and rapid changes leading to a high cost of vulnerability (Frankel et al. 2008). However, in the past decade, only a few studies have addressed the issue of vulnerability in the context of supply chains (e.g., Peck 2005; Sheffi 2005), and even fewer studies have addressed the methodological issues faced therein. In current literature (e.g., Vlajic et al. 2012), researchers have emphasized the need for integrated frameworks to support analyses for overcoming supply chain vulnerability and supply chain disturbances. Therefore, this chapter aims to provide insights on supply chain vulnerability using analyses with a discrete-event-based simulation. Specifically, it shows how a simulation method can be used to gain a more holistic view of supply chain vulnerability. For this purpose, a conceptual framework is developed and tested to analyze supply chain vulnerability, and its feasibility is evaluated. This chapter focuses on process-level disturbances (consequences of unwanted and unexpected events) and how these impact wider supply chain level operations.

The rest of this chapter is organized as follows. Section 7.2 presents relevant concepts and their definitions. Section 7.3 introduces the research process used for simulating supply chain vulnerability. Then, Sect. 7.4 presents a simulation analysis. Finally, Sect. 7.5 presents the conclusions and discussions.

7.2 Literature Review

The theoretical part of this study contains two main perspectives: supply chain vulnerability theory with related concepts and applying a simulation in the supply chain vulnerability context.

7.2.1 Supply Chain Vulnerability

A supply chain is defined as a system of suppliers, manufacturers, distributors, retailers, and customers in which material, financial, and information flows connect participants in both directions (Fiala 2005). Waters (2007) described a supply chain as consisting of a series of activities and organizations through which material moves on its journey from initial suppliers to final customers. Material can include everything that an organization moves and can be both tangible and intangible.

To define supply chain vulnerability, it is essential to first examine the characteristics of risk. Risks have been defined in numerous ways in literature. Waters (2007) defined risks as a threat of disruption to normal activities that stop these activities from happening as planned. A standard formula for the quantitative definition of supply chain risk is (Mitchell 1995)

$$\text{Risk} = \text{P} \times \text{I} \tag{7.1}$$

where P is the probability of a risk event, and I is the impact of the risk event.

Depending on the context, the sources of risk can be categorized in several ways. The sources of risk are generally categorized as endogenous and exogenous, depending on whether they derive from within or outside the system, which in this case is the supply network (Trkman and McCormack 2009). Risks can arise from organizations, supply chain partners, or the external environment (Waters 2007). The sensitivity of a supply chain to these disturbances is measured by its vulnerability.

From the perspective of supply chain risk management, an organization incurs loss as a result of its supply chain's vulnerability to a risk event (Wagner and Neshat 2010). Asbjørnslett (2008) defined vulnerability as "the properties of a supply chain system; its premises, facilities and equipment, including human resources, human organization and all its software, hardware, netware that may weaken or limit its ability to endure threats and survive accidental events that originate both within and outside system boundaries." Previous definitions were somewhat different. For example, Peck (2005) described vulnerability as an "exposure to serious disturbance, arising from risks within the supply chain as well as risks external to the supply chain." Furthermore, according to Waters (2007), "supply chain vulnerability reflects the susceptibility of a supply chain to disruption and is a consequence of the risks to the chain." Jüttner et al. (2003) described supply chain vulnerability as the propensity of risk sources and risk drivers to outweigh risk-mitigating strategies, thus causing adverse supply chain consequences and jeopardizing the supply chain's ability to effectively serve the end customer market.

According to Asbjørnslett (2008), the difference between vulnerability analysis and risk analysis arises from the focus of the analysis. While vulnerability analysis focuses on the more holistic supply chain perspective in terms of the system's mission and supply security, risk analysis focuses more on the impacts of individual events. When examined from a quantitative perspective, the difference between risk and vulnerability arises from the exposure element, which reflects the extent of the impact with regard to a specific supply chain actor. The benefit of this type of examination is that it allows the differentiation of both the general risk (e.g., for the supply chain) and an individual actor's vulnerability to a specific risk. In doing so, the illustration of these different perspectives allows a better understanding of different actors' views on different risks and therefore allows mitigation actions to be adjusted accordingly in the entire supply chain. Currency risk is a practical example of the benefit of adding the exposure element to risk management examination: if a company faces a currency risk in its supply chain, its risk exposure is determined by the risk management actions it conducts. If the company acknowledges the risk but does not manage it in any way, its risk exposure can be considered to be 100%. Accordingly, we define supply chain vulnerability as follows:

$$\text{Vulnerability} = \mathrm{P} \times \mathrm{I} \times \mathrm{E} \tag{7.2}$$

where E is the risk exposure.

In reality, when considering supply chain vulnerability, the actors can better affect the probability of a risk event when they have control over the operations (risk arising inside the supply chain) or the exposure to risk events (risk that enters from outside the supply chain). Thus, when analyzing the proper responses to supply chain vulnerability, the origin of the risk event needs to be taken into account.

7.2.2 *Simulation of Supply Chain Vulnerability*

Few studies have attempted to use simulations to analyze supply chain vulnerability. The lack of research can be illustrated by a simple comparison with other related areas through a keyword search in Google Scholar (Table 7.1).

While some studies have reported on the use of simulations, the feasibility of their application has not yet been thoroughly investigated. To gain deeper insights into the state-of-the-art in analyzing supply chain vulnerability using simulations, we systematically analyzed existing literatures using Elsevier's Sciencedirect as the

Table 7.1 Keyword searches (using Google Scholar on 10.4.2015)

Keyword combination	Search results
“supply chain vulnerability analysis” and simulation	2
“supply chain risk analysis” and simulation	117
“supply chain vulnerability” and simulation	547
“supply chain risk management” and simulation	1950
“supply chain analysis” and simulation	2290
“supply chain risk” and simulation	2970
“supply chain management” and simulation	52,600

main search tool With the keywords *supply chain*, *simulation*, and *vulnerability*. As a result, 26 studies were found, of which 16 were relevant (Table 7.2 and Fig. 7.1).

Simulations have been used for analyzing vulnerability-related issues in various applications during the last decade; studies have used various research approaches to this end. In Table 7.2, Conceptual approach refers to a purely conceptual contemplation of concepts and terms; Hypothetical approach, to a simulation research conducted with hypothetical models (without real-world cases or data); and Empirical approach, to real-world case examples in which simulations are used in different ways. The first case found in our search was by Gnoni et al. (2003), who analyzed only risks involving demand-side uncertainty. Marquez and Blanchar (2004) concentrated on a portfolio of contracts for procuring strategic parts. Wilson (2007) studied the effect of transportation disruptions on the performance of different parts of the supply chain. Biehl et al. (2007) concentrated on the carpet manufacturing industry with a focus on reverse logistics.

Kull and Closs (2008) studied a generic supply chain; their results highlighted the importance of true systematic analyses when risks need to be managed and of coordination to manage supply risks.

Galasso and Thierry (2009) concentrated on risk analysis from the viewpoints of suppliers, customers, and cooperation among all parties involved. They also noted how different criteria could be taken into account in a decision support system. Tuncel and Alpan (2010) used more traditional risk management tools, including a Petri net.

Supply chain risks can also depend on global issues. Jacxsens et al. (2010) developed a conceptual framework that can be used to enhance research on the impact of climate change on fresh produce supply chains. In this case, the risks are greatly different from those in most analyses where some physical disruption or demand uncertainty is evaluated. Carvalho et al. (2012) used Supply Chain Operations Reference (SCOR) for constructing a simulation model. SCOR is a supply chain management tool used to address, improve, and communicate supply chain management decisions within a supply chain (Huan et al. 2004).

Vilko and Hallikas (2012) concentrated on multimodal supply chains; their approach allowed the identification of issues that had the highest impact in a maritime supply chain. Li and Liu (2013) used dynamic programming to model a multitier supply chain with various sources of uncertainty; this was one of the few

Table 7.2 Review of literature on supply chain vulnerability simulation

Author (Year)	Venue	Main research method (discrete-event simulation, system dynamics, agent-based modelling, or other method)				Research objective	Research approach (conceptual/ hypothetical/ empirical)		
		DES	SD	ABM	Other*		C	H	E
Shu et al. (2014)	ESWA				MP	Supply chain construction optimization in production uncertainty and different product		x	
Burgholzer et al. (2013)	DSS		X	X		Analysis of intermodal transport network flows under disruption			x
Li and Liu (2013)	AMM				DP	Bullwhip effect control in supply chain system		x	
Shi et al. (2013)	EJOR	x				Supply chain distribution performance and risk optimization			x
Villada and Olaya (2013)	EP	x		x		Evaluating alternative policies for increasing the security of gas supply			x
Carvalho et al. (2012)	C&IE	x				Design support for supply chain resiliency			x
Schmitt and Singh (2012)	IJPE	x				The impact of disruptions in different nodes of the network			x
Vilko and Hallikas (2012)	IJPE				MC	Supply chain risk assessment			x
Jacxsens et al. (2010)	FRI				N/A	Safety and security of food supply chain	x		
Tuncel and Alpan (2010)	CI				PN	Supply chain risk management and real-time control			x
Galasso and Thierry (2009)	EAAI				MC&MP	Decision and cooperation support of planning processes		x	
Kull and Closs (2008)	EJOR	x				Interaction of inventory and supply risk on system performance		x	

(continued)

Table 7.2 (continued)

Author (Year)	Venue	Main research method (discrete-event simulation, system dynamics, agent-based modelling, or other method)				Research objective	Research approach (conceptual/ hypothetical/ empirical)		
		DES	SD	ABM	Other*		C	H	E
Wilson (2007)	TRE		**x**			Transportation disruptions' effect on supply chain performance		**x**	
Biehl et al. (2007)	COR	**x**				Design of reverse logistics system			**x**
Marquez and Blanchar (2004)	IJPE		**x**			Managing and valuing supplier contract portfolio		**x**	
Gnoni et al. (2003)	IJPE	**x**			**MP**	Demand stochastic variability effects on production systems' technical and economic performance			**x**

**PN* PetriNet, *MC* Monte Carlo simulation, *MP* Mathematical programming, *DP* Dynamic programming

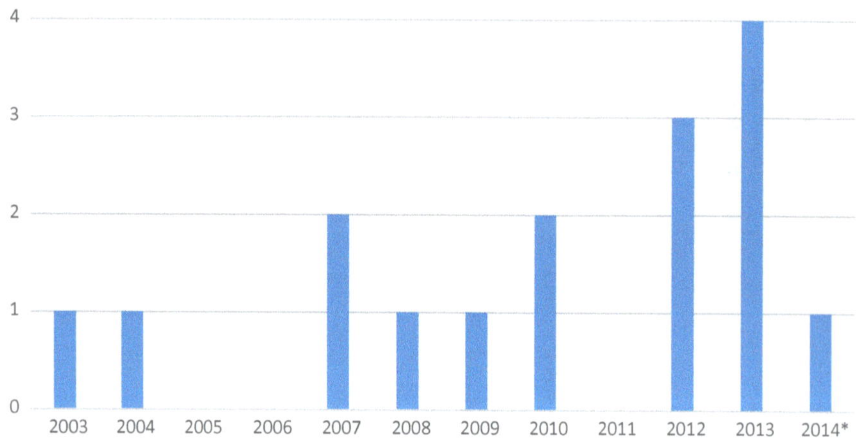

Fig. 7.1 Supply chain vulnerability simulation studies in Sciencedirect

attempts to apply a holistic approach to risk management and robust network design.

In recent years, areas other than traditional supply chains have attracted interest in supply chain vulnerability simulations. For example, Villada and Olaya (2013) evaluated the short-term security of natural gas supply with a contracts-based simulation model by representing different parts of the supply chain. Burgholzer et al. (2013) concentrated on intermodal transport networks with a microlevel perspective. Shi et al. (2013) analyzed a JIT-based cross-docking distribution center by minimizing supply uncertainty in the cross-docking activities. Shu et al. (2014) proposed a generic tool that is based on a bill-of-materials and covers production disruptions and supply chain optimization.

Overall, the above examples clearly show that simulations are mostly applied on the demand or supply side or from a single actor's perspective of the supply network; only a few studies take into account the supply chain vulnerability holistically. Previous simulation-based analyses have typically concentrated on a specific part of a supply chain or a certain perspective of it. Herein, our aim is to contribute to the current body of knowledge with a more holistic perspective of supply chain vulnerability by developing and testing a model that illustrates the concrete benefits of collaboration in a supply chain. Specifically, our holistic perspective involves taking into account the complete supply chain system by examining the perspective of a larger supply chain as well as the perspective of individual actors, thus allowing a more comprehensive view of vulnerability for simulation analysis. In doing so, the risk mitigation actions of the entire supply chain can be more carefully measured and planned for each actor.

7.3 Research Process

The research process involved two main phases: literature review and model development.

The literature review revealed the scarcity of scientific literature on supply chain vulnerability management. A Google Scholar search with the keywords "supply chain vulnerability management" and simulation only yielded 6 results, and a search with the keywords "supply chain risk management" and simulation yielded 1850 results. This also illustrates the state of maturity of the concepts, namely, that while both are still developing (Vilko 2012), supply chain vulnerability is clearly still in its early stages. Therefore, to provide better clarity for our study, we developed our own definition for the concept and thereafter used it in the simulation model. To have a proper conceptual foundation, we used a vulnerability-related concept with an integrated literature review strategy.

The main message from the literature reviewed on supply chain vulnerability management is that further studies with a systematic approach should be developed. For example, Peck (2005) noted that there is a need to develop more complete predictive simulations that can estimate the impact of various actions in dynamic supply chain networks. These types of complex simulation studies should be able to estimate how the entire supply chain reacts to different types of issues. These systems would be aimed towards managers, who currently do not have adequate tools to cope with supply chain vulnerability analyses. Similar issues have also been noted by Wu et al. (2006) and Bernadel and Panizzollo (2012).

The model development involved three steps following the basic principles given by Banks et al. (2005). The first was the selection of the model, which was based on a previous smaller study (Vilko and Lättilä 2013). The supply chain case was observed from a wider perspective to gain a more complete view of the supply chain events. The hypothetical supply chain case was built based on 40 interviews from the STOCA (Study of Cargo flows in the Gulf of Finland in Emergency Situations) project. The second step was the actual development of the model by two logistics researchers with different backgrounds (one focused on supply chain risk management and the other, on supply chain simulations). The development was conducted as an iterative process, in which the main focus was on material flows. The final step of model development was testing. It included several runs of the model, fine-tuning of the factorial relationships, and top-down verification of the model and code.

As the main rule for a disruption, we use the concept of supply security. According to the Finnish National Emergency Supply Agency (NESA), supply security refers to "the capacity to maintain the basic activities that are indispensable for safeguarding the population's living conditions, for sustaining the functioning of critical infrastructures, and the material preconditions for maintaining national preparedness and defence in case of serious disturbances and emergency situations." Thus, ensuring capacity and delivery can be considered essential, as is the case in business as well. However, in complex and long supply chains, it is difficult to identify the chain reactions produced by different types of disturbances. A simulation can be used to discover the systemic structures and causalities of the network; this, in turn, can provide valuable information about the role of different factors in the supply chain.

7.4 Vulnerability Simulation

7.4.1 Case Description

The supply chain consists of multiple suppliers, a manufacturing unit, distribution warehouses, and sales offices, as shown in Fig. 7.2. Two of the suppliers are located offshore. When the manufacturing unit places an order, the goods arrive in 30–41 days (Table 7.3); two of the suppliers had a delivery lead time of 7–14 days; and the last supplier had a lead time of 2–4 days. We assume that the lead time is uniformly distributed and that it should reflect real operations as deliveries tend to be optimized. The distribution warehouses also have different lead times; the last distribution warehouse had a lead time of 14 days. Each distribution warehouse

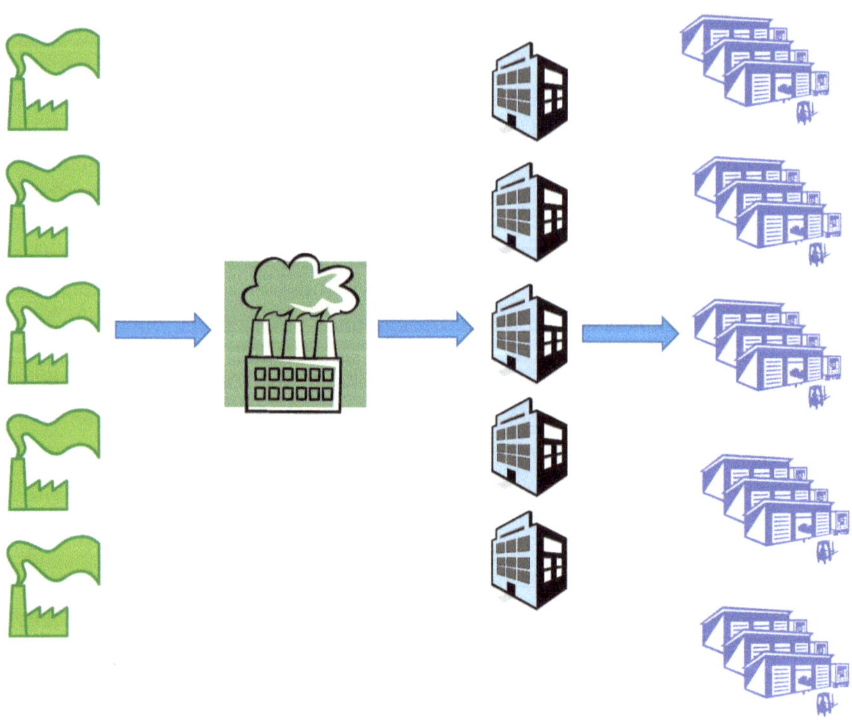

Fig. 7.2 Basic supply chain structure

serves three sales offices. These sales offices are supplied with a lead time of 1–3 days. The actual simulation is run for 11 years, in which the first year is a warm-up period and the last ten years are the actual simulation period.

Both the factory and the distribution warehouse reserve their stock according to the orders received from the next tier in the supply chain. All tiers inform the previous tier by using their own sales data. For instance, as soon as a sales office sells one product, it sends information to its own distribution warehouse, which in turn reserves one product from the warehouse for that particular sales office. As soon as an entire order is ready, the supplier/factory/distribution warehouse sends the delivery to the customer. The actual warehousing policies and distribution lead times are summarized in Table 7.3.

Supply chain costs arise from three different sources: lost sales, warehousing costs, and ordering costs. These costs are location dependent, for example, an order from an offshore supplier has much higher cost than an order from a supplier located nearby. Warehousing costs start accumulating as soon as the raw materials arrive at the factory, and it is assumed that all raw materials have a similar cost. All cost elements are listed in Table 7.4.

In addition to the supply chain nodes, simplified production is also modelled. Producing one unit takes 6 min, and the factory operates in two shifts per day from

Table 7.3 Warehousing policy and distribution lead times

Node	Batch size (units)	Delivery lead time (days)
Suppliers 1 and 2	400	30–41
Suppliers 3 and 4	150	7–14
Supplier 5	30	2–4
Distribution warehouse 1	60	2
Distribution warehouses 2 and 3	75	5
Distribution warehouse 4	90	7
Distribution warehouse 5	120	14
Sales offices	30	1–3

Table 7.4 Cost elements in supply chain

Cost element	Amount
Cost of lost sales	$1000/unit
Ordering cost from suppliers 1 and 2	$3000/order
Ordering cost from suppliers 3 and 4	$700/order
Ordering cost from supplier 5	$200/order
Ordering cost for distribution warehouse 1	$500/order
Ordering cost for distribution warehouses 2 and 3	$625/order
Ordering cost for distribution warehouse 4	$750/order
Ordering cost for distribution warehouse 5	$1000/order
Ordering cost for sales offices	$500/order
Warehousing cost	$200/unit/year

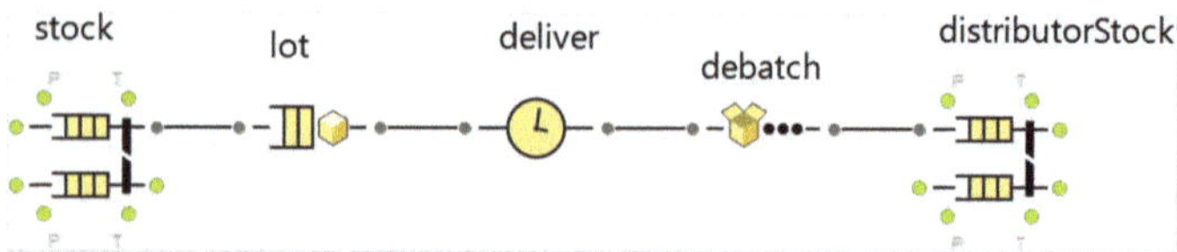

Fig. 7.3 Basic connections in simulation model

Monday to Friday. This is used to ensure that the production is not instant and that it reflects normal operating conditions.

The actual simulation model was constructed using Anylogic. The distribution warehouses and sales offices are almost identical, with the only difference between them being that the demand at the sales offices is stochastic and random whereas that at the distribution warehouses is dependent on the demand at the sales offices. Figure 7.3 shows an example of these nodes. The suppliers' warehouses are not modelled and have infinite capacity; however, in the simulation model, they are completely dependent on the demand from the factory. The factory has a simple assembly operation in which all goods from the suppliers are assembled to make final products. The factory itself operates on a push principle; however, the raw materials arrive based on a pull principle. The factory stock is then connected to the distribution warehouses.

"Stock" represents physical stock. Products arrive at the location and wait in the queue for an order. When an order arrives, they are moved to the "lot" element. The "lot" element batches the products depending on the batch size, and when the correct batch size is reached, the goods are delivered. The "deliver" element contains a node-dependent delay. In the case of a disruption, the delay contains additional time in addition to the actual delivery lead time. When the goods arrive, they are removed from the batch in the "debatch" element to become individual products. Finally, the products arrive at the next stock called "distributorStock." The distributor has a similar chain for the sales offices.

7.4.2 Disruptions in the Model

We want to analyze how the supply chain behaves when different partners react to changes in the likelihood of disruptions. We analyze multiple different scenarios, in which either only one party will change their amount of safety stock or all parties will cooperate. By doing so, we can understand the benefits that can be achieved when supply chain partners cooperate to manage changes in supply-chain-related risks.

We assume that there is an inherent likelihood of having an excess delay between the raw material suppliers and the factory. The actual disruption will double the delivery time to the factory. The three scenarios use different likelihoods for this disruption: 5, 15, and 25%. In each case, we use the OptQuest optimization engine to minimize the supply chain costs.

Overall, there are nine different scenarios. We use the scenario with a disruption likelihood of 5% as a baseline scenario. The baseline scenario defines the used safety stocks; these are used in the other scenarios as well. If all supply chain partners cooperate, we can allow all safety stocks to change. However, if only one tier tries to cope with the change in the environment, we assume that the other tiers do not change their safety stock policies but instead rely on the values optimized in the baseline scenario.

7.4.3 Results

Table 7.5 presents the results in millions over a ten-year period. These results clear show the benefits of cooperating in supply chain risk management. Depending on the scenario, different partners have a larger impact on the results. In the scenario with 15% likelihood, the sales offices have the best tools to manage disruptions as they can keep their costs the lowest if the tiers do not cooperate. However, in the scenario with 25% likelihood, the factory has the best impact on the supply chain cost structure. The nonlinear dependencies place different importance on different actors in different scenarios.

Cooperation between supply chain partners should be encouraged. This creates some issues with incentives as the tier that increases the amount of safety stocks has to carry more costs. Table 7.6 provides the optimized safety stocks when cooperation is used. In the 15% scenario, the sales offices hold lesser inventory than in the baseline scenario, whereas the factory and distribution warehouses hold more inventory. In the 25% scenario, the factory and sales offices hold more inventory.

If a supply chain tier tries to mitigate the change alone, the safety stocks need to increase. In particular, the sales offices needs to hold much more inventory than in the cooperative scenario, as shown in Table 7.7. These values should be compared to the 5% likelihood scenario in the cooperative scenario as it serves as the baseline for the other scenarios.

Table 7.5 Supply chain costs in millions during ten-year period when different partners react to changes in the supply chain environment

	5%	15%	25%
Factory		8.387	8.473
Warehouse		8.339	8.475
Sales office		8.294	8.525
Cooperation	7.885	8.264	8.336

Table 7.6 Optimized safety stock levels in the scenario where different partners cooperate

	5%	15%	25%
Factory	200	450	350
Warehouse	125	175	125
Sales office	10	5	16

Table 7.7 Optimized safety stock levels if only one tier mitigates

	15%	25%
Factory	450	500
Warehouse	150	200
Sales office	19	36

7.5 Discussion and Conclusions

Owing to lengthier and more complex supply chains, vulnerability against disruptions has clearly increased. Even though this has increased the need for advanced vulnerability analyses among practitioners, there is still a clear need for further research. To address this gap in scientific literature, this chapter developed and tested a vulnerability analysis framework based on a simulation approach. This chapter contributes to both theory and practice as follows.

From a theoretical perspective, we make three main contributions. First, we provide a definition for supply chain vulnerability using an integrated literature review. Second, we demonstrate the current state-of-the-art of using simulations in scientific studies. Finally, and most importantly, we develop and test our discrete-event simulation model that enables one to test the benefits of collaboration in supply chain risk management and thus reduce the overall vulnerability. Our method seemed to work particularly well when analyzing the key components of vulnerability, namely, disruptions and exposure risk.

From a practical perspective, we make two main contributions. First, we demonstrate how simulations can be used to illustrate complex structures in long supply chains without losing process-level factors, which is especially important for gaining a holistic view of supply chain vulnerability. Second, we illustrate how the model can be used to run "what-if" experiments and how it can be used to increase the supply chain performance by influencing the factors a supply chain is most sensitive to.

This model includes some obvious limitations owing to the research design. However, when considering the illustrative purposes of this research, the examples used are considered appropriate. Moreover, the companies considered as examples in the simulation might have multiple suppliers for the same components, in which case a backup supplier would be used; the model built cannot take this into account.

References

Asbjørnslett, B. E. (2008). Assessing the vulnerability of supply chains. In G. A. Zsidisin & B. Ritchie (Eds.), *Supply chain risk: A handbook of assessment*. Management and Performance, US: Springer.

Banks, J., Carson II, J. S., Nelson, B. L., & Nicol, D. M. (2005). *Discrete-Event System Simulation* (5th ed.,). Upper Saddle River, NJ, USA: Pearson Education.

Bernadel, F., & Pannizolo, R. (2012). Approaching risk management: An overview of critical success factors and challenges. *The International Journal on Management Science and Information Technology, 1*(4), 1–27.

Biehl, M., Prater, E., & Realff, M. J. (2007). Assessing performance and uncertainty in developing carpet reverse logistics system. *Computers & Operations, 34*(2), 443–463.

Blome, C., & Schoenherr, T. (2011). Supply chain risk management in financial crises—a multiple case-study approach. *International Journal of Production Economics, 134*(1), 43–57.

Burgholzer, W., Bauer, G., Posset, M., & Jammernegg, W. (2013). Analysing the impact of disruptions in intermodal transport networks: A micro simulation-based model. *Decision Support Systems, 54*(4), 1580–1586.

Carvalho, H., Barroso, A. P., Machado, V. M., Azevedo, S., & Cruz-Machado, V. (2012). Supply chain redesign for resilience using simulation. *Computers & Industrial Engineering, 62*(1), 329–341.

Edwards, P., Peters, M., & Sharman, G. (2001). The effectiveness of information systems in supporting the extended supply chain. *Journal of Business Logistics, 22*(1), 1–28.

Fiala, P. (2005). Information sharing in supply chains. *The International Journal of Management Science, 33*(3), 419–423.

Frankel, R., Yemisi, A. B., Reham, A. E., Paulraj, A., & Gundlach, G. T. (2008). The domain and scope of SCMs foundational disciplines—insights and issues to advance research. *Journal of Business Logistics, 29*(1), 1–30.

Galasso, F., & Thierry, C. (2009). Design of cooperative processes in a customer-supplier relationship: An approach based on simulation and decision theory. *Engineering Applications of Artificial Intelligence, 22*(6), 865–881.

Gnoni, M. G., Iavagnilio, R., Mossa, G., Mummolo, G., & Di Leva, A. (2003). Production planning of a multi-site manufacturing system by hybrid modelling: A case study from the automotive industry. *International Journal of Production Economics, 83*(2), 251–262.

Hendricks, K., Singhal, V., & Zhang, R. (2009). The effect of operational slack diversification, and vertical relatedness on the stock market reaction to supply chain disruptions. *Journal of Operations Management, 273*(3), 233–246.

Huan, S., Sheoran, S., & Wang, G. (2004). A research and analysis of supply chain operations reference (SCOR) model. *Supply Chain Management: An International Journal, 9*(1), 23–29.

Jacxsens, L., Luning, P. A., van der Vorst, J. G. A. J., Devlieghere, F., Leemans, R., & Uyttendaele, M. (2010). Simulation modelling and risk assessment as tools to identify the impact of climate change on microbiological food safety—the case study of fresh produce supply chain. *Food Research International, 43*(7), 1925–1935.

Jüttner, U., Peck, H., & Christopher, M. (2003). Supply chain risk management: Outlining an agenda for future research. *International Journal of Logistics: Research and Applications, 6*(4), 197–210.

Kull, T., & Closs, D. (2008). The risk of second tier supplier failures in serial supply chains: Implications for order policies and distributor autonomy. *European Journal of Operational Research, 186*(3), 1158–1174.

Li, C., & Liu, S. (2013). A robust optimization approach to reduce the bullwhip effect of supply chains with vendor order placement lead time delays in an uncertain environment. *Applied Mathematical Modelling, 37*(3), 707–718.

Marquez, A. C., & Blanchar, C. (2004). The procurement of strategic parts. Analysis of portfolio of contracts with suppliers using a system dynamics simulation model. *International Journal of Production Economics, 88*(1), 29–49.

Mitchell, V. W. (1995). Organisational risk perception and reduction: a literature review. *British Journal of Management, 6*(2), 115–133.

Narasimhan, R., & Talluri, S. (2009). Perspectives on risk management in supply chains. *Journal of Operations Management, 27*(2), 114–118.

Peck, H. (2005). Drivers of supply chain vulnerability: an integrated framework. *International Journal of Physical Distribution and Logistics Management, 35*(4), 210–232.

Schmitt, A. J., & Singh, M. (2012). A quantitative analysis of disruption risk in a multi-echelon supply chain. *International Journal of Production Economics, 139*(1), 22–32.

Sheffi, Y. (2005). *The resilient enterprise: overcoming vulnerability for competitive advantage*. Cambridge, MA: MIT Press Books.

Shi, W., Liu, Z., Shang, J., & Cui, Y. (2013). Multi-criteria robust design of a JIT-based cross-docking distribution center for an auto parts supply chain. *European Journal of Operational Research, 229*(3), 695–706.

Shu, T., Chen, S., Wang, S., & Lai, K. K. (2014). GBOM-oriented management of production disruption risk and optimization of supply chain construction. *Expert System with Applications, 41*(1), 59–68.

Soosay, C., Hyland, P., & Ferrer, M. (2008). Supply chain collaboration: capabilities for continuous learning. *Supply Chain Management: An International Journal, 13*(2), 160–169.

Svensson, G. (2001). A conceptual framework for the analysis of vulnerability in supply chains. *International Journal of Physical Distribution and Logistics Management, 30*(9), 731–750.

Thun, J.-H., & Hoenig, D. (2011). An empirical analysis of supply chain risk management in the German automotive industry. *International Journal of Production Economics, 131*(1), 242–249.

Trkman, P., & McCormack, K. (2009). Supply chain risk in turbulent environments—a conceptual model for managing supply chain network risk. *International Journal of Production Economics, 119*(2), 247–258.

Tuncel, G., & Alpan, G. (2010). Risk assessment and management for supply chain networks: A case study. *Computers in Industry, 61*(3), 250–259.

Villada, J., & Olaya, Y. (2013). A simulation approach for analysis of short-term security of natural gas supply in Colombia. *Energy Policy, 53,* 11–26.

Vilko, J. (2012). *Supply chain risk management: Identification*. Lappeenranta, Finland: Analysis and Control. Acta Universitalis Lappeenrantaelis.

Vilko, J., & Lättilä, L. (2013). Vulnerability in supply chain risk management. In *The 5th International Conference on Logistics and Transport,* Kyoto, Japan.

Vilko, J., & Hallikas, J. (2012). Risk assessment in multimodal supply chains. *International Journal on Production Economics, 140*(2), 586–595.

Vlajic, J., van der Vorst, J., & Haijema, R. (2012). A framework for designing robust food supply chains. *International Journal of Production Economics, 137*(1), 176–189.

Wagner, S. M., & Neshat, N. (2010). Assessing the vulnerability of supply chains using graph theory. *International Journal of Production Economics, 126*(1), 121–129.

Waters, D. (2007). *Supply chain risk management: Vulnerability and resilience in logistics*. London: Kogan Page Limited.

Wilson, M. C. (2007). The impact of transportation disruptions on supply chain performance. *Transportation Research Part E, 43*(4), 295–320.

Wu, T., Blackhurst, J., & Chidambaram, V. (2006). A model for inbound risk analysis. *Computers in Industry, 57*(4), 350–365.

Chapter 8
Supply Chain Disruptions Preparedness Measures Using a Dynamic Model

Amit Sonar and Cameron A. Mackenzie

Abstract Supply chain risk management has recently seen extensive research efforts, but questions such as "How should a firm plan for each type of disruption?" and "What are the strategies and the total cost incurred by the firm if a disruption occurs?" continue to deserve attention. This chapter analyzes different disruption cases by considering the impacts of disruptions at a supplier, a firm's warehouse, and at the firm's production facility. The firm can prepare for each type of disruption by buying from an alternate supplier, holding more inventory, or holding inventory at a different warehouse. The Wagner-Whitin model is used to solve the optimal ordering strategy for each type of disruption. Since the type of disruption is uncertain, we assign probabilities for each disruption and use the Wagner-Whitin model to find the order policy that minimizes the firm's expected cost.

8.1 Introduction

Disruptions are unpredictable events and can occur at any facility location of a plant at any point of time. A supply chain is vulnerable to different types of disruptions, which can take the form of supply disruptions, operational problems at warehouses, demand uncertainty, transportation difficulties, or catastrophic events that close a firm's manufacturing facilities. Since a firm does not know what type of disruption will occur, if any, planning for disruptions should account for this uncertainty.

This chapter addresses disruptions occurring at three major locations: a supplier, a warehouse, and a firm's production facility. Two important questions are: (1) How should a firm plan for each type of disruption? and (2) How should a firm prepare for the possibility of all three disruptions? This chapter presents a model

A. Sonar (✉) · C.A. Mackenzie
Department of Industrial and Manufacturing Systems Engineering,
Iowa State University, Ames, USA
e-mail: amitrs@iastate.edu

Y. Khojasteh (ed.), *Supply Chain Risk Management*,
DOI 10.1007/978-981-10-4106-8_8

that seeks to answer these questions by exploring the firm's planning horizon and preparation strategies. First, the firm can prepare itself from calamity by holding inventory, possibly at different locations. Second, the firm can have an alternate supplier for its product.

Preparation strategies may also account for how the firm and other entities may respond if a disruption occurs. For example, a multinational firm may be able to rely on suppliers from other countries that are not impacted by a disruption. For example, if the firm's manufacturing plant is located in one part of world, the firm could increase productions at other facilities. Selecting international suppliers as an alternate supplier may incur higher ordering cost, however.

Each of the preparation strategies has a cost, and the cost of implementing all these strategies might be higher than the disruption itself. This chapter models this decision using the Wagner-Whitin model to incorporate the uncertainty around the type of disruption and to select a strategy that minimizes the firm's expected cost. This research is novel because we look at preparedness strategies of a firm during disruptions, which will reduce the overall disruption losses. It uses the idea of the Wagner-Whitin model to think about different disruption scenarios. A firm can use this Wagner-Whitin model with disruptions to make profitable decisions before and after a disruption.

Section 8.2 reviews the literature on supply chain disruptions. Section 8.3 introduces the supply chain model, the Wagner-Whitin algorithm, and the three disruption scenarios. Section 8.4 applies probabilities to each disruption and finds the firm's order policy that minimizes its expected cost. Section 8.5 discusses the results of this analysis.

8.2 Literature Review

Supply chain risk management and supply chain disruptions have received a lot of attention both in academia and in industry. A supply chain disruption can be defined as an internal or external event that alters the normal or planned flow of goods and services in a supply chain. Literature reviews on supply chain disruptions and supply chain risk management can be found in Tang (2006), Snyder et al. (2006), Vakharia and Yeniparzarli (2008), Natarajarathinam et al. (2009), Schmitt and Tomlin (2012), and Snyder et al. (2016). Supply chain disruptions can take many different forms, including production difficulties or operational risks (Xia et al. 2004), wholesale prices impacted by cost fluctuations (Xiao and Qi 2008), supply shortages (Xiao and Yu 2006), and sudden drops in demand based on the market conditions (Xiao et al. 2005). Much of the academic literature on supply chain disruptions focuses on understanding and modeling strategies that firms can use to mitigate a disruption, such as holding inventory (Song and Zipkin 1996; Tomlin 2006) purchasing from alternate suppliers (Tomlin 2006; Song and Zipkin 2009; Babich et al. 2007; Hopp et al. 2009), rescheduling production (Bean et al. 1991; Adhyitya et al. 2007), rerouting transportation (MacKenzie et al. 2012), and producing at an alternate facility (MacKenzie et al. 2014). A firm can attempt to build a supply chain resilient to disruptions (Sheffi 2005) by reconfiguring resources or improving its infrastructure (Ambulkar et al. 2015).

Understanding characteristics that make firms more or less vulnerable to supply chain disruptions is another important area of research. Bode and Wagner (2015) empirically found that the complexity of a supply chain, to include the horizontal and vertical complexity, can increase the frequency of disruptions and exacerbate them. Make-to-order supply chains may be more vulnerable to disruptions than make-to-forecast supply chains (Papadakis 2006). Supply chain disruptions may be more severe for firms that are more geographically diverse or undertake a lot of outsourcing (Hendricks et al. 2009). This chapter explores some of the potential impacts that could occur in a complex supply chain with multiple suppliers and different warehouses.

The model in this chapter uses the model developed by Wagner and Whitin (1958) which provides a production or ordering plan with varying but known demand. If demand and order lead time are uncertain to small extent, a modified Wagner-Whitin model can still be applied (Kazan et al. 2000; Jeunet and Jonard 2000). The Wagner-Whitin model was recently extended to situations with variable manufacturing and remanufacturing cost (Richter and Sombrutzki 2000; Richter and Weber 2001). To our knowledge, no research has extended the Wagner-Whitin model to supply chain disruptions to understand how a firm can use a manufacturing resource planning system to prepare for potential disruptions.

8.3 Supply Chain Model and Illustrative Example

8.3.1 The Model

We consider a supply chain (see Fig. 8.1) in which a manufacturing firm requires several suppliers. These suppliers transform raw materials into goods that are delivered to the firm. The firm stores these supplies in a warehouse. The firm also operates two smaller warehouses that are located further away but can be used if the main warehouse is short of supplies or unusable. The firm depends on a single primary supplier for parts. An alternate supplier is also available to deliver parts at a more expensive price if the primary supplier cannot meet demand. Since this chapter assumes that at most one supplier is disrupted, the analysis focuses on the firm's ability to obtain parts for its manufacturing process.

We assume that the firm's forecasted demand D_t in time period t is deterministic but changes in each time period where $t = 1, 2, \ldots, T$ and T represents the planning horizon. The firm develops a plan to order quantity Q_t in each period in order to minimize its cumulative cost over the time horizon. The firm's cost is composed of a per-unit ordering cost C_t, a fixed cost per order A_t, and a per-unit holding or inventory cost H_t. All costs are in U.S. dollars. Given the assumptions in this

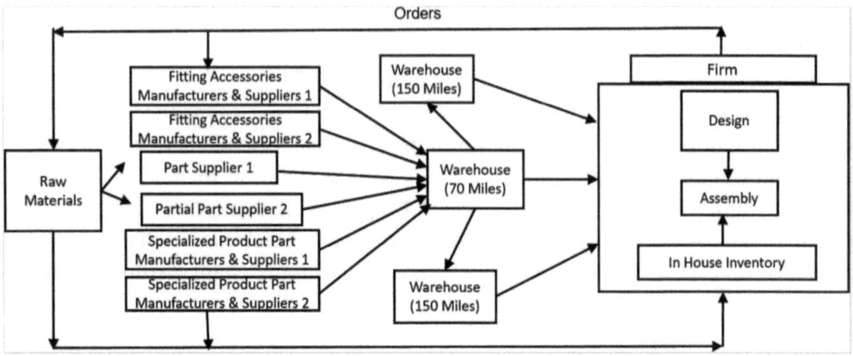

Fig. 8.1 Supply chain map

framework, the model developed by Wagner and Whitin (1958) provides an appropriate solution for the firm's planning. The Wagner-Whitin model is a dynamic lot-sizing model that produces an optimal lot size for each period. A notional example is developed for a firm using the "RoadHog" example from Hopp and Spearman (2008, pp. 58–64). The example without a disruption is explained first. We extend the example to three possible scenario disruptions: (1) a supplier disruption, (2) a firm closure, and (3) a warehouse disruption.

8.3.2 No Disruptions

Table 8.1 depicts the parameters for a 10-period model. The demand changes in each period, but the variable ordering cost, the fixed order cost, and the holding cost remain the same for each period. The cost in period t equals $A_t 1_{Q_t > 0} + C_t Q_t + H_t I_t$ where $1_{Q_t > 0}$ is in the indicator function that equals 1 if $Q_t > 0$ and where I_t is the amount of inventory being held from period t to $t + 1$. We assume the revenue for the firm is the product of the demand and a per-unit selling price.

Under an optimal lot-sizing policy, the inventory carried from period $t - 1$ to t will be zero, or the order quantity in period t will be zero (Hopp and Spearman 2008). In the Wagner-Whitin model, the per-unit ordering cost C_t is constant and can be ignored in the calculations. When no disruption occurs, C_t is constant, but as

Table 8.1 Data representing demand, variable order cost, fixed order cost, and holding cost

Time period	1	2	3	4	5	6	7	8	9	10
D_t	20	50	10	50	50	10	20	40	20	30
C_t	10	10	10	10	10	10	10	10	10	10
A_t	100	100	100	100	100	100	100	100	100	100
H_t	1	1	1	1	1	1	1	1	1	1

will be explained later, C_t can change during a supply chain disruption. Thus, C_t is included in this model's calculations. The basic recursive algorithm is outlined below. The algorithm goes forward in time by calculating $X_{\tau,t}$ the cost of ordering in period τ to satisfy demand in all periods from τ through t. The cumulative minimum cost Z_t^* in each period t is selected, and $j_t^* \epsilon \{1, 2, \ldots, t\}$ represents the period in which to order parts to meet demand in t. The third and fourth steps in the algorithm ensures that the optimal order period j_t^* is selected in cost calculations.

Wager-Whitin algorithm:

1. Satisfy demand in first period D_1, … $Z_1^* = X_{1,1} = A_1 + C_1 D_1 \ldots j_1^* = 1$
2. Determine minimum cost for periods $t = 2, 3, \ldots, T$

$$X_{\tau,t} = \begin{cases} X_{\tau-1,t} + D_t\left(C_\tau + \sum_{t'=\tau}^{t-1} H_{t'}\right) & \text{if} \quad \tau < t \\ Z_{t-1}^* + D_t C_t + A_t & \text{if} \quad \tau = t \end{cases}$$

$$Z_t^* = \min_\tau X_{\tau,t}$$

$$j_t^* = \operatorname*{argmin}_\tau X_{\tau,t}$$

3. Begin with $t = T$ and continuing with $t = T - 1, T - 2, \ldots, 2$
   If $j_t^* < j_\tau^*$ for any $\tau = j_t^*, \ldots, t - 1$, then set $j_\tau^* = j_t^*$
4. For periods $t = 2, 3, \ldots, T$, repeat calculation for $X_{\tau,t}$ from step 2 and set $Z_t^* = X_{j_t^*,t}$.

As shown in Table 8.2 (which replicates the result from Hopp and Spearman 2008, pp. 58–64), the firm should order 80 units in period 1 to satisfy demand in

Table 8.2 Planning horizon with total costs for each possible ordering period

Last period with order	Planning horizon (t)									
	1	2	3	4	5	6	7	8	9	10
1	300	850	970	1620	2320	2470	2790	3470	3830	4400
2		900	1010	1610	2260	2400	2700	3340	3680	4220
3			1050	1600	2200	2330	2610	3210	3530	4040
4				1570	2120	2240	2500	3060	3360	3840
5					2170	2280	2520	3040	3320	3770
6						2320	2540	3020	3280	3700
7							2540	2980	3220	3610
8								3000	3220	3580
9									3300	3630
10										3620
Z_t^*	300	850	970	1570	2120	2240	2500	3000	3220	3580
j_t^*	1	1	1	4	4	4	4	8	8	8

periods 1, 2, and 3; 130 units in period 4 to satisfy demand in 4, 5, 6, and 7; and 90 units in period 8 to satisfy demand in 8, 9, and 10.

8.3.3 Supplier Disruption

We first consider that a disruption occurs with the primary parts supplier in period 5 and lasts through the rest of the planning horizon. The firm is able to order from the secondary parts supplier, but the ordering cost C_t increases from 10 to 20 for periods 5 through 10. All other values from Table 8.1 remain the same. If we assume that the firm knows the primary supplier will be disrupted in period 5, we can use the Wagner-Whitin algorithm to calculate the optimal order period given this disruption (Table 8.3).

When the cost is 20 the firm should order 80 units in period 1 to satisfy demand in periods 1, 2, and 3; and 220 units in period 4 to satisfy demand in periods 4 through 10. It is cheaper for the firm to hold inventory than to purchase from the alternate supplier.

We explore the impact of changing the ordering cost from 10 to 20 for the alternate supplier. Figure 8.2 illustrates the relationship between total cost and the per-unit ordering cost. As the ordering cost increases, the total cost initially increases until the ordering cost equals 13, at which point the total cost remains the same. When the cost is 13, the firm changes its strategy from ordering in periods 1, 4, and 8 to ordering in periods 1 and 4 only. The cost of holding inventory from

Table 8.3 Optimal planning horizon with local supplier disruption

	Planning horizon (t)									
	1	2	3	4	5	6	7	8	9	10
Z_t^*	300	850	970	1570	2120	2240	2500	3060	3360	3840
j_t^*	1	1	1	4	4	4	4	4	4	4

Fig. 8.2 Total cost as the ordering cost changes for period 5 through 10

periods 4 through 10 is less than the cost of ordering in period 8 when the cost is 13 or greater. Since the firm is ordering all of its parts before the disruption in period 5, the total cost remains the same even when the ordering cost increases beyond 13.

8.3.4 Firm Disruption

The second type of disruption occurs when the firm itself is impacted and cannot produce. We model this type of disruption by setting $D_t = 0$ for those periods when the firm is disabled. The firm's revenue will be 0 until the firm recovers from the disruption. If the impact due to the disruption is large, the firm will take more time to recover from it. The purchase and holding costs remain the same as in Table 8.1. Table 8.4 illustrates the notional data in which the disruption takes place in period 5 and the firm recovers in period 9. The firm is disabled in periods 5 through 8 (Table 8.5).

Since the firm is losing revenue when it is not producing, we examine the impact of the firm disruption on the firm's revenue and profit. We assume the firm receives a revenue of 50 for each unit it produces. Table 8.6 shows how the firm's profit changes based on when it recovers and resumes ordering and production. If the firm reopens in periods 6 or 7, the firm orders enough supplies in period 4 to cover the initial periods when it reopens. If the firm reopens in periods 8, 9, or 10, the firm holds no additional inventory from period 4 and orders supplies when it completely recovers.

8.3.5 Main Warehouse Disruption

The third type of disruption occurs when the main warehouse is impacted. If the main warehouse is closed, the firm will need to arrange for additional warehouse space. We assume that the firm can use one of its two other warehouses as depicted in Fig. 8.1, but using either of these facilities increases H_t the holding cost.

Table 8.4 Demand with a firm disruption

t	1	2	3	4	5	6	7	8	9	10
D_t (units)	20	50	10	50	0	0	0	0	20	30

Table 8.5 Optimal planning horizon with firm disruption

	Planning horizon (t)									
	1	2	3	4	5	6	7	8	9	10
Z_t^*	300	850	970	1570	1570	1570	1570	1570	1870	2200
j_t^*	1	1	1	4	4	4	4	4	9	9

Table 8.6 Recovery period and ordering strategy in case of a firm disruption (~ means the firm is closed)

Recovery period	Cost	Revenue	Profit	Ordering strategy j_t^*
No disruption	3580	15,000	11,420	1, 1, 1, 4, 4, 4, 4, 8, 8, 8
6	3030	12,500	9470	1, 1, 1, 4, ~, 4, 4, 8, 8, 8
7	2910	12,000	9090	1, 1, 1, 4, ~, ~, 4, 8, 8, 8
8	2650	11,000	8350	1, 1, 1, 4, ~, ~, ~, 8, 8, 8
9	2200	9000	6800	1, 1, 1, 4, ~, ~, ~, ~, 9, 9
10	1970	8000	6030	1, 1, 1, 4, ~, ~, ~, ~, ~, 10

Table 8.7 illustrates the increase in holding cost when the main warehouses closes from periods 5 through 10.

If the holding cost is 5 beginning in period 5, the firm is incentivized to make more frequent orders. As depicted in Table 8.8, the firm should order 80 units in period 1 to satisfy demand in periods 1, 2, and 3; 110 units in period 4 to satisfy demand in periods 4, 5, and 6; 20 units in period 7 to satisfy demand in period 7; 60 units in period 8 to satisfy demand in periods 8 and 9; and 30 units in period 10 to satisfy demand in period 10.

Figure 8.3 shows the relationship between the firm's total cost and the holding cost. Not surprisingly, as the holding cost increases, the total cost also increases.

Table 8.7 Holding cost with a main warehouse disruption

t	1	2	3	4	5	6	7	8	9	10
H_t	1	1	1	1	5	5	5	5	5	5

Table 8.8 Optimal planning horizon with warehouse disruption

	Planning horizon (t)									
	1	2	3	4	5	6	7	8	9	10
Z_t^*	300	850	970	1570	2120	2280	2580	3080	3380	3780
j_t^*	1	1	1	4	4	4	7	8	8	10

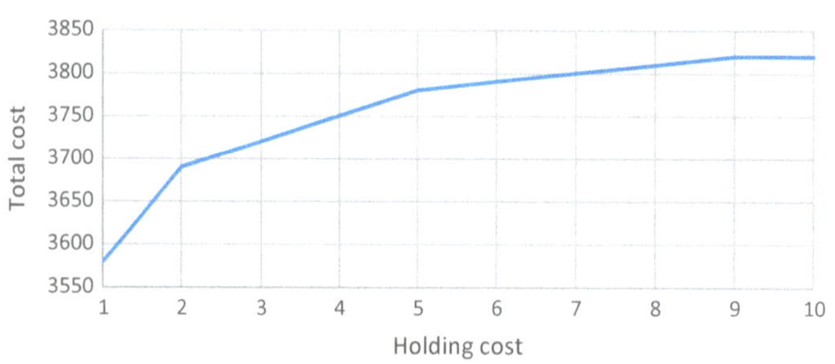

Fig. 8.3 Total cost as the holding cost changes for periods 5 through 10

Table 8.9 Optimal planning horizon with warehouse disruption

Holding cost	Ordering strategy j_t^*
1	1, 1, 1, 4, 4, 4, 4, 8, 8, 8
2	1, 1, 1, 4, 4, 4, 4, 8, 8, 10
3	1, 1, 1, 4, 4, 4, 7, 8, 8, 10
4	1, 1, 1, 4, 4, 4, 7, 8, 8, 10
5	1, 1, 1, 4, 4, 4, 7, 8, 8, 10
6	1, 1, 1, 4, 4, 4, 7, 8, 9, 10
7	1, 1, 1, 4, 4, 4, 7, 8, 9, 10
8	1, 1, 1, 4, 4, 4, 7, 8, 9, 10

When the holding cost increases from 5 to 6, the ordering strategy changes from 1, 4, 7, 8, 10 to 1, 4, 7, 8, 9, 10 as represented in Table 8.9. As the holding cost increases, it is cheaper to order more frequently.

8.3.6 Disruption Occurs in Different Periods

The previous section assumes that the disruption always occurs in period 5, but the disruption could occur in any period. This section analyzes the impact on the firm's cost and profit if the disruption occurs in different periods for each of the three types of disruptions.

Supplier Disruption

The initial period in which the primary parts supplier experiences a disruption is varied from periods 3 through 8. The primary supplier is always closed through period 10. As in Sect. 8.3.3, the firm can order from the secondary parts supplier, but the ordering cost increases to 20. The holding cost and fixed cost are the same as in Table 8.1. Figure 8.4 illustrates the relationship between the firm's total cost and when the disruption begins. The last ordering period for the firm should occur in the previous immediately prior to the disruption (Table 8.10).

Firm Disruption

The disruption disables the firm, and it cannot produce for a number of periods. The firm's revenue will be 0 until the firm recovers from the disruption, and we continue to assume that the firm recovers in the 10th period. The period in which the disruption begins is varied from periods 3 to 8. Table 8.11 and Fig. 8.5 illustrate the relationship among the period in which the disruption begins, the firm's profit, and its ordering strategy. The firm's profit increases as the period in which the disruption occurs increases. The firm continues to order in periods 1 and 4 irrespective of the length of the disruption (as long as the disruption occurs after period 4).

Main Warehouse Disruption

If the firm's main warehouse is disrupted, we assume the firm can use alternate warehouses, but its holding cost increases to 10. The disruption can begin in periods 3 through 8 but always continues through period 10. The ordering cost and fixed cost remain the same as in Table 8.1. Table 8.12 and Fig. 8.6 illustrate that the total

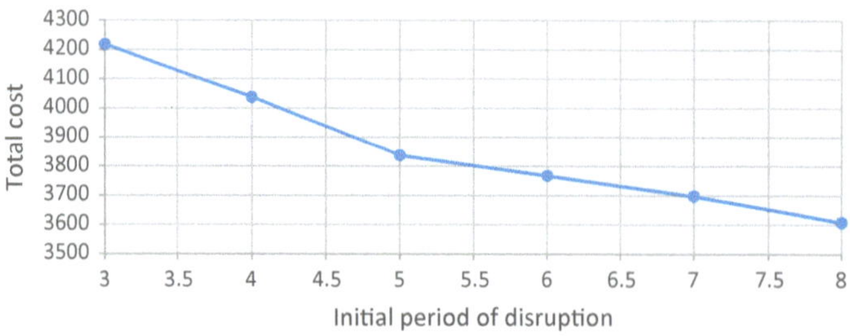

Fig. 8.4 Total cost as the initial period of disruption changes from 3 through 8

Table 8.10 Total cost and ordering strategy with different period of disruption

Periods during which primary supplier is disabled	Total cost	Ordering strategy
3–10	4220	1, 2, 2, 2, 2, 2, 2, 2, 2, 2
4–10	4040	1, 1, 3, 3, 3, 3, 3, 3, 3, 3
5–10	3840	1, 1, 1, 4, 4, 4, 4, 4, 4, 4
6–10	3770	1, 1, 1, 4, 5, 5, 5, 5, 5, 5
7–10	3700	1, 1, 1, 4, 4, 6, 6, 6, 6, 6
8–10	3610	1, 1, 1, 4, 4, 4, 7, 7, 7, 7

Table 8.11 Profit and ordering strategy in case of a firm disruption with different periods of disruption (~ means the firm is closed)

Periods during which firm is unable to produce	Cost	Revenue	Profit	Ordering strategy j_t^*
3–9	1250	5000	3750	1, 1, ~, ~, ~, ~, ~, ~, ~, 10
4–9	1370	5500	4130	1, 1, 1, ~, ~, ~, ~, ~, ~, 10
5–9	1970	8000	6030	1, 1, 1, 4, ~, ~, ~, ~, ~, 10
6–9	2520	10,500	7980	1, 1, 1, 4, 4, ~, ~, ~, ~, 10
7–9	2640	11,000	8360	1, 1, 1, 4, 4, 4, ~, ~, ~, 10
8–9	2900	12,000	9100	1, 1, 1, 4, 4, 4, 4, ~, ~, 10

cost decreases as the length of the disruption decreases. The firm should always order in periods 1 and 4, but whether or the not the firm orders in other periods changes as the length of disruption changes. For most cases, the firm should order in each period after the first disruption period. For example, if the disruption lasts from periods 5–10, the firm should order in each period from 6 through 10.

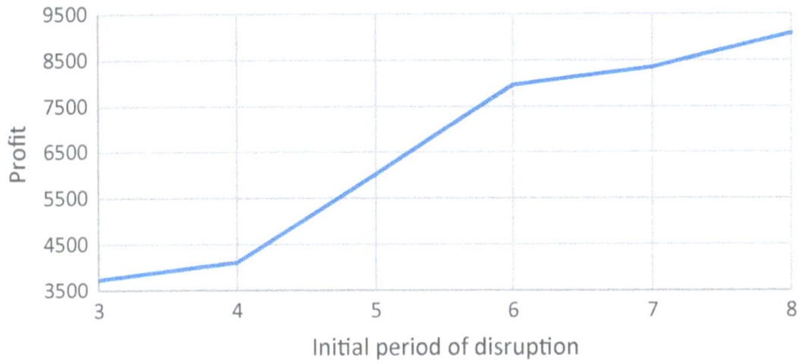

Fig. 8.5 Profit as the initial period of disruption changes from 3 through 8

8.4 Unknown Disruption and Period

The previous section assumes that the firm plans for each disruption individually and knows the type and timing of the disruption. In reality, the firm will not know which disruption, if any, will occur or when it will occur. This section explores how the chance and timing of one of these disruptions should impact the firm's planning. We assume that one of the three disruptions could occur: the local supplier disruption, the firm disruption, or the main warehouse disruption. Given that a disruption occurs, the probability the local supplier is disabled is 0.5, the probability the firm is closed is 0.2, and the probability the main warehouse is closed is 0.3.

We assume there is an equal probability that the disruption will begin in period 3, 4, 5, 6, 7, or 8, equivalent to a 1/6 probability for each period. If the local supplier is disrupted, the firm can order from the alternate supplier at a per-unit cost of 20. If the firm is disrupted, we assume the firm cannot satisfy any demand while it is closed. If the main warehouse is disrupted, the firm can store inventory at the alternate warehouses, but the holding cost increases to 5. We use the probabilities of disruption to calculate the expected costs for each possible ordering strategy. The Wagner-Whitin algorithm is deployed to find the order policy that minimizes the firm's total expected cost. Since this is a planning problem, the firm establishes an

Table 8.12 Total cost, holding cost and ordering strategy in case of a main warehouse disruption with different periods of disruption

Periods during which main warehouse is closed	Total cost	Ordering strategy j_t^*
3–10	3870	1, 1, 1, 4, 5, 5, 7, 8, 9, 10
4–10	3870	1, 1, 1, 4, 5, 5, 7, 8, 9, 10
5–10	3820	1, 1, 1, 4, 4, 6, 7, 8, 9, 10
6–10	3740	1, 1, 1, 4, 4, 4, 7, 8, 9, 10
7–10	3700	1, 1, 1, 4, 4, 4, 4, 8, 9, 10
8–10	3680	1, 1, 1, 4, 4, 4, 7, 7, 9, 10

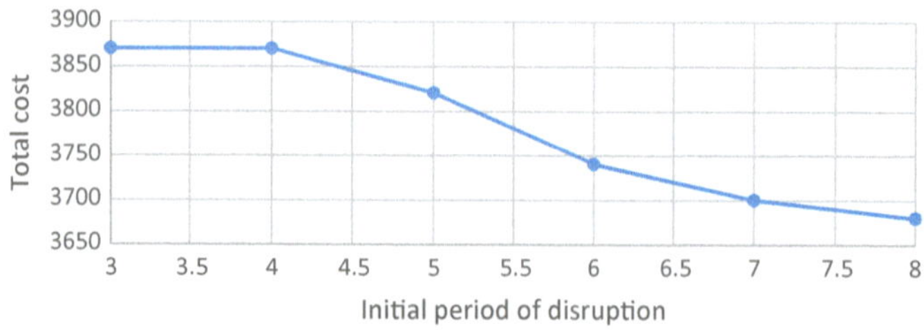

Fig. 8.6 Total cost as the initial period of disruption changes from 3 through 8

order before knowing whether a disruption occurs, which disruption will occur, or when the disruption will occur.

We vary the probability of a disruption between 0 and 1. The optimal ordering strategy for the firm for different probabilities of disruptions is illustrated in Table 8.13. If the probability of a disruption is less than 0.3, the firm should not change its ordering policy from the case without a disruption. If the probability of a disruption is greater than or equal to 0.3, the firm should order in periods 1, 4, 8, and 10. It becomes optimal to order in period 10 because the firm is incentivized to plan for the firm being closed and for the main warehouse being closed. With such a large probability of disruption, it becomes more likely that the firm will have a disrupted warehouse, which increases its holding cost. Thus, it becomes more advantageous to hold less inventory and order in period 10. (If the disruption disables the primary supplier, the firm's cost of ordering does not change based on whether it orders in period 8 or 10 because both periods require ordering from the more expensive alternate supplier.) The expected profit decreases in a linear fashion as the probability of a disruption increases as displayed in Fig. 8.7.

Table 8.13 Probability of disruption and optimal planning for uncertain periods

Probability of disruption	Expected profit	Ordering strategy j_t^*
0	11,420	1, 1, 1, 4, 4, 4, 4, 8, 8, 8
0.1	11,318	1, 1, 1, 4, 4, 4, 4, 8, 8, 8
0.2	11,215	1, 1, 1, 4, 4, 4, 4, 8, 8, 8
0.3	11,121	1, 1, 1, 4, 4, 4, 4, 8, 8, 10
0.4	11,035	1, 1, 1, 4, 4, 4, 4, 8, 8, 10
0.5	10,949	1, 1, 1, 4, 4, 4, 4, 8, 8, 10
0.6	10,862	1, 1, 1, 4, 4, 4, 4, 8, 8, 10
0.7	10,776	1, 1, 1, 4, 4, 4, 4, 8, 8, 10
0.8	10,690	1, 1, 1, 4, 4, 4, 4, 8, 8, 10
0.9	10,603	1, 1, 1, 4, 4, 4, 4, 8, 8, 10
1	10,517	1, 1, 1, 4, 4, 4, 4, 8, 8, 10

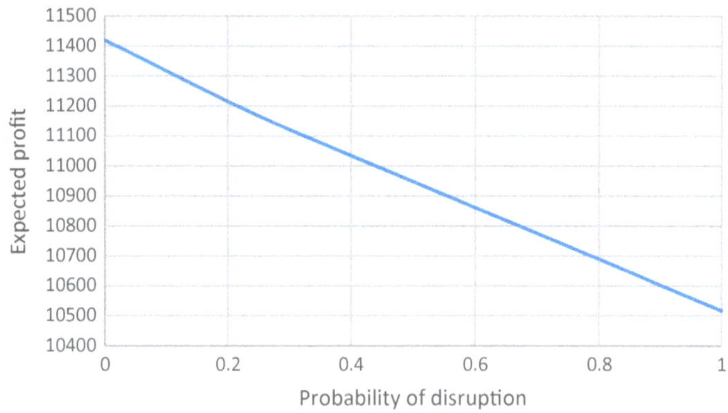

Fig. 8.7 Expected profit as the probability of disruption changes from 0 through 1

8.5 Discussions and Conclusions

This research addresses an important question of how a firm should plan for the possibility of several disruptions. The Wagner-Whitin model is appropriate with the assumption that demand is varying but deterministic. Three possible disruption scenarios are studied: a supply disruption, a disruption in the firm's production facility, and a warehouse disruption. If the firm can anticipate that the supplier cannot deliver its supplies, the firm is incentivized to hold more inventory, depending on the cost of the alternate supplier. If the firm's primary warehouse closes, the firm should hold less inventory and order more frequently from its suppliers. The application explores how the firm's cost and order strategies change as the parameters change.

Since a firm will not know in advance which disruption occurs, it will need to decide for which, if any, disruption to plan. The period in which the disruption occurs is also uncertain. The model applies probabilities to each disruption and the timing, and the firm chooses an order policy in order to minimize its expected cost. Total profit is calculated based on the different probabilities of disruptions. The firm's ordering strategy may change as the probability of a disruption increases.

A firm who uses a manufacturing resource planning system that resembles the Wagner-Whitin model could forecast possible disruptive events and explore if its ordering and production schedule should change based on the possible disruptions. The incorporation of probability to account for the uncertainty in the type and timing of disruptions allows a firm to understand how the likelihood of a disruption should impact its planning and ordering strategy. For the illustrative example in this chapter, the firm should slightly modify its ordering strategy as the probability of a disruption occurs. Further research can seek to understand if generalized results can be derived from the model about how the probability of disruption should impact a firm's ordering strategy. Though the Wagner-Whitin model generates an optimal planning horizon, it has some drawbacks. It has a fixed setup cost and deterministic demand.

In the future, we plan to extend our methodology to more complex supply chains, which may involve multiple suppliers. Future extensions can apply the algorithm to a real case study rather than considering notional data. Having longer planning horizons and allowing the firm to respond based on what disruption occurs may also impact the firm's optimal planning.

References

Adhyitya, A., Srinivasan, R., & Karimi, I. A. (2007). Heuristic rescheduling of crude oil operations to manage abnormal supply chain events. *American Institute of Chemical Engineers Journal, 53*(2), 397–422.

Ambulkar, S., Blackhurst, J., & Grawe, S. (2015). Firm's resilience to supply chain disruptions: Scale development and empirical examination. *Journal of Operations Management, 33,* 111–122.

Babich, V., Burnetas, A. N., & Ritchken, P. H. (2007). Competition and diversification effects in supply chains with supplier default risk. *Manufacturing & Service Operations Management, 9* (2), 123–146.

Bean, J. C., Birge, J. R., Mittenthal, J., & Noon, C. E. (1991). Matchup scheduling with multiple resources, release dates and disruptions. *Operations Research, 39*(3), 470–483.

Bode, C., & Wagner, S. M. (2015). Structural drivers of upstream supply chain complexity and the frequency of supply chain disruptions. *Journal of Operations Management, 36,* 215–228.

Hendricks, K. B., Singhal, V. R., & Zhang, R. (2009). The effect of operational slack, diversification, and vertical relatedness on the stock market reaction to supply chain disruptions. *Journal of Operations Management, 27*(3), 233–246.

Hopp WJ, Iravani SMR, Liu Z (2009) Strategic risk from supply chain disruptions. Working paper. Department of Industrial Engineering and Management Sciences, Northwestern University. Retrieved from http://webuser.bus.umich.edu/whopp/working%20papers/Strategic%20Risk%20from%20Supply%20Chain%20Disruptions.pdf

Hopp, W. J., & Spearman, M. L. (2008). *Factory physics* (3rd ed.). Boston, MA: McGraw-Hill.

Jeunet, J., & Jonard, N. (2000). Measuring the performance of lot-sizing techniques in uncertain environments. *International Journal of Production Economics, 64*(1), 197–208.

Kazan, O., Nagi, R., & Rump, C. M. (2000). New lot-sizing formulations for less nervous production schedules. *Computers & Operations Research, 27*(13), 1325–1345.

MacKenzie CA, Barker K, Grant FH (2012) Evaluating the consequences of an inland waterway port closure with a dynamic multiregional interdependence model. *IEEE Transactions on Systems, Man, and Cybernetics—Part A: Systems and Humans, 42*(2), 359–370.

MacKenzie, C. A., Barker, K., & Santos, J. R. (2014). Modeling a severe supply chain disruption and post-disaster decision making with application to the Japanese earthquake and tsunami. *IIE Transactions, 46*(12), 1243–1260.

Natarajarathinam, M., Capar, I., & Narayanan, A. (2009). Managing supply chains in times of crisis: A review of literature and insights. *International Journal of Physical Distribution & Logistics Management, 39*(7), 535–573.

Papadakis, I. S. (2006). Financial performance of supply chains after disruptions: An event study. *Supply Chain Management: An International Journal, 11*(1), 25–33.

Richter, K., & Weber, J. (2001). The reverse Wagner/Whitin model with variable manufacturing and remanufacturing cost. *International Journal of Production Economics, 71,* 447–456.

Richter, K., & Sombrutzki, M. (2000). Remanufacturing planning for the reverse Wagner/Whitin models. *European Journal of Operational Research, 121*(2), 304–315.
Sheffi, Y. (2005). *The resilient enterprise: Overcoming vulnerability for competitive advantage*. Cambridge: The MIT Press.
Schmitt, A. J., & Tomlin, B. (2012). Sourcing strategies to manage supply disruptions. In H. Gurnani, A. Mehrotra, & S. Ray (Eds.), *supply chain disruptions: Theory and practice of managing risk* (pp. 51–72). London: Springer.
Snyder, L. V., Atan, Z., Peng, P., Rong, Y., Schmitt, A. J., & Sinsoysal, B. (2016). OR/MS models for supply chain disruptions: A review. *IIE Transactions, 48*(2), 89–109.
Snyder LV, Scaparra MP, Daskin MS, Church RL (2006) Planning for disruptions in supply chain networks. *Tutorials in Operations Research*, 234–257.
Song, J.-S., & Zipkin, P. H. (1996). Inventory control with information about supply conditions. *Management Science, 42*(10), 1409–1419.
Song, J.-S., & Zipkin, P. (2009). Inventories with multiple supply sources and networks of queues with overflow bypasses. *Management Science, 55*(3), 362–372.
Tang, C. S. (2006). Perspectives in supply chain risk management. *International Journal of Production Economics, 103*(2), 451–488.
Tomlin, B. (2006). On the value of mitigation and contingency strategies for managing supply chain disruption risks. *Management Science, 52*(5), 639–657.
Vakharia, A. J., & Yenipazarli, A. (2008). Managing supply chain disruptions. *Foundations and Trends in Technology, Information and Operations Management, 2*(4), 243–325.
Wagner, H. M., & Whitin, T. M. (1958). Dynamic version of the economic lot size model. *Management Science, 9*(1), 89–96.
Xia, Y., Yang, M.-H., Golany, B., Gilbert, S. M., & Yu, G. (2004). Real-time disruption management in a two-stage production and inventory system. *IIE Transactions, 36,* 111–125.
Xiao, T., & Qi, X. (2008). Price competition, cost and demand disruptions and coordination of a supply chain with one manufacturer and two competing retailers. *Omega, 36*(5), 741–753.
Xiao, T., & Yu, G. (2006). Supply chain disruption management and evolutionarily stable strategies of retailers in the quantity-setting duopoly situation with homogeneous goods. *European Journal of Operational Research, 173*(2), 648–668.
Xiao, T., Yu, G., Sheng, Z., & Xia, Y. (2005). Coordination of a supply chain with one-manufacturer and two-retailers under demand promotion and disruption management decisions. *Annals of Operations Research, 135*(1), 87–109.

Chapter 9
A Quantitative Model for Analyzing Market Response During Supply Chain Disruptions

Arun Vinayak and Cameron A. Mackenzie

Abstract Supply chain disruptions can lead to firms losing customers and consequently losing profit. We consider a firm facing a supply chain disruption due to which it is unable to deliver products for a certain period of time. When the firm is restored, each customer may choose to return to the firm immediately, with or without backorders, or may purchase from other firms. This chapter develops a quantitative model of the different customer behaviors in such a scenario and analytically interprets the impact of these behaviors on the firm's post-disruption performance. The model is applied to an illustrative example.

9.1 Introduction

Supply chain disruptions have garnered increased attention, both in academia and in practice, since the early 2000s. Modern production methodologies, globalized supply chains, shorter product life cycle, and the emphasis on efficiency have increased the risk faced by many supply chains. Managing the risk facing a supply chain is vital to the success of any company.

A supply chain is an integrated system of companies involved in the upstream and downstream flows of products, services, finances, and/or information from a source to a customer (Mentzer et al. 2001). Figure 9.1 presents a basic supply chain model from the firm's perspective. A supply chain is characterized by the flow of resources—typically material, information, and money—with the primary purpose of satisfying the needs of a customer, who are the source of revenue for a firm. A supply chain will ideally maximize the total value generated from customers and minimize the cost of meeting consumer demand.

A. Vinayak (✉) · C.A. Mackenzie
Department of Industrial and Manufacturing Systems Engineering,
Iowa State University, Ames, USA
e-mail: vinayak@iastate.edu

Y. Khojasteh (ed.), *Supply Chain Risk Management*,
DOI 10.1007/978-981-10-4106-8_9

Fig. 9.1 A simple supply chain model

Major disruptions, such as those that occur from natural disasters, terrorist acts, and labor strikes, can interrupt the flow of materials for several firms. Sodhi and Tang (2012) categorized supply chain risk into supply risks, process risks, demand risks, and corporate-level risks. These risks often materialize all together during a major supply chain disruption, and decision makers need to consider all of these risks. Kilubi and Haasis (2015) conducted a systematic literature review on supply chain risk management (SCRM) and identified ten different definitions of SCRM. Lavastre et al. (2012, p. 839) defined SCRM as "the management of risk that implies both strategic and operational horizons for long-term and short-term assessment." As implied by this definition, decision makers need to consider both the long-term and short-term impacts from a supply chain disruption.

The marketplace or customers can play a significant role in the long-term impacts as their needs, values, and opinions will affect the firm's decisions during the disruption. The volatility of consumer demand is a major form of risk (Jüttner et al. 2003). Firms face a risk of being penalized by their customers if their suppliers default and firms are unable to deliver on their obligations. Assessing how consumers react to such disruptions helps to forecast the long-term profits for the firm and can help it make sound risk management decisions. Modeling consumer behavior is useful not only when a disaster occurs but also to build flexibility within the supply chain as a proactive measure to anticipate such threats and quickly respond.

This chapter presents a probabilistic model to quantify the risk from a severe supply chain disruption with an explicit focus on how consumers or the marketplace's demand for a product should influence a firm's risk management strategies. Many supply chain disruption models assume some type of demand function, which may be constant or random. However, that demand function does not usually change when the disruption occurs, or simple assumptions are made about whether or not customers are willing to wait for a final product. Less research has focused on how the final customers should influence how a firm determines what risk management strategies are appropriate. This chapter models the demand function using a probabilistic approach to customer behavior in a post-disruption scenario. The model assumes that a disruption causes a supplier to default, and a firm is unable to deliver its product to consumers. The market responds with defined probabilities and time delays. The model attempts to measure the extent to which a firm can be penalized due to a default from its supplier and recommends strategies or practices to build resilience to such disruptions.

This chapter is organized as follows: a literature review is given in Sect. 9.2. Section 9.3 presents the mathematical model framework, and Sect. 9.4 describes an illustrative example and performs sensitivity analysis. Section 9.5 concludes the chapter with recommendations, insights, and conclusions drawn from the study.

9.2 Literature Review

Supply chain management has seen a variety of trends, including Just-in-Time, global sourcing, and outsourcing. These methods are aimed at cutting costs in a firm's supply chain and enabling the firm to compete more effectively. Increasing supply chain efficiency can also make supply chains more vulnerable to disruptions (Christopher 2005). In the race to increase their market share, firms may ignore that their supply chains are susceptible to disruptions.

A wide variety of events can disrupt a supply chain, including supply-side difficulties, demand-side variability, operational problems, and large-scale disruptions such as natural disasters (Manuj et al. 2007). Qualitative studies to manage these disruptions recommend excess inventory, additional capacity, redundant suppliers, flexible production and transportation, and dynamic pricing (Sheffi and Rice 2005; Stecke and Kumar 2009). Managing one type of risk may exacerbate another risk, and identifying the best strategy relies on the manager's ability to identify the most crucial risk and understand the trade-offs in SCRM (Chopra and Sodhi 2004). Quantitative studies in SCRM generally model the trade-off between purchasing from alternate suppliers and holding inventory (Tomlin and Wang 2005), or they model the interaction between suppliers and customers (Babich et al. 2007; Xia et al. 2011). MacKenzie et al. (2014) used simulation to model the interactions among supply chain entities where each entity can take different actions such as holding inventory or purchasing from alternate suppliers. Interested readers should refer to Snyder et al. (2016) for an in-depth review of the recent models of supply chain disruptions and disruption management strategies.

Although research has focused on the impacts of supply chain disruptions based on stock returns (Hendricks and Singhal 2005) or based on the economic linkages (MacKenzie et al. 2012), less research has focused on how customers behave during and after a supply chain disruption. Nagurney et al. (2005) examined the impact of unforeseen customer demands on the supply chain, but this research assumes the customer behavior causes the disruption. Ellis et al. (2010) surveyed managers and buyers of materials to study how customers may perceive supply chain risk. Modern supply chain management is very sensitive to customer demand (Nishat Faisal et al. 2006), but examining the relationship between customer demand sensitivity and a manufacturer or retailer during a disruption has not been fully explored. An important exception to this lack of research is the modeling and analysis of consumer behavior following a food contamination (Beach et al. 2008; Arnade et al. 2009).

This chapter seeks to fill the gap in the existing literature by probabilistically modeling customer behavior following a supply chain disruption. Whereas much of the current literature focuses on the interaction between the supplier and the firm, the focus of this chapter is the market response to the disruption and its impact on the firm. The model examines the decisions customers make after the interruption of a firm's service due to a supply chain disruption. Possible customer behaviors are fused within a probabilistic model to assess the expected lost revenue of the firm. A firm can use this forecasted measure of average lost revenue to decide what it should do to prepare and respond to such a disruption in its supply chain.

9.3 The Model

This section presents an overall profile of a supply chain disruption and develops a probabilistic model to focus on the market response to the disruption. A supply chain disruption occurs when a firm's supplier defaults. A major disruption impacts a firm in distinct phases (Sheffi and Rice 2005). It may take time for the final consumer to be impacted by the supply disruption. If the firm does not have enough inventory or cannot purchase from alternate suppliers, it will not be able to satisfy demand for its goods. Consequently, consumers may choose to purchase from other firms. The consumers' loyalty depends on a number of factors such as their relationship to the product. To get back to standard performance levels, a firm may adopt various response actions such as working at over-capacity levels. If the firm is prepared for such a disruption (e.g., having multiple suppliers or having more inventory), it should be able to respond more effectively (Yu et al. 2009).

9.3.1 Model Framework

We develop a probabilistic model to quantify the reaction of customers following a supply chain disruption that causes a temporary production shut down. Before the disruption, there are n customers (they could also be retailers) who purchase from a firm in each time period before a disruption. In the base model, we assume the demand equals the number of customers. In other words, every customer buys exactly one product. This assumption is relaxed in Sect. 9.4.3, which considers varying demands from each customer. An unexpected disruptive event causes one or more of the firm's suppliers to default, and the firm is unable to satisfy any demand beginning at time period $t = 1$. The disruption continues for M time periods, and the firm does not deliver to its n customers for $t = 1, 2, \ldots, M$. The firm recovers from the disruption at $t = M + 1$ and will be able to deliver at its full capacity C orders per time period, where $C \geq n$.

In the post-disruption time period beginning at $t = M + 1$, each customer decides whether or not to return to the firm in each time period $t = M + i$. Note that

$i = 1, 2, \ldots$ since the customer cannot buy from the firm during time periods $t = 1, 2, \ldots, M$. Each customer comes back to the firm with a constant probability p in each time period. The value of p depends upon the type of product as well as the firm's response actions such as qualifying alternate suppliers and making up for lost production by running at maximum capacity. If a customer decides not to return to the firm at a particular time period, the model assumes that it will return to the firm in the next period with the same probability p. Once a customer returns to the firm, it will continue to purchase from the firm in all future time periods.

If a customer buys from the firm at time $t = M + i$, it will return with one of the following behaviors:

1. Customers can return right away without backorders at time $t = M + 1$. This category of customers might have used inventory from safety stock, not used the product, or purchased the product from other firms during the time periods 1 through M.
2. Customers who come back immediately and have backorders.
3. Customers who do not return immediately but return later to the firm with no backorders.

The probability q represents the conditional probability that the customer who comes back immediately at $t = M + 1$ will require backorders for $t = 1, 2, \ldots, M$. In other words, given the customer has returned to the firm, the probability that he or she will have backorders is q. The revenue from backorders is accounted for at $t = M + 1$ since backorders are taken only in that time period. We assume that customers who wait longer to return do not have backorders (behavior number 3). The initial model assumes the firm can satisfy all the backorders. This could be because the firm is able to monitor activity and make plans to increase capacity to satisfy backorders. If q is small, the firm can be reasonably confident the backorders will not exceed its capacity. Since this assumption may not be realistic, Subsection 9.3.3 discusses how the model might change if a capacity constraint limits the number of backorders the firm can accept. Even if the lack of a capacity constraint may not be realistic, modeling the situation without this constraint generates useful insights into the potential benefits of increasing capacity after reopening.

9.3.2 Calculating the Firm's Post-impact Revenue

The revenue at time periods $t = 1, 2, \ldots, M$ is zero since the firm is not delivering any product to its customers. The total expected revenue after the firm reopens is calculated by estimating the number of customers who decide to buy from the firm at each period after it reopens at $t = M + 1$. Let X_t be the number of customers who decide to come back and purchase from the firm at time t. $X_t = 0$ for $t = 1, 2, \ldots, M$

For $t = M+1, M+2, \ldots$ each of the n customers returns with a constant probability p and X_t follows a binomial distribution.

$$\begin{aligned}
\text{At}\, t = M+1, \quad & X_{M+1} \sim Binom(n, p) \\
& with E[X_{M+1}] = np \\
\text{At}\, t = M+2, \quad & X_{M+2} \sim Binom(n - X_{M+1}, p) \\
& with E[X_{M+2}] = np(1-p) \\
\text{At}\, t = M+3, \quad & X_{M+3} \sim Binom(n - X_{M+1} - X_{M+2}, p) \\
& with E[X_{M+3}] = np(1-p)^2
\end{aligned}$$

$$\begin{aligned}
\text{At}\, t = M+i, \quad & X_{M+i} \sim Binom\left(n - \sum_{j=1}^{i-1} X_{M+j}, p\right) \\
& \text{with } E[X_{M+i}] = np(1-p)^{i-1}
\end{aligned}$$

Since the model assumes that a customer who returns to the firm will continue to purchase from the firm in subsequent periods, the expected number of customers who purchase from the firm at $t = M+i$ is:

$$\begin{aligned}
& np\left(1 + (1-p) + (1-p)^2 + (1-p)^3 + \cdots + (1-p)^{(i-1)}\right) \\
& = np\left(\frac{1-(1-p)^i}{1-(1-p)}\right) \\
& = n(1-(1-p)^i)
\end{aligned}$$

Since customers that return at $t = M+1$ may return with backorders, the number of orders for the firm may exceed the number of customers X_{M+1}. The number of customers who return with backorders is represented by the random variable Z. The model assumes that backorders are placed only once at time $t = M+1$ and $Z \sim Binom(X_{M+1}, q)$.

Although it makes intuitive sense to assume that customers who did not return to the firm immediately satisfied their demand during the shutdown period, $t = 1, 2, \ldots, M$, from another firm, a further extension to this model may consider situations where customers who do not return immediately but return later to the firm also places backorders. In that case Z would need to be indexed by time t.

Since each customer orders exactly 1 product in each time period, a customer who returns with backorders is assumed to have M backorders (one backorder for each period that the firm was closed). Thus, the total number of orders at time $M+1$ is $M * Z + X_{M+1}$. Using the expected number of customers from the above results and the conditional probability of placing a backorder, we calculate the expected number of orders at $t = M+1$:

$$
\begin{aligned}
&= \begin{pmatrix}\text{Expected number of}\\ \text{customers who return}\\ \text{with backorders}\end{pmatrix} * \begin{pmatrix}\text{Backorder}\\ \text{quantity}\\ \text{per customer}\\ + \\ \text{Regular order}\\ \text{quantity per}\\ \text{customer}\end{pmatrix}\\
&\quad + \begin{pmatrix}\text{Expected number of}\\ \text{customers who return}\\ \text{without backorders}\end{pmatrix} * \begin{pmatrix}\text{Regular order}\\ \text{quantity per}\\ \text{customer}\end{pmatrix}\\
&= (np * q) * (M+1) + np * (1-q) * 1\\
&= np(qM + q + 1 - q)\\
&= np(qM+1)
\end{aligned}
$$

The expected cumulative orders at time $t = M + i$ for $i > 1$ equals $n(1-(1-p)^i)$, which is equivalent to the expected cumulative number of customers who have returned by time $t = M + i$.

If the firm's per-unit selling price is c, we calculate R_t the lost revenue at time t:

$$
R_t = \begin{cases} cn & \text{if } t = 1, 2, \ldots, M \\ c(n - X_{M+1} - Z) & \text{if } t = M+1 \\ c\left(n - \sum_{i=1}^{t} X_{M+i}\right) & \text{if } t = M+i; i > 1 \end{cases}
$$

The expected lost revenue at time t is denoted by $\bar{R}_t$.

9.3.3 *Production Capacity Considerations*

In the proposed model, it is important to look at the production capacity of the firm, especially at time $t = M + 1$, when backorders may be received. The number of orders $M * Z + X_{M+1}$ must not exceed the available capacity C. If $M * Z + X_{M+1} > C$, the excess orders will be carried forward to the next time period, $t = M + 2$, but capacity restrictions require that $M * Z + X_{M+1} + X_{M+2} \leq 2C$.

Similarly, the firm can estimate and forecast the production capacity levels for future time periods. Depending on the willingness of customers to wait for the backorder delivery, the firm needs to prioritize production with the goal of meeting customer needs. If customers are likely to be lost in case of a late delivery, the firm will have to consider whether it can temporarily increase its production capacity or other alternatives to meet the spike in demand due to backorders.

9.4 Illustrative Example

This model can be applied to several situations. For example, a consumer-product manufacturing firm could face a supply chain disruption forcing it to shut down production. The firm's customers could react in different ways. One, a retailer who uses inventory during this period may come back to the firm immediately with backorders to replace its inventory. Two, a retailer who temporarily switches to another supplier may decide to come back when the firm starts producing again. Three, a retailer who switches to another supplier may decide not to come back when the firm starts producing again. The latter retailer may come back at a later stage depending on the firm's performance. By estimating the probability that the retailer takes any of these actions, the model can account for each of these scenarios.

9.4.1 *Lost Revenue with Backorders*

We illustrate the application of this model to a scenario in which a firm experiences a supply disruption and must stop production for $M = 4$ periods. Table 9.1 provides values for the parameters in this example.

The average value and standard deviation of lost revenue at each time period were obtained via 10,000 simulations of the supply chain disruption model for customer reactions using the parameters in Table 9.1. Since the firm is unable to produce during $t = 1, 2, \ldots, M$, the lost revenue at each time period equals the total revenue per period at undisrupted production rates. Because some of the lost revenue in the first M periods may be recaptured via backorders, the lost revenue may not actually be completely lost. In the model, this is accounted for at $t = M + 1$.

Since the binomial distribution can be approximated by the normal distribution, we calculate 90% probability intervals for the lost revenue $\bar{R}_t \pm 1.64 S_t$, where $\bar{R}_t$ is the average lost revenue and S_t is the standard deviation for time period t.

Table 9.1 Parameters

	Symbol	Value
Number of customers or demand per period	n	100
Per unit selling price in dollars	c	1000
Probability with which customers return in each period	p	0.15
Conditional probability of backorder requirement	q	0.50
Duration of the disruption in periods	M	4

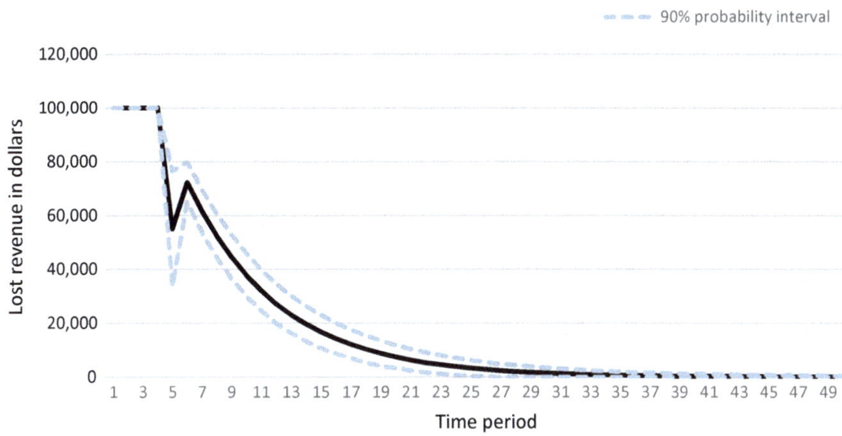

Fig. 9.2 The firm's expected lost revenue per period from the supply chain disruption

The results are illustrated in Fig. 9.2. The expected lost revenue reduces to less than 1% of the total pre-disruption revenue after $t = 34$, and the revenue from sales is almost completely restored to pre-disruption levels. If each time period is a week, the firm returns to its full performance in approximately 8 months.

As depicted by the probability interval, there is a 5% probability the lost revenue will be less than $1000 within 24 periods and a 5% probability the lost revenue will be greater than $1000 for at least 42 time periods. The expected lost revenue is at its maximum value for the first four periods, which is equal to the total pre-disruption revenue per period and then drops from $100,000 to $55,000. The downward spike in the expected lost revenue is due to the backorders. The lost revenue at $t = 5$ has a 5% probability of being as low as $33,444, which would occur if many customers return with backorders. If very few customers return with backorders, the lost revenue could be $76,556, which is the 95% upper bound for lost revenue in that time period. At time $t = 6$, the expected lost revenue increases to $72,250 and then gradually decreases over time as the firm recovers from the disruption.

9.4.2 *Lost Revenue Without Backorders*

Certain disruptions may not allow for backorders. For instance, a restaurant could be closed for a period of time because of food poisoning, and when it reopens, backorders are not realistic because the delivered product is a service that cannot be backordered. We can assign $q = 0$ in the simulation model to reflect such a situation. Figure 9.3 illustrates this scenario without backorders. Here, the expected cumulative lost revenue is higher because of the lack of backorders.

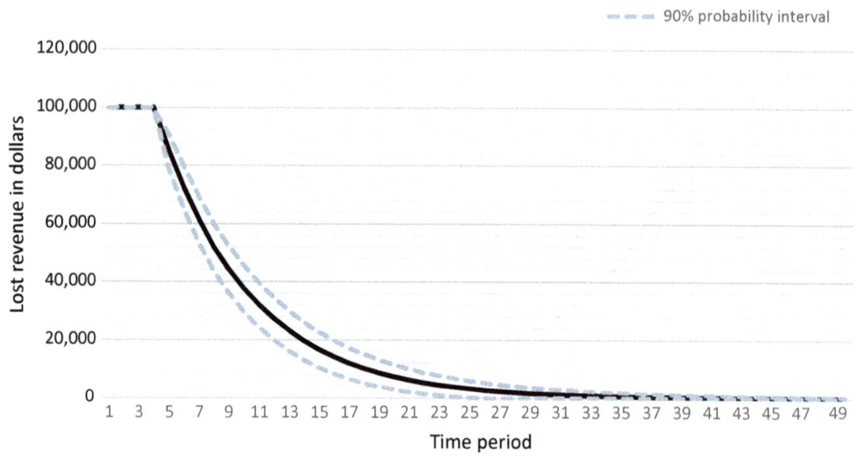

Fig. 9.3 The firm's expected lost revenue without backorders

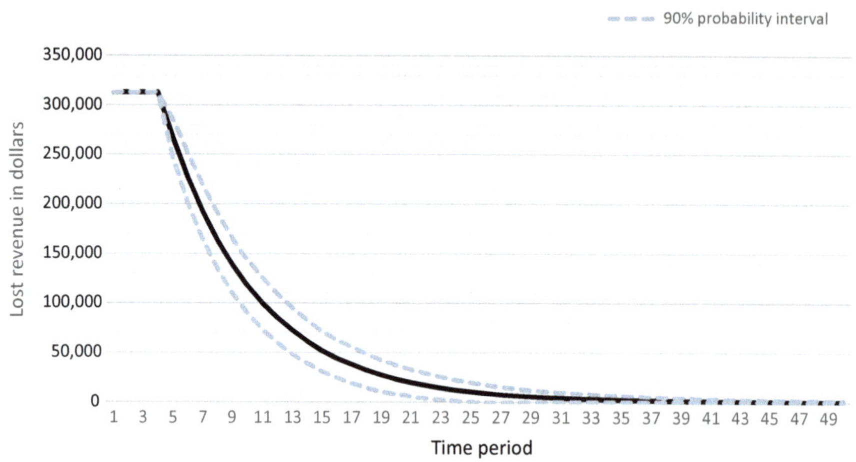

Fig. 9.4 The firm's expected lost revenue with varying demand from customers

9.4.3 Customers with Varying Demand

The assumption that each customer buys exactly one product may not be valid. This sub-section extends the simulation model to accommodate varying demands from the firm's customers. The demand from customer l is n_l where $l = 1, 2, \ldots, n$. We assume each n_l follows a discrete uniform distribution between 1 and 5, i.e., $n_l \sim U(1, 5)$. Backorders are ignored for simplicity. Parameters from Table 9.1 along with a simulation of $n_l \sim U(1, 5)$ were used in the model with varying demand from different customers to run 1000 simulations. The results are illustrated in Fig. 9.4.

The maximum total expected lost revenue is much higher than the previous cases because the total initial demand is more than in the previous cases. The shape of recovery is very similar to the model in Sect. 9.4.1 because each customer returns with the same probability. The expected lost revenue reduces to less than 1% of the total pre-disruption revenue after time period 25. This is comparable to the results from the model in Sects. 9.4.1 and 9.4.2. The results might look different if customers returned with different probabilities. For example, perhaps customers with more demand from the firm might be more likely to return because it may be more difficult for these customers to get all of their demand satisfied from the firm's competitors.

9.4.4 Risk Management Insights

A firm can use this model to understand how parameters impact the firm's expected lost revenue. The results discussed are highly sensitive to the value of p. As illustrated in Fig. 9.5, the firm recovers more quickly when the probability with which customers are gained back in each period is larger. This makes intuitive sense since firms with loyal customers tend to recover faster. We observe that the downward spike at time $t = M + 1$ is directly correlated with p. At $t = M + 1$, the cumulative expected number of orders including the backorders is directly proportional to the probability of customers buying from the firm at a given time period after the disruption.

The expected lost revenue in time period $t = 5$ is negative when $p = 0.4$. This negative value represents revenue greater than $100,000 in that period, a trend that continues as the value of p increases. Such situations may require the firm to work

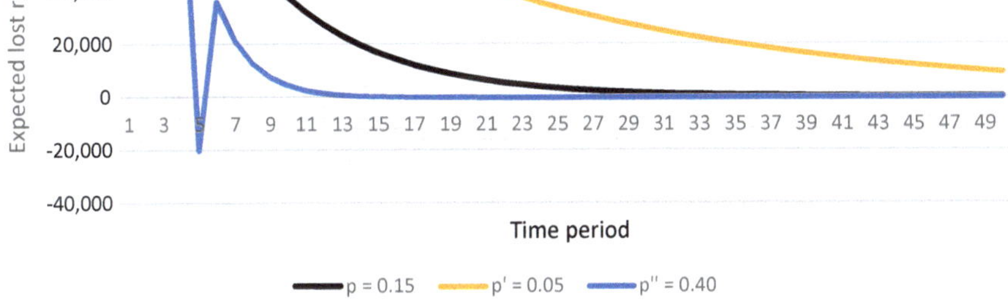

Fig. 9.5 Sensitivity of expected lost revenue to p

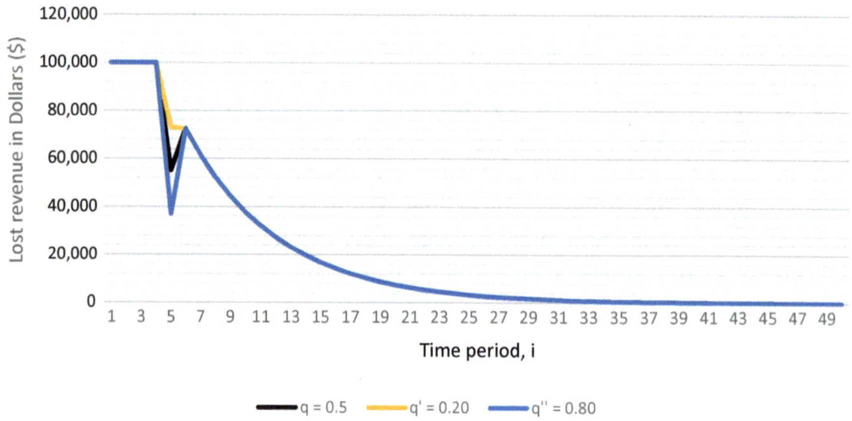

Fig. 9.6 Sensitivity of expected lost revenue to q

at overcapacity immediately after reopening to meet the sudden increase in demand, which is an integral part of the firm's recovery process (Sheffi and Rice 2005). This provides an important insight to the firm's management that in case of a production shut down, it may need to be prepared to temporarily increase its production capacity after reopening. The model also helps to estimate the maximum production the firm would need in order to meet the demand.

A similar trend can be observed with the sensitivity analysis on q, as illustrated in Fig. 9.6. The time of recovery remains the same since p is constant. This is also an important insight since firms need to think about the likelihood that their customers will place backorders. Accordingly, they can devise suitable production plans.

Firms can prepare for disruptions by using this quantitative model to estimate the potential loss in revenue due to a shutdown of operations from a supply chain disruption. Moreover, the model can be used to evaluate whether preparation strategies are economical. Investments to reduce the chances of a supply chain disruption itself may not be practical or economically reasonable. In such cases, firms can use the expected lost revenue from the model to decide whether or not investments to reduce the risk of a disruption are cost effective. Preparedness measures can help reduce the probability of a disruption and/or allow the firm to regain more of its revenue following a disruption. Even if the disruption cannot be avoided, preparedness measures could reduce the shutdown length M. It is logical to assume that the probability of customers returning depends on M. Decision makers can make decisions about investing in preparedness measures based on understanding how much revenue will be lost if the disruption occurs as well as the chances of the disruption itself.

For example, the cumulative expected lost revenue in the illustrative example is \$536,667. A risk-neutral firm should spend at most \$536,667 in preparing for this type of disruption and should spend much less once the probability of a disruption is considered. Investing in risk reduction strategies such as inventory or an additional supplier could reduce the time the firm is closed. The chances of customers returning immediately to the firm are higher if the firm is not closed as long. This would increase the probability p and reduce the cumulative expected lost revenue. In the example, increasing the value of p from 0.15 to 0.2 decreases the total expected lost revenue from $536,667 to $360,000. Strategies that could reduce p from 0.15 to 0.2 are economically wise if these strategies cost less than $176,667, assuming an extremely high probability of disruption.

9.5 Conclusions

This chapter proposes a model to quantitatively represent the way customers or the marketplace reacts to a supply chain disruption. The model is used to identify the impact of such an event on the firm's revenue. From the firm's perspective, the total expected lost revenue is a measure of the impact of the supply chain disruption and can be analyzed to draw useful insights to manage the risk of such an event.

The results obtained from applying the model serves as an illustration of the usefulness of the model. The simulation of the customer response model allows the firm to anticipate how customers might react to a supply chain disruption. The model can inform decision making to manage the risks of a supply chain disruption. Insights from the model can reveal how a disruption can affect the firm's revenue depending on the customers' decisions and the time a firm takes to recover to its pre-disruption revenue levels. Sensitivity analysis on the model parameters reveals how the probability at which customers return to the firm impacts the recovery time. Firms that expect most of its customers to return with backorders may need to temporarily increase production capacity. Management can use the cumulative expected lost revenue projections to evaluate investments aimed at increasing the firm's resilience to supply chain disruptions.

The proposed model could be developed further by relaxing some of the assumptions. For instance, customers may return with different probabilities or probabilities that change over time. Further extensions to this research can include the development of a decision-making framework to utilize the mathematical model to determine the most effective risk management decisions during a supply chain disruption. Another extension is to model the probability of a supply chain disruption along with the total expected lost revenue to make sound management decisions regarding investments in preparedness measures. An optimization model that minimizes the lost revenue during the disruption periods can also serve as a future extension to this chapter.

References

Arnade, C., Calvin, L., & Kuchler, F. (2009). Consumer response to a food safety shock: The 2006 food-borne illness outbreak of *E. coli* O157: H7 linked to spinach. *Applied Economic Perspectives and Policy, 31*(4), 734–750.

Babich, V., Burnetas, A. N., & Ritchken, P. H. (2007). Competition and diversification effects in supply chains with supplier default risk. *Manufacturing & Service Operations Management, 9* (2), 123–146.

Beach, R. H., Kuchler, F., Leibtag, E. S., & Zhen, C. (2008). The effects of avian influenza news on consumer purchasing behavior: A case study of Italian consumers' retail purchases (no. 56477). United States Department of Agriculture, Economic Research Service.

Chopra, S., & Sodhi, M. S. (2004). Managing risk to avoid supply-chain breakdown. *MIT Sloan Management Review, 46*(1), 53.

Christopher, M. (2005). *Logistics and supply chain management: creating value-adding networks* (3rd ed.). Harlow, England: Pearson Education.

Ellis, S. C., Henry, R. M., & Shockley, J. (2010). Buyer perceptions of supply disruption risk: A behavioral view and empirical assessment. *Journal of Operations Management, 28*(1), 34–46.

Hendricks, K. B., & Singhal, V. R. (2005). Association between supply chain glitches and operating performance. *Management Science, 51*(5), 695–711.

Jüttner, U., Peck, H., & Christopher, M. (2003). Supply chain risk management: Outlining an agenda for future research. *International Journal of Logistics: Research and Applications, 6*(4), 197–210.

Kilubi, I., & Haasis, H. D. (2015). Supply chain risk management enablers: A framework development through systematic review of the literature from 2000 to 2015. *International Journal of Business Science & Applied Management, 10*(1), 35–54.

Lavastre, O., Gunasekaran, A., & Spalanzani, A. (2012). Supply chain risk management in French companies. *Decision Support Systems, 52*(4), 828–838.

MacKenzie, C. A., Barker, K., & Santos, J. R. (2014). Modeling a severe supply chain disruption and post-disaster decision making with application to the Japanese earthquake and tsunami. *IIE Transactions, 46*(12), 1243–1260.

MacKenzie, C. A., Santos, J. R., & Barker, K. (2012). Measuring changes in international production from a disruption: Case study of the Japanese earthquake and tsunami. *International Journal of Production Economics, 138*(2), 293–302.

Manuj, I., Dittmann, P., & Gaudenzi, B. (2007). Risk management. In J. T. Mentzer, M. B. Myers, & T. P. Stank (Eds.), *Handbook of global supply chain management* (pp. 319–336). Thousand Oaks, Calif.: Sage Publications.

Mentzer, J. T., DeWitt, W., Keebler, J. S., Min, S., Nix, N. W., Smith, C. D., et al. (2001). Defining supply chain management. *Journal of Business Logistics, 22*(2), 1–25.

Nagurney, A., Cruz, J., Dong, J., & Zhang, D. (2005). Supply chain networks, electronic commerce, and supply side and demand side risk. *European Journal of Operational Research, 164*(1), 120–142.

Nishat Faisal, M., Banwet, D. K., & Shankar, R. (2006). Mapping supply chains on risk and customer sensitivity dimensions. *Industrial Management & Data Systems, 106*(6), 878–895.

Sheffi, Y., & Rice, J. B., Jr. (2005). A supply chain view of the resilient enterprise. *MIT Sloan Management Review, 47*(1), 41.

Snyder, L. V., Atan, Z., Peng, P., Rong, Y., Schmitt, A. J., & Sinsoysal, B. (2016). OR/MS models for supply chain disruptions: A review. *IIE Transactions, 48*(2), 89–109.

Sodhi, M. S., & Tang, C. S. (2012). *Managing supply chain risk.* New York: Springer Science & Business Media.

Stecke, K. E., & Kumar, S. (2009). Sources of supply chain disruptions, factors that breed vulnerability, and mitigating strategies. *Journal of Marketing Channels, 16*(3), 193–226.

Tomlin, B., & Wang, Y. (2005). On the value of mix flexibility and dual sourcing in unreliable newsvendor networks. *Manufacturing & Service Operations Management, 7*(1), 37–57.
Xia, Y., Ramachandran, K., & Gurnani, H. (2011). Sharing demand and supply risk in a supply chain. *IIE Transactions, 43*(6), 451–469.
Yu, H., Zeng, A. Z., & Zhao, L. (2009). Single or dual sourcing: Decision-making in the presence of supply chain disruption risks. *Omega, 37*(4), 788–800.

Chapter 10
Supply Chain Risk Management in the Transmission and Amplification of Disruptions

Artur Swierczek

Abstract The concept of risk management within the supply chain framework ought to involve indirect effects of disruptions. In other words, not only should it take into consideration the risk sources and their direct consequences, but also look into the indirect disruptions that may be transmitted and amplified in the supply chain structure. The transmission of disruptions means that the negative effects of risk are extended to a larger number of participants in a supply chain. If the negative risk effects are additionally magnified during the transmission, this suggests the occurrence of the amplification of disruptions. In other words, the subsequent links in a supply chain are exposed to a stronger impact of disruptions in the transmission. Thus, the supply chain management needs to apply a certain approach that enables to mitigate the negative consequences of the transmission and amplification of disruptions in supply chains. In this chapter, we review the extant literature on the essence, sources and factors of the transmission and amplification of disruptions in supply chains. In particular, we put emphasis on the issue of supply chain integration that may either drive or inhibit the transmission and amplification of disruptions. Having linked the obtained findings with the classical concepts of risk management, we develop and assess a framework of risk management that aims at mitigating the transmission and amplification of disruptions in supply chains.

10.1 Introduction

A myriad of examples derived from the practice of supply chain management evidence that risk consequences at the interorganizational level may be very pricey, especially when they take the form of transmission and amplification of disruptions. For instance, the supply chain of Ericsson lost an estimated $2 billion in 10 min

A. Swierczek (✉)
Department of Business Logistics, University of Economics in Katowice, Katowice, Poland
e-mail: artur.swierczek@uekat.pl

Y. Khojasteh (ed.), *Supply Chain Risk Management*,
DOI 10.1007/978-981-10-4106-8_10

when a fire that happened at its manufacturer of chips left Ericsson with no alternative source of supplies (Norrman and Jansson 2004). On the other hand, the supply chain of Boeing was affected by the loss of $2.6 billion when its two key suppliers failed to deliver critical parts on time (Radjou et al. 2002). The aforementioned and other examples, not cited here, indicate the magnitude of losses that affect supply chains in the result of the transmission and amplification of disruptions. However, the literature concerning this issue is still scarce, and the existing works refer to the problem partially, without employing a holistic approach. Consequently, to the best of our knowledge, there is no framework that shows how to deal with the phenomenon of the transmission and amplification of disruptions in supply chains.

The core issue for mitigating the transmission and amplification of disruptions is to establish the appropriate level of integration in supply chains. The transmission of disruptions is determined by its range, while the amplification is indicated by the strength of disruptions. Therefore, this phenomenon refers to supply chain integration that may either drive or inhibit the range of transmission and strength of disruptions. In other words, the supply chain integration demonstrates a *trade-off* between the pursuit of efficiency/effectiveness and the negative consequences of transmitted and amplified disruptions. Consequently, the concept of risk management in the transmission and amplification of disruptions should take into account that integration contributes to mitigating the transmission and amplification of disruptions, without an excessive drop in the supply chain efficiency/effectiveness.

Based on the traditional risk management concepts, we develop subsequent steps in the process of risk management in the transmission and amplification of disruptions, including identification of potential and actual disruptions, estimation of disruptions, evaluation of the most appropriate approach to deal with the identified and estimated disruptions, as well as application of the mitigating strategy. Having described the activities performed in each of the steps, we assess the research model of risk management in the transmission and amplification of disruptions, and draw conclusions significant for the practice of supply chain risk management.

10.2 The Phenomenon of the Transmission and Amplification of Disruptions in Supply Chains

The concept of the transmission and amplification of disruptions in supply chains has not yet been a subject of intense research either in theoretical or empirical frameworks. Therefore, there are very few previous works describing multidimensional aspects of this issue. This problem was partially raised by Juttner et al. (2003) who mention the "network effect" which is linked to the negative consequences of risks emanating from the supply chain relationships. Similarly, Kersten et al. (2012) mention that supply chain risks are the risks that affect at least two companies in a supply chain, and it is irrelevant whether a company is affected by supply chain risk directly or indirectly. Therefore, the transmission of disruptions is not limited to one level of a supply chain, and the companies that are only affected indirectly emit these risks to subsequent links of their network (Kersten et al. 2012). The problem has also been addressed by Cheng and Kam (2008) who suggest that risk may arise at the node or link and affect other links and nodes in the structure of a supply chain. In general, the transmission of disruptions means that the negative effects of risk are extended to a larger number of participants in a supply chain. The primary sources of these disruptions are external and internal risk factors. The external risk factors are located outside the supply chain, while the internal factors remain within the supply chain (Rao and Goldsby 2009).

The transmission of negative effects originating from the risk factors requires at least two companies in a supply chain to be involved in a process. One company is affected by a direct impact of these risk factors, whereas the other one is affected by an indirect influence. The risk factors affect a supplier directly, causing a certain disruption, which is then transmitted to other participants inside the structure of the supply chain. In this case, the supplier is the initial link, while the actors at the other levels of the physical flow of products in the supply chain—producer and customer —are exposed to an indirect impact of these risk factors. Consequently, an indirect impact of risk factors constitutes the transmission of disruptions.

The negative risk effects may spread out to a larger number of participants in a supply chain. Following the opinion of Svensson (2000), the range can be varied, but it generally falls within two types of disruptions located at the extreme positions of the continuum:

- limited range of disruptions, usually bilateral;
- widespread disruptions, generally holistic.

In the limited range of disruptions, the negative effects of risks are transmitted to a small number of links in a supply chain (Svensson 2000). For the purpose of this chapter, this range consists of only two companies, which indicates the transmission of disruptions from one company to the other (Kersten et al. 2007). At the other extreme continuum outlining the range of the transmission of negative effects are widespread disruptions. The transmission of these disruptions affects all actors in a supply chain structure. In general, the effects of risks are positioned between the two poles of limited range and widespread disruptions. As a result, a certain number of actors participating in a supply chain will be exposed to the negative effects of risk (Swierczek 2014). In terms of the direction of transmission, the propagation of supply chain disruptions may take the form of forward or backward transmission (Swierczek 2012). The forward transmission denotes that the disruptions caused by the risk factors in the initial link are then transferred to the other echelons downstream in a supply chain. The backward transmission is originated when disruptions in the ultimate link of a supply chain are transferred upstream to the initial echelons.

The transmission of negative risk effects often results in the amplification of disruptions. This is consistent with the outcome of the analysis carried out by

Juttner (2005) who points out that supply chain risk is likely to affect several organizations through the 'rippling effect'. According to Juttner et al. (2003), the strength of disruptions may be either absorbed or amplified during transmission. In general, the amplification of disruptions means that each affected link in a supply chain can be exposed to stronger effects of risks. In other words, smaller disruptions can snowball into stronger effects (Tsai et al. 2013), setting off the 'snowball effect'. It means that subsequent links are exposed to a stronger impact of disruptions in the forward transmission. The transmission and amplification of disruptions may also be manifested in the form of new disruptions, different from the original ones.

10.3 The Concept of Risk Management in the Transmission and Amplification of Disruptions

10.3.1 Conceptual Framework of the Risk Management Concept

Risk management is the concept used to identify, characterize, quantify, evaluate and mitigate risk and its negative consequences that may produce undesired outcomes (Aven and Kristensen 2005). The framework of risk management in the transmission and amplification of disruptions might be developed on the basis of traditional risk management concepts. However, in practice, the accurate use of risk management in the transmission and amplification of disruptions is a daunting task.

Based on the previous concepts of risk management, we identify the following steps in the process of risk management in the transmission and amplification of disruptions: formulation of the goals of risk management, analysis of the environment in terms of disruptions that either currently exist or will emerge in the near future, including: identification of potential and actual disruptions that may be transmitted to and amplified in other supply chain links, estimation of disruptions, evaluation of the most appropriate approach for each of the identified and estimated disruptions, and finally, application of mitigating strategies congruent with one of the following approaches: passive, reactive or proactive. The conceptual framework of risk management in the transmission and amplification of disruptions is depicted in Fig. 10.1.

The concept consists of five constructs and relationships. The constructs, described in the following sections of the chapter, are anchored in the literature and embrace a number of activities performed in each step. In general, the model investigates whether and how subsequent steps are determined by the risk management activities, and how each step in the sequence of activities affects the following step of the risk management process in the transmission and amplification of disruptions.

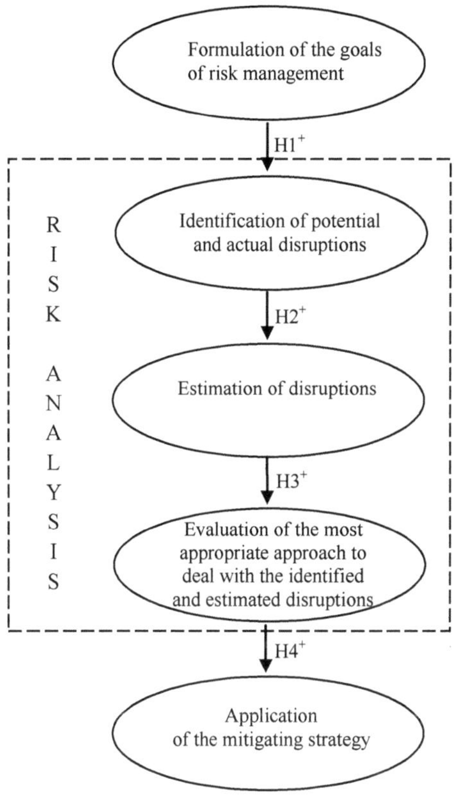

Fig. 10.1 Conceptual framework of supply chain risk management in the transmission and amplification of disruptions

10.3.2 Formulation of the Goals of Risk Management

Formulation of the goals is the first step in the process of risk management. As the phenomenon of the transmission and amplification of disruptions is determined by the range of transmission and strength of disruptions, it is inextricably linked to the issue of supply chain integration. In other words, the supply chain integration may either drive or inhibit the range of transmission and strength of disruptions. For instance, the study carried out by Swierczek (2014) suggests that the intensity of supply chain integration contributes to increasing the strength of disruptions in the flow of product and information. This issue has also been highlighted by Spekman and Davis (2004) who suggest that interdependency carries risk and its negative effects into supply chains. Juttner et al. (2003) demonstrates that the 'network effect' in the transmission of disruptions may arise from the relationships among supply chain partners. In the same vein, Swierczek (2016) asserts that based on the relationships between integration and the transmission and amplification of disruptions, one may identify specific clusters of supply chains demonstrating that the more intense supply chain integration contributes to the amplification of disruptions in the material flows in the forward and backward transmission. Drawing on these findings, we posit that a lower level of integration may mitigate the phenomenon of the transmission and amplification of disruptions by decreasing the mutual dependence of companies in a supply chain (Tang 2006). However, it will simultaneously bring a lower level of the supply chain efficiency/effectiveness.

In the light of the aforementioned, supply chain integration, to a different extent, contributes to the transmission and amplification of disruptions, having both augmentative and mitigating character. Therefore, supply chain integration is a milestone in searching for the appropriate strategy to deal with the transmission and amplification of disruptions in contemporary supply chains.

The establishment of optimal integrative relationships among the supply chain partners may contribute to mitigating the negative effects of the transmission and amplification of disruptions (Hult et al. 2004), thus ensuring the satisfactory efficiency/effectiveness. Consequently, the concept of supply chain risk management in the transmission and amplification of disruptions should pertain to supply chain integration. Therefore, we posit that ensuring the appropriate level of integration may contribute to obtaining the goals of risk management. The optimal level of integration allows to mitigate the transmission and amplification of disruptions, without an excessive drop in the supply chain efficiency. Most of the relationships between the factors concerning supply chain integration demonstrate *a trade-off* between the efficiency/effectiveness and disruptions (Zsidisin and Ritchie 2009), which requires looking for balance between the extreme values of a specific factor.

Consequently, we highlight the specific role of the relationship between the efficiency/effectiveness of supply chain management on the one hand, and the extent of transmission and strength of disruptions on the other hand. Christopher (2002) mentions the following major factors of supply chain integration that indicate a specific relationship between the supply chain efficiency/effectiveness, and the transmission and amplification of disruptions: the number of supply chain partners, outsourcing, globalization of supply chains, backup infrastructure and extra capacity/inventory, as well as transparency of the flow of information among the supply chain links. The first three factors concern the structure of links constituting integrative relationships, whilst the remaining factors refer to the intensity of supply chain integration. For instance, decreasing a number of supply chain partners may lead to single sourcing, whereby one supplier is solely responsible for all supplies of an item. Several well-documented studies show that the major supply chain disruptions have been caused by a failure at a single source (Nishiguchi and Baaudet 1998). Even though there are many benefits of reducing the partner base of supply chains, it is also widely recognized that it brings an increased risk (Christopher 2002).

Outsourcing, as another factor of integration, produces the higher efficiency/effectiveness of supply chain management; however, it also simultaneously results in the increased supply chain complexity that may be a driver of the transmission and amplification of disruptions (Peck 2004). The study conducted by Juttner (2005) shows that globalization is the most important factor increasing the exposure of supply chains to disruptions. The next factor—an increased level of inventory—usually goes hand in hand with the tendency to maintain excessive capacity of technical infrastructure used in the physical flow of products. This is another way to reduce the increased susceptibility of contemporary supply chains to the transmission and amplification of disruptions.

Therefore, the fundamental goal of risk management in the transmission and amplification of disruptions is to achieve two tightly-related objectives of the efficient/effective supply chain management and limited transmission and amplification of disruptions. The first step of risk management should then be followed by the analysis of risk, including identification of potential and actual disruptions, estimation of disruptions and evaluation of the most appropriate approach to deal with the identified and estimated disruptions. Therefore, we hypothesize as follows:

H1 *Formulation of the goals of risk management is positively related to the identification of potential and actual disruptions.*

10.3.3 Identification of Potential and Actual Disruptions

The purpose of the identification of disruptions is to determine all disruptions that are likely to be transmitted and amplified in the structures of supply chains (Khan and Burns 2007). In practice, one can use several methods for collecting information about the negative risk effects. These include: experience of managers, use of decision support systems, performance of surveys, "brainstorming" or recourse to the external consultants (Hillson 2002). However, from the institutional point of view, the use of such methods should be complemented with determination of the scope of diagnosis. In other words, it is important to identify the specific characteristics of links relevant from the perspective of the transmission and amplification of disruptions. Gilbert and Gips (2000) argued that while it makes sense to consider potential disruptions at the supplier's suppliers, it is less understandable and may be more costly to read the effects of risk at further stages of a supply chain structure. Hence, the key issue is to determine the scope of diagnosis for the purpose of outlining how many links are to be involved in the identification process. The problem is that the phenomenon of the transmission and amplification of disruptions may not even be observable in particular situations. It means that the negative risk effects occurring in a specific link of a supply chain are not necessarily amplified during the transmission. In this case, time and financial expenditures incurred in connection with identification of such disruptions are not justified, because they do not lead to a higher level of efficiency in the entire supply chain.

The issue of the transmission and amplification of disruptions in supply chains is complex and multifaceted, as there are two closely related phenomena involved, namely the range of transmission and the amplification of disruptions. The most interesting situation concerns the disruptions which were amplified and transmitted to a larger number of firms in a supply chain. However, the relations between the range of transmission and the strength of disruptions are only illustrative—Fig. 10.2.

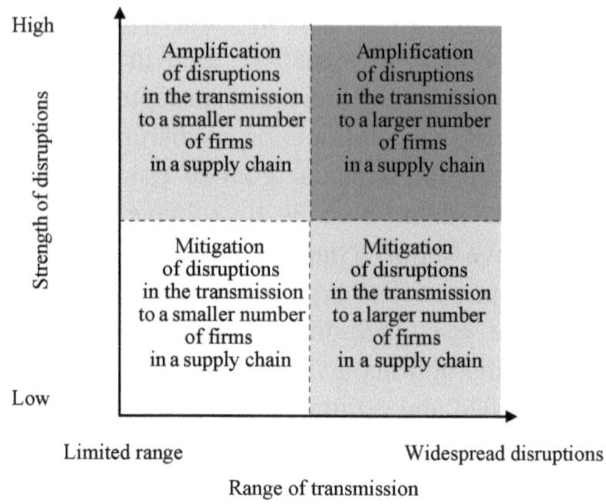

Fig. 10.2 Matrix of the range of transmission and the strength of disruptions. *Source* Reproduced from Swierczek (2013)

It is rather uncommon that the effects of risk are transmitted to all companies in a supply chain, having a holistic impact. On the other hand, the disruptions are not only amplified in the transmission, but they may also be mitigated.

It is also important to identify the risk factors that form the sources of disruptions amplified during the transmission. The most difficult to identify is the transmission of disruptions caused by the risk factor which directly affects a larger number of companies in a supply chain (Cheng and Kam 2008). The risk factors such as natural disasters or financial crises often simultaneously and directly affect a larger number of links (van Dorp 2004). The disruptions caused by this group of risk factors are not sequential in nature and they are often interdependent (van Dorp and Duffey 1999).

The particular risk factor which affects a larger number of companies in a supply chain may be referred to as 'common risk factor'. The identification of potential and actual disruptions is a critical step in the risk management process (Kliendorfer and Saad 2005) that should then be followed by the estimation of disruptions (Berg et al. 2008). Kern et al. (2012) argues that supply chains have to develop the capability to predict disruptions early, so that they can be duly assessed and mitigated. Therefore, risk estimation is highly dependent on the quality of risk identification. Consequently, we define the following hypothesis:

H2 *Identification of potential and actual disruptions has a positive effect on the supply chain risk estimation.*

10.3.4 Estimation of Disruptions

The estimation of the phenomenon of transmission and amplification of disruptions should be preceded by the identification of risk factors, whose negative effects can be transferred with amplified strength to the subsequent supply chain links.

The managers usually pay special attention to the effects caused by the impact of a specific factor, at the same time underestimating its indirect impact. It may suggest that the strength of disruption caused by the direct impact of an external risk factor is similar to the strength of impact of the same disruption during the transmission. This evokes the tendency to ignore the phenomenon of amplification during transmission and to focus attention solely on the strength of disruptions caused by the direct impact of an external risk factor. It is also more difficult to determine the degree of amplification of a disruption caused by a 'common risk factor' as a result of transmission from one unit to another, if the same disruption has a direct impact on the other link, causing a higher level of disruptions in this link. In such a situation, the estimation intended to determine to what degree the disruption transferred from one link caused the amplification of disruption in another link is practically impossible.

The strength of disruption in a particular link depends on the effects caused by the direct impact of the risk factor on this link, as well as on the same disruption transferred during the transmission. The determination of the degree of the amplification of disruption is additionally hindered by the fact that common risk factor effects can be potentially transferred from several companies at the same time. Christou and Amendale (1998) propose to include the following activities in the estimation of disruptions: considering the goals of risk management, determining the probability of failure to achieve these goals, and finally, defining consequences resulting from any failure to achieve the goals of risk management.

In order to estimate the extent of the transmission of disruptions, Juttner (2005) asked the respondents to rate the extent to which each of a range of prominent disruptive events affected their own organization, their suppliers and customers. The analysis concerning the extent of the transmission of disruptions may also be determined by the number of supply chain links indirectly affected by the negative risk effects. The estimation of the amplification of transferred disruptions may in turn consist in assigning the scores indicating the strength of risk effects that indirectly affect all supply chain partners. If no difference between the scores in the subsequent links is revealed, the crisis affects the whole supply chain equally. On the other hand, an increase in the value of scores between suppliers, manufacturers and customers demonstrates the amplification of transmitted disruptions.

The estimation should serve in the first place as a reliable foundation for taking decisions concerning the mitigation of the transmission and amplification of disruptions. The main idea is to enable the comparison of the estimation results concerning the range of transmission and strength of amplified disruptions with the purpose of risk management. As a result of this comparison, a specific attitude should be adopted towards the identified and potential disruptions, in the form of a developed and implemented strategy (Khan and Burnes 2007). This will enable taking efficient and effective decisions that will make the supply chain unsusceptible to risk factors and their negative effects, whose range of transmission may increase and strength may be amplified (Stecke and Kumar 2009). Kern et al. (2012) demonstrate that the estimation of disruptions should result in classifying all identified disruptions and putting them in order of priority to select the most appropriate approach to deal with the identified and estimated disruptions. Thus, the following relationship is hypothesized.

H3 *Estimation of disruptions has a positive impact on evaluation of the approach that is supposed to deal with the identified and estimated disruptions.*

10.3.5 Evaluation of the Most Appropriate Approach to Deal with the Identified and Estimated Disruptions

Evaluation should follow the estimation of disruptions and pertain to integration as a driver of the transmission and amplification of disruptions. Based on the study of Rice and Caniato (2003), we distinguish between the following types of attitudes as ways to deal with disruptions: passive, reactive and proactive.

Employing the passive approach denotes avoiding any activities that would potentially or effectively contribute to the transmission and amplification of disruptions. This approach is more popular if the likelihood of risk and severity of its negative effects are high. The reactive approach tends to ensure the optimal structure and intensity of supply chain integration (Mentzer 2004). In practice, it pertains to classical means of mitigating the transmission and amplification of disruptions in supply chains, such as establishing an appropriate structure of supply chain network, increasing the transparency in the information flow, maintaining backup infrastructure and excessive capacity/inventory. The proactive approach denotes ensuring responsiveness and time compression of information and physical flow of products (Christopher and Peck 2004). In line with the opinion of Smeltzer and Siferd (1998), the proactive approach provides unique capabilities for supply chains operating worldwide. As demonstrated by the study of Blackhurst et al. (2005), the tenets of proactive initiatives enable to mitigate the severity of disruptions. The identification and estimation of the negative risk effects, followed by evaluation of the relevant approach to deal with the disruptions, are necessary to initiate the mitigating activities. The selected mitigating strategy will only work well if all previous steps of risk management are performed carefully and correctly (Kern et al. 2012). Therefore, we define the following hypothesis.

H4 *Evaluation of the most appropriate approach that tends to deal with disruptions has a positive effect on the application of the mitigating strategy in supply chains.*

10.3.6 Application of the Mitigating Strategy

The application of the mitigating strategy is the last step of risk management in the transmission and amplification of disruptions. The mitigating strategy should follow the appropriate approach that aims to deal with the identified and estimated disruptions. The application of the mitigating strategy consistent with the passive approach denotes that some business opportunities are too risky as compared to the potential benefits. For instance, supply chains may refuse to sell products to the customers with unhealthy financial standing, abandon the markets whose future perspective is uncertain, or give up the idea to enter the international markets due to high risk and strength of negative effects (Sheehan 2009). Therefore, employing the mitigating strategy consistent with the passive approach may result in lowering the intensity of integration among geographically-dispersed supply chain partners, or dropping the idea of closer collaboration with other companies in manufacturing and product distribution.

Among the strategies consistent with the reactive approach, one may enumerate the following: joint efforts to share risk-related information, increased stockpiling and use of buffer stock, maintaining the excess capacity of technical infrastructure and selective outsourcing operations (Soler and Bassetto 2008). These strategies ought to ensure balance between the supply chain efficiency and the negative consequences of the transmission and amplification of disruptions.

Mitigating strategies consistent with the proactive approach include establishing a flexible base of partners, flexible transportation and manufacturing, as well as an agile configuration of the supply chain structure. The cornerstone of the proactive approach is flexible and agile integration in supply chains. For instance, maintaining a flexible base of partners is described by Billington et al. (2002) who give the example of a supply chain that uses double sourcing for its manufacturing process. The first manufacturing facility assembles the product in the quantity that meets the base (average) customer demand, while the second one delivers the product if the demand exceeds its base value. Similarly, as noted by Tang (2006), the strategy of flexible transportation consists in using multi-modal transportation, multi-carrier transportation and multiple routes.

Aside from the strategy of flexible resources, it is also worth mentioning the strategy of agile configuration of a supply chain structure. As highlighted by Blackhurst et al. (2005), if one link in a supply chain structure may cause a certain risk, then it is necessary to conduct quick reconfiguration of the supply chain structure in order to prevent the transmission of disruptions.

The aforementioned strategies are not unique in the sense that they serve as a means of mitigating the transmission and amplification of disruptions (Ellegaard 2008). On the contrary, they may be successfully used in other decision making situations. However, from the standpoint of using supply chain integration to deal with the transmission and amplification of disruptions, the described strategies appear to be the most suitable and adequate, as they concern both the structure and the intensity of integration.

10.4 Methodology

10.4.1 Sample and Measures

In order to assess the research model that depicts the concept of risk management in the transmission and amplification of disruptions, we conducted an exploratory study with a quantitative survey as a method of data collection. The structure of the interview questionnaire corresponds to the goal of the paper and enables to test the research hypotheses. It consists of several sections examining subsequent steps in the concept of risk management: formulation of the goals of risk management, identification of potential and actual disruptions that may be transmitted to and amplified in other supply chain links, estimation of disruptions, evaluation of the most appropriate approach for each of the identified and estimated disruptions, as well as application of the mitigating strategy. Each step consisted of detailed variables demonstrating certain managerial activities. The variables were measured with the 7-point Likert scale, indicating the intensity of particular activities in the risk management process, and anchored between the values of "never" and "always".

The research had a non-exhaustive character. The set of data was collected in 2015. The target sample included 122 companies operating in European supply chains. The companies had at least one supplier and one customer, and were leaders or major links in their respective supply chains, having a relatively strong position as compared to the preceding and subsequent links in the supply chain structure. The obtained responses were additionally processed in order to reveal if the managers of companies were aware of risk factors, their sources and consequences that may potentially affect the investigated companies and their upstream and downstream partners. The solicited companies represented the manufacturing (55% of the sample) and trading (45% of the sample) sectors. Most manufacturers operated in the fabricated metal products sector, mining industry, industrial and commercial machinery sector and automotive industry. The trading companies distributed cross-industry products, mainly household goods and clothes, chemicals, groceries and electronic equipment. In terms of size, the sample consisted of medium and large companies. The prevailing share of 37% of the sample employed from 50 to 249 staff, while the rest employed above 250 people.

10.4.2 Partial Least Square (PLS) Path Model

In order to assess the research model, the PLS Path Model procedure was employed. In the opinion of Ainuddin et al. (2007), the use of PLS is especially suited to exploratory studies, where the measures are new and the relationships have not been previously tested. This is confirmed by Tsang (2002) who argues that the PLS procedure is particularly suitable for data analysis at the early stage of a theory development, where the conceptual model and its measures are not well developed. In addition, the study carried out by Kern et al. (2012) used the PLS Path Model to investigate the relationships between the steps in the classical risk management concept in supply chains. All these support the use of PLS as a method of model assessment. As a rule of thumb for PLS, the sample size should be ten times larger than the largest number of indicators of the construct in the outer model, or ten times larger than the largest number of structural paths directed at a particular construct in the inner path model (Chin 1998).

The sample size used in the study is 122, whereas the largest number of indicators in the proposed outer model is 5, and the largest number of structural paths directed at a particular construct in the proposed path model is 1. Therefore, the study meets the criterion of a sample size.

PLS requires that the dependent and independent variables should be specified before carrying out any analysis. In order to check the hypothetical structure of constructs in the model, the Exploratory Factor Analysis (*EFA*) with the Principal Component Analysis (*PCA*) and Varimax Rotation was conducted. There were 5 factors chosen for the analysis. The inspection of anti-image correlation matrix demonstrated that the measure of individual sampling adequacy (*MSA*) was above a nominal cut-off point of 0.5. In addition, the factor analysis confirmed that variables demonstrated sufficient factor loadings above the value of 0.6. Consequently, the model presented in Fig. 10.3 was obtained and used for the further PLS analysis.

The PLS Path Model of this study consists of the inner model, which is comprised of constructs and their hypothesized relationships, and the outer model, describing the relationship between latent and manifest variables (Tenenhaus et al. 2005). The reliability and validity of the outer model was assessed first, and then followed by the assessment of the inner model (Hulland 1999).

10.5 Results

10.5.1 Outer Path Model

The proposed model has reflective items from the latent variable to the manifest variables in their blocks. An in-depth study of the theory provides a clarification of the generative nature of constructs (Fornell and Bookstein 1982). In the study conducted by Kern et al. (2012), the steps in the classical concept of risk management in supply chains are also manifested by reflective items. The application of the reflective outer model posits that changes in constructs are expected to be manifested by changes in all of their indicators. In the model, the observed items ought to be highly correlated, as they explain the same construct (Jarvis et al. 2003). Consequently, removing any item from the block of variables should not have a significant effect on the latent variable. In other words, the observed items constituting a reflective block do not need to represent all the aspects that form the

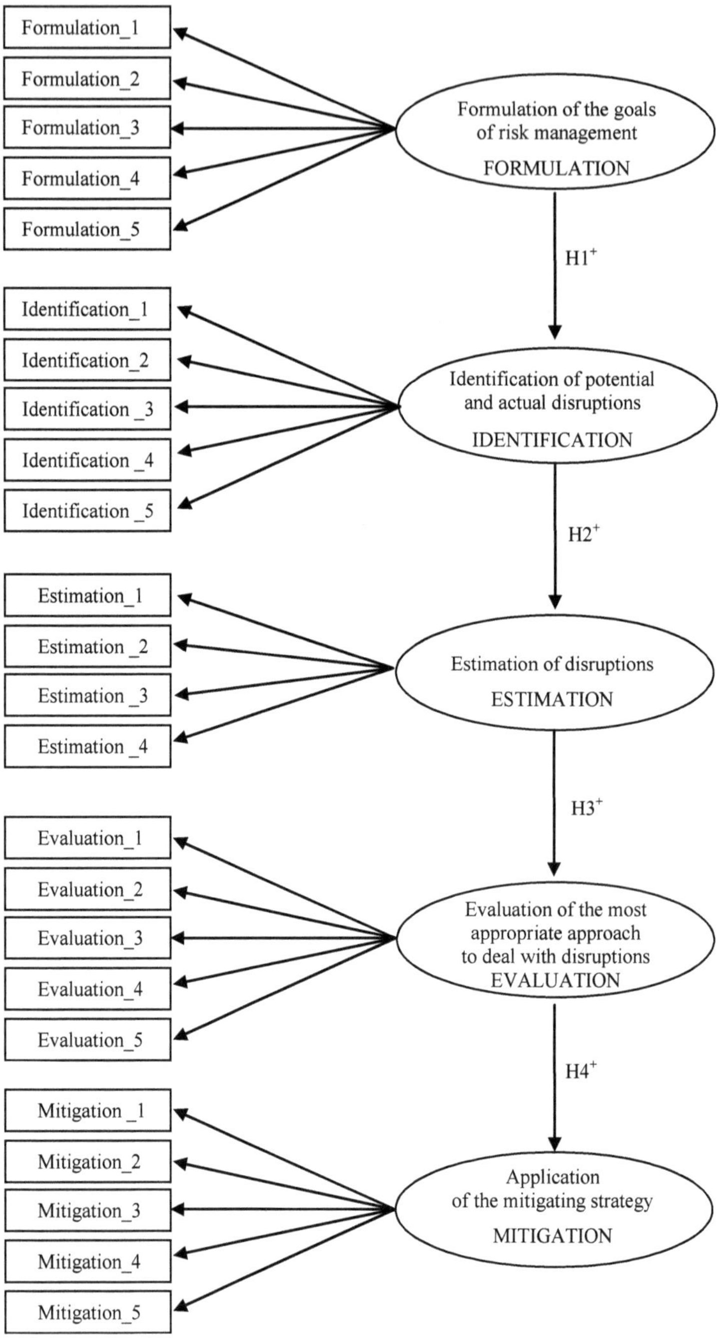

Fig. 10.3 PLS Path model

concept (McDonald 1996). In fact, the items are interchangeable and share the same construct.

The reflective outer model was assessed with respect to its reliability and construct validity. Reliability testing usually includes internal consistency and composite reliability (*CR*). Each of five constructs indicates Cronbach's alpha coefficient exceeding 0.7. As Cronbach's in PLS path models may provide a significant underestimation of the internal consistency of the constructs, it is recommended to complement the outcome of calculated Cronbach's alpha with the application of composite reliability (Werts et al. 1974). The coefficients of *CR* estimated for the underlying constructs in an outer model are above the value of 0.7. Therefore, the reliability of results is satisfactory for an early stage of the study (Nunnally and Bernstein 1994)—Table 10.1.

For the assessment of validity, the convergent validity (Straub et al. 2004) and the discriminant validity are examined (O'Leary-Kelly and Vokurka 1998). The convergent validity, as measured by the coefficients of average variance extracted (*AVE*), is equal to or above a nominal cut-off point of 0.5 across all constructs. It indicates that all latent variables in the model are able to explain more than half of the variance of its indicators on average (Chin 1998), which is acceptable for an exploratory study. The discriminant validity has been assessed to explore if the appropriate items load substantially on their hypothesized constructs and load no larger than 0.3 on any other component (Hair et al. 2006). Although the outcome of the analysis demonstrates that the observed items used for measuring the specified constructs load high (above 0.6) on their assigned components, the threshold of 0.3 is not met for all cross-loadings. It may suggest that some variables load substantially on more constructs. The discriminant validity also meets the *Fornell–Larcker* criterion that posits that the *AVE* coefficient of one construct is larger than the highest square of its correlation with the other constructs (Fornell and Larcker 1981). Table 10.2 shows the AVEs in italics in the diagonal of the correlation matrix and the values off-diagonal are the squared correlations between the constructs.

The squared values of correlations amount to less than the corresponding *AVE*, which indicates discriminant validity of the measures. Employing the *Fornell-Larcker* criterion, each construct in the outer model shares more variance with its assigned indicators than with any other latent variable criterion (Fornell and Larcker 1981). Overall, as the criteria for reliability and construct validity have been met, the obtained measurement results in the outer model are satisfactory and appropriate for proceeding with an estimation of the inner model.

10.5.2 Inner Path Model

The reliable and valid outer model estimations are followed by the evaluation of the inner path model. In order to assess the model, the coefficients of determination (R^2) of the constructs, standardized path coefficients and prediction relevance of the model have been determined. In general, as shown in Table 10.3, the subsequent

Table 10.1 The results summary for the outer model

Latent variables	α	CR	AVE	Factor loadings
Formulation of the goals of risk management (FORMULATION)	0.72	0.83	0.50	
We investigate over-dependency among partners in our supply chain that may lead to the transmission and amplification of disruptions in our supply chain (Formulation_1)				0.59
We consider that the structure of the supply chain (e.g. supply chain globalization, outsourcing, number of supply chain partners) may either drive or inhibit the range of the transmission of disruptions (Formulation_2)				0.72
We examine the effects of the intensity of supply chain integration (ensuring backup infrastructure and maintaining extra capacity/inventory) on the strength of disruptions in our supply chains (Formulation_3)				0.62
We weight a trade-off between the supply chain efficiency/effectiveness and the extent of the transmission/strength of disruptions (Formulation_4)				0.72
We are looking for a certain degree of compromise in ensuring both the supply chain efficiency/effectiveness and mitigation of the transmission and amplification of disruptions (Formulation_5)				0.85
Identification of the potential and actual disruptions (IDENTIFICATION)	0.73	0.84	0.50	
We monitor the potential and actual disruptions that may affect our supply chain partners (Identification_1)				0.78
We try to identify the disruptions (usually induced by the internal risk factors) that might be transferred from the other supply chain partners (Identification_2)				0.75
We tend to identify if the effects of the direct impact of a particular risk factor (usually external) differ from the disruptions transmitted indirectly from other supply chain partners (Identification_3)				0.72
We have a database storing the historical disruptions transmitted and amplified in our supply chain (Identification_4)				0.62
Based on our previous experience, we implement warning indicators that may be used if disruptions are transmitted and amplified in our supply chain (Identification_5)				0.67
Estimation of disruptions (ESTIMATION)	0.87	0.81	0.51	
We investigate the extent of the transmission of disruptions in our supply chain (Estimation_1);				0.75
We examine the severity of the strength of disruptions transmitted from other links in our supply chain (Estimation_2)				0.62

(continued)

Table 10.1 (continued)

Latent variables	α	CR	AVE	Factor loadings
While estimating the disruptions, we look into the goals of risk management (Estimation_3)				0.75
We try to classify and prioritize the transmitted and amplified disruptions in our supply chain (Estimation_4)				0.73
Evaluation of disruptions (EVALUATION)	0.68	0.84	0.51	
We regularly evaluate the most adequate approach in order to deal with the transmitted and amplified disruptions in our supply chains (Evaluation_1)				0.62
We consider each transmitted and amplified disruption uniquely and individually, and try to apply the most appropriate approach to mitigate it (Evaluation_2)				0.77
As a result of the evaluation of disruptions, we apply the approach that tends to avoid any activities that would potentially or effectively contribute to the transmission and amplification of disruptions in our supply chain (Evaluation_3)				0.59
As a result of the evaluation of disruptions, we undertake activities to ensure the optimal balance between the structure of supply chain and the intensity of integration, i.e. to establish the appropriate structure of supply chain network and maintain the appropriate intensity of integration in our supply chain (Evaluation_4)				0.72
As a result of the evaluation of disruptions, we focus on the responsiveness and time compression of information and physical flow of products in order to perform fast and agile interorganizational activities that aim to mitigate the transmission and amplification of disruptions in our supply chain (Evaluation_5)				0.85
Application of the mitigating strategy (MITIGATION)	0.67	0.85	0.53	
In order to mitigate the transmission and amplification of disruptions, we refuse to sell products to the customers with unhealthy financial standing, abandon the markets whose future perspective is uncertain, or give up the idea to enter into the international markets due to high risk and strength of negative effects (Mitigation_1)				0.62
In order to mitigate the transmission and amplification of disruptions, we conduct joint efforts to share risk-related information, increase stockpiling and use of buffer stock, maintain the excess capacity of technical infrastructure and employ selective outsourcing operations (Mitigation_2)				0.79
In order to mitigate the transmission and amplification of disruptions, we employ a flexible base of partners (e.g. by using double sourcing for the replenishment/manufacturing and/or distribution processes in which one source ensures the quantity of goods that meets base or average customer demand, while the second one provides the product if demand exceeds its base value) (Mitigation_3)				0.74

(continued)

Table 10.1 (continued)

Latent variables	α	CR	AVE	Factor loadings
In order to mitigate the transmission and amplification of disruptions, we apply flexible transportation that consists in using multi-modal transportation, multi-carrier transportation and multiple routes (Mitigation_4)				0.75
In order to mitigate the transmission and amplification of disruptions, we use an agile configuration of the supply chain structure that denotes establishing open and reconfigurable organizations, striving to precisely simulate the volatility of markets and environment through a quick reconfiguration of the supply chain structure (Mitigation_5)				0.72

Table 10.2 Correlation matrix

Constructs	Formulation	Identification	Estimation	Evaluation	Mitigation
Formulation	*0.50*				
Identification	0.42	*0.50*			
Estimation	0.21	0.47	*0.51*		
Evaluation	0.18	0.23	0.50	*0.61*	
Mitigation	0.15	0.19	0.32	0.60	*0.53*

Note The AVE is provided in italics in the diagonal; the squared correlations between the constructs are given off-diagonal

steps of risk management explain a diverse amount of variance in the five constructs with R^2 values of 0.412 for the identification of disruptions, 0.571 for the estimation of disruptions, 0.477 for the evaluation of disruptions, and 0.468 for the selection of the appropriate mitigating strategy.

The findings suggest that the coefficients of determination for the following steps of risk management are moderate. In the opinion of Chin (1998), if any endogenous latent variable is explained only by a few exogenous latent variables, moderate value of R^2 may be accepted. Aczel (1993) proposes using lower R^2 values (around 0.5) to indicate the relationships between variables. Therefore, the R^2 values for the following five steps of risk management in the transmission and amplification of disruptions provided an indication of the predictive ability of independent variables (Cohen and Cohen 1975).

In order to determine the standardized path coefficients of the model and their statistical significance, the bootstrapping re-sampling technique was employed (Davison and Hinkley 2003). The obtained results from 500 re-samples revealed that four links in the model were significant at the level of $p = 0.05$.

The PLS results depicted in Table 10.3 indicate a strong support to the proposed hypotheses. The first step of risk management—formulation of the goals of risk management - has a positive and significant effect on the following step consisting in the identification of disruptions (path coefficient is +0.373 at $p < 0.05$).

Table 10.3 Inner model results

	Proposed effect	Stand. path coefficient	*t*-value	Significance (*p*-values)	Hypothesis
Effects on the identification of disruptions ($R^2 = 0.412$)					
Formulation of the goals of risk management	+	0.373	3.85	$p < 0.05$	Supported
Effects on the estimation of disruptions ($R^2 = 0.571$)					
Identification of disruptions	+	0.598	5.04	$p < 0.05$	Supported
Effects on the evaluation of disruptions ($R^2 = 0.477$)					
Estimation of disruptions	+	0.487	6.42	$p < 0.05$	Supported
Effects on the application of mitigating strategy ($R^2 = 0.468$)					
Evaluation of disruptions	+	0.512	6.89	$p < 0.05$	Supported

Consequently, the obtained findings support *H1*. The identification of disruptions has, in turn, a positive and significant impact on the estimation of disruptions (path coefficient is +0.598 at $p < 0.05$), offering a support to *H2*. The results also indicate a positive and significant effect of the estimation of disruptions on the evaluation of disruptions (path coefficient is +0.487 at $p < 0.05$), giving a support to *H3*. Finally, the evaluation of disruptions has a positive and significant impact on the last step in the proposed concept, that is, the application of mitigating strategy (path coefficient is +0.512 at $p < 0.05$). Accordingly, this research outcome lends a support to *H4*.

10.6 Discussion of the Results and Managerial Implications

10.6.1 Steps of Supply Chain Risk Management in the Transmission and Amplification of Disruptions

The PLS Path analysis provides some interesting findings concerning the transmission and amplification of disruptions. Based on the extensive literature review, we have developed and empirically evaluated a conceptual framework for risk management in the transmission and amplification of disruptions. The assessment of the outer path model indicating the sequence of activities in the risk management process that have been classified into a certain number of steps shows a sufficient level of reliability and construct validity. It demonstrates that the identified managerial activities are classified correctly into specific steps, filling in each step with substantial and consistent content. Among these steps one may enumerate: formulation of the goals of risk management, identification of disruptions, estimation and evaluation of disruptions, and application of the mitigating strategy.

In the first step—formulation of the goals of risk management, supply chains should investigate over-dependency among partners that may lead to the transmission and amplification of disruptions in our supply chain, consider whether the structure of a supply chain is driving or inhibiting the range of the transmission of disruptions, examine the effects of the intensity of supply chain integration on the strength of disruptions, weight a trade-off between the supply chain efficiency/effectiveness and the extent of the transmission/strength of disruptions, and finally look for a certain degree of compromise in ensuring both the supply chain efficiency/effectiveness and mitigation of the transmission and amplification of disruptions.

Among important activities in the identification of disruptions in a supply chain, one may enumerate the following: monitoring the potential and actual disruptions that may affect our supply chain partners, identifying the disruptions that might be transferred from the other supply chain partners, determining if the effects of the direct impact of a particular risk factor differ from the disruptions transmitted indirectly from other supply chain partners, maintaining a database storing the historical disruptions transmitted and amplified in a supply chain, as well as implementing warning indicators that may be used if disruptions are transmitted and amplified in a supply chain.

The third step of the proposed concept is the estimation of disruptions. It should consist of the following activities: investigating the extent of the transmission of disruptions, examining the severity of the strength of disruptions transmitted from other links in a supply chain, considering the goals of risk management while estimating the disruptions, as well as classifying and prioritizing the transmitted and amplified disruptions in a supply chain.

The fourth step, the evaluation of disruptions, should include selection of the most adequate approach in order to deal with the transmitted and amplified disruptions, unique and individual selection of each transmitted and amplified disruption, an attempt to apply the most appropriate approach to mitigate them, application of the approach that tends to avoid any activities that would potentially or effectively contribute to the transmission and amplification of disruptions in a supply chain, undertaking activities to ensure the optimal balance between the structure of a supply chain and the intensity of integration, as well as focusing on the responsiveness in order to perform fast and agile interorganizational activities that aim to mitigate the transmission and amplification of disruptions in a supply chain.

The fifth step in the proposed concept of risk management, that is, the application of the mitigating strategy, covers the combination of the following activities: refusing to sell products to the customers with unhealthy financial standing, abandoning the markets whose future perspective is uncertain, or giving up the idea to enter into international markets due to high risk and strength of negative effects, conducting joint efforts to share risk-related information, increasing stockpiling and using a buffer stock, maintaining the excess capacity of technical infrastructure and employing the selective outsourcing operations, employing a flexible base of partners, applying flexible transportation that consists in using multi-modal transportation, multi-carrier transportation and multiple routes, using an agile configuration of the supply chain structure that denotes establishing open and reconfigurable organizations, as well as striving to precisely simulate the volatility of markets and environment through a quick reconfiguration of the supply chain structure.

Based on the estimation of convergent validity for constructs, we argue that the list of enumerated activities classified into certain steps is demonstrative and open. It means that it should be additionally complemented with the activities stemming from the unique and diverse character of each supply chain. In other words, the list of activities in the risk management process should be modified and extended to cover the specificity of the transmission and amplification of disruptions in the examined supply chain. The study also evidences that the employed scales of items and the way the activities are grouped into certain steps provide a sound empirical foundation for the evaluation of the proposed framework of risk management in the transmission and amplification of disruptions.

10.6.2 The Relationships Between the Subsequent Steps of Supply Chain Risk Management

The analysis of the inner path model shows that the coefficients of determination for the subsequent steps in the concept of the transmission and amplification of disruptions are moderate, meaning that they enable to indicate general relationships between the subsequent steps of risk management in the transmission of disruptions. It means that each construct manifesting a certain step in risk management is closely connected with its preceding and following steps, which supports the significance of the issue of integration in the risk management process. For instance, the estimation step requires to identify the disruptions that may be transmitted to and amplified in other supply chain links, and concomitantly provides a basis for the next step of evaluation of the most appropriate approach for each of the identified and estimated disruptions. In other words, the bundle of the activities of risk management ought to be performed in a certain logical sequence due to a high level of interdependence between the steps and corresponding activities of risk management. Moreover, we investigated potential relationships among all steps of risk management in order to highlight the importance of performing the activities in the correct sequence. The obtained variances demonstrate a significantly lower level of the strength of relationships among all constructs. It additionally supports the necessity to perform the activities of risk management in the right order.

The findings also show that in order to mitigate the transmission and amplification of disruptions, managers should employ the traditional risk management concept, adapted to the new content-related circumstances and managerial conditions. In other words, if the companies already use a certain model of risk management in their supply chains, there is no necessity to build the concept of risk management in the transmission and amplification of disruptions from scratch. It should rather be extended to involve a wider analysis of disruptions that might be transmitted and amplified in the supply chain structure. In other words, the proposed concept complements the existing, traditional frameworks of risk management with new, hitherto disregarded and unappreciated aspects.

The traditional concept of risk management in supply chains has *ex-ante* character, as it focuses on decreasing the probability of occurrence of risk and mitigating its direct negative consequences. On the other hand, risk management in the transmission and amplification of disruptions should provide a response to the disruptions, amplified during the transmission, whose sources and direct effects have not been captured and neutralized in a timely manner by the traditional risk management process. In this vein, the concept of risk management in the transmission and amplification of disruptions has *ex-post* character aimed at reducing the negative effects of deviations from the desired condition. This is particularly important when a supply chain is exposed to the risk effects that have a strong and devastating impact, or there is a lack of effectiveness in preventing disruptions at the earlier stages of risk management.

Acknowledgements The study was financed by the National Science Centre as a research project no. DEC-2012/05/E/HS4/01598.

References

Aczel, A. D. (1993). *Complete business statistics* (2nd ed.). Massachusetts: Boston.

Ainuddin, R., Beamish, P., Hulland, J., & Rouse, M. (2007). Resource attributes and firm performance in international joint ventures. *Journal of World Business, 42*(1), 47–60.

Aven, T., & Kristensen, V. (2005). Perspectives on risk: Review and discussion of the basis for establishing a unified and holistic approach. *Reliability Engineering and System Safety, 90*(1), 1–14.

Berg, E., Knudsen, D., & Norrman, A. (2008). Assessing performance of supply chain risk management programs: A tentative approach. *International Journal of Risk Assessment and Management, 9*(3), 288–310.

Billington, C., Johnson, B., & Triantis, A. (2002). A Real options perspective on supply chain management in high technology. *Journal of Applied Corporate Finance, 15*(2), 32–43.

Blackhurst, J., Craighead, C., Elkins, D., & Handfield, R. (2005). An empirically derived agenda of critical research issues for managing supply-chain disruptions. *International Journal of Production Research, 43*(19), 4067–4081.

Cheng, S., & Kam, B. (2008). A conceptual framework for analyzing risk in supply networks. *Journal of Enterprise Information Management, 22*(4), 345–360.

Chin, W. (1998). The partial least squares approach for structural equation modeling. In G. A. Marcoulides (Ed.), *Modern methods for business research* (pp. 295–336). NJ: Lawrence-Erlbaum, Mahwah.

Christopher, M. (2002). *Supply chain vulnerability*. Cranfield: Research Report.

Christopher, M., & Peck, H. (2004). The five principles of supply chain resilience. *Logistics Europe*, February, 16–21.

Christou, M., & Amendale, A. (1998). *How lessons learned from exercises can improve the quality of risk studies*. In A. Mosleh & R. A. Bari (Eds.), *Proceedings of the 4th International Conference on Probabilistic Safety Assessment and Management*, New York, NY.

Cohen, J., & Cohen, P. (1975). *Applied multiple regression/correlation analysis for the behavioural science*. Mahwah, NJ: Lawrence Erlbaum Associates.

Davison, A., & Hinkley, D. (2003). *Bootstrap methods and their application*. New York, NY: Cambridge University Press.
Ellegaard, Ch. (2008). Supply risk management in a small company perspective. *International Journal of Supply Chain Management, 13*(6), 425–434.
Fornell, C., & Bookstein, F. (1982). Two structural equation models: LISREL and PLS applied to consumer exit-voice theory. *Journal of Marketing Research, 19*(4), 440–452.
Fornell, C., & Larcker, D. (1981). Evaluating structural equation models with unobservable variables and measurement error. *Journal of Marketing Research, 18*(1), 39–50.
Gilbert, G., & Gips, M. (2000). Supply-side contingency planning. *Security Management, 44*(3), 70–74.
Hair, J., Black, W., Babin, B., Anderson, R., & Tatham, R. (2006). *Multivariate data analysis*. Upper Saddle River, NJ: Pearson Prentice Hall.
Hillson, D. (2002). *The risk breakdown structure (RBS) as an aid to effective risk management.* In: 5th European Project Management Conference. Cannes, France, 1–11.
Hulland, J. (1999). Use of partial least squares (PLS) in strategic management research: A review of four recent studies. *Strategic Management Journal, 20*(4), 195–204.
Hult, G., Hurley, R., & Knight, G. (2004). Innovativeness: Its antecedents and impact on business performance. *Industrial Marketing Management, 33*(5), 429–438.
Jarvis, C., Mackenzie, S., Podsakoff, P., Mick, D., & Bearden, W. (2003). A critical review of construct indicators and measurement model misspecification in marketing and consumer research. *Journal of Consumer Research, 30*(2), 199–218.
Juttner, U. (2005). Supply chain risk management. Understanding the business requirements from a practitioner perspective. *International Journal of Logistics Management, 16*(1), 120–141.
Juttner, U., Peck, H., & Christopher, M. (2003). Supply chain risk management: Outlining an agenda for future research. *International Journal of Logistics: Research and Applications, 6*(4), 197–210.
Kern, D., Moser, R., Hartmann, E., & Moder, M. (2012). Supply risk management: Model development and empirical analysis. *International Journal of Physical Distribution & Logistics Management, 42*(1), 60–82.
Kersten, W., Hohrath, P. H., & Böger, M. (2007). *An empirical approach to supply chain risk management: Development of a strategic framework.* In *18th Annual POMs Conference, Dallas, TX.*
Kersten, W., Schroeder, M., Skirde, H., & Feser, M. (2012). *The development of supply chain risk management (SCRM) implementation model.* In *23rd Annual POMs Conference, Chicago, IL.*
Khan, O., & Burns, B. (2007). Risk and supply chain management: Creating a research agenda. *International Journal of Logistics Management, 18*(2), 197–216.
Kleindorfer, P., & Saad, G. (2005). Disruption risk management in supply chains. *Production and Operations Management, 14*(1), 53–68.
McDonald, R. (1996). Path analysis with composite variables. *Multivariate Behavioral Research, 31*(2), 239–270.
Mentzer, J. (2004). *Global supply chain risk management*. White Paper: University of Tennesee. September 30.
Nishiguchi, T., & Baaudet, A. (1998). The Toyota Group and the Aisin fire. *Sloan Management Review*, 49–59.
Norrman, A., & Jansson, U. (2004). Ericsson's proactive supply chain risk management approach after a serious sub-supplier accident. *International Journal of Physical Distribution and Logistics Management, 34*(5), 434–456.
Nunnally, J., & Bernstein, I. (1994). *Psychometric theory*. New York, NY: McGraw-Hill.
O'Leary-Kelly, S., & Vokurka, R. (1998). The empirical assessment of construct validity. *Journal of Operations Management, 16*(4), 387–405.
Peck, H. (2004). Resilience—surviving the unthinkable. *Logistics Manager*, March, 16–18.
Radjou, N., Orlov, L., & Nakashima, T. (2002). *Adapting to supply network change*. The TechStrategy TM Report, March.

Rao, S., & Goldsby, T. J. (2009). Supply chain risk: A review and typology. *Journal of Logistics Management, 20*(1), 97–123.

Rice, J., & Caniato, F. (2003). Building a secure and resilient supply chain. *Supply Chain Management Review, 7*(5), 22–30.

Sheehan, N. T. (2009). Making risk pay: The boards' role. *Journal of Business Strategy, 30*(1), 33–39.

Smeltzer, L., & Siferd, S. (1998). Proactive supply management: The management of risk. *International Journal of Purchasing and Material Management, 34*(1), 38–45.

Soler, M., & Bassetto, S. (2008). *Analyse des risques de la chaine d'approvisionnements.* Janvier.

Spekman, R., & Davis, E. (2004). Risky business: Expanding the discussion on risk and the extended enterprise. *International Journal of Physical Distribution and Logistics Management, 34*(5), 414–433.

Stecke, K., & Kumar, S. (2009). Sources of supply chain disruptions, factors that breed vulnerability, and mitigating strategies. *Journal of Marketing Channels, 16*(3), 193–226.

Straub, D., Boudreau, M., & Gefen, D. (2004). Validation guidelines for IS positivist research. *Communications of the Association for Information Systems, 13*(1), 380–427.

Svensson, G. (2000). A conceptual framework for the analysis of vulnerability in supply chains. *International Journal of Physical Distribution and Logistics Management, 30*(9), 731–749.

Swierczek, A. (2012). *Propagation of amplified disruptions in supply chains. Conceptual perspective and practical implications*. In 23rd Annual POMS Conference, Chicago, IL.

Swierczek, A. (2013). An identification of the 'rippling effect' in the transmission of disruptions. The dilemmas of theoretical study and empirical research. *Journal of Economics & Management 12,* 83–96.

Swierczek, A. (2014). The impact of supply chain integration on the 'snowball effect' in the transmission of disruptions: An empirical evaluation of the model. *International Journal of Production Economics, 157,* 89–104.

Swierczek, A. (2016). The 'snowball effect' in the transmission of disruptions in supply chains: The role of intensity and span of integration. *International Journal of Logistics Management, 27*(3), 1002–1038.

Tang, C. S. (2006). Perspectives in supply chain risk management. *International Journal of Production Economics, 103*(2), 451–488.

Tenenhaus, M., Esposito, V., Chatelin, Y., & Lauro, C. (2005). PLS path modelling. *Computational Statistics & Data Analysis, 48*(1), 159–205.

Tsai, J., Bowring, E., Marsella, S., & Tambe, M. (2013). Empirical evaluation of computational fear contagion models in crowd dispersions. *Autonomous Agents and Multi-Agent Systems, 27* (2), 200–217.

Tsang, E. (2002). Acquiring knowledge by foreign partners from international joint ventures in a transition economy: Learning-by-doing and learning myopia. *Strategic Management Journal, 23*(9), 835–854.

van Dorp, J., & Duffey, M. (1999). Statistical dependence in risk analysis for project networks using Monte Carlo methods. *International Journal of Production Economics, 58*(1), 17–29.

van Dorp, J. (2004). Statistical dependence through common risk factors: With applications in uncertainty analysis. *European Journal of Operations Research, 16*(1), 240–255.

Werts, C., Linn, R., & Joreskog, K. (1974). Intraclass reliability estimates: Testing structural assumptions. *Educational and Psychological Measurement, 34*(1), 25–33.

Zsidisin, G., & Ritchie, B. (Eds.). (2009). *Supply chain risk. A handbook of assessment, management, and performance.* New York: Springer Verlag.

Chapter 11
Strategic Sourcing Under Supply Disruption Risk

S. Prasanna Venkatesan and Mark Goh

Abstract Disruption in the upstream of any supply chain affects the productivity and reputation of suppliers in that chain. Supply disruption risk is prevalent and affects more suppliers especially since these suppliers tend to be grouped geographically or as clusters for greater economies of scale. With attention paid to disaster management and business contingency planning, many firms are reassessing their supply chain strategies to effectively handle such risks, contain cost, and maintain service levels. This chapter presents a Mixed Integer Linear Programming (MILP) model for supplier selection and order quantity allocation (SSOA) for suppliers who bear different disruption likelihood, capacity, upside flexibility and operate under different price discount regimes. The objective is to minimize the expected total cost comprising supplier management cost, purchasing cost, and an expected loss if a supplier's reliability to serve is compromised by disruptions. As the SSOA problem under supply disruption risk is NP-hard, particle swarm optimization with time varying inertia weight and acceleration coefficients is applied. Numerical tests are conducted to illustrate the proposed approach and the results obtained are compared with Genetic Algorithm (GA). Sensitivity analysis is conducted on the disruption likelihood, supplier upside flexibility, and the price discount regimes.

11.1 Introduction

Today's supply chain being global suffers from more risks which come from sources within and outside of the chain. Indeed, empirical studies suggest that supply chain risk is an important component of a firm's strategic decision-making

S. Prasanna Venkatesan (✉)
Department of Production Engineering, National Institute of Technology, Tiruchirappalli, TamilNadu, India
e-mail: prasanna@nitt.edu

M. Goh
NUS Business School, National University of Singapore, Singapore, Singapore
e-mail: mark.goh@nus.edu.sg

Y. Khojasteh (ed.), *Supply Chain Risk Management*,
DOI 10.1007/978-981-10-4106-8_11

process (Marchese and Paramasivam 2013). The literature categorizes supply chain risks to be either operational or disruption. Operational risks are the inherent uncertainties in the system e.g., demand, supply, and cost. Disruption risks are the outcomes of natural or man-made disasters. The effort to identify and mitigate supply chain risks has traditionally focused on operational risks as disruption risks often had a small likelihood of occurrence. Recently, disruption risks occur more frequently and as such receive more attention as suppliers tend to be grouped geographically or as clusters for greater economies of scale. Succumbing to disruption risk can affect the productivity, market share, and reputation of the suppliers (Chopra and Sodhi 2014). For instance, the disasters (Japanese tsunami and Thailand flood) in 2011 have forced many leading automotive and computer manufacturers to reassess their supply network strategies in Asia to effectively mitigate the risks arising from the clustering of suppliers in these two locations, so as to contain disruption cost and maintain service levels (Matsuo 2015). Thus far, the literature on SSOA tends under disruption is scant and tends to overlook supply disruption (Meena and Sarmah 2014; Sawik 2014). Planning for disruptions typically requires a proactive process to identify the key locations for catastrophic risks in a supply chain and to estimate the likelihood of its occurrence and the impact (Knemeyer et al. 2009).

Supply disruption can be modeled as either a super, semi-super, or unique event (Sarkar and Mohapatra 2009). A super event occurs when the suppliers at all locations are disrupted i.e. they all fail at the same time exhibiting a total effect. A semi-super event is location/region specific and occurs when a set of suppliers at a location are disrupted exhibiting a regional effect. A unique event occurs when only one supplier at a location is disrupted exhibiting a local effect. The literature on supply disruptions concerns mostly super and unique events with equal and unequal failure likelihoods (see Table 11.1). Disruption risks can be measured by the expected monetary loss to the supply chain (Heckmann et al. 2015). The SSOA models under supply disruption risk are classified based on the objective, decision variables, model parameters, and solution methodology. Usually such SSOA models are formulated to minimize the expected total cost considering either all or partial supplier disruptions as shown in Table 11.1. Only some studies have simultaneously considered supplier location, selection and order allocation under disruption. For completeness, Chai et al. (2013) presented a good review of the techniques used to select suppliers. While the decision tree technique is most used to capture the different disruption scenarios an arbitrary allocation of orders is proposed to determine the optimum supply base. Meena and Sarmah (2013) showed that the SSOA problem under supply disruption risk is NP-hard as the computational complexity increases with the number and locations of suppliers, disruption likelihoods, supply capacity, price discounts, and supplier flexibility; hence, they proposed a Genetic Algorithm (GA) approach.

Particle Swarm Optimization (PSO), drawn from swarm intelligence, is another technique used by researchers given its simplicity and performance (Poli 2008). However, the work on PSO for SSOA under disruption is scant. Kamali et al. (2011) applied PSO on multi objective buyer-vendor coordination. Che (2012) used

Table 11.1 SSOA models under supply disruption risk

Source	Model description																
	Objective	Decision variables			Parameters												Solution approach
		Number of suppliers	Order allocation		Cost				Supplier location	Supplier disruption		Supply disruption events				Suppliers upside flexibility	
			Equal	Unequal	FC	VC	LC	CD		All	Partial	Su	Se	Uq			
														Equal	Unequal		
Berger et al. (2004)	ETC	●	–	–	●	–	●	–	–	●	–	●	–	●	–	–	Decision tree
Zeng et al. (2005)	ETC	●	–	–	●	–	●	–	–	●	–	●	–	●	–	–	
Ruiz-Torres and Mahmoodi (2006)	ETC	●	–	●	●	●	●	●	●	–	●	–	–	●	●	●	Decision tree and arbitrary order allocation
Ruiz-Torres and Mahmoodi (2007)	ETC	●	–	–	●	–	●	–	–	–	●	●	–	●	●	●	Decision tree
Sarkar and Mohapatra (2009)	ETC	●	–	–	●	●	●	–	●	●	–	●	●	●	–	–	Decision tree and tabular method
Meena et al. (2011)	ETC	●	●	–	●	●	●	–	–	–	●	●	–	●	–	●	Problem specific algorithm

(continued)

Table 11.1 (continued)

Source	Model description																Solution approach
	Objective	Decision variables			Parameters												
		Number of suppliers	Order allocation		Cost				Supplier location	Supplier disruption		Supply disruption events				Suppliers upside flexibility	
			Equal	Unequal	FC	VC	LC	CD		All	Partial	Su	Se	Uq			
														Equal	Unequal		
Meena and Sarmah (2013)	ETC	●	–	●	●	●	●	●	–	–	●	●	–	–	●	●	GA
Ruiz-Torres et al. (2013)	ETC	●	●		●	●	●	–	–	–	●	–	–	●	–	●	Decision tree and Excel solver
Meena and Sarmah (2014)	ETC	●	–	●	●	●	●	●	–			●	–	–	●	●	GA, BONMIN solver
Sawik (2014)	ETC/CSL	●	–	●	●	●	●	–	●	●	–	–	●	–	●	–	Stochastic programming

Note: *ETC* Expected Total Cost, *CSL* Customer Service Level, *FC* Fixed Cost, *VC* Variable Cost, *LC* Loss Cost, *CD* Cost Discount, *Su* Super event, *Se* Semi-super event, *Uq* Unique event, *BONMIN* Basic open-source Mixed Integer Non-Linear programming

PSO to solve a multi-echelon unbalanced supply chain planning problem. PrasannaVenkatesan and Kumanan (2012) applied a multi objective binary PSO algorithm on sourcing with price and exchange rate risks.

In this chapter, we formulate an MILP model for SSOA under disruption risk for super, semi-super, and unique events. We minimize the expected total cost (ETC) comprising supplier management cost, raw material purchase cost, and expected supplier loss.

This chapter is organized as follows. Section 11.2 presents an overview of PSO and GA. Section 11.3 describes the problem and model formulation. Section 11.4 details the adoption of PSO and GA for the SSOA problem. Section 11.5 provides an illustrative example. Section 11.6 discusses the results. Section 11.7 concludes with some future research directions.

11.2 Overview of PSO and GA

In this section, we present a brief description of the PSO and GA algorithms

11.2.1 Particle Swarm Optimization (PSO)

Developed by Kennedy and Eberhart (1995), PSO is inspired by the social behavior of a flock of migrating birds trying to reach an unknown destination. In PSO, each solution is a 'bird' in the flock and is referred to as a 'particle'. Each bird looks in a specific direction. When communicating with each other, they identify the bird that is in the best location. Accordingly, each bird speeds towards the best bird with a velocity that depends on its current position. Each bird, then, investigates the search space from its new local position, and the process repeats until the flock reaches their desired destination. The search process involves both social interaction and intelligence so that the birds learn from their own experience (local search) and from the experience of the others around them (global search).

The pseudo code for the PSO algorithm is as follows:

Begin

Initialize the swarm of size (*N*);
While maximum iteration (*max_it*) is not attained

Do
For each particle in the swarm;
Calculate fitness value;
If fitness value is better than best fitness value (pBest) in history;
Set current value as new pBest;
Choose particle with best fitness value of all particles as the gBest

For each particle
Calculate particle velocity using velocity update equation

Update particle position using position update equation

End

End

11.2.2 Genetic Algorithm (GA)

GA is a stochastic search technique inspired by a biological system's improved fitness through evolution (Goldberg 1989). GA starts with a random population of solutions (chromosomes). The chromosomes are evaluated using the given objective function. The best chromosomes exchange information through selection, crossover and mutation to produce offspring chromosomes. The offspring chromosomes are then evaluated and used to evolve the population if they provide better solutions than a weak population (Gen and Cheng 1997). The process is continued until the maximum number of generations or the termination criteria is attained.

The pseudo code of the GA algorithm is as follows:

Begin

Initialize population of N' chromosomes;
Evaluate fitness for each chromosome;
While maximum iteration (*max_it*) is not attained

Do
Recombine N' using selection, crossover and mutation;
Generate offspring N'';
Evaluate offspring;
Remove worst chromosome from N' and N''
Select population of size N' for next iteration
End
End

11.3 Problem Description and Model Formulation

Firms keep a set of preferred suppliers based on cost, quality, and service level. Such suppliers tend to be clustered geographically, for reasons of pooling of labor and technology sharing (Fig. 11.1). Siting reliable alternative suppliers and sourcing from both preferred and alternate suppliers is common when minimizing ETC.

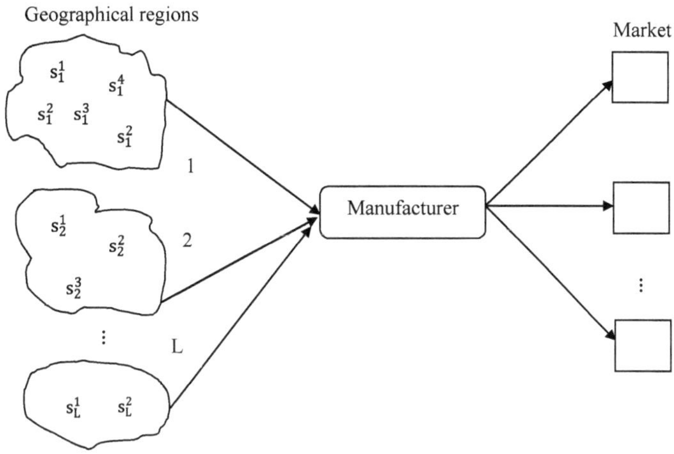

Fig. 11.1 Typical supply chain setup

Model formulation: An MILP model is formed to find the choice of suppliers and their order allocations subject to the constraints on capacity and demand. The objective is to minimize the ETC. ETC includes supplier management cost, purchasing cost, and an expected loss cost (ELC) if a supplier is disrupted. While sourcing from multiple suppliers increases the supplier management cost with supply disruption, the expected loss incurred by the manufacturer is less, as the order is now allocated to many suppliers.

We assume the followings in our model:

1. Single product with quantity discounts and a single period planning horizon;
2. Manufacturer produces functional products which have stable demand;
3. We include only Tier-1 suppliers who are independent;
4. Number of suppliers and their geographical regions, capacities are known and fixed;
5. Acquisition and transportation cost of raw materials from suppliers to manufacturer is known and fixed;
6. A semi-super event is region specific and each region has its disruption likelihood;
7. If some supplier(s) fails to deliver the units ordered due to a disruption, the other un-disrupted suppliers will make up the shortfall at no extra cost (Meena and Sarmah 2013);
8. Each supplier has a different capacity, unique event likelihood, and compensation potential (which is the ability of the supplier to make up for the supply shortfall);

9. We estimate the disruption likelihood of super, semi-super, and unique events by combining the expert/decision maker's opinion with historical data (Knemeyer et al. 2009);
10. Supplier management cost comprising the cost of meetings, negotiation and quality monitoring is a linear function of the number of suppliers (Meena and Sarmah 2013);

Indices

s	Supplier ($s = 1, 2, \ldots, S$)
l	Region ($l = 1, 2, \ldots, L$); x_l^s denotes supplier s in region l

Parameters

D	Total demand of raw materials for the planning period
C_s	Capacity of supplier s
ts_l	Total number of suppliers in region l
F_s	Fixed cost of managing supplier s
r_s	Base purchasing cost per item from supplier s
d_s^{pb}	Percentage discount offered by supplier s in price break pb
r'	Financial loss per item due to the failure of a supplier(s) to deliver
p^{su}	Likelihood of a super event causing all suppliers to disrupt
p_l^{se}	Likelihood of a semi-super event causing all suppliers in region l to disrupt
p_s^{uq}	Likelihood of a unique event causing only supplier s to disrupt
Q_s^{min}	Minimum order for supplier s as a proportion of the total demand
$B(f)$	Set of all subsets (different from the empty set) of region l $\{l = 1, 2, \ldots, L\}$ in which all suppliers fail due to a semi-super event with, $B(f) = \{B(f_1), B(f_2), \ldots, B(f_L)\}$, where $B(f_1)$ = Subset containing each single region in which all suppliers are disrupted; $B(f_2)$ = Subset containing each pair of regions in which all suppliers are disrupted; Subsets of regions that can be affected by a semi-super event are $(2^L - 1)$ being the number of subsets of the set of regions $\{1, 2\ldots L\}$ and assuming at least one supplier from a region is selected (Sarkar and Mohapatra 2009). For example with three regions l_1, l_2, and l_3, $B(f_1) = \{\{l_1\},\{l_2\},\{l_3\}\}$; $B(f_2) = \{\{l_1, l_2\},\{l_1, l_3\},\{l_2, l_3\}\}$ and $B(f_3) = \{l_1, l_2, l_3\}$.
$B'(f')$	Set of all subsets of regions in which all suppliers are not disrupted due to a semi-super event where $B'(f') = \{B'(f'_1), B'(f'_2), \ldots, B'(f'_L)\}$, where

$B'(f'_1)$ = subset containing un-disrupted regions when all suppliers at a single region are disrupted; and $B'(f'_2)$ = Subset containing un-disrupted regions when all suppliers at a pair of regions are disrupted;
For the above example, $B'(f'_1) = \{\{l_2, l_3\}, \{l_1, l_3\}, \{l_1, l_2\}\}$; $B'(f'_2) = \{\{l_3\}, \{l_2\}, \{l_1\}\}$ and $B'(f'_3) = \{\}$;

$A(f)$ Set of all subsets (different from the empty set) of suppliers (s = 1,…,S) who are disrupted due to a unique event, $A(f) = \{A(f_1), A(f_2), \ldots, A(f_S)\}$ where
$A(f_1)$ = Subset containing each of a single supplier who are disrupted; $A(f_2)$ = Subset containing each of a pair of suppliers who are disrupted etc. The total number of subsets composed of f_s suppliers that can be subjected to a unique event is $\frac{S!}{f_s!(S-f_s)!}$ where $S = \sum_{l=1}^{L} ts_l$ (Ruiz-Torres and Mahmoodi 2007). For example, with 6 suppliers, $A(f_1) = \{\{1\}, \{2\}, \{3\}, \{4\}, \{5\}, \{6\}\}$; Similarly $A(f_2)$ has 15 elements with two suppliers who fail.

$A'(f')$ Set of all subsets of suppliers who are undisrupted due to a unique event,$A'(f') = \{A'(f'_1), A'(f'_2), \ldots, A'(f'_s)\}$ $A'(f'_1)$ = Subset of undisrupted suppliers when one of S suppliers is disrupted; $A'(f'_1)$ has 6 elements with 5 un-disrupted suppliers in each
$A'(f'_2)$ = Subset of un-disrupted suppliers when any two of S suppliers fail; etc.

o_s Output flexibility index for supplier s

Decision Variables

X_s 1, if supplier s is selected; 0, else
Q_s Proportion of the total demand assigned to supplier s
q_s Compensation received from an un-disrupted supplier s

Objective

$$\mathrm{Min}(f_1) = \sum_{s=1}^{S} F_s X_s + \sum_{s=1}^{S} r_s\left(1 - d_s^{pb}\right) Q_s D + ELC, \tag{11.1}$$

where ELC (Expected Loss Cost) is given by

$$ELC = \{ELC^{su} + ELC^{se} + ELC^{uq}\} Dr' \text{ and}$$
$$ELC^{su} = p^{su}$$

$$\mathrm{ELC^{se}} = (1-p^{su})\left(\begin{array}{l}\left(\mathrm{I}_{\left(\sum_{i\in B(f_1)}\left(\sum_{s=1}^{ts_i}Q_s\right)_i-\sum_{j\in B'(f'_1)}\left(\sum_{s=1}^{ts_j}q_s\right)_j\ge 0\right)}\left(\sum_{i\in B(f_1)}\left(\sum_{s=1}^{ts_i}Q_s\right)_i-\sum_{j\in B'(f'_1)}\left(\sum_{s=1}^{ts_j}q_s\right)_j\right)\left(\sum\left(\prod_{i\in B(f_1)}p_i^{se}\prod_{j\in B'(f'_1)}\left(1-p_j^{se}\right)\right)\right)\right)\\ +\left(\mathrm{I}_{\left(\sum_{i\in B(f_2)}\left(\sum_{s=1}^{ts_i}Q_s\right)_i-\sum_{j\in B'(f'_2)}\left(\sum_{s=1}^{ts_j}q_s\right)_j\ge 0\right)}\left(\sum_{i\in B(f_2)}\left(\sum_{s=1}^{ts_i}Q_s\right)_i-\sum_{j\in B'(f'_2)}\left(\sum_{s=1}^{ts_j}q_s\right)_j\right)\left(\sum\left(\prod_{i\in B(f_2)}p_i^{se}\prod_{j\in B'(f'_2)}\left(1-p_j^{se}\right)\right)\right)\right)\\ +\cdots+\left(\mathrm{I}_{\left(\sum_{i\in B(f_L)}\left(\sum_{s=1}^{ts_i}Q_s\right)_i\ge 0\right)}\left(\sum_{i\in B(f_L)}\left(\sum_{s=1}^{ts_i}Q_s\right)_i\right)\left(\sum\left(\prod_{i\in B(f_L)}p_i^{se}\right)\right)\right)\quad \text{where } i\neq j\end{array}\right)$$

$$\mathrm{ELC^{uq}} = (1-\mathrm{p^{su}})\prod_{l=1}^{L}\left(1-\mathrm{p}_l^{se}\right)\times\left(\begin{array}{l}\left(\mathrm{I}_{\left(\sum_{m\in A(f_1)}(Q_s)_m-\sum_{n\in A'(f'_1)}(q_s)_n\ge 0\right)}\left(\sum_{m\in A(f_1)}(Q_s)_m-\sum_{n\in A'(f'_1)}(q_s)_n\right)\left(\sum\left(\prod_{m\in A(f_1)}\mathrm{p_m^{uq}}\prod_{n\in A'(f'_1)}\left(1-\mathrm{p_n^{uq}}\right)\right)\right)\right)+\\ \left(\mathrm{I}_{\left(\sum_{m\in A(f_2)}(Q_s)_m-\sum_{n\in A'(f'_2)}(q_s)_n\ge 0\right)}\left(\sum_{m\in A(f_2)}(Q_s)_m-\sum_{n\in A'(f'_2)}(q_s)_n\right)\left(\sum\left(\prod_{m\in A(f_2)}\mathrm{p_m^{uq}}\prod_{n\in A'(f'_2)}\left(1-\mathrm{p_n^{uq}}\right)\right)\right)\right)\\ +\cdots+\left(\mathrm{I}_{\left(\sum_{m\in A(f_L)}(Q_s)_m\ge 0\right)}\left(\sum_{m\in A(f_L)}(Q_s)_m\right)\left(\sum\left(\prod_{m\in A(f_L)}\mathrm{p_m^{uq}}\right)\right)\right)\quad \text{where m}\neq\text{n}\end{array}\right)$$

Constraints

$$\mathrm{Q_sD \le C_sX_s,\ \forall s} \tag{11.2}$$

$$\sum_{s=1}^{S}\mathrm{Q_s} = 1 \tag{11.3}$$

$$Q_s \geq Q_s^{min} \geq 0, \forall s \tag{11.4}$$

$$q_s \leq (C_s/D - Q_s)o_s, \forall s \tag{11.5}$$

The objective function defined in Eq. (11.1) minimizes the expected total cost that includes the supplier management cost, purchasing cost from the suppliers, and an expected loss to the manufacturer if a supplier disrupts (ELC). The loss due to a super, semi-super, and unique event is denoted as ELC^{su}, ELC^{se}, and ELC^{uq} respectively. To ensure a non-negative value for ELC an indicator function I_y is used in Eq. (11.1) following Meena et al. (2011) where $I_{(y)} = 1$ if (y) holds, 0 else. Equations (11.2) and (11.3) are the capacity and demand satisfaction constraints for the suppliers respectively. Equation (11.4) states that the portion of the total demand assigned to supplier *s* must not be less than the minimum order assigned to the same supplier. Each un-disrupted supplier can compensate a short fall up to an amount of $k_s = (C_s/D - Q_s)o_s$. Hence, the compensation received from a supplier who does not disrupt should be less or equal to the compensation potential for the supplier given in Eq. (11.5). The output flexibility index (o_s) in Eq. (11.5) refers to a supplier's ability to compensate for the shortfall should the other suppliers disrupt (Ruiz-Torres and Mahmoodi 2006). The output flexibility index could be measured based on suppliers' production, logistics capabilities and geographic proximity.

11.4 Proposed PSO

The steps of the proposed PSO are described below. The parameters of the proposed algorithms are swarm size (*N*), maximum number of iterations (*max_it*), time varying inertia weight (ω_t), acceleration coefficients (C_{1t} and C_{2t}) and random parameters (r_1 and r_2).

Step 1 Particle representation and Swarm initialization: In the PSO algorithm, each particle is a feasible allocation of demand to the suppliers. The position and velocity of each particle are initialized randomly. The length of a particle depends on the number of suppliers and each bit of a particle represents the fraction of demand assigned to a supplier. Figure 11.2 is an example of a particle with 2 suppliers, each sited in three regions. Supplier 1 located in Region 1 receives maximum allocation. A set of feasible particles represents the swarm.

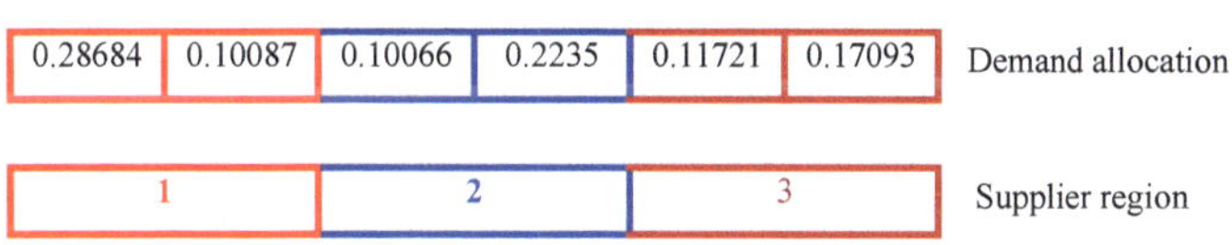

Fig. 11.2 Representation of a particle for SSOA problem

Step 2 Fitness evaluation: The fitness values of the particles are computed. The individual experience of the particle is captured in the pBest attribute that corresponds to the best performance attained by a particle in its flight. In the first iteration (t), the current position of particle $p_{i[t]}$ is set as the pBest particle $pBest_{i[t]}$. In subsequent iterations, $pBest_{i[t]}$ is replaced if a better fitness value is found. The best particle in the whole swarm is selected as the global best *gBest* ($g_{i[t]}$).

Step 3 Velocity and position update: The velocity and position update equations are used to update the velocity and position of each particle during the iterations. The velocity update relation is given in Eq. (11.6) with r_1 and r_2 uniformly distributed on (0, 1). The inertia weight ω_t controls the impact of the previous velocity $V_{i[t]}$ on the current velocity $V_{i[t+1]}$ and is allowed to decrease linearly with iteration from the initial value ω_1 to the final value ω_2 as shown in Eq. (11.7). This ensures global exploration of the search space at the initial stages and local exploration at later stages. C_{1t} is called the cognitive acceleration coefficient which represents the private thinking of a particle when comparing its current position to its own best. C_{2t} is called the social acceleration coefficient which denotes the social collaboration among the particles when comparing a particle's current position to that of the best particle. C_{1t} is allowed to decrease from its initial value of C_{1i} to a final value C_{1f} as shown in Eq. (11.8). C_{2t} is allowed to increase from its initial value of C_{2i} to a final value C_{2f} as shown in Eq. (11.9). The particle's current position $p_{i[t]}$ is updated with Eq. (11.10) and the particle then moves towards the new position $p_{i[t+1]}$. The particles are then evaluated for feasibility. Infeasible particles are repaired subject to the constraints on demand, capacity, and minimum order allocation. Equations (11.6–11.10) are defined following the work of Tripathi et al. (2007).

$$V_{i[t+1]} = \omega_t * V_{i[t]} + r_1 * C_{1t}\left(pBest_{i[t]} - P_{i[t]}\right) + r_2 * C_{2t}\left(gBest_{i[t]} - P_{i[t]}\right) \quad (11.6)$$

$$\omega_t = (\omega_1 - \omega_2)(\max\_it - t)/(\max\_it) + \omega_2 \quad (11.7)$$

$$C_{1t} = \left(C_{1f} - C_{1i}\right)(t/\max\_it) + C_{1i} \quad (11.8)$$

$$C_{2t} = \left(C_{2f} - C_{2i}\right)(t/\max\_it) + C_{2i} \quad (11.9)$$

$$P_{i[t+1]} = P_{i[t]} + V_{i[t+1]} \quad (11.10)$$

11.5 Illustrative Example

A manufacturer plans to procure materials from a set of suppliers. To avoid depending on a single supply region, the manufacturer decides to consider alternate suppliers from multiple regions. Scenarios are generated using simulated data as shown in Table 11.2 following the SSOA literature. The number of suppliers and their regions vary between (6, 12) and (3, 5) respectively. The total demand varies

Table 11.2 Scenarios generated using simulated data

Scenario	Number of regions	Number of suppliers in each region					Total number of suppliers	Total Demand
		1	2	3	4	5		
1	3	2	2	2	–	–	6	7000
2	3	3	3	2	–	–	8	8000
3	4	3	3	2	2	–	10	10,000
4	5	3	3	2	2	2	12	12,000

from 7000 to 12,000 units. The capacity of the suppliers is generated in the interval (1200, 3500). Supplier management cost is selected in the interval (1000, 3500). The unit purchase cost is drawn in the interval (12, 18). The loss per unit is set to vary between 2 and 4 times of the purchase cost. The minimum order quantity for any supplier is set at 10% of the total demand. All unit quantity discounts with three price breaks are considered following Meena and Sarmah (2013). The price discount varies from 5 to 25% of the base price and the order quantities for a price break is set to vary between 1.5 and 3 times the minimum order quantity. Table 11.3 gives the capacity, disruption likelihoods, output flexibility index of the suppliers, supplier management cost and unit purchase cost of the materials for Scenario 3. It is assumed that Region 1 has established suppliers with good market reputation and is the primary procurement source. The manufacturer intends to locate alternate suppliers from Regions 2, 3 and 4 as Region 1 is prone to disruption risk. It is assumed that the suppliers in Regions 3 and 4 are new and expensive. The suppliers in Regions 1 and 2 are located outside of the manufacturer's geographical proximity.

11.6 Results and Discussion

The proposed PSO and GA algorithms are coded in Matlab 7.1.0. The swarm size (*N*)/population (*N*′) and the maximum number of iterations (*max_it*) are set as 250 and 500, respectively. Based on the random trials, the inertia weight is set to vary linearly from 1.0 to 0.3 and the acceleration coefficients are set as $C_{1i} = 1.5$, $C_{1f} = 0.5$, $C_{2i} = 0.5$, $C_{2f} = 1.5$. Tables 11.4 and 11.5 show the optimal solutions for the scenarios using PSO and GA, respectively. From the results of scenarios 1 and 2, the demand is assigned to all suppliers located in Regions 1, 2 and 3 in order to avoid the loss due to disruption. Supplier 1 located in Region 1 is assigned more than 25% of the total demand in all scenarios except Scenario 2 solved by GA as the purchase cost is a minimum. Suppliers located in Regions 4 and 5 are not used in Scenarios 4 as the purchase cost is high and for the restriction of minimum order quantity. For Scenarios 3, supplier 3 of Region 2 (x_2^3) is assigned 20% of the total demand as the unique event disruption likelihood is less albeit at a higher purchase cost.

Table 11.3 Data for Scenario 3

Supplier		Supplier capacity	Disruption likelihood of event			Output flexibility index	Supplier management cost ($)	Base purchase price/unit ($)	Price break quantities (multiple of minimum order quantity)			Associated discount (%)		
			Super	Semi-super	Unique									
Region 1	x_1^1	3500	0.010	0.030	0.05	0.7	2000	12	2	2.5	3	15	20	25
	x_1^2	3000			0.15	0.8	1000	14	2	2.5	3	12	15	18
	x_1^3	2500			0.10	0.6	2500	15	1.5	2	2.5	15	17	20
Region 2	x_2^1	2200		0.025	0.10	0.8	2000	15	2	2.5	3	15	20	25
	x_2^2	2500			0.08	0.7	1500	17	2	2.5	3	12	15	18
	x_2^3	2200			0.05	0.5	2500	16	1.5	2	2.5	15	17	20
Region 3	x_3^1	2000		0.020	0.06	0.6	1200	18	1.5	2	2.5	18	20	25
	x_3^2	1800			0.03	0.5	3500	17	1.5	2	2.5	5	7	9
Region 4	x_4^1	1800		0.020	0.05	0.4	2500	18	1.5	1.75	2	5	10	12
	x_4^2	1500			0.04	0.4	2400	15	1.5	1.75	2	5	10	12

Table 11.4 Optimal solution for scenarios using PSO

Scenarios	Demand allocation to suppliers												SC	PC	ELC	ETC ($)
	x_1^1	x_1^2	x_1^3	$x_{2\cdot}^1$	x_2^2	$x_{2\cdot}^3$	$x_{3\cdot}^1$	$x_{3\cdot}^2$	$x_{4\cdot}^1$	$x_{4\cdot}^2$	x_5^1	x_5^2				
1	0.28684	0.10087	–	0.10066	0.2235	–	0.11721	0.17093	–	–	–	–	12,700	84,710	41,035	138,445
2	0.25367	0.10354	0.1	0.10204	0.10342	0.10048	0.13028	0.10657	–	–	–	–	16,200	103,106	47,574	166,880
3	0.27336	0.10659			0.10416	0.20081	0.10204	0	0	0	–	–	12,700	121,244	62,568	196,512
4	0.27691	0.10312	0.10271	0.10248	0.10417	0.10859	0.10202	0.1	0	0	0	0	15,000	143,938	83,503	242,441

Table 11.5 Optimal solution for scenarios using GA

Scenarios	Demand allocation to suppliers												SC	PC	ELC	ETC ($)
	x_1^1	x_1^2	x_1^3	x_2^1	x_2^2	x_2^3	x_3^1	x_3^2	x_4^1	x_4^2	x_5^1	x_5^2				
1	0.30176	0.10072	–	0.10103	0.21722	–	0.10784	0.17143	–	–	–	–	12,700	84,068	41,427	138,195
2	0.20046	0.10205	0.10091	0.10531	0.10042	0.1577	0.10796	0.12512	–	–	–	–	16,200	103,492	46,806	166,498
3	0.28677	0.10015	0.10029	0.10029	0.10021	0.21186	0.10045	0	0	0	–	–	12,700	120,656	61,698	195,054
4	0.28997	0.10071	0.10045	0.10161	0.10227	0.10103	0.10071	0.10324	0	0	0	0	15,000	140,514	82,925	238,439

11.6.1 Comparison of PSO and GA Results

The parameters of GA are population size, maximum number of iterations, cross-over and mutation probabilities. The strings are initialized as described in Sect. 11.4. The population size and the number of iterations in GA are the same as the proposed PSO. Roulette wheel selection, segment based cross over and a mutation operator are used (Gen and Cheng 1997). In roulette wheel selection a fitter chromosome has a large chance to be reproduced into the next generation (Khojasteh-Ghamari 2012). Traditionally, crossover and mutation probabilities are selected in the range (0.6, 1.0) and (0.05, 0.2), respectively. The cross over and mutation probabilities for the GA are set as 0.7 and 0.2, respectively.

These values are set based on preliminary computations. An illustration of the segment based cross over operator for six suppliers located in three regions is shown in Fig. 11.3. A binary mask is generated and its length is equal to the number of regions. The first parent will transfer its genetic material to the offspring if '0' occurs in the binary mask. Similarly parent 2 will transfer its genetic material to the offspring if '1' occurs in the binary mask. This segment based cross over operator tends to preserve good gene segments of both parents and generate one off spring (Altiparmak et al. 2006). An illustration of a mutation operator is shown in Fig. 11.4. A binary mask is randomly generated and a decision about which segment will be mutated is reached. Selected segments are then mutated. Infeasible

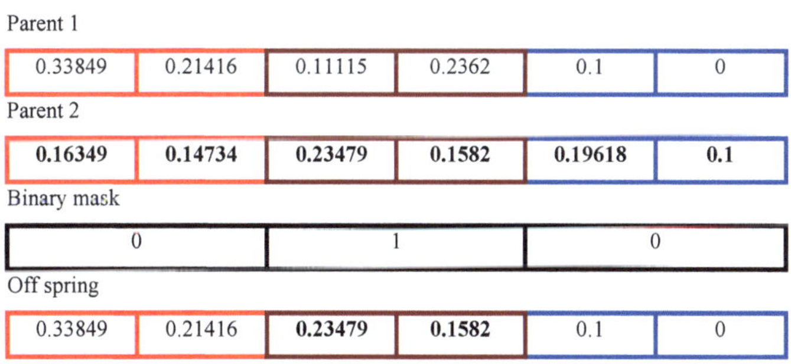

Fig. 11.3 Illustration of segment based cross over operator

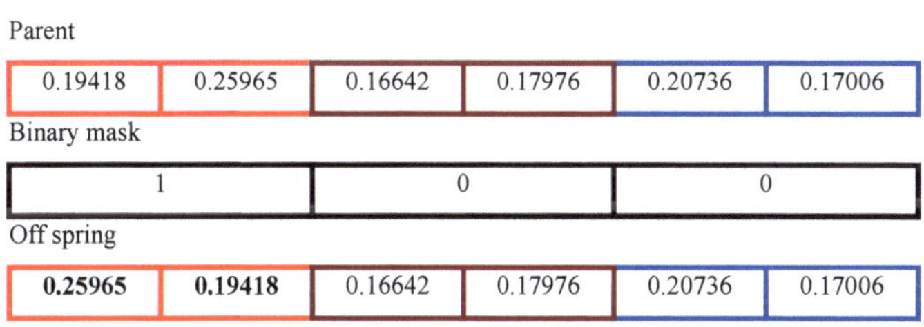

Fig. 11.4 Illustration of mutation operator

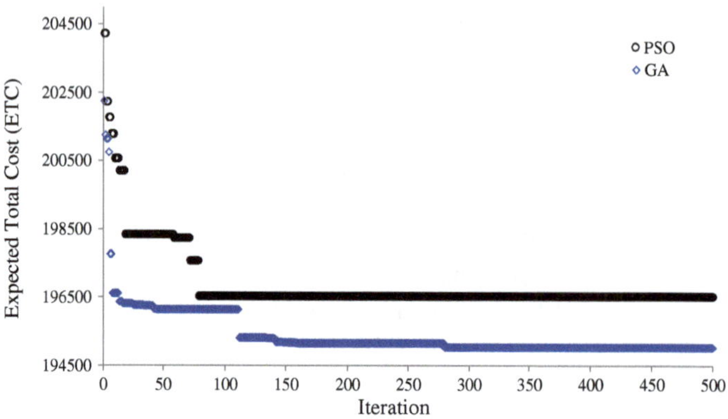

Fig. 11.5 Convergence of solutions using PSO and GA for Scenario 3

strings generated after cross over and mutation are repaired. The convergence of solutions for Scenario 3 is shown in Fig. 11.5. It is observed that PSO converges to the optimal solution in less iteration compared to the GA. The deviation in PSO solution quality is found to be less than 1%.

Sensitivity analysis: A sensitivity analysis is performed on Scenarios 3 to study the effect of variations in disruption likelihood, output flexibility and price discount offered by the suppliers on the ETC.

Disruption likelihood: The disruption likelihood of the suppliers is varied at four levels while the other parameters presented in Table 11.3 are kept constant. The individual and combined effect of mis-estimating the failure likelihood of super event (p_{su}), semi-super event (p_{se}), and unique event (p_{uq}) on ETC are analyzed. Figure 11.6 shows that the combined effect of all events yields a larger deviation in ETC. The disruption likelihood of a unique event has more impact on ETC than the other two events. Larger deviations in the ETC are observed when the error in estimating the disruption likelihood is more than 50% in either direction. Further, underestimating the disruption likelihood leads to a slightly larger deviation than over-estimating the failure likelihood.

Output flexibility: The output flexibility index of the suppliers is varied at four levels while the other parameters reported in Table 11.3 are kept constant. The ETC is robust to changes in output flexibility as demand is allocated to multiple suppliers to minimize the expected loss under disruption. The deviation in ETC is slightly higher when the output flexibility of suppliers is reduced by 25% as shown in Fig. 11.7.

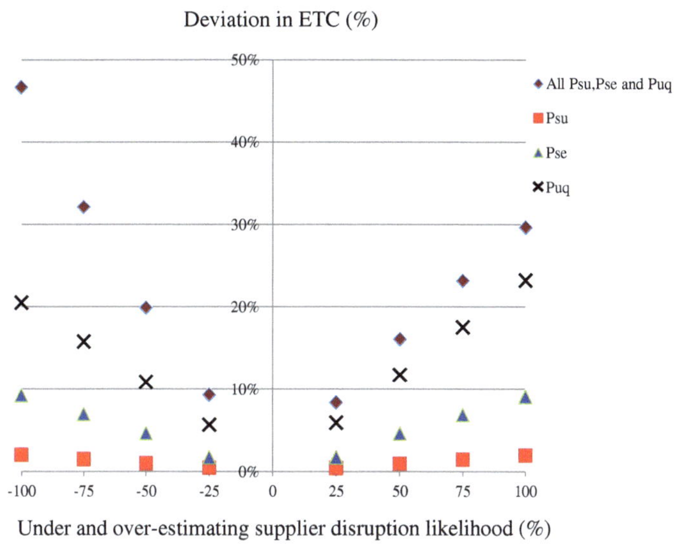

Fig. 11.6 Effect of mis-estimating supplier disruption likelihood on the ETC

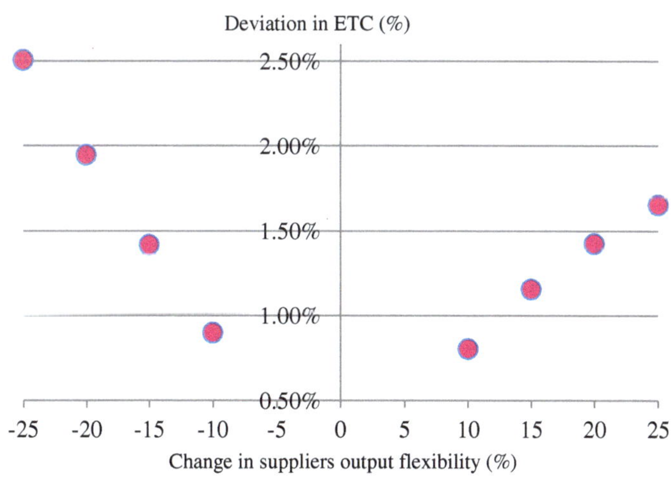

Fig. 11.7 Effect of suppliers output flexibility on the ETC

Price discounts: The price discount offered by the suppliers is varied at four levels while the other parameters reported in Table 11.3 are kept constant. The ETC is less sensitive to variations in price discounts as shown in Fig. 11.8. This is due to the higher allocation of the total demand (around 50%) to suppliers x_1^1 and x_2^3.

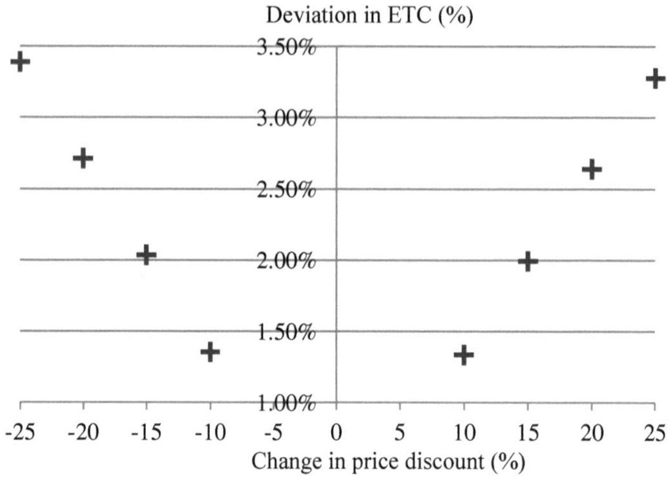

Fig. 11.8 Effect of price discounts on the ETC

11.7 Conclusions

Sourcing under supply disruption risk is an important research topic and needs attention. We developed a MILP model to select suppliers and allocate order quantity under disruption risk. Four scenarios were generated using simulated data and PSO was used to minimize the expected total cost. The results were compared against a GA generated set of results. The results suggest that to minimize the ETC, suppliers from different regions who are less prone to disruption and offering minimum purchase cost should be assigned greater demand. Sensitivity analysis on ETC shows that the combined effect of mis-estimating the disruption likelihood of super, semi-super, and unique events yields a larger deviation in ETC. The ETC is found to be less sensitive to the variation in the output flexibility of the suppliers when multiple suppliers are selected. The ETC is less sensitive to a variation in price discounts when more demand is assigned to a few suppliers. We assumed that un-disrupted suppliers have buffer capacity and will compensate the shortfall at no extra cost. In practice, suppliers may charge a premium to supply additional quantities. Several extensions to this work are possible. Our model could be extended to include stochastic demand with multiple objectives considering service level. A model for a multi-tier supply network under disruption could be also developed.

Acknowledgements The first author acknowledges the National Institute of Technology, Trichy, India for providing a travel grant to visit the second author under the Technical Education Quality Improvement Programme (TEQIP-II), in which this work was done. The authors thank the editor for the constructive comments.

References

Altiparmak, F., Gen, M., Lin, L., & Paksoy, T. (2006). A genetic algorithm approach for multi-objective optimization of supply chain networks. *Computers & Industrial Engineering, 5,* 197–216.

Berger, P. D., Gerstenfeld, A., & Zeng, A. Z. (2004). How many suppliers are best? A decision-analysis approach. *Omega, 32,* 9–15.

Chai, J., Liu, J. N. K., & Nagi, E. W. T. (2013). Application of decision making techniques in supplier selection: A systematic literature review. *Expert Systems with Applications, 40,* 3872–3885.

Che, Z. H. (2012). A particle swarm optimization algorithm for solving unbalanced supply chain planning problems. *Applied Soft Computing, 12,* 1279–1287.

Chopra, S., & Sodhi, M. S. (2014). Reducing the risk of supply chain disruptions. *MIT Sloan Management Review, 55,* 73–80.

Gen, M., & Cheng, R. (1997). *Genetic algorithms and engineering design.* USA: Wiley.

Goldberg, D. E. (1989). *Genetic algorithms in search, optimization and machine learning.* Reading, MA: Addison-Wesley Publishing.

Heckmann, I., Comes, T., & Nickel, S. (2015). A critical review on supply chain risk—Definition, measure and modeling. *Omega, 52,* 119–132.

Kamali, A., Fatemi Ghomi, S. M. T., & Jolai, F. (2011). A multi-objective quantity discount and joint optimization model for coordination of a single-buyer multi-vendor supply chain. *Computers & Mathematics with Applications, 62,* 3251–3269.

Kennedy, J., Eberhart, R. C. (1995). Particle swarm optimization. In *Proceedings of IEEE International Conference on Neural Networks (Perth, Australia)* (Vol. IV, pp. 1942–1948).

Khojasteh-Ghamari, Y. (2012). Warehouse management: Productivity improvement in automated storage and retrieval systems. In R. Manzini (Ed.), *Warehousing in the global supply chain* (pp. 233–260). London: Springer.

Knemeyer, A. M., Zinn, W., & Eroglu, C. (2009). Proactive planning for catastrophic events in supply chains. *J Oper Manage, 27,* 141–153.

Marchese K, Paramasivam S (2013) The ripple effects how manufacturing and retail executives view the growing challenge of supply chain risk. http://www2.deloitte.com/content/dam/Deloitte/global/Documents/Process-and-Operations/gx-operations-consulting-the-ripple-effect-041213.pdf. Accessed on 21 May 2014.

Matsuo, H. (2015). Implications of the Tohoku earthquake for Toyota's coordination mechanism: Supply chain disruption of automotive semiconductors. *Int J Prod Econ, 161,* 217–227.

Meena, P. L., Sarmah, S. P., & Sarkar, A. (2011). Sourcing decisions under risks of catastrophic event disruptions. *Transp Res Part E, 47,* 1058–1074.

Meena, P. L., & Sarmah, S. P. (2013). Multiple sourcing under supplier failure risk and quantity discount: A genetic algorithm approach. *Transp Res Part E, 50,* 84–97.

Meena, P. L., & Sarmah, S. P. (2014). Mitigating the risks of supply disruption under stochastic demand. *Int J Manage Sci Eng Manage, 9,* 157–168.

Poli, R. (2008). Analysis of the publications on the applications of particle swarm optimization. *J Artif Evol Appl, 8,* 1–10.

PrasannaVenkatesan, S., & Kumanan, S. (2012). Multi-objective supply chain sourcing strategy design under risk using PSO and simulation. *Int J Adv Manuf Technol, 61,* 325–337.

Ruiz-Torres, A. J., & Mohmoodi, F. (2006). A supplier allocation model considering delivery failure, maintenance and supplier cycle costs. *Int J Prod Econ, 103,* 755–766.

Ruiz-Torres, A. J., & Mohmoodi, F. (2007). The optimal number of suppliers considering the cost of individual supplier failures. *Omega, 35,* 104–115.

Ruiz-Torres, A. J., Mohmoodi, F., & Zeng, A. Z. (2013). Supplier selection model with contingency planning for supplier failures. *Comp Indus Eng, 66,* 374–382.

Sawik, T. (2014). Joint supplier selection and scheduling of customer orders under disruption risks: single vs. dual sourcing. *Omega, 43,* 83–95.

Sarkar, A., & Mohapatra, P. K. J. (2009). Determining the optimal size of supply base with the consideration of risks of supply disruptions. *Int J Prod Econ, 119,* 122–135.

Tripathi, P. K., Bandyopadhyay, S., & Pal, S. K. (2007). Multi-objective particle swarm optimization with time variant inertia and acceleration coefficients. *Inf Sci, 177,* 5033–5049.

Zeng AA, Berger PD, Gerstenfeld A (2005) Managing the supply side-risks in supply chains: Taxonomies, processes and examples of decision making modeling In: Geunes J, Akcali E, Pardalos PM, Romeijn HE, Shen ZJ (eds) Applications of supply chain management and e-commerce research. Springer, Berlin, pp 141–160.

Chapter 12
Design and Evaluation of Global Supply Chain Considering Disruption Risk

Yasutaka Kainuma

Abstract With the rapid advancement of businesses into overseas markets in recent years, the scope of supply chain configuration is expanding globally. Supply chain disruption due to natural disasters such as the 2011 Great East Japan Earthquake and the flooding in Thailand has become a serious problem. Under the impact of these natural disasters, risk evaluation has been recognized as an important element of supply chain management. In this chapter, we consider disruption risk and develop a model by incorporating supplier decentralization that assumes a global supply chain spanning two countries and consisting of three levels: supplier, manufacturer, and customer. We assume three types of disruption of varying frequency and effectiveness, generated by random numbers by the Poisson process. We assess the global supply chain designed by verifying the effectiveness of supplier decentralization in response to disruptions.

12.1 Introduction

The assumption that whatever is manufactured can be sold is no longer true. Today, the manufacturing industry needs to determine optimal output and supply levels for production efficiency because of factors such as diversification of consumer needs, globalization of business competition, and decreasing life cycle of products entering into the market. Up until now, the manufacturing industry aimed to improve production efficiency by shortening lead time and reducing costs through efficient management of the supply chain, from raw material procurement to manufacture, distribution, and sales.

The breakdown in production following the Great East Japan Earthquake and the floods in Thailand in 2011 was inevitable, especially for automobile and semiconductor manufacturers. This disrupted the supply chain for these manufacturers,

Y. Kainuma (✉)
Faculty of System Design, Tokyo Metropolitan University, Hino, Tokyo, Japan
e-mail: kainuma@tmu.ac.jp

Y. Khojasteh (ed.), *Supply Chain Risk Management*,
DOI 10.1007/978-981-10-4106-8_12

seriously affecting not only Japan but the whole world (METI 2014). Thus, supply chain disruption became a serious issue at the time, but it was supposedly due to the fact that supply chain management stressed efficiency and aimed at shorter lead times and lower costs, and risk management was not seriously considered.

However, with increasing globalization of business, the environment of supply chain management is transforming in a significant way. This is because one must take into account not only certain new factors, such as natural disasters, exchange rate fluctuations, and the uncertainty of demand, but also the unique components of a global supply chain, such as political risks, corporation taxes, and transfer prices.

In addition to optimizing the supply chain used so far, this chapter aims at designing a global supply chain model incorporating disruption risks. We also conduct numerical experiments using the model designed, and obtain insight about disruption risk reduction.

The remainder of this chapter is as follows. Section 12.2 reviews the literature and discusses some related published works. A global supply chain model is designed and developed in Sect. 12.3. Numerical experiments are conducted in Sect. 12.4. Section 12.5 presents the results, and Sect. 12.6 concludes the chapter.

12.2 Literature Review

Vidal and Goetschalckx (2001) determined the traffic, transfer price, and shipping cost distribution ratio for global supply chains, and proposed a determination process to maximize post-tax profits. Transfer price is the price applied for transactions within a given company. By skillfully using this transfer price, it becomes possible to transfer profits from one country to another. As a result, by gathering pre-tax profits into countries with low corporate tax rates, it is possible to maximize profits for the entire company.

Figure 12.1 shows categorized risks considered in the recent 50 studies concerning supply chain risk management. Of these, 87 risks could be considered repeated; they can be categorized, in descending order of repetition, as disruption risk, supply risk, demand risk, and operating risk. Furthermore, Liu and Anna (2011) considered the conceivable risks in the supply chain: (1) foreign exchange risks, (2) quality risks, (3) production interruption risks, and (4) supplier debt default risk. By focusing on foreign exchange risk, they developed determination models for in-house manufacturing and outsourcing. From the viewpoint of creating a supply chain, there is a great number of risks other than the ones considered by Liu and Anna (2011). Christopher and Peck (2004) classified sources of supply chain risk into four risks (supply risk, process risk, demand risk, and control risk) and identified the relationship among them as depicted in Fig. 12.2.

Chopra and Sodhi (2004) broadly categorized risks into delays, disruptions, forecast inaccuracies, systems breakdowns, intellectual property breaches, procurement failures, inventory problems, and capacity issues. Sheffi and Rice (2005) indicated that the significant disruption has a typical profile in terms of its effect on

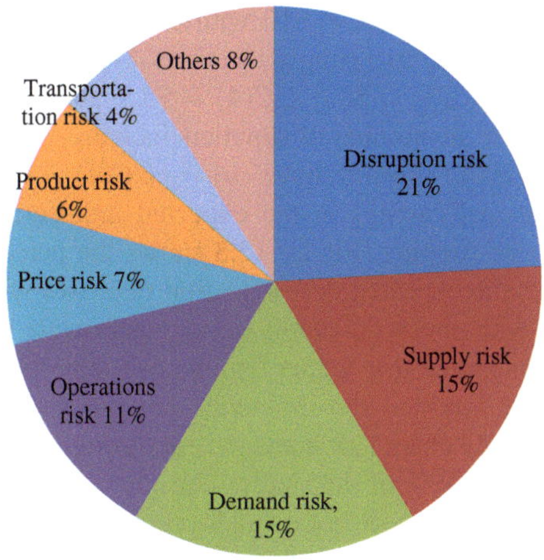

Fig. 12.1 Classification of supply chain risks

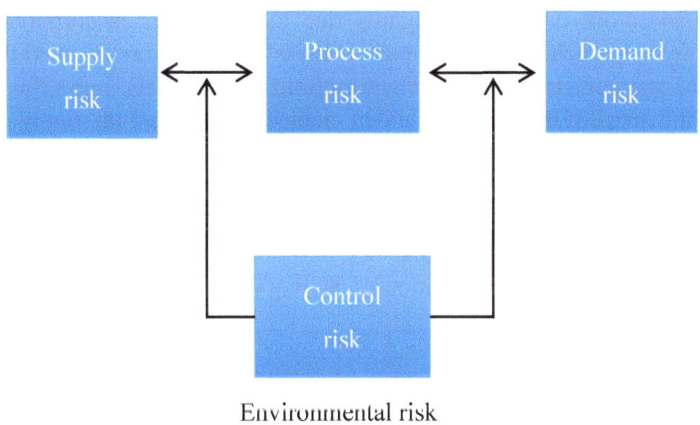

Fig. 12.2 Sources of supply chain risk (Christopher and Peck 2004)

company performance. They pointed out that the nature of the disruption and dynamics of the company response can be divided into eight phases as follows: preparation, disruptive event, first response, initial impact, time of full impact, preparation for recovery, recovery and long-term impact.

Tang and Tomlin (2008) conducted a study on flexibility in supply chain risk mitigation. They assumed five positions $C_j (j = 1, 2, \ldots, 5)$ with uncertain supply costs ($\$5, \$10, \$15$), generated by uniform random numbers. In this case, the expected cost is $UC(1) = 1/3(5+10+15) = \$10$ with one supply location and $UC(2) = E(\mathrm{Min}\{C_1, C_2\}) = \$7.8$ with two supply locations. With the same calculations, the expected cost comes to $UC(3) = \$6.6$, $UC(4) = \$5.9$, and $UC(5) = \$5.6$, with further reduction possible if the number of suppliers increases.

Tang and Tomlin (2008) showed that $V(n) = (UC(1) - UC(n))/UC(1)$, where $V(n)$ is the percentage of savings in the expected unit cost by ordering from n suppliers instead of one supplier. Figure 12.3 shows the percentage of saving unit cost. From the figure, the expected cost reduction rate rises with an increase in the number of suppliers with uncertain supply costs, but because this result produces a concave line, they concluded that a small number of suppliers is sufficient.

Sodhi et al. (2012) reported the difference among researchers' opinions and future directions of supply chain risk management through a literature review and a survey. As a result, about 50% of the studies considered the risk of natural disaster and fire, which have a big impact but a small probability to occur.

Considering the unique components of global supply chains, Kubo (2006) covered such things as (1) the great uncertainty of demand and foreign exchange, (2) the risk of disasters or accidents such as terrorism and flooding, (3) product supply and production considerations such as import taxes and import substitution rates, and (4) profit distribution legality due to differences in corporate tax. He demonstrated approaches based on each of these factors and researched the current status and issues of global supply chain optimization models. Lee (2004) defined agility as the speedily reaction to sudden changes in demand or supply.

Cui (2013) determined that in order to remove supply chain vulnerability, supply chain resilience (SCR) is necessary. He carried out a systematic analysis of supply chain risk, investigated supply chain vulnerability, classified abilities necessary to implement SCR, performed case analyses, and presented a decision-making model for operational strategic determination of SCR implementation.

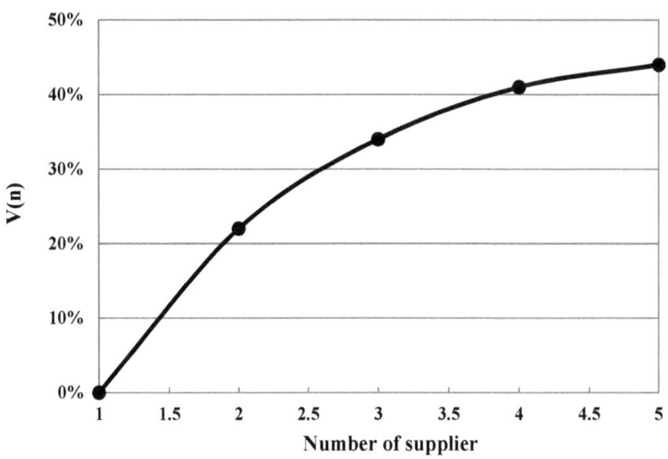

Fig. 12.3 Flexibility by multi-suppliers (Tang and Tomlin 2008)

12.3 The Model

12.3.1 Model Design

According to the relevant studies, many risks need to be considered in a global supply chain, but this chapter focuses only on disruption risk, and designs a model that takes into account supplier decentralization for risk response. Figure 12.4 shows the model, which considers supplier decentralization.

This chapter supposes a global supply chain that spans two countries, a developed and a developing country, and consists of three levels: supplier, manufacturer, and customer. In both cases, we assume one manufacturer location and one customer location, with two locations possible for suppliers only. Of the suppliers s_1, s_2, s_3, s_4, suppliers s_1, s_3 are located in the developed country and s_2, s_4 are located in the developing country. Similarly, manufacturers are m_1, m_2, customers are c_1, c_2, with m_1, c_1 being a manufacturer and customer located in the developed country, and m_2, c_2 being a manufacturer and customer in the developing country.

12.3.2 Notations

The following notations are used in the proposed model.

Sets

S set of all suppliers s ($s \in S$)
M set of all manufacturers m ($m \in M$)
C set of all customers c ($c \in C$).

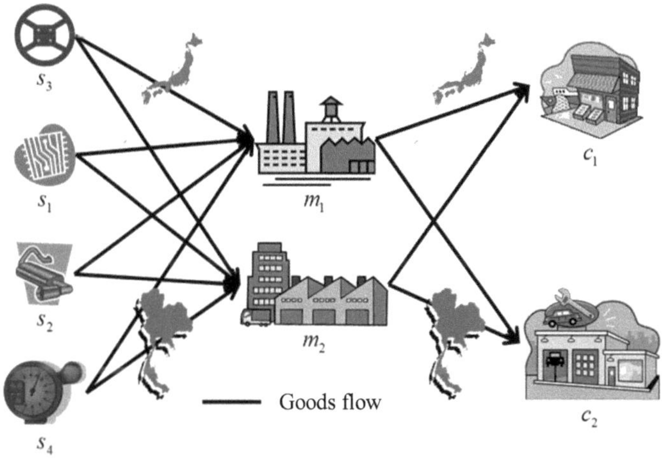

Fig. 12.4 Supply Chain Risk Model

Parameters

CAP_{st}	potential supply from supplier s in period t
CAP_{mt}	potential supply from manufacturer m in period t
D_{ct}	demand from customer c in period t
TC_{sm}	shipping costs from supplier s to manufacturer m
TC_{mc}	shipping costs from manufacturer m to customer c
SP_{sm}	sales price from supplier s to manufacturer m
SP_{mc}	sales price from manufacturer m to customer c
SC_m	inventory costs of manufacturer m
PC_s	supply costs of supplier s
PC_m	manufacturing costs of manufacturer m
FC_s	fixed costs of supplier s
FC_m	fixed costs of manufacturer m
CT_s	corporate tax rate of supplier s
CT_m	corporate tax rate of manufacturer m
IT_m	import tax rate of manufacturer m
E_{st}	exchange rate concerning supplier s in period t
E_{mt}	exchange rate concerning manufacturer m in period t
CL_c	penalty for unmet demand for customer c
T	target period.

Variables

x_{smt}	amount of supply sent from supplier s to manufacturer m in period t
y_{mct}	amount of supply sent from manufacturer m to customer c in period t
z_{mt}	inventory level at manufacturer m in period t
n_{ct}	unmet demand for customer c in period t
w_s^+	pre-tax profit of supplier s (when positive)
w_s^-	pre-tax profit of supplier s (when negative)
w_m^+	pre-tax profit of manufacturer m (when positive)
w_m^-	pre-tax profit of manufacturer m (when negative).

12.3.3 Formulation

In this section, we formulate the proposed model with the objective function of maximizing profit. The three terms in Eq. (12.1) below represent supplier's pre-tax profit, manufacturer's pre-tax profit, and the penalty for unmet customer demand, respectively. The pre-tax profit of supplier s is w_s^+, w_s^-, and that of manufacturer m is w_m^+, w_m^-. Since the pre-tax profit of the supplier is $w_s^+ > 0, w_s^- = 0$ when positive, and $w_s^+ = 0, w_s^- > 0$ when negative, thus it can be solved as a non-negative variable, because the model allows for appropriate levy of corporate tax.

Furthermore, the equality constraints related to the supplier's and manufacturer's pre-tax profits are demonstrated in Eqs. (12.2) and (12.3), respectively. Constraints related to the volume of demand are shown in Eq. (12.4), and those related to potential supply quantity are given in Eqs. (12.5) and (12.6). Constraints related to inventory and output preservation are given in Eq. (12.7). Those related to unmet demand that occurs when supply is low relative to demand are shown in formula (12.8). Equality constraints on each variable are shown in formula (12.9).

$$\begin{aligned} Maximize\,profit = & \sum_{s\in S}\{(1-CT_s)w_s^+ - w_s^-\} \\ & + \sum_{m\in M}\{(1-CT_m)w_m^+ - w_m^-\} - \sum_{t=1}^{T}\sum_{c\in C} CL_c n_{ct} \end{aligned} \tag{12.1}$$

Subject to

$$w_s^+ - w_s^- = \sum_{t=1}^{T}\sum_{m\in M}\left(\frac{SP_{sm}}{E_{st}}x_{smt}\right) - \sum_{t=1}^{T}\sum_{m\in M}\left\{\frac{(PC_s + TC_{sm})}{E_{st}}x_{smt}\right\} - FC_s \tag{12.2}$$

$$\begin{aligned} w_m^+ - w_m^- = & \sum_{t=1}^{T}\sum_{c\in C}\left(\frac{SP_{mc}}{E_{mt}}y_{mct}\right) - \sum_{t=1}^{T}\sum_{s\in S}\left\{\frac{(1+IT_m)SP_{sm}}{E_{mt}}x_{smt}\right\} \\ & - \sum_{t=1}^{T}\sum_{c\in C}\left\{\frac{(PC_m + TC_{mc})}{E_{mt}}y_{mct}\right\} - \sum_{t=1}^{T}\left(\frac{SC_m}{E_{mt}}z_{mt}\right) - FC_m \end{aligned} \tag{12.3}$$

$$\sum_{m\in M} y_{mc(t-2)} \le D_{ct} \tag{12.4}$$

$$\sum_{s\in S} x_{smt} \le CAP_{st} \tag{12.5}$$

$$\sum_{m\in M} y_{mct} \le CAP_{mt} \tag{12.6}$$

$$z_{mt} = z_{m(t-1)} + \sum_{s\in S} x_{sm(t-2)} - \sum_{c\in C} y_{mct} \tag{12.7}$$

$$n_{ct} = D_{ct} - \sum_{m\in M} y_{mc(t-2)} \tag{12.8}$$

$$x_{smt}, y_{mct}, z_{mt}, w_s^+, w_s^-, w_m^+, w_m^- \ge 0 \tag{12.9}$$

12.4 Numerical Experiments

12.4.1 Disruption Occurrence

We generated disruptions through random numbers using Poisson process to hypothesize that they seldom occur. Regarding their frequency and effect, we assumed three types of disruption. We assumed that they occur with probabilities of once in 25 periods, once in 50 periods, or once in 100 periods, each with a different impact level.

12.4.2 Recovery from Disruption

Regarding recovery from a disruption, we set ranked recovery rates of 0, 10, 40, and 70% for the potential supply in normal times, as shown in Table 12.1. For each recovery rate, the period of recovery varies, in the descending order of disruption frequency, from 1 ± 1, to 2 ± 1, and to 4 ± 1. The interval from disruption to recovery is determined as one third of the probability of the respective uniform random numbers, regardless of frequency of occurrence. We can construct a more realistic model not only by incorporating disruptions but also by making the disruption period probabilistic. We considered the scale of disruption damage by setting short disruption periods with a higher frequency and long disruption periods with a lower frequency, as shown in Table 12.1.

12.4.3 Establishment of Parameters

For the proposed model, we carry out numerical experiments using the parameters given in Table 12.2. We generate demand D_{ct} from customer c in period t using random numbers by normal distribution given the assumption that the demand in the developed country is higher than that in the developing country. Furthermore, we set the parameter values for each cost low, assuming that the products can be made less expensive in the developing country than in the developed country.

Concerning the exchange rates in each period, the rate of the developing country's currency relative to the developed country's one is shown in Fig. 12.5. The exchange rates were generated using uniform random numbers. We performed numerical experiments by dividing the suppliers into four scenarios. The scenarios are shown in Table 12.3.

Table 12.1 Period of recovery from disruption

Recovery rate	0%	10%	40%	70%
Once in 25 periods	1 ± 1	1 ± 1	1 ± 1	1 ± 1
Once in 50 periods	2 ± 1	2 ± 1	2 ± 1	2 ± 1
Once in 100 periods	4 ± 1	4 ± 1	4 ± 1	4 ± 1

Table 12.2 Respective parameters

	Developed country	Developing country
CAP_{st}	700	600
CAP_{mt}	800	700
D_{ct}	$N(500, 10)$	$N(400, 8)$
TC_{sm}	20	8
TC_{mc}	30	12
SP_{sm}	80	27
SP_{mc}	165	55
SC_s	15	5
PC_s	10	3
PC_m	25	8
FC_s	600,000	400,000
FC_m	600,000	400,000
CT_s	0.35	0.25
IT_m	0.05	0.03
CL_c	150	150
T	200	200

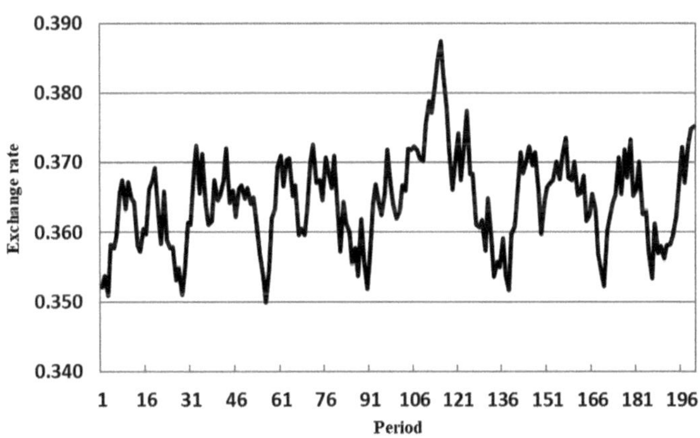

Fig. 12.5 Exchange rate of the developing country relative to the developed country

Table 12.3 Experimental scenarios

Scenarios	Developed country suppliers	Developing country suppliers
1	1 location	1 location
2	2 locations	1 location
3	1 location	2 locations
4	2 locations	2 locations

Because we use a method that probabilistically determines both disruption occurrence and period, we repeat the experiment 20 times in each scenario. Using the average of these experiment results, we verify the effectiveness of supplier decentralization by comparing the objective function values in each scenario.

12.5 Experimental Results and Observations

The results for three types of disruption of varying frequency in Scenarios 1 through 4 are depicted in Fig. 12.6. As it can be seen in the figure, the post-tax profit rose each time when the number of supplier locations increased from two to three and to four.

Figure 12.7 shows an example of the transition in potential supply and unmet demand in cases of a 1-in-25 disruption occurrence. It follows that disruptions occur

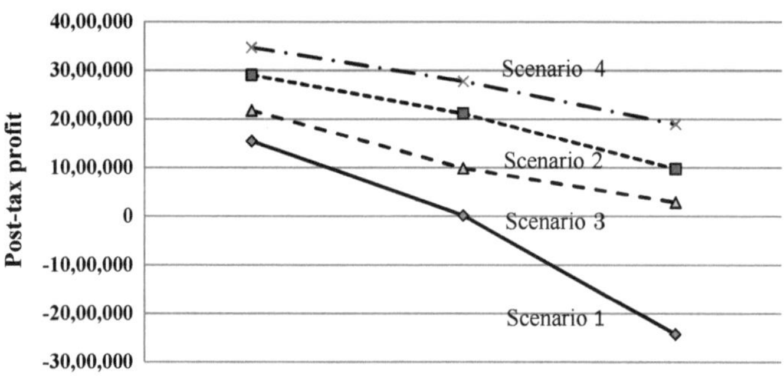

Fig. 12.6 Post-tax profit by frequency of occurrence

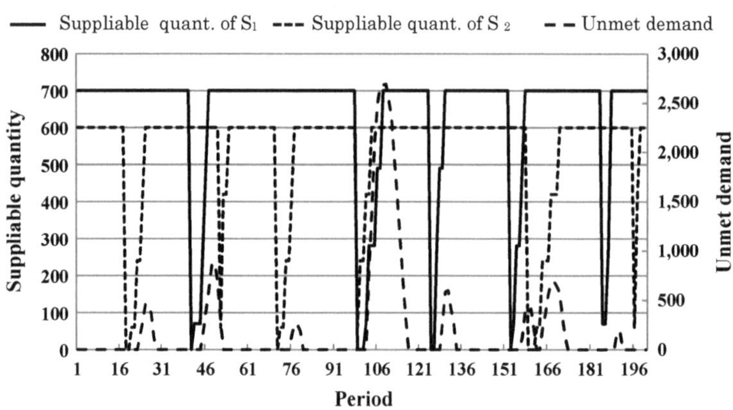

Fig. 12.7 Potential supply with a 1-in-25 disruption

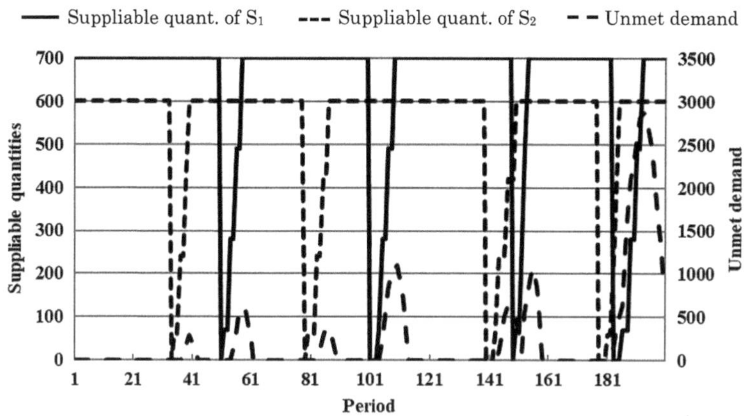

Fig. 12.8 Potential supply with a 1-in-50 disruption

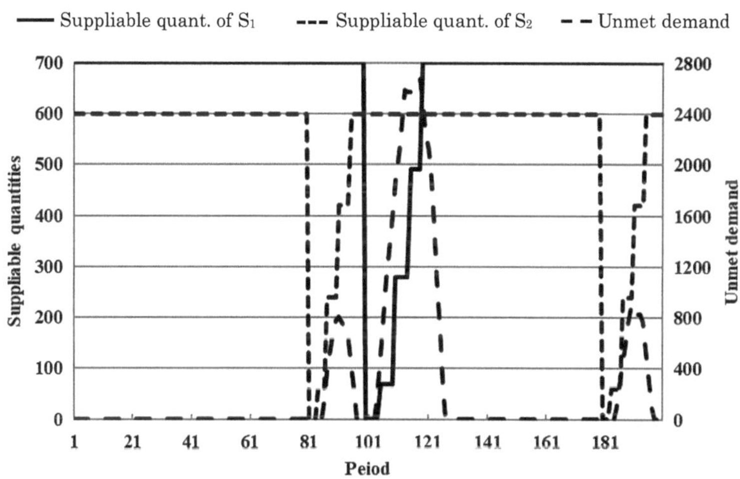

Fig. 12.9 Potential supply with a 1-in-100 disruption

eight times for each of developed and developing countries suppliers. In this case, when a disruption occurred at the supplier location, the effect would reach the customer four periods later because we set the lead time between each location (supplier-manufacturer, manufacturer-customer) to one period. Consequently, we can verify from the experiment results that an unmet demand occurs belatedly. Figure 12.8 shows a case with a 1-in-50 disruption occurrence, and Fig. 12.9 with a 1-in-100 disruption occurrence. As Figs. 12.7, 12.8 and 12.9 show, the unmet demand from one disruption occurrence grows larger in Figs. 12.7, 12.8 and 12.9.

From the results obtained by the numerical experiments, we can confirm the effectiveness of supplier decentralization in reducing penalties for unmet demand.

Furthermore, the frequency of occurrence is low when large-scale, high-impact disruptions in the supply chain are assumed leading to confirm that strategies to decentralize suppliers are indispensable.

12.6 Conclusions

In this chapter, we designed a global supply chain model based on the current conditions of advancing business globalization considering disruption risk. We investigated three types of disruption of varying frequency and impact, and compared post-tax profits depending on the occurrence of disruption. Through numerical experiments, we showed that profits increase when suppliers are decentralized, which supports the effectiveness of decentralization policy. Moreover, we showed that supplier decentralization is even more effective when disruption frequency is low and the impact is high.

We investigated only disruptions of the same frequency, in 200 periods, however more studies are needed to assess supplier decentralization using a model that combines disruptions with varying frequencies of occurrence.

References

Christopher, M., & Peck, H. (2004). Building the resilient supply chain. *International Journal of Logistics Management, 15*(2), 1–13.

Chopra, S., & Sodhi, S. M. (2004). Managing risk to avoid supply-chain breakdown. *MIT Sloan Management Review, 46*(1), 52–61.

Cui, Y. (2013). A decision-making model for supply chain resilience. *Japan Society for Information and Management Journal, 34*(1), 77–88.

Kubo, M. (2006). Global supply chain optimization models. *Communication of Japan Industrial Management Association, 16*(2), 56–61.

Lee, H. L. (2004). The triple-A supply chain. *Harvard Business Review, 82*(10), 22–30.

Liu, Z., & Anna, N. (2011). Supply chain outsourcing under exchange rate risk and competition. *Omega, 39,* 539–549.

METI (Ministry of Economy, Trade and Industry of Japan). (2014). website: http://www.meti.go.jp/. Retrieved on August 14, 2014.

Sheffi, J., & Rice, J. B. (2005). A supply chain view of the resilient enterprise. *MIT Sloan Management Review, 47*(1), 40–49.

Sodhi, S. M., Son, B., & Tang, C. S. (2012). Researchers' perspectives on supply chain risk management. *Production and Operations Management, 21*(1), 1–13.

Tang, C., & Tomlin, B. (2008). The power of flexibility for mitigating supply chain risks. *International Journal of Production Economics, 116,* 12–27.

Vidal, C. J., & Goetschalckx, M. (2001). A global supply chain model with transfer pricing and transportation cost allocation. *European Journal of Operational Research, 129,* 134–158.

Part III
Toward a Resilient Supply Chain

Chapter 13
Supply Chain Resiliency: A Review

Srinivasan Radhakrishnan, Benjamin Harris and Sagar Kamarthi

Abstract This chapter provides a broad overview of the field of supply chain resiliency. First, we define the concept of resiliency from the perspective of a supply chain. Next the terms *risk* and *vulnerability* are defined in the context of a resilient supply chain. This connects previous studies in supply chain engineering to the emerging field of resiliency. The second section of the chapter outlines components that contribute to the resiliency of a supply chain. Supply chain *flexibility*, *velocity*, *visibility*, and *collaboration* are defined and references to additional sources are provided. The third section of the chapter outlines processes that are used for building resilient supply chains. A number of relationships between supply chain risk and profitability are explored, along with their impact on supply chain resiliency. This section further provides a unifying exploration of the various aspects and perspectives on supply chain engineering, including how they can be utilized for developing and measuring the resiliency of a supply chain. The chapter concludes with remarks ongoing research on supply resiliency and identifies knowledge gaps and topics for future research.

13.1 Introduction

A recent movement in supply chain engineering is the development and incorporation of a concept called *Supply Chain Resiliency* (SCR). This chapter presents a brief review of SCR. Section 13.2 of the chapter defines SCR as well as outlines the components from each definition that contribute to supply chain engineering. Section 13.3 reviews the literature to identify the components that constitute a resilient supply chain. Section 13.4 examines recent attempts to design a supply

S. Radhakrishnan · B. Harris · S. Kamarthi (✉)
Department of Mechanical and Industrial Engineering, Northeastern University,
Boston, MA 02115, USA
e-mail: sagar@coe.neu.edu

Y. Khojasteh (ed.), *Supply Chain Risk Management*,
DOI 10.1007/978-981-10-4106-8_13

chain that incorporates one or more resiliency components discussed in this chapter. Section 13.5 concludes with a summary of current resiliency definitions, and identifies a number of research areas for future research.

13.2 Definition of Resiliency

In this section we discuss the multifaceted aspects of the term resiliency and funnel a set of definitions that are used in the supply chain engineering literature.

13.2.1 Resiliency from a Supply Chain Perspective

The challenge in defining *resiliency* for a supply chain lies in the fact that the terms uncertainty, risk, vulnerability and resilience are often used interchangeably to define supply chain characteristics. This chapter discusses the boundaries and scope of the aforementioned terms. Supply chain uncertainty is often used in place of supply chain risk and vice versa. Some authors make a clear distinction between uncertainty and risk (Simangunsong et al. 2012; Courtney et al. 1997; Juttner et al. 2003), while others do not give much importance to the distinction because of blurring lines between those two terms (Juttner et al. 2003; Peck 2006; Li and Hong 2007; Ritchie and Brindley 2007). The distinction between uncertainty and risk mainly emerges from the directionality of the outcomes, either positive or negative. Risk is associated with negative outcomes whereas uncertainty can lead to negative or positive outcomes (Wagner and Bode 2008). For example natural disaster based disruptions to supply chain will have serious negative consequences however demand based disruptions may either swing towards positive or negative side. Knight (1965) gave a clear distinction between uncertainty and risk: “if you don’t know the for sure what will happen, but you know the odds, that’s risk, and if you don’t even know the odds, that’s uncertainty.” A suitable definition for supply chain uncertainty according to Simangunsong et al. (2012) and van der Vorst and Beulens (2002) given as follows:

> Decision-making situations in the supply-chain in which the decision-maker does not know definitely what to decide as he [or she] is indistinct about the objectives; lacks information about (or understanding of) the supply-chain or its environment; lacks information processing capacities; is unable to accurately predict the impact of possible control actions on supply-chain behavior; or, lacks effective control actions (non-controllability)

Rosenhead et al. (1972) developed three classifications of decision processes, delineated by supply chain information available; certainty, risk and uncertainty. Under certainty all parameters are deterministic and known. The relationship between input and output is unambiguous. Decision making under risk relies on probability distributions, which govern the relation between input and output.

Decision making under uncertainty needs to be made despite the lack of information about the likelihood of parameter changes.

Most authors adopt this categorization and refer to supply chain risk as how much information is available about randomly changing supply chain parameters—assuming probability specifications are at hand. Yet information processing needs to respect the fact that supply chain scenarios are dynamic and the information contained therein has varying degree of relevance and reliability. Supply chain managers, however, still need to make decisions in the absence of pertinent information about the risk of a supply chain. Supply chain risk therefore addresses both decision-making under risk and decision-making under uncertainty (Heckmann et al. 2015).

The type of process used to describe the development of uncertain parameters is depicted by uncertainty models. The literature analysis follows the categorization of Owen and Daskin (1998). They distinguished between probabilistic approaches and scenario planning approaches. While the former explicitly considers probability distributions, the latter evaluates generated sets of possible future values, which can be, but are not required to be, weighted by discrete probability values (Heckmann et al. 2015).

The international engineering standard ISO14971 defines and measures a risk R as the product of probability and harm of an event e: $R = P_e \cdot S_e$, where P_e and S_e refer to the probability and severity of e, respectively (ISO 2015). In assessing supply chain risk, triggering events are modeled as a function of their severity in terms of impact on the supply chain goals and their frequency of occurrence. Different terms are often used synonymously to refer to triggering events, e.g. disturbance (Svensson 2000), disruption (Sheffi and Rice 2005), disaster, hazard or crisis. Wagner and Bode (2008) stated that a disruption is characterized by its probability, severity and effects. A disruption is further described as a combination of the triggering event, which is characterized through frequency of occurrence and magnitude, and a consequential situation, which threatens the normal course of business operations. A disruption is regarded as more severe and often persists for a longer period in time than a disturbance. Klibi and Martel (2012) combined the availability of probability information and the extent of impact related to each triggering event. The authors distinguish between random, which have a single instance, hazardous events, which occur repeatedly, and uncertain events, about which very little information exists.

13.2.2 Supply Chain Risk and Vulnerability

Often in academic literature the term *vulnerability* is used in conjunction with the term *risk*. Svensson (2000) defined supply chain vulnerability (SCV) as "exposure to serious disturbance, arising from risks within the supply chain as well as risks external to the supply chain" and as "a condition that is caused by time and relationship dependencies in a company's activities in a supply chain." In another work Svensson (2002) incorporated supply chain disturbances (unexpected deviations from the norm) and their negative consequences into vulnerability. Svensson's seminal work was followed by other works (Peck 2005, 2006) that treated SCV as a multifaceted term rather than encompassing it in a single term definition. Peck (2005, 2006) defined SCV in relation to risk as "at risk; vulnerable: likely to be lost or damaged." They suggested that supply chains link organizations, industries and economies, and hence SCV should be addressed at multiple levels of analysis. What is "at risk" could be the performance or survival of a process, vital assets or infrastructure, an organization, an inter-organizational network, an economy, or society (Peck 2005).

In general, SCV is the susceptibility of the supply chain to the likelihood and consequences of disruptions (Svensson 2000, 2002; Blos et al. 2009; Christopher and Peck, 2004) and hence often coupled with risk. In some papers SCV is defined as the exposure of the supply chain to risks characteristic of any supply chain system. SCV is a *latent condition* which only becomes manifest if a disruptive event occurs (Juttner and Maklan 2011). Higher SCV is more likely to lead to a disruptive event with severe consequences. As a latent condition, SCV can be analyzed by measuring the exposure of the supply chain to environmental, supply network and organizational risks (Briano et al. 2009). As a manifest condition, the impact of a supply chain disruption indicates the degree of vulnerability (Juttner and Maklan 2011).

13.2.3 Supply Chain Resilience

Supply chain *resilience* (SCR) addresses the supply chain's ability to cope with the consequences of unavoidable risk events in order to return to its original operational state or to move to a new, more desirable state after being disturbed (Peck 2005; Christopher and Peck 2004; Juttner and Maklan 2011). Ponomarov and Holcomb (2009) defined supply chain resilience as "the adaptive capability of the supply chain to prepare for unexpected events, respond to disruptions, and recover from them by maintaining continuity of operations at the desired level of connectedness and control over structure and function." SCR focuses on the system's adaptive capability to deal with temporary disruptive events (Briano et al. 2009; Smith 2004). These disruptions imply a certain level of turbulence (Hamel and Valikangas 2003) and uncertainty in the supply chain (van der Vorst and Beulens 2002), which together cause threats to the current operations (Sheffi 2005). Depending on the magnitude of these threatening events, the terms disruption (Sheffi and Rice 2005), crisis or even disaster are used (Natarajarathinam et al. 2009; Richey 2009). In addition to how SCR is defined, we need to understand its relationship with SCV and supply chain risk management (SCRM). Juttner and Makalan (2011) gave a clear relationship map between the above mentioned three concepts (see Fig. 13.1).

Since lowering the impact of a supply chain disruption is also the key target of SCR, it can be assumed that both concepts are related. More specifically, if SCR

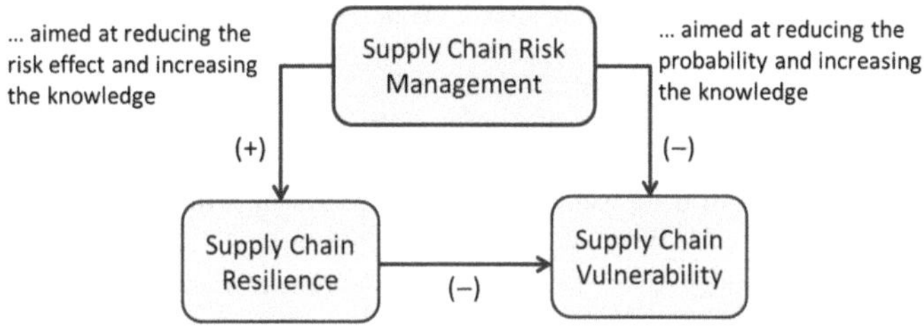

Fig. 13.1 Relation between SCRM, SCR and SCV (Juttner and Maklan 2011)

decreases the negative consequences of supply chain risk events by ensuring a fast return to its original or improved operation, it should, at the same time, decrease the SCV in the case of a manifest risk event (Juttner and Maklan 2011). The main objective of SCRM is to reduce SCV (Juttner and Maklan 2011) and increase SCR (Sheffi and Rice 2005; Rao and Goldsby 2009). Juttner and Maklan (2011) noted that this essentially puts emphasis on managing and mitigating risk and thereby fostering resilience of the supply chain. However, the authors also note that a supply chain risk measure does not necessarily reduce the vulnerability of the supply chain and, at the same time, increase its resilience. Likewise, a supply chain with high vulnerability could either have high or low resilience. If a SCRM initiative only lowers the probability of a disruptive event, the SCV, here defined as the supply chain's latent exposure to supply chain risks, is reduced but will not necessarily have an effect on the SCR. In this sense, a supply chain risk strategy which avoids certain geographical risk areas has lowered the likelihood of a disruption caused, e.g. by political instability in the region. It has, however, not increased its capability to response to recover from a disruption if it still occurred. However, if a supply chain risk initiative successfully addresses the risk effects, the SCR increases as well (Juttner and Maklan 2011).

13.3 Components of a Resilient Supply Chain

In the case of ecological system *resiliency*, the components of resiliency are clearly defined (see Table 13.1).

Similarly, components of SCR are also detailed in the literature. Alternative terminologies for SCR include: capabilities of resilient supply chain, characteristics of resilient supply chain, and formative resilient capabilities. Sheffi and Rice (2005) divided supply chain disruptions into three phases: (1) readiness, (2) responsiveness, and (3) recovery. In order to secure these three disruption phases, four key resilient capabilities are frequently discussed in the literature. They are (1) flexibility, (2) velocity, (3) visibility, and (4) collaboration (Juttner and Maklan 2011).

Table 13.1 Components of ecological resilience (Ponomorov and Holcomb 2009)

Components of resilience	
Elasticity	Rapidity of restoration of a stable state following disturbance (Orians 1975; Westman 1978)
Amplitude	The zone of deformation from which the system will return to its initial state (Orians 1975; Westman 1978)
Hysteresis	The extent to which the path of degradation under chronic disturbance, and a recovery when disturbance ceases, are not mirror-images of each other (Westman1978, 1986)
Malleability	Degree to which the steady state established after disturbance differs from the original steady-state (Westman 1978)
Damping	The degree and manner by which the path of restoration is altered by any forces that change the normal restoring force (Clapham 1971)

13.3.1 Supply Chain Flexibility

Peck (2005) defined *flexibility* as "being able to bend easily without breaking." Flexibility ensures that changes caused by the risk event can be absorbed by the supply chain through effective responses (Skipper and Hanna 2009). It is hence the ability to encounter, resolve and, when appropriate, exploit unexpected emergencies (Juttner and Maklan 2011). Flexibility can amount to an organic capability, which also supports sensing disruptions and, as such, relates to the event readiness dimension of supply chain resilience (Juttner and Maklan 2011; Sheffi and Rice 2005). Sheffi and Rice (2005) proposed "redundancy" as a separate formative resilience capability. In agreement with Rice and Canioato (2003), Juttner and Maklan (2011) proposed redundancy as "duplications of capacity so that operations can continue following failure" as route to flexibility. Other authors included "velocity" and speed into their flexibility definition and emphasized that flexibility means doing things fast (Christopher 2005; Li et al. 2006). However, Juttner and Maklan (2011) have maintained that both are distinct, yet mutually reinforcing capabilities.

13.3.2 Supply Chain Velocity

Christopher and Peck (2004) defined *velocity* as "speed of motion, action, or operation, rapidity and swiftness." Velocity in a risk event determines the loss that happens per unit of time. Compared to flexibility, velocity places a stronger emphasis on the efficiency rather than effectiveness of the supply chain's response and recovery throughout and after a disruption (Smith 2004). In the context of flexibility reconfiguration is the number of possible states a supply chain can take, robustness is the number of changes it is able to cope with, and velocity is the pace of flexible adaptations (Stevenson and Spring 2007). Lead-time is therefore seen as a key indicator of supply chain velocity (Cranfield School of Management 2003). From a global supply chain risk perspective, Manuj and Mentzer (2008) categorized three forms of velocity: the rate at which a risk event happens, the rate at which losses happen and how quickly the risk event is discovered. In a resilience context, a fourth form was added by Juttner and Maklan (2011): the speed with which a supply chain can recover from a risk event. Velocity thus supports the adaptive capacity in all three phases of the risk event: before, throughout and after the supply chain disruption.

13.3.3 Supply Chain Visibility

Francis (2008) defined supply chain *visibility* as "the identity, location and status of entities transiting the supply chain, captured in timely messages about events, along with the planned and actual dates/times of these events". Supply chain visibility addresses information about entities and events regarding end-to-end orders, inventory, transportation and distribution as well as any events in the environment (Sheffi and Rice 2005; Smith 2004; Wei and Wang 2010). Visibility ensures confidence into the supply chain and prevents overreactions, unnecessary interventions and ineffective decisions in a risk event situation (Christopher and Lee 2004). As such, visibility is related to effective disruption response and recovery. Furthermore, the ability to see from one end of the pipeline to the other is an important element of event readiness because the right signals are picked up in a timely manner (van der Vorst and Beulens 2002). Visibility, velocity and flexibility together are sometimes captured under "agility" (Li et al. 2009; Chopra and Sodhi 2004; Faisal et al. 2006; Tang and Tomlin 2008; Christopher and Peck 2004). However, in order to have a clear view on all dimensions of resilience we decide to target all three formative capabilities separately.

13.3.4 Supply Chain Collaboration

Since supply chain resilience is a network-wide, inter-organizational concept, its formative capabilities have to adopt the predisposed attitudes of the parties to align forces in the case of a risk event. *Collaboration* is related to visibility in the sense that it includes the parties' willingness to share even sensitive risk and risk event-related information (Faisal et al. 2006). As such, collaboration contributes to reduced uncertainty and event readiness (Cranfield School of Management 2003). Furthermore, collaboration has been suggested as the "glue that holds supply chain organizations in a crisis together" (Richey 2009). It prevents opportunistic behavior on behalf of individual parties which would adversely affect the whole system's response capability. Sheffi (2005) stressed that collaboration is equally important, after a disruption was overcome, to share experiences among the parties. Such post disruption collaboration is likely to have an effect on the system's ability to deal with future disruptions along all three phases: before, throughout and after the event (Juttner and Maklan 2011). The four formative resilience capabilities echo rather than contradict widely accepted principles of good supply chain management. However, the literature suggests that disruptions are a strong moderator for the positive effect of these formative capabilities on smooth supply chain operations (Juttner and Maklan 2011).

13.4 Building Supply Chain Resiliency (SCR)

The field of operations research has contributed much to the study and development of SCR. Pettit (2008) provided a framework by which contributions to SCR can be categorized and analyzed, which we align within the review below. It is important for organizations to have an SCR framework which forms the basis for evaluating the health of supply chain when subjected to various disruptions. Pettit (2008) proposed a comprehensive SCR framework that included two main dimensions, shown in Table 13.2: (1) vulnerability and (2) capabilities.

The zone of balanced resilience as proposed by Pettit (Pettit 2008) is shown in Fig. 13.2. This figure illustrates the importance of building resilience by balancing profitability and risk. Low vulnerabilities and high capabilities lead to an erosion of profits, indicating that the supply chain is over-equipped for a given amount of risk. On the other hand, high vulnerability combined with low capability takes on more supply chain risk than the system is capable of withstanding. With this relationship in mind, it is important for an organization to have a clear vulnerability and capability map.

Table 13.2 Vulnerabilities and capabilities according to Pettit (2008)

Vulnerability factors	Capabilities
Turbulence	Flexibility in sourcing
Deliberate threats	Flexibility in order fulfillment
External pressures	Capacity
Resource limits	Efficiency
Sensitivity	Visibility
Connectivity	Adaptability
Supplier/customer disruptions	Anticipation
	Recovery
	Dispersion
	Collaboration
	Organization
	Market position
	Security
	Financial strength

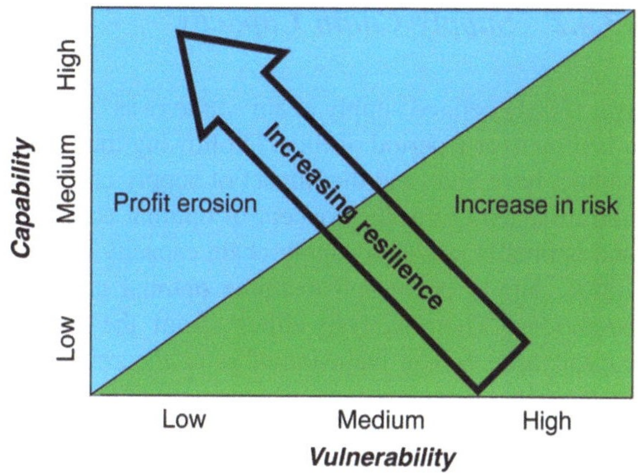

Fig. 13.2 Measurement of Resilience and Resilience Fitness Space (Pettit 2008)

A number of researchers have sought to bring the mathematical tools provided by operations research to bear on the problem of designing resilient supply chains. Following the capability framework outlined in by Pattit (2008), we provide a brief survey of current results.

13.4.1 Flexibility in Sourcing

A number of operations research and econometric techniques have been brought to bear on analyzing *sourcing flexibility* in supply chain management. The concept of supply chain flexibility is theoretically and practically explained by Ka-Leung Moon et al. (2012), who defined supply chain flexibility metrics and then used them in an analysis of textile and clothing companies. Benaroch et al. (2012) utilized a combination of econometrics and unconstrained nonlinear programming to solve optimal sourcing problems while incorporating supply chain flexibility considerations. Pen-Her Pei (2011) included methods found in computational game theory and mechanism design to understand and evaluate sourcing flexibility conditions under a variety of contact structures. Purvis et al. (2014) examined the concept of supply chain flexibility from the perspective of lean and agile engineering. While the previous work in supply chain flexibility concerns individual contracts and transactions, the work of Chiang et al. (2012) sought to use a high-level strategic view to examine the impact of sourcing and strategic flexibility. In doing so, they fill a key gap in demonstrating supply chain flexibility as a discriminator, both from the individual transaction basis to high-level strategic considerations.

13.4.2 Supply Chain Capacity

Iyer (2014) defined supply chain *capacity* as "the designed maximum flow through a facility over a period of time." Following the trend of this definition, a number of authors have analyzed the impact of supply chain capacity on overall supply chain performance. Using the concept of optimal control, Ivanov et al. (2015) described and optimally solved a supply chain capacity model. Li et al. (2014) constructed a simple supply chain and examine optimal capacity decisions under competitive conditions. Their analysis differs from the traditional notion of supply chain capacity due to their inclusion of game-theoretic concepts. Kamath and Roy (2007) incorporated a system dynamics modeling methodology and utilize it to analyze the information required to make optimal supply chain capacity decisions. In the literature for this survey, Mazzola and Neebe (2012) most closely linked operations research techniques with supply chain capacity planning in a theoretical sense. The model they developed incorporated nonlinear and network programming to solve the Generalized Assignment Problem (GAP) over finite time with discrete time steps. Due to the level of generality, their result finds applicability in many supply chain capacity planning problems.

13.4.3 Supply Chain Efficiency

The concept of supply chain *efficiency* has existed in the literature for a few of decades. A number of metrics have been developed through which engineers can gauge the efficiency of a supply chain. More recently, the following authors have contributed additionally to the concept. Martinez-de-Albeniz and Simchi-Levi (2013) took the concept of supply chain efficiency and posed the problem in a two-player stochastic game and pricing and demand. They then solved the problem using stochastic dynamic programming. Qiu (2012) took an alternative approach to measuring supply chain efficiency phenomenon, using a statistical instrument to measure organizational support and how it correlates to cross-boundary (that is, inter, intra, and extra-organizational) activities. The observed number of activities was then correlated to the associated efficiency of the supply chain. Lo et al. (2008) followed a method similar to that of Qiu to measure improvements in supply chain efficiency following the implementation of the ISO 9000 manufacturing standards. Feng and Zhang (2014) incorporated the proven concept of modular manufacturing into a study on how a firm can improve its supply chain efficiency under a modular manufacturing framework. Finally, Li and O'Brien (1999) examined supply chain efficiency from a hierarchical perspective, seeking to optimize decisions at both the supply chain and operational levels of an organization. In the context of SCR, the above mentioned publications add to the computational toolkit available for analysts and engineers to quantify and improve resilience.

13.4.4 Supply Chain Visibility

While the exact definition differs across sources, one online source (Rouse 2015) defines supply chain visibility as "the ability of parts, components, or products in transit to be tracked from the manufacturer to their final destination." While the study of supply chain *visibility* is a field of research in its own right, Pettit (2008) defined it as only one of a number of capabilities that characterize a resilient supply chain. Zhang et al. (2011) further expanded the above definition using set notation and operations. They defined atom, single, and compound visibility and use the definitions to build a conceptual framework that can be used for building a system to build and measure supply chain visibility in a large operation. The impact of implementing improvements in supply chain visibility was explored by Caridi et al. (2014), who correlated changes in supply chain visibility with changes in key performance indicators (KPIs). The authors also provided a structured method to estimate the level of visibility within a company's supply chain. Many other sources (Barratt and Oke 2007; Williams et al. 2013; Caridi et al. 2014; Yu and Goh 2014; Zhang et al. 2011; Caridi et al. 2010) contributed to the theoretical and practical understanding of supply chain visibility.

13.4.5 Supply Chain Adaptability

Supply *adaptability* refers to the ability of a supply chain to augment and re-organize itself in the face of possible disruptions. This ability is crucial to supply chain analysis in a number of areas, highlighted by humanitarian and medical systems. Dubey and Gunasekaran (2015) presented the differences between a humanitarian supply chain and one commonly encountered in the commercial world. Consequently, they pointed out characteristics of the supply chain that are critical to operation, among them the ability of the supply chain to adapt to stochastic events. Supplementing the previous work, Makris et al. (2011) utilized a Bayesian network approach to enhance adaptability through improved decision making under uncertainty. A common theme in these research programs is the presence of uncertainty in the supply chain and mitigation of the impact of the uncertainty. Along a different line of analysis, Fan et al. (2008) connected the concept of self-organization in large systems to how supply chains incorporate adaptability. While they also used the concept of information entropy to explain the tendency of supply chains to adapt to external stimuli, they did not include an empirical example. This indicates that the concept of self-organization in supply chains, and adaptability in this context, still has room for research. Returning to an empirical and statistical set of studies, Eckstein et al. (2014) analyzed a broad cross-section of German industrial firms and demonstrated that firms displaying higher levels of supply chain adaptability (and agility as well) perform better with regard to cost and performance than firms that do not. While intuitive, their insights into how product complexity affects the performance of each supply chain factor (adaptability and agility) provided valuable information to supply chain managers and practitioners.

13.4.6 Supply Chain Anticipation

Again returning to the common thread of stochastic behavior in a supply chain, a number of researchers have developed methods by which a supply chain manager can *anticipate* (and hopefully respond to) changes and disruptions in the enterprise. Jansen et al. (2013) incorporated operations research techniques into supply chain anticipation by developing a two-stage linear programming that captures demand uncertainty to optimize subsequent production decisions. Chauhan et al. (2011) also utilized linear programming techniques to optimize a decision process with applications in the forestry industry. The impact of supply chain anticipation is examined by a more complicated example by Tanrisever et al. (2012), who used the ability to anticipate changes in a supply chain to investigate the interplay between process flexibility, defined as "the ability to produce multiple products on multiple production lines," and operational flexibility, which they defined it as "the ability to dynamically change capacity allocations among different product families over time." The authors reached one interesting conclusion in particular, that most analyses assume that firms will operate optimally after a supply chain decision has been made. The validity of that assumption is shown to have a large impact on how supply chain anticipation will impact key performance indicators. Another example of innovative research involving supply chain anticipation was provided by Boulaksil et al. (2011). They examined a contractual environment between a provider and a customer, and demonstrate a decision toolkit for dealing with customers with heterogeneous demand levels. A number of interesting conclusions are drawn, key among them (for this literature survey) being demand uncertainty and penalty costs are directly proportional to the importance of integrating supply chain anticipation techniques.

13.4.7 Supply Chain Recovery

The term *recovery* has come to have two different meanings in the supply chain literature over the last decade. The first refers to the recycling and recovery of products that are processed in the supply chain, while the second refers to the rebuilding of the actual supply chain following a stochastic event. Within the context of SCR, we shall focus on the second definition. The concept of supply chain resilience implies the response to or recovery from an unforeseen event that impacts the key performance indicators of the supply chain. The recovery of the supply chain is a field of research in its own right, though the literature examining disastrous events is not as widespread. Vahdani et al. (2011) considered the process of supply chain recovery from the initial operation of the supply chain pre-collapse, and develop a model to measure the probability that the supply chain can feasibly recover in the time required to maintain a customer base. Macdonald and Corsi (2013) performed a qualitative survey among supply chain managers to identify and understand the factors that led up to a supply chain collapse, as well as a number of best practices for managing the recovery of the supply chain to pre-collapse levels.

13.4.8 Supply Chain Dispersion

Under stochastic supply chain *disruptions*, one method for mitigating the impact on supply chain performance is dispersing supply chain elements globally. This question has attracted a lot of research in the last decade. Park et al. (2013) used the Japanese economy and its recovery from a number of natural disasters as a case study in the effectiveness of supply chain dispersion, among other methods. Their conclusion that none of the Japanese firms have reached an appropriate responsiveness level indicates that the concept of supply chain dispersion is only recently beginning to take hold commercially. Applying dispersion to supply chain management has also been explored in the theoretical arena. Mokashi and Kokossis (2003) used directed graphs and dispersion algorithms to develop optimal planning and distribution solution for supply chain management. Lorentz et al. (2012) showed that geographic dispersion in a supply chain can have vastly different effects, depending on the desired performance indicators. While supply chain dispersion can reduce a supply chain's susceptibility to natural disasters, it also tends to drive up holding and storage costs due to the increased need for transportation. Seuring and Muller (2008) used the concept of supply chain dispersion as one component of a sustainable supply chain architecture. While not explicitly called out, the authors implied that global supply chains have a greater ability to be architected in a sustainable fashion, implying an additional benefit from geographic supply chain dispersion.

13.4.9 Supply Chain Collaboration

The concept of supply chain *collaboration* has been studied extensively as an enabling factor for improving the key performance indicators of a supply chain. Ramanathan (2013) provided a framework by which participants in a supply chain can understand how information exchanged between them can be of mutual benefit for improving supply chain anticipation and risk mitigation. Moving from a qualitative analysis and report to numerical simulation, Ramanathan (2014) used a simulation environment as a heuristic tool to enable interested companies to develop collaboration capabilities without having extensively invest. Ramanathan also identified and provided metrics for how to measure different levels of collaboration, showing that companies can expect to gain different levels of supply chain key performance indicator improvement as a function of their collaboration level. On a practical level, Ramanathan (2012) collected empirical retail data to examine and recommend how some factors, when shared between firms in collaboration, will result in increased forecast accuracy, while other factors may not. Zacharia et al. (2011) envisioned supply chain collaboration using both knowledge-based (meaning that knowledge is the most strategically important resource of a firm) and relational (where links between firms are a strategic resource) views of firms. They then utilized structural equation modeling to understand which factors among firms prove to be the most impactful in terms of supply chain collaboration and improvements in key performance indicators. In their empirical study, Cao and Zhang (2011) arrived at a conclusion similar to that of Ramanathan (2012), showing that supply chain collaboration has the potential to provide competitive advantage to companies that intelligently utilize it. One distinction they noted, however, is that the size of firm affects the level to which supply chain collaboration can impact firm performance.

13.4.10 Supply Chain Organization

The *organization* of a supply chain plays a major role in its performance, especially in a competitive environment. Ketchen and Hult (2007) explored multiple indicators of supply chain performance instead of analyzing based on a single supply chain key performance indicator. Their goal is to understand how to create a "best value" supply chain. The computational aspect of this is a subject of future, but the authors identified a number of factors and theories that contribute to improved supply chain organization. Miles and Snow (2007) also brought concepts from organization theory to bear on supply chain management. They trace the evolution of modern supply chains over the last three decades, concluding that supply chain management will continue to become more collaborative in the future. From a qualitative standpoint, Tangpong (2011) suggested content analysis to determine improvement in a supply chain organization, while Whitten et al. (2012) defined the presence of agility, adaptability, and alignment as components of a well-organized supply chain ("Triple-A Supply Chain"). Along a different track, Singhal and Singhal (2012) proposed using concept from supply chain management, including organization theory, to build and pursue innovation in multiple industries and commercial settings.

13.4.11 Supply Chain Market Position

Literature tying *market position* to supply chain management is not as widely available as the literature on other aspects of supply chain resilience are. Nevertheless, a number of papers give insight into the idea. Sharifi et al. (2013) tied supply chain management and performance into a firm's ability to enhance its market position. This differs slightly from our viewpoint of a resilient supply chain in that we are seeking to analyze a firm's market position as an independent variable with regard to supply chain resilience, not vice versa. The work of Lorentz, et al. (2013) examined international food supply chains in emerging markets in order to understand what supply chain management techniques must be brought to bear in order to optimize the process as the marketplace evolves.

13.4.12 Supply Chain Security

The *security* of a supply chain can also be grouped in the broader area of risk management. Yang (2011) examined a number of incidents in the Taiwanese maritime supply chain and suggested risk mitigation strategies appropriate to the impact and likelihood of the events. Similarly, Speier et al. (2011) identified security factors in a general sense with the intent of developing a framework by which risks to the supply chain can be efficiently and effectively mitigated. Tang and Musa (2011) noted one factor lacking in other literature on the subject: information flow risk. They then proceed to analyze the supply chain impact when information is blocked in a global enterprise. Looking back at the literature regarding supply chain collaboration, Lee et al. (2011) demonstrated how supply chain collaboration can actually improve supply chain security.

13.4.13 Supply Chain Financial Strength

The *financial strength* of a supply chain is difficult to define, but it follows intuitively that a supply chain with financial reserves and liquidity will be able to withstand disruption events. Randall and Farris II (2009) demonstrated how techniques from financial analysis and financial management can benefit a supply chain by reducing the costs associated with it. This will in turn increase the supply chain's ability to withstand something unforeseen.

Table 13.3 provides an overview of the previously discussed factors along with citations to major works on the topic.

Table 13.3 An overview of supply chain resiliency attributes and corresponding references

Resiliency factor	Analysis type		
	Conceptual proposal	Survey instrument w/quantitative analysis	Other (specified)
Supply chain flexibility	Benaroch et al. (2012), Pen-Ehr Pei, et al. (2011)	Purvis et al. (2014), Ka-Leung Moon et al. (2012), Chiang et al. (2012)	
Supply chain capacity	Ivanov et al. (2015), Li et al. (2014), Mazzola and Neebe (2012)		System dynamics modeling—Kamath and Roy (2007)
Supply chain efficiency	Li and O'Brien (1999), Feng and Zhang (2014), Martinez-de-Albeniz and Simchi-Levi (2013)	Qiu (2012), Lo et al. (2008)	
Supply chain visibility	Zhang et al. (2011), Yu and Goh (2014)	Williams et al. (2013), Barratt and Oke (2007), Caridi et al. (2014)	Case studies—Caridi et al. (2010)
Supply chain adaptability	Fan et al. (2008), Makris et al. (2011), Dubey and Gunasekaran (2015)	Eckstein et al. (2014)	
Supply chain anticipation	Boulaksil et al. (2011), Tanrisever et al. (2012), Jansen et al. (2013)		Case study—Chauhan et al. (2011)
Supply chain recovery		Macdonald and Corsi (2013)	
Supply chain dispersion	Mokashi and Kokossis (2003)	Lorentz et al. (2012)	Case studies—Park et al. (2013), Lit review—Seuring and Muller (2008)
Supply chain collaboration	Ramanathan (2013, 2014)		Case study—Ramanathan (2012)
Supply chain organization	Ketchen and Hult (2007), Tangpong (2011), Singhal and Singhal (2012)	Whitten et al. (2012)	Historical review—Miles and Snow (2007)
Supply chain market position			Case studies—Lorentz et al. (2013), Sharifi et al. (2013)
Supply chain security	Speier et al. (2011), Lee et al. (2011)		Lit review—Tang and Musa (2011), Case study—Yang, (2011)
Supply chain financial strength		Randall and Farris II (2009)	

13.5 Conclusions

This chapter provides a literature review of resiliency definitions from fields other than supply chain engineering and demonstrates how these concepts from disparate fields have influenced supply chain practitioners in defining resiliency in supply chain engineering. Table 13.3 summarizes the SCR attributes and their analysis types and the corresponding references. As shown in Sects. 13.1 and 13.2, resiliency definitions from fields as disparate as ecology and psychology provide valuable insight into what constitutes supply chain resilience. Transitioning from those definitions to applications in supply chain engineering has occurred in a piecewise fashion under labels such as SCRM. Due to this fact, a unifying effort in defining and developing SCR as a field of study is necessary.

Beyond the review of literature presented in this chapter, there are a number of research gaps that must be covered before SCR can be integrated into SCM operations on a large scale. For example, proactive SCM, competitive supply chain interactions, and resiliency metrics, are some of the important areas in which academic researchers can contribute to the growth of the supply chain resiliency concept. Given the necessity of managing a supply chain in an increasingly competitive and volatile market space, the impact of disruptive events must be understood and mitigated effectively. The main goal of this chapter is to review concepts, information, and benchmarks so that researchers can leverage this body of knowledge to develop robust computational tools and to identify directions for future research in supply chain resiliency.

Acknowledgements This work is supported by the research initiation grant for "Supply chain engineering for neutralizing threats to resiliency (SENTRY)" project. We are very thankful to Dr. Michael Silevitch, the Director of the DHS Center of Excellence for Awareness and Localization of Explosives Related Threats, and Mr. John Beaty, the Director of Technology Programs, for facilitating SENTRY project discussions and for their valuable intellectual inputs.

References

Barratt, M., & Oke, A. (2007). Antecedents of supply chain visibility in retail supply chains: A resource-based theory perspective. *Journal of Operations Management, 25,* 1217–1233.

Benaroch, M., Webster, S., & Kazaz, B. (2012). Impact of sourcing flexibility on the outsourcing of services under demand uncertainty. *European Journal of Operational Research, 219,* 272–283.

Blos, M., Quaddus, M., Wee, H., & Watanabe, K. (2009). Supply chain risk management: A case study of automotive and electronic industries in Brazil. *Supply Chain Management: An International Journal, 14*(4), 247–252.

Boulaksil, Y., Grunow, M., & Fransoo, J. (2011). Capacity flexibility allocation in an outsourced supply chain with reservation. *International Journal of Production Economics, 129,* 111–118.

Briano, E., Caballini, C., and Revetria, R. (2009). *Literature review about supply chain vulnerability and resilience.* s.l., s.n., pp. 191–197.

Cao, M., & Zhang, Q. (2011). Supply chain collaboration: Impact on collaborative advantage and firm performance. *Journal of Production Management, 29,* 163–180.

Caridi, M., et al. (2010). Do virtuality and complexity affect supply chain visibility? *International Journal of Production Economics, 127,* 372–383.

Caridi, M., Moretto, A., Perego, A., & Tumino, A. (2014). The benefits of supply chain visibility: A value assessment model. *International Journal of Production Economics, 151,* 1–19.

Chauhan, S. S., Frayret, J.-M., & LeBel, L. (2011). Supply network planning in the forest supply chain with bucking decisions anticipation. *Annals of Operations Research, 190,* 93–115.

Chiang, C.-Y., Kocabasoglu-Hillmer, C., & Suresh, N. (2012). An empirical investigation of the impact of strategic sourcing and flexibility on firm's supply chain agility. *International Journal of Operations and Production Management, 32*(1), 49–78.

Chopra, S., & Sodhi, M. (2004). Managing risk to avoid supply chain breakdown. *MIT Sloan Management Review, 46*(1), 53–61.

Christopher, M. (2005). Managing risk in the supply chain. In: *Logistics and supply chain management: Creating value—Adding networks.* Harlow: FT Prentice-Hall.

Christopher, M., & Lee, H. (2004). Mitigating supply chain risk through improved confidence. *International Journal of Physical Distribution and Logistics Management, 34*(5), 386–388.

Christopher, M., & Peck, H. (2004). Building the resilient Supply Chain. *The International Journal of Logistics Management, 15*(2), 1–13.

Clapham, W., Jr. (1971). *Natural ecosystems.* New York: Macmillan.

Courtney, H., Kirkland, J., & Viguerie, P. (1997). Strategy under uncertainty. *Harvard Business Review, 75*(6), 66–79.

Cranfield School of Management. (2003). *Creating resilient supply chains: A practical guide.* Cranfield: Department of Transport, Cranfield School of Management.

Dubey, R., & Gunasekaran, A. (2015). The sustainable humanitarian supply chain design: Agility, adaptability, and alignment. *International Journal of Logistics: Research and Applications, 19* (1), 62–82.

Eckstein, D., Goellner, M., Blome, C., & Henke, M. (2014). The performance impact of supply chain agility and supply chain adaptability: The moderating effect of product complexity. *International Journal of Production Research, 53*(10), 3028–3046.

Faisal, N., Banwet, D., & Shankar, R. (2006). Supply chain risk mitigation: Modeling the enablers. *Business Process Management Journal, 12*(4), 535–552.

Fan, Y., Mu, D., Feng, X., and Yu, L. (2008). Analysis of supply chain adaptability based on self-organization. *IEEE,* Oct, Vol. 2, pp. 2197–2200.

Feng, T., and Zhang, F. (2014). The impact of modular assembly on supply chain efficiency. *Production and Operations Management, November, 23*(11), 1985–2001.

Francis, V. (2008). Supply chain visibility: Lost in translation? *Supply Chain Management: An International Journal, 13*(3), 180–184.

Hamel, G., and Valikangas, L. (2003). The quest for resilience. *Harvard Business Review,* pp. 52–63.

Heckmann, I., Comes, T., and Nickel, S. (2015). A critical review on supply chain risk-definition, measure, and modeling. *Omega* 119–132.

ISO. (2015). *ISO14971:2007 medical devices—Application of risk management to medical devices.* [Online] Available at: http://www.iso.org/iso/catalogue_detail?csnumber=38193

Ivanov, D., Hartl, R., Dolgui, A., Pavlov, A., & Sokolov, B. (2015). Integration of aggregate distribution and dynamic transportation planning in a supply chain with capacity disruptions and the ripple effect consideration. *International Journal of Production Research, 53*(23), 6963–6979.

Iyer, A. (2014). *Introduction to the 4 Cs of supply chain management: Chain structure, competition, capacity, and coordination.* New York: Business Expert Press.

Jansen, M. M., de Kok, T. G., & Fransoo, J. C. (2013). Lead time anticipation in supply chain operations. *Operations Research Spectrum, 35,* 251–290.

Juttner, U., & Maklan, S. (2011). Supply chain resilience in the global financial crisis: An empirical study. *Supply Chain Management: An International Journal, 16*(4), 246–259.

Juttner, U., Peck, H., and Christopher, M. (2003). Supply chain risk management: Outlining an agenda for future research. *International Journal of Logistics: Research and Applications* 197–210.

Ka-Leung Moon, K., Ying Yi, C., & Ngai, E. (2012). An instrument for measuring supply chain flexibility for the textile and clothing companies. *European Journal of Operational Research, 222,* 191–203.

Kamath, N. B., & Roy, R. (2007). Capacity augmentation of a supply chain for a short lifecycle product: A system dynamics framework. *European Journal of Operational Research, 179,* 334–351.

Ketchen, D. J., Jr., & Hult, G. T. M. (2007). Bridging organization theory and supply chain management: The case of best value supply chains. *Journal of Operations Management, 25,* 573–580.

Klibi, W., & Martel, A. (2012). Scenario-based supply chain network risk modeling. *European Journal of Operational Research, 223,* 644–658.

Knight, F. (1965). *Uncertainty and risk.* New York: Harper and Row.

Lee, J., Palekar, U. S., & Qualls, W. (2011). Supply chain efficiency and security: Coordination for collaborative investment in technology. *European Journal of Operational Research, 210,* 568–578.

Li, D., & O'Brien, C. (1999). Integrated decision modelling of supply chain efficiency. *International Journal of Production Economics, 59,* 147–157.

Li, G., et al. (2014). Make-or-buy service capacity decision in a supply chain providing after-sales service. *European Journal of Operational Research, 239,* 377–388.

Li, G., Li, Y., Wang, S., & Yan, H. (2006). Enhancing agility by timely sharing of supply information. *Supply Chain Management: An International Journal, 11*(5), 425–435.

Li, J., & Hong, S. (2007). Towards a new model of supply chain risk management: The cross-functional process mapping approach. *International Journal of Electronic Customer Relationship Management, 1*(1), 91–107.

Li, X., Goldsbby, T., & Holsapple, C. (2009). Supply chain agility: Scale development. *The International Journal of Logistics Management, 20*(3), 408–424.

Lo, C. K., Yeung, A. C., & Cheng, T. (2008). ISO 9000 and supply chain efficiency: Empirical evidence on inventory and account receivable days. *International Journal of Production Economics, 118,* 367–374.

Lorentz, H., Kittipanta-ngam, P., & Srai, J. S. (2013). Emerging market characteristics and supply network adjustment in internationalising food supply chains. *International Journal of Production Economics, 145,* 220–232.

Lorentz, H., et al. (2012). Effects of geographic dispersion on intra-firm supply chain performance. *Supply Chain Management: An International Journal, 17*(6), 611–626.

Macdonald, J. R., & Corsi, T. M. (2013). Supply chain disruption management: Severe events, recovery, and performance. *Journal of Business Logistics, 34*(4), 270–288.

Makris, S., Zoupas, P., and Chryssolouris, G. (2011). Supply chain control logic for enabling adaptability under uncertainty. *International Journal of Production Research, January, 49*(1), 121–137.

Manuj, I., & Mentzer, J. (2008). Global supply chain risk management strategies. *International Journal of Physical Distribution and Logistics Management, 38*(3), 192–223.

Martinez-de-Albeniz, V., & Simchi-Levi, D. (2013). Supplier-buyer negotiation games: Equilibrium conditions and supply chain efficiency. *Production and Operations Management, March-April, 22*(2), 397–409.

Mazzola, J. B., and Neebe, A. W. (2012). A generalized assignment model for dynamic supply chain capacity planning. *Naval Research Logistics, August, 59*(6), 470–485.

Miles, R. E., & Snow, C. C. (2007). Organization theory and supply chain management: An evolving research perspective. *Journal of Operations Management, 25,* 459–463.

Mokashi, S., & Kokossis, A. (2003). Application of dispersion algorithms to supply chain optimisation. *Computers and Chemical Engineering, 27,* 927–949.

Natarajarathinam, M., Capar, I., & Narayanan, A. (2009). Managing supply chains in times of crisis: A review literature and insights. *International Journal of Physical Distribution and Logistics Management, 39*(7), 619–628.

Orians, G. (1975). Diversity, stability, and maturity in natural ecosystems. In: L. Van Dobben (Ed.), *Unifying concepts in ecology* (pp. 139–150). The Hague, The Netherlands: Springer.

Owen, S., & Daskin, M. (1998). Strategic facility location: A review. *European Journal of Operational Research, 111,* 423–447.

Park, Y., Hong, P., & Roh, J. J. (2013). Supply chain lessons from the catastrophic natural disaster in Japan. *Business Horizons, 56,* 75–85.

Peck, H. (2005). Drivers of supply chain vulnerability: An integrated framework. *International Journal of Physical Distribution and Logistics Management, 35,* 210–232.

Peck, H. (2006). Reconciling supply chain vulnerability, risk and supply chain management. *International Journal of Logistics: Research and Applications, 9*(2), 127–142.

Pen-Ehr Pei, P., Simchi-Levi, D., & Tunca, T. I. (2011). Sourcing Flexibility, spot trading, and procurement contract structure. *Operations Research, 59*(3), 578–601.

Pettit, T. (2008). *Supply chain resilience: Development of a conceptual framework, an assessment tool and an implementation process*. Columbus: The Ohio State University.

Ponomorov, S., & Holcomb, M. (2009). Understanding the concept of supply chain resilience. *The International Journal of Logistics Management, 20*(1), 124–143.

Purvis, L., Gosling, J., & Naim, M. M. (2014). The development of a lean, agile, and leagile supply network taxonomy based on differing types of flexibility. *International Journal of Production Economics, 151,* 100–111.

Qiu, T. (2012). Managing boundary-spanning marketing activities for supply-chain efficiency. *Journal of Marketing Management, 28*(9–10), 1114–1131.

Ramanathan, U. (2012). Supply chain collaboration for improved forecast accuracy of promotional sales. *International Journal of Operations and Production Management, 32*(6), 676–695.

Ramanathan, U. (2013). Aligning supply chain collaboration using analytic hierarchy process. *Omega, 41,* 431–440.

Ramanathan, U. (2014). Performance of supply chain collaboration—A simulation study. *Expert Systems with Applications, 41,* 210–220.

Randall, W. S., & Farris, M. T., II. (2009). Supply chain financing: using cash-to-cash variables to strengthen the supply chain. *International Journal of Physical Distribution and Logistics Management, 39*(8), 669–689.

Rao, S., & Goldsby, T. (2009). Supply chain risks: A review and typology. *The International Journal of Logistics Management, 20*(1), 97–123.

Rice, J., and Canioato, F. (2003). Building a secure and resilient supply network. *Supply Chain Management Review, September, 7*(5), 22–30.

Richey, R. (2009). The supply chain crisis and disaster pyramid. *International Journal of Physical Distribution and Logistics Management, 39*(7), 619–628.

Ritchie, B., & Brindley, C. (2007). Supply chain risk management and performance: A guiding framework for future development. *International Journal of Operations and Production Management, 27*(3), 303–323.

Rosenhead, J., Elton, M., & Gupta, S. (1972). Robustness and optimality as criteria for strategic decisions. *Operational Research Quarterly, 23*(4), 413–430.

Rouse, M. (2015). *TechTarget.com.* [Online] Available at: http://searchmanufacturingerp.techtarget.com/definition/supply-chain-visibility-SCV

Seuring, S., & Muller, M. (2008). From a literature review to a conceptual framework for sustainable supply chain management. *Journal of Cleaner Production, 16,* 1699–1710.

Sharifi, H., Ismail, H. S., Qiu, J., & Tavani, S. N. (2013). Supply chain strategy and its impacts on product and market growth strategies: A case study of SMEs. *International Journal of Production Economics, 145,* 397–408.

Sheffi, Y. (2005). *The resilient enterprise: Overcoming vulnerability for competitive advantage*. Cambridge: MIT Press.

Sheffi, Y., & Rice, B. (2005). A supply chain view of the resilient enterprise. *MIT Sloan Management Review, 47*(1), 41–49.

Simangunsong, E., Hendry, L., & Stevenson, M. (2012). Supply-chain uncertainty: A review and theoretical foundation for future research. *International Journal of Production Research, 50* (16), 4495–4523.

Singhal, K., & Singhal, J. (2012). Imperatives of the science of operations and supply-chain management. *Journal of Operations Management, 30,* 237–244.

Skipper, J., & Hanna, J. (2009). Minimizing supply chain disruption risk through enhanced visibility. *International Journal of Physical Distribution and Logistics Management, 39*(5), 404–427.

Smith, R. (2004). Operational capabilities for the resilient supply chain. *Supply Chain Practice, 6* (2), 24–35.

Speier, C., Whipple, J. M., Closs, D. J., & Voss, M. D. (2011). Global supply chain design considerations: Mitigating product safety and security risks. *Journal of Operations Management, 29,* 721–736.

Stevenson, M., & Spring, M. (2007). Flexibility from a supply chain perspective: Definition and review. *International Journal of Operations and Production Management, 27*(7), 685–713.

Svensson, G. (2000). A conceptual framework for the analysis of vulnerability of supply chains. *International Journal of Physical Distribution and Logistics Management, 30*(9), 731–750.

Svensson, G. (2002). Dyadic vulnerability in companies inbound and outbound logistics flows. *Journal of Logistics: Research and Applications, 5*(1), 81–113.

Tang, C., & Tomlin, B. (2008). The power of flexibility for mitigating supply chain risks. *International Journal of Production Economics, 116,* 12–27.

Tang, O., & Musa, S. N. (2011). Identifying risk issues and research advancements in supply chain risk management. *International Journal of Production Economics, 133,* 25–34.

Tangpong, C. (2011). Content analytic approach to measuring constructs in operations and supply chain management. *Journal of Operations Management, 29,* 627–638.

Tanrisever, F., Morrice, D., & Morton, D. (2012). Managing capacity flexibility in make-to-order production environments. *European Journal of Operational Research, 216,* 334–345.

Vahdani, B., Zandieh, M., & Roshanaei, V. (2011). A hybrid multi-stage predictive model for supply chain network collapse recovery analysis: A practical framework for effective supply chain network continuity management. *International Journal of Production Research, 49*(7), 2035–2060.

van der Vorst, J., & Beulens, A. (2002). Identifying sources of uncertainty to generate supply chain redesign strategies. *International Journal of Physical Distribution and Logistics Management, 32*(6), 409–430.

Wagner, S., & Bode, C. (2008). An empirical examination of supply chain performance along several dimensions of risk. *Journal of Business Logistics, 29*(1), 307–325.

Wei, H.-L., & Wang, E. (2010). The strategic value of supply chain visibility: Increasing the ability to reconfigure. *European Journal of Information Systems, 19,* 238–249.

Westman, W. (1978). Measuring the inertia and resilience of ecosystems. *BioScience, 28*(11), 705–710.

Westman, W. (1986). Resilience: Concepts and measures. In: W. Perth (Ed.), *Resilience in mediterranean type ecosystems* (pp. 5–19). The Hague, The Netherlands: Springer.

Whitten, G. D., Green, K. W., Jr., & Zelbst, P. J. (2012). Triple-A supply chain performance. *International Journal of Operations and Production Management, 32*(1), 28–48.

Williams, B. D., Roh, J., Tokar, T., & Swink, M. (2013). Leveraging supply chain visibility for responsiveness: The moderating role of internal integration. *Journal of Operations Management, 31,* 543–554.

Yang, Y.-C. (2011). Risk management of Taiwan's maritime supply chain security. *Safety Science, 49,* 382–393.

Yu, M.-C., & Goh, M. (2014). A multi-objective approach to supply chain visibility and risk. *European Journal of Operational Research, 233,* 125–130.

Zacharia, Z. G., Nix, N. W., & Lusch, R. F. (2011). Capabilities that enhance outcomes of an episodic supply chain collaboration. *Journal of Operations Management, 29,* 591–603.

Zhang, A. N., Goh, M., & Meng, F. (2011). Conceptual modelling for supply chain inventory visibility. *International Journal of Production Economics, 133,* 578–585.

Chapter 14
The Role of Resiliency in Managing Supply Chains Disruptions

Anirban Ganguly, Debdeep Chatterjee and Harish Rao

Abstract Current day business organizations, symbolized by complex and global supply chains, are often subjected to unforeseen threats that result in huge financial losses. There are no sure ways of assessing these threats, especially the "black swans" (high-impact, but low-probability events like natural disasters, terrorist attacks, outbreaks, etc.), as the severe dearth of historical data excludes the use of forecasting tools to evaluate those disruptions. However, it has been observed that some organizations cope far better than others in addressing these unforeseen and unquantifiable disruptions. This is not because they have a 'secret formula', but due to them sharing a critical trait known as *resilience*. The notion of supply chain resiliency, which is the ability of a supply chain to recover to the 'pre-disruption' or a better state after suffering through a disruption process, has always been considered as a core element in the success of an organization. The primary objective of this chapter is to familiarize the readers with the concept of supply chain resiliency and its role in mitigating supply chain disruptions. The chapter will also reveal the advantages of a resilient supply chain through insightful examples from a wide range of industries.

A. Ganguly (✉)
Jindal Global Business School, O. P. Jindal Global University,
Sonipat, Haryana 131001, India
e-mail: aganguly@jgu.edu.in

D. Chatterjee
Schneider Electric, 1st Main Rd, Electronic City, Bengaluru
Karnataka 560100, India

H. Rao
International Management Institute, B-10, Qutab Institutional Area,
Tara Crescent, New Delhi, Delhi 110016, India
e-mail: harish.rao@imi.edu

Y. Khojasteh (ed.), *Supply Chain Risk Management*,
DOI 10.1007/978-981-10-4106-8_14

14.1 Introduction

In the current day global business environment marked by uncertainty and turbulence, the vulnerability of supply chain has become a major cause of concern for organizations. Increase in the size and complexity of supply chains, coupled with globalization and unpredictable market trends, have greatly increased the risks associated with an organization's supply chain. These risks, which might include natural disasters, terrorism, cyber-attacks and credit crunch among others, could yield to a drastic loss in productivity, revenue, competitive advantage and profitability if not managed appropriately (Mensah and Merkuryev 2014). In order to combat these risks, supply chains are being designed to withstand disruptions, provide an efficient and effective response, and be capable of recovering to their original state or even better, post the disruptive event (Christopher and Peck 2004; Ponomarov and Holcomb 2009). This is whole essence of supply chain resiliency, which is concerned with improving the adaptability of global supply chains, effective collaboration with the various components of the supply chain and leveraging information technology to assure continuity in the face of catastrophic disruptions (Fiskel et al. 2015). Resilience allows firms to manage supply chain disruptions and continue to deliver their products and services to the customer (Ambulkar et al. 2015). In the current day business scenario, supply chain resiliency goes beyond just mitigating risks to being a major tool for competitive advantage and financial gains, along with serving as an avenue to reduce customer perception of assumed risks and moving companies from simple risk management to risk resilient growth.

According to Ponomarov and Holcomb (2009), supply chain resilience aims at developing the adaptive capability to prepare for unexpected events and to respond and recover from disruptions. Supply chain resilience has gained momentum as a competitive characteristic of supply chains due to increasing uncertainty in its operations (Carvalho et al. 2012). It is based on the underlying assumption that not all risk events can be prevented (Jüttner and Maklan 2011), and can be both proactive and reactive in nature. While some researchers' state that resilience comprises of reactive capabilities for use after a disruption, others argue that resilience is a more proactive effort toward being prepared for disruptions (Falasca et al. 2008; Kamalahmadi and Parast 2016). However, whether reactive or proactive in nature, resilience is often perceived as a highly desirable quality of supply chains, as it increases a firm's readiness in dealing with risks that can emerge from the customers' side, the suppliers' side, the internal processes adopted or the integration mechanisms employed or a combination of the above (Purvis et al. 2016).

Organizations that concentrate on building a resilient supply chain often end up combating disruptions far better than their non-resilient counterparts. Two notable examples of supply chain resiliency aiding an organization to bounce back from disruption effectively and more efficiently that their competitors can be cited as Toyota and DHL. In 1997, after a devastating fire roared through Aisin Seiki Co. factory, which was then the largest manufacturer of brake fluid valves for Toyota

Corporation, most of the people thought Toyota couldn't recover for weeks (Reitman 1997). However, due to the resiliency of their supply chain, five days after the fire, its car factories started up again. Similarly, after the eruption of the Eyjafjallajökull volcano in Iceland in 2010, DHL activated its emergency plan and rescheduled one hundred flights from its hub in Leipzig, Germany, toward destinations in southern Europe that did not experience airspace closures. Furthermore, it quickly shifted transport to ground vehicles by deploying a fleet of trucks to Leipzig to retrieve shipments, while providing continuous status updates to its customers, thereby avoiding significant financial impacts due to the sheer resilience of their supply chain (Fiskel 2015).

Other examples of resilient supply chain includes ON Semiconductor Corp, an Arizona based chip maker, who kept their business moving after the devastating earthquake and tsunami hit Japan in 2011 (Dipietro 2015) and Seagate, post the Thailand floods of 2012, who managed not only to absorb the pressure that the floods caused in their inventory and operations management, but also was able to displace Western Digital, the then market leaders, as the global leader in hard drives (Mearian 2012).

This chapter traces the concept of supply chain resiliency and its contribution towards addressing disruption in organizations. This chapter aims to address two key facets in supply chain resiliency: (1) an overview of supply chain resiliency and (2) its role is mitigating supply chain disruption. Additionally, it also discusses the critical phases and attributes of a resilient supply chain along with discussing important supply chain resiliency strategies. Conclusions on the current state of supply chain resiliency are provided based on the findings. The chapter is divided into four sections. While the first section introduces the chapter to the readers along with laying down the organization of the chapter, Sect. 14.2 discusses the definitions and characteristics of supply chain resiliency. Section 14.3 provides the role of resiliency in addressing supply chain disruption along with stating the critical strategies for designing a resilient supply chain. Section 14.4 is devoted toward discussing the findings and drawing conclusions and recommendations from it.

14.2 Definition and Characteristics of a Resilient Supply Chain

Resilience, which traces its origin to the Latin word *resilīre* meaning 'to spring back or rebound', can be stated as the ability of a substance or object to spring back into shape. The concept of resilience has its origins in development theory of social psychology and is directly related to important issues such as ecological and social vulnerability, the politics and psychology of disaster recovery, and risk management under increasing threats (Ponomarov and Holcomb 2009). One of the early conceptualization of resilience stated it as a degree, manner, and pace of restoration of initial structure and function in an ecosystem after disturbance (Clapham 1971). The concept of resilience, over the years, has gradually evolved and diffused into a variety of domains, with supply chain being one of the newest members to adapt the concept.

The concept of resilience in supply chains combines previous tenets with studies of supply chain vulnerability, defined by Svensson (2002) as "*unexpected deviations from the norm and their negative consequences*". Therefore, it can be concluded that resiliency addresses the supply chain's ability to cope with the consequences of unavoidable risk events in order to return to its original operations or move to a new, more desirable state after being disturbed (Christopher and Peck 2004; Peck 2005). A resilient supply chain must therefore develop capabilities to react to the negative consequences of unexpected events and to return quickly to its original state, the one before disruption, or to move to a new best state after being affected by the disruption, and continue business operations as efficiently as possible (Barroso et al. 2015). A resilient supply chain may not be the lowest cost supply chain, but one that is more capable of coping with the uncertainties in the business environment (Carvalho et al. 2012). According to Melnyk et al. (2014), resilience can either consist of a system's ability to minimize the impact of a disruption by evading it entirely (avoidance) or by minimizing the time between the onset of disruption and the start of recovery from that disruption (containment) and the ability of a system to find a return path (recovery) to a steady state of functionality (stabilization) once a disruption has occurred. Therefore, resilience is not only about responding to a one time disruption, but is concerned with continuously anticipating and adjusting to severe disruptions that can permanently impair the earning power of an organization (Hamel and Valikangas 2003). Table 14.1 provides the readers with some of the key definitions of supply chin resiliency.

As seen from the set of definitions provided in Table 14.1, there exists a significant overlap as most of the definitions agree in the adaptive and adjustable nature of resilience. Furthermore, it has been observed that the developmental nature of resilience should guide supply chains not only to recover from a disruptive event or crisis but moreover to find stability in a better state than before (Ponis and Koronis 2012). In essence, supply chain resiliency can be addressed on four aspects —preparation for a disruptive event; response to an event; recovery from the event; and, growth/competitive advantage after the event (Tukamuhabwa et al. 2015). The definitions provided in Table 14.1 also exhibit certain characteristics of a resilient supply chain. According to most of the definitions, a resilient supply chain needs to be ready to adapt and adjust to unforeseen changes in business environment (Bhamra et al. 2011). Additionally, being proactively ready for an unforeseen event and responding to them in an efficient manner, not to forget about recovering from disruptions, are also considered as important characteristics of resilient supply chains (Ponomarov and Holcomb 2009). Furthermore, flexibility of the supply chain can also serve as an important weapon for combating supply chain disruptions. Finally, it can be also stated that capability of sustained response to sudden and significant shift in input is another major characteristics of resilient supply chains (Christopher and Rutherford 2004). Therefore, the essential characteristics of a resilient supply chain, based on extant literature, are as follows.

Table 14.1 Some key definitions of supply chain resilience

Author(s) (Year)	Definition
Ates and Bititci (2011)	The ability of a firm's supply chain network to absorb disruptions and subsequently return to its initial state condition
Barroso et al. (2011)	Ability to react to the negative effects caused by disturbances that occur at a given moment in order to maintain the supply chain's objectives
Brandon-Jones et al. (2014)	Ability of a system to return to its original state, within an acceptable period of time, after being disturbed
Christopher and Peck (2004)	The ability of a system to return to its original state or move to a new, more desirable state after being disturbed
Datta et al. (2007)	The ability of the production–distribution system to meet each customer demand for each product on time and to quantity
Falasca et al. (2008)	Ability of a supply chain system to reduce the probabilities of a disruption, to reduce the consequences of those disruptions once they occur, and to reduce the time to recover normal performance
Fiksel et al. (2015)	The capacity for an enterprise or set of business entities to survive, adapt, and grow in the face of turbulent change
Kamalahmadi and Parast (2016)	The adaptive capability of a supply chain to reduce the probability of facing sudden disturbances, resist the spread of disturbances by maintaining control over structures and functions, and recover and respond by immediate and effective reactive plans to transcend the disturbance and restore the supply chain to a robust state of operations
Kim et al. (2015)	A network-level attribute to withstand disruptions that may be triggered at the node or arc level
Ponomarov and Holcomb (2009)	The adaptive capability of the supply chain to prepare for unexpected events, respond to disruptions, and recover from them by maintaining continuity of operations at the desired level of connectedness and control over structure and function
Ponis and Koronis (2012)	The ability to proactively plan and design a supply chain network for anticipating unexpected disruptive (negative) events, respond adaptively to disruptions while maintaining control over structure and function and transcending to a post event robust state of operations, if possible, more favorable than the one prior to the event, thus gaining competitive advantage
Rice and Caniato (2003)	Ability of the supply chain to react to a disruption or disturbance and restore normal operations
Xiao et al. (2012)	supply chain's ability to return to the original or ideal status after external disruption and includes both the abilities of adaptability to the environment and recovery from the disruption

- Adjustability
- Adaptability
- Responsiveness
- Sustainability
- Flexibility/Agility

Next section will discuss the strategies required to build a resilient supply chain.

14.3 Building a Resilient Supply Chain to Combat Disruptions

Supply chain disruption can be stated as unplanned and unanticipated events that negatively affect the normal flow of goods and materials within a supply chain (Craighead et al. 2007; Kleindorfer and Saad 2005). Therefore, disruption is a fundamental pre-requisite of supply chain resiliency (with vulnerability being the other). Sheffi and Rice (2005), in their seminal work concerning resiliency, illustrated a disruption profile as exhibited in Fig. 14.1.

According to Sheffi and Rice (2005), a serious disruption in an organization (and its supply chain) can be dissected into eight components—starting from the event itself to the stage of full recovery and long term impact. Figure 14.1 also illustrates that a disruptive event can render a supply chain vulnerable and it generally takes a while for the supply chain to bounce back to its 'pre-disruption' state after the disturbance. Therefore, it can be stated that a proper understanding of the supply chain disruptions, coupled with a clear assessment of the accompanying risks, can serve as a key building block of a resilient supply chain. Supply chain risks identification lies at the foundation of building a resilient supply chain and risks can be categorized into different types and also from different perspectives. Understanding the risks associated with supply chain and developing mitigation strategies accordingly can aid an organization to understand and design their resiliency strategies.

One of the key initiatives for addressing these risks is fostering a risk management culture in organizations (Christopher and Peck 2004). Owing to the multi-level complications and multi-faceted interactions along the length of a supply chain, it becomes extremely difficult for the risk managers (or the risk management team) to monitor and identify all risks. As a result, nurturing the culture of risk management is an integral component in the success of an organization and risk assessment forms an important part of the decision making process. Therefore, organizations often create a cross-functional supply chain risk management team to report to the top management on a periodic basis through the supply chain managers.[1]

---

[1]It should be worthwhile to mention here that the risk exposure index, developed by David Simchi-Levi at Massachusetts Institute of Technology (MIT) enables companies for the first time to fully quantify their maximum risk exposure under any unpredictable supply chain disruptions. Ford has already implemented this in collaboration with the MIT team, by developing their

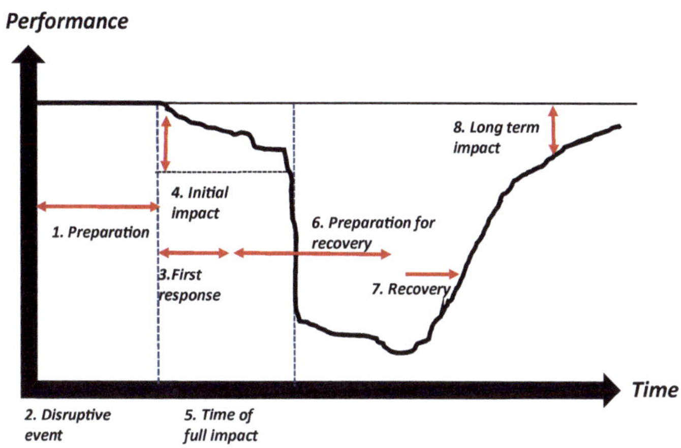

Fig. 14.1 The disruption profile. *Source* Sheffi and Rice (2005)

In recent years, supply chain disruption management has become one of the major concerns of many organizations and supply chain managers that direct its efforts to improve the resilience of their organization's supply chains (Barroso et al. 2010). Because complex global supply networks are characterized by limited visibility, the potential risks are hidden and their potential cascading effects may not be understood (Fiskel 2015). An often-cited example is Nokia's cell phone business, which discovered in 2000 that one of its key suppliers in New Mexico was concealing the fact that its facility had been destroyed by fire. However, early recognition of the crisis enabled Nokia to secure alternative supplies, and it modified the product design to broaden its sourcing options, ultimately gaining significant market share while Ericsson, which relied on the same supplier, lost about $400 million in sales due to slowness in crisis recognition and response, and eventually exited the cell phone business (Fiskel 2015; Fiskel et al. 2015). Therefore, one of the main objectives of building a resilient supply chain is to recover from any disruption caused due to known or unknown/unforeseen events, and organizations, over the years, have developed a set of strategies to make their supply chain more resilient and thus, more adaptable to unforeseen disruptions. Hamel and Vailikangas (2003), Christopher and Peck (2004) and Sheffi and Rice (2005), in their seminal articles concerning enterprise and supply chain resiliency, were one of

(Footnote 1 continued)

Decision Support System (DSS) for risk management, which is used daily. The system is used by procurement managers and directs in three ways—(1) strategically, to identify exposure to risk associated with parts and suppliers, prioritize and allocate resources effectively, segment suppliers, and develop risk mitigation plans, (2) tactically, to track daily changes in risk exposure in order to alert procurement executives to changes in their risk position; and (3) operationally, to respond to a disruptions by identifying an effective way to allocate resources after a disruption (Simchi-Levi et al. 2014; Simchi-Levi 2015).

the earliest proponents of resiliency strategies in organizations and supply chains. While Hamel and Vailikangas (2003) and Sheffi and Rice (2005) focused their attention on enterprise resiliency, Christopher and Peck (2004) did so more towards the resiliency of supply chains. Other notable works on supply chain resiliency strategies includes the research conducted by Barroso et al. (2010), Johnson et al. (2013), McKinnon (2014), Mensah and Merkuryev (2014), Ole-Hohenstein et al. (2015), Ponomarov and Holcomb (2009), Scholten et al. (2014) and Purvis et al. (2016), to name a few. However, with the blurring boundary between the resiliency of an enterprise and its supply chain, the strategies are being held true both in the case of an enterprise as well as its supply chain. The remainder of this section will be devoted towards enlisting and discussing the strategies that form essential building blocks of a resilient supply chain.

14.3.1 Making the Supply Chain Flexible/Agile in Nature

Resilience implies agility, or the flexibility (which can be stated as "being able to bend easily without breaking") and ability to adapt speedily (also referred to as "velocity") to both positive and negative environmental influences (Peck 2005; Ponomarov and Holcomb 2009). It is the ability of a supply chain to encounter, resolve, and when appropriate, exploit unexpected emergencies (Jüttner and Maklan 2011). Furthermore, it has been suggested that flexibility can amount to an organic capability, which also supports sensing disruptions and, as such, relates to the event readiness dimension of supply chain resilience (Sheffi and Rice 2005). According to Sheffi (2005), flexibility, coupled with redundancy, can be considered as the two important approaches for building resilience. Similarly, agility, defined as the ability of an organization's supply chain to respond rapidly to unpredictable changes in demand or supply (Christopher and Peck 2004), is another important strategy for building a resilient supply chain and involves continuous search for the most appropriate response to change, uncertainty and unpredictability within the business environment. The essence of flexibility and agility lies in a supply chains capability of reallocating resources when needed and developing good relationship with suppliers (Mensah and Merkuryev 2014). These characteristics along with velocity, which is considered as an important antecedent of agility, are essential in a resilient supply chain (Christopher and Peck 2004; Scholten et al. 2014).

Fashion giant, Zara, thrives on supply chain agility. Zara is renowned for replenishing stocks to each of its store twice a week in small batches thus producing close to 450 million items a year. However in order to reach on the rapid change in consumer demand, Zara has developed an efficient agile supply chain, with all designers, buyer experts and management in one place and production facility close to them, assuring full flexibility and agility (Zhelyazkov 2011).

14.3.2 Increasing the Redundancy of the Supply Chain

Some researches argue that redundancy, which can be stated as having excess capacity and back-up systems to maintain the core functionality of a system in the event of disturbances, ensures that an enterprise will be less likely to experience a collapse in the wake of unforeseen stresses. According to some researchers on supply chain resiliency, increasing the redundancy of an organization's supply chain can be a useful strategy in building a resilient supply chain. For example, Christopher and Peck (2004) argues that strategic disposition of additional capacity and/or inventory at potential 'pinch points' can be extremely beneficial in the creation of resilience within the supply chain (Christopher and Peck 2004). Purvis et al. (2016), in their research on supply chain resiliency strategy, established the fact that redundancy is a function of supply chain resiliency. Redundancy could be achieved through holding additional inventory (thereby preventing stockouts), ensuring excess supplier capacity, having multiple supply source and/or geographically dispersing the business (Christopher and Peck 2004; Ole-Hohenstein et al. 2015; Rice and Caniato 2003; Tomlin 2006), all with the intention of increasing a firm's ability to deal with disruptions. However, an overreliance on redundancy and its buffers to achieve resilience is also perceived as an expensive strategy, which should only be used temporarily in situations in which the disruption is predictable or more likely to occur in the near future (Sheffi 2005).

> An example of using supply chain redundancy to its advantage can be cited of Intel, one of the world's largest semiconductor chip makers. Intel builds semiconductor fabrication factories with identical layouts for machinery and production processes. Because of its standard fabrication design, Intel can switch production among facilities if the need arises (Sheffi 2005).

14.3.3 Increasing the Visibility of the Supply Chain

A clear understanding of upstream and downstream demand and customer expectation helps the supply chain to respond better to market changes more quickly. According to Christopher and Peck (2004), visibility implies a clear view of upstream and downstream inventories, demand and supply conditions, and production and purchasing schedules. Information sharing and collaboration between different entities in the supply chain is a pre-requisite to achieve visibility. An example of supply chain opaqueness caused due to each entity making their decision to respond to market flux without having proper information of the customer demand is bullwhip effect. A significant barrier to supply chain visibility is often encountered within the focal firm's internal organization structure. The presence of 'functional silos' inhibit the free flow of information leading to 'second guessing' and a general lack of communication (Christopher and Peck 2004).

For example, Cisco revamped its supply chain post hurricane Katrina in 2005, which paid major dividends in the aftermath of 2011 Japanese earthquake and tsunami. Within 40 minutes after the tsunami hit the shores, Cisco supply chain managers were aware of it and started forming their continuity plan. This catastrophe resulted in one of the largest supply chain disruptions in modern history, with economic losses crossing $200 billion. Yet, CISCO suffered almost no revenue loss. Within 12 hours, CISCO's managers could identify all their suppliers in the affected region, assess the impact of the disaster on more than 300 suppliers, list more than 7000 affected parts, assign a risk rating to each part and create a mitigation response. By the time the day drew to a close, CISCO had setup a solid supply chain resiliency program that addressed not only the impact of the tsunami but also the aftereffects the tsunami would cause on its worldwide value chain (Manners-Bell 2014).

14.3.4 Effective Knowledge Management and Collaboration Among the Supply Chain Entities

Researchers on supply chain resiliency have repeatedly stressed on the importance of effective knowledge management and information sharing as one of the key strategies in building a resilient supply chain. Information sharing, which can be stated as exchange of ideas between various organizations, people and technologies, can reduce uncertainty in supply chains and in turn, vulnerability to disruptions. Thus a key priority for supply chain risk reduction is the creation of a supply chain community to enable the exchange of information between members of that community (Christopher and Peck 2004). Additionally, sharing knowledge about supply chain disruptions has a positive impact on its resiliency as it can improve the event readiness through increasing the visibility and reducing the time for detection of the events (Jüttner and Maklan 2011; Manuj and Mentzer 2008). Furthermore, collaboration to share crucial information and valuable knowledge and establish joint efforts can also be considered as an important resiliency strategy (Johnson et al. 2013; Jüttner and Maklan 2011; Ole-Hohenstein et al. 2015; Pettit et al. 2010, 2013; Sheffi 2005). However, since supply chain resilience can't be achieved in silos, so the exchange of information has to be timely and accurate. Traditionally, different entities in a supply chain have different objectives which are often opposite in nature and therefore infuse a kind of adversarial relationship between them. Positive collaborative relations positively impacts smooth supply chain performance at times of disruption.

14.3.5 Inventory Management and Control

The use of inventory redundancy in situations of supply uncertainty is, in most cases, recognized as a possible risk mitigation strategy (Barroso et al. 2010) and aids in building up the resiliency of a supply chain. Although it might lead to an increase in the cost, building redundant inventory in the supply chain might function as a buffer to maintain continuous operations (Barroso et al. 2010). Therefore, researches on supply chain resiliency has enlisted stocking surplus inventory as one of the important strategies in ensuring supply chain resiliency (McKinnon 2014; Ole-Hohenstein et al. 2015).

For example, Walmart's vendor managed inventory model has been a major contributor towards the success of its supply chain. This benefit is achieved because suppliers can directly access data about the inventory of their goods at Walmart stores. As a result, multiple supplier can intervene in case of a supply chain disruption and ensure that the inventory reaches the stores on time, thereby eliminating the possibility of any breakdown of the supply chain. Furthermore, Walmart's policy of stockpiling to combat possible anticipated disasters had also been a key to their success, which they did in October 2002 prior to the West Coast port lockout, and in the process prevented any disruptions that could have affected their holiday sales (Sheffi 2005).

14.3.6 Changing the Corporate Culture

According to Christopher and Peck (2004), every organization should instill a culture of 'supply chain continuity management' in order to make sure that the supply chain disruptions are well understood and addressed. They further stated that a cross-functional supply chain risk management team should be created within the organization, whose primary responsibility will be to audit risks using a set of framework and tools and provided feedback on their analysis. Furthermore, Mensah and Merkuryev (2014) also stressed the importance of a strong corporate culture in building a resilient supply chain. According to them, developing a strong corporate culture will lead to empowering employees to make quick decisions, which might lead to quick recovery after disruptions. The role of developing a corporate culture to facilitate resiliency has also been discussed in the works of Sheffi (2005), Sheffi and Rice (2005) and Scholten et al. (2014). Table 14.2 provides the readers with the key supply chain resiliency strategies.

Table 14.2 Supply chain resiliency strategies

	Resiliency strategies
1	Making the supply chain flexible/agile in nature
2	Increasing the redundancy of the supply chain
3	Increasing the visibility of the supply chain
4	Effective knowledge management & collaboration among the supply chain entities
5	Inventory management and control
6	Changing the corporate culture

14.4 Conclusions

This chapter set out to familiarize the readers with the concept of supply chain resiliency and various strategies to achieve the same. In the present day business scenario marred by constant uncertainty and elephantine complexity, supply chain disruptions are increasing in frequency, thereby affecting their normal operation and stability and hence the ability of the business to fulfill commitments. This has been further complicated by the fact that the competition among business entities has gradually transitioned into competitions among their supply chains, thereby compelling organizations towards the daunting task of designing resilient supply chain strategies, which has fast become an essential component of business continuity. As a result, supply chains are being designed to be resilient to disruptions and react effectively to its negative effects (Barroso et al. 2015).

As discussed in this chapter, one of the key elements of being resilient is to anticipate, prepare, adapt and recover from disruptions. There have also been instances where organizations were able to treat potential disruptions as opportunities for gaining competitive advantage in the market. However, the key elements of supply chain resiliency and the strategies for managing these key issues are still not clearly understood. Additionally, in order to justify the need for resilient supply chains, one needs to have an understanding and clear definition of the phenomenon of resilience. This chapter tries to shed some light on these issues and is expected to serve as a starting block for students and researchers who wish to embark on the journey of exploring supply chain resiliency. The definitions, characteristics, strategies and the importance of resiliency in combating disruption as discussed in this chapter will serve as a valuable weapon in the hands of researchers who can subsequently use this as a roadmap for further research activities in supply chain resiliency. This chapter also has a twofold implication for managers as well. Firstly, practicing managers and executives can use the information provided in this chapter to respond to disruptive events more effectively and with increased confidence. Secondly, managers are encouraged to examine the strategies of designing a resilient supply chain as provided in this chapter as an avenue to ensure more effective structure and more efficient response to supply chain disruption.

Finally, it can be stated that just as the market is constantly changing, threats to our supply chains are evolving, adapting, and changing as well (Petit et al. 2010). Therefore, resilience has not only become a mandatory characteristic of a supply chain in order to survive in the short-term, but also provides the ability to adapt to change and thrive in the long-term (Petit et al. 2010) and is expected to prove to be the ultimate competitive advantage in an age of turbulence (Hamel and Valikangas 2003). The authors' expect that the theoretical foundation of the concept of supply chain resiliency as laid down in this chapter will help in building up future research activities that will open up new windows for research, in the process leading to the development of new theories and empirical studies on supply chain resiliency.

References

Ambulkar, S., Blackhurst, J., & Grawe, S. (2015). Firm's resilience to supply chain disruptions: Scale development and empirical examination. *Journal of Operations Management, 33,* 111–122.
Ates, A., & Bititci, U. (2011). Change process: A key enabler for building resilient SMEs. *International Journal of Production Research, 49*(18), 5601–5618.
Barroso, A. P., Machado, V. H., Barros, A. R., & Machado, V. C. (2010). Toward a resilient supply chain with supply disturbances. In *IEEE International Conference on Industrial Engineering and Engineering Management (IEEM)* (pp. 245–249). Macao, China.
Barroso, A. P., Machado, V. H., Carvalho, H., & Cruz Machado, V. (2015). Quantifying the supply chain resilience. In H. Tozan, & A. Erturk (Eds.), *Applications of contemporary management approaches in supply chains*. ISBN: 978-953-51-2045-2.
Barroso, A. P., Machado, V. H. & Machado, V. C. (2011). Supply chain resilience using mapping approach. In P. Li (Ed.), *Supply chain Management*. InTech Open Access Publishers on April 26, 2011 under CC BY-NC-SA 3.0 license. ISBN 978-953-307-184-8.
Bhamra, R., Dani, S., & Burnard, K. (2011). Resilience: The concept, a literature review and future directions. *International Journal of Production Research, 49*(18), 5375–5393.
Brandon-Jones, E., Squire, B., Autry, C. W., & Petersen, K. (2014). A contingent resource-based perspective of supply chain resilience and robustness. *Journal of Supply Chain Management, 50*(3), 55–73.
Carvalho, H., Azevedo, S. G., & Cruz-Machado, V. (2012). Agile and resilient approaches to supply chain management: Influence on performance and competitiveness. *Logistics Research, 4*(1–2), 49–62.
Christopher, M., & Peck, H. (2004). Building the resilient supply chain. *International Journal of Logistics Management, 15*(2), 1–14.
Christopher, M., & Rutherford, C. (2004). Creating supply chain resilience through agile six sigma. *Critical Eye*, 24–28.
Clapham, W. B. (1971). *Natural ecosystems*. New York, NY: Macmillan.
Craighead, C. W., Blackhurst, J., Rungtusanatham, M. J., & Handfield, R. B. (2007). The severity of supply chain disruptions: Design characteristics and mitigation capabilities. *Decision Sciences, 38*(1), 131–156.
Datta, P., Christopher, M., & Allen, P. (2007). Agent-based modelling of complex production/distribution systems to improve resilience. *International Journal of Logistics: Research and Applications, 10*(3), 187–203.
Dipietro, B. (2015, October 21). When manufacturing means building supply-chain resilience. *The Wall Street Journal*.
Falasca, M., Zobel, C. W., & Cook, D. (2008, May). A decision support framework to assess supply chain resilience. In *Proceedings of the 5th International ISCRAM Conference* (pp. 596–605).
Fiksel, J. (2015). *Resilient by design: Creating businesses that adapt and flourish in a changing world*. USA: Island Press.
Fiksel, J., Polyviou, M., Croxton, K. L., & Pettit, T. J. (2015). From risk to resilience: Learning to deal with disruption. *MIT Sloan Management Review, 56*(2), 79–86.
Hamel, G., & Välikangas, L. (2003). The quest for resilience. *Harvard Business Review, 81*(9), 52–65.
Johnson, N., Elliott, D., & Drake, P. (2013). Exploring the role of social capital in facilitating supply chain resilience. *Supply Chain Management: An International Journal, 18*(3), 324–336.
Jüttner, U., & Maklan, S. (2011). Supply chain resilience in the global financial crisis: An empirical study. *Supply Chain Management: An International Journal, 16*(4), 246–259.
Kamalahmadi, M., & Parast, M. M. (2016). A review of the literature on the principles of enterprise and supply chain resilience: Major findings and directions for future research. *International Journal of Production Economics, 171*(1), 116–133.

Kim, Y., Chen, Y. S., & Linderman, K. (2015). Supply network disruption and resilience: A network structural perspective. *Journal of Operations Management, 33–34,* 43–59.

Kleindorfer, P., & Saad, G. (2005). Managing disruption risks in supply chains. *Production and Operations Management, 14*(1), 53–68.

Manners-Bell, J. (2014). How does cisco manage supply chain risk? Accessed from http://electronicspurchasingstrategies.com/2014/08/12/cisco-manage-supply-chain-risk

Manuj, I., & Mentzer, J. (2008). Global supply chain risk management. *Journal of Business Logistics, 29*(1), 133–155.

McKinnon, A. (2014). *Building supply chain resilience: A review of challenges and strategies.* New Zealand: Christchurch.

Mearian, L. (2012, February 29). Thai floods catapult Seagate into hard drive market lead. Computerworld. Accessed from http://www.computerworld.com/article/2501937/data-storage-solutions/thai-floods-catapult-seagate-into-hard-drive-market-lead.html

Melnyk, S. A., Closs, D. J., Griffis, S. E., Zobel, C. W., & Macdonald, J. R. (2014). Understanding supply chain resilience. *Supply Chain Management Review, 18*(1), 34–41.

Mensah, P., & Merkuryev, Y. (2014). Developing a resilient supply chain. *Procedia-Social and Behavioral Sciences, 110,* 301–319.

Ole-Hohenstein, N., Feisel, E., Hartmann, E., & Giunipero, L. (2015). Research on the phenomenon of supply chain resilience: A systematic review and paths for further investigation. *International Journal of Physical Distribution & Logistics Management, 45* (1/2), 90–117.

Peck, H. (2005). Drivers of supply chain vulnerability: An integrated framework. *International journal of Physical Distribution & Logistics Management, 35*(4), 210–232.

Pettit, T. J., Croxton, K. L., & Fiksel, J. (2013). Ensuring supply chain resilience: Development and implementation of an assessment tool. *Journal of Business Logistics, 34*(1), 46–76.

Pettit, T. J., Fiksel, J., & Croxton, K. L. (2010). Ensuring supply chain resilience: Development of a conceptual framework. *Journal of Business Logistics, 31*(1), 1–21.

Ponis, S. T., & Koronis, E. (2012). Supply chain resilience: Definition of concept and its formative elements. *Journal of Applied Business Research, 28*(5), 921–929.

Ponomarov, S. Y., & Holcomb, M. C. (2009). Understanding the concept of supply chain resilience. *The International Journal of Logistics Management, 20*(1), 124–143.

Purvis, L., Spall, S., Naim, M., & Spiegler, V. (2016). Developing a resilient supply chain strategy during 'boom' and 'bust'. *Production Planning & Control.* doi:10.1080/09537287.2016.1165306:1-12.

Reitman, V. (1997, May 8). Toyota motor shows its mettle after fire destroys parts plant. *The Wall Street Journal.*

Rice, J. B., & Caniato, F. (2003). Building a secure and resilient supply network. *Supply Chain Management Review, 7*(5), 22–30.

Scholten, K., Sharkey, P., & Fynes, S. B. (2014). Mitigation processes—Antecedents for building supply chain resilience. *Supply Chain Management: An International Journal, 19*(2), 211–228.

Sheffi, Y. (2005). *The resilient enterprise: Overcoming vulnerability for competitive advantage.* Cambridge, MA: MIT Press.

Sheffi, Y., & Rice, J. B., Jr. (2005). A supply chain view of the resilient enterprise. *MIT Sloan Management Review, 47*(1), 41–48.

Simchi-Levi, D. (2015, June 9). Find the weak link in your supply chain. *Harvard Business Review.* Accessed from https://hbr.org/2015/06/find-the-weak-link-in-your-supply-chain

Simchi-Levi, D., Schmidt, W., & Yehua Wei, Y. (2014). From superstorms to factory fires: Managing unpredictable supply-chain disruptions. *Harvard Business Review, 92*(1–2), 96–102.

Svensson, G. (2002). Dyadic vulnerability in companies' inbound and outbound logistics flows. *International Journal of Logistics and Research Applications, 5*(1), 13–44.

Tomlin, B. (2006). On the value of mitigation and contingency strategies for managing supply chain disruption risks. *Management Science, 52*(5), 639–657.

Tukamuhabwa, B. R., Stevenson, M., Busby, J., & Zorzini, M. (2015). Supply chain resilience: Definition, review and theoretical foundations for further study. *International Journal of Production Research, 53*(18), 5592–5623.
Xiao, R., Yu, T., & Gong, X. (2012). Modeling and simulation of ant colony's labor division with constraints for task allocation of resilient supply chains. *International Journal on Artificial Intelligence Tools, 21*(3), 1–19.
Zhelyazkov, G. (2011). Agile supply chain: Zara's case study analysis. *Personal Website*. Accessed from http://www.galinzhelyazkov.com

Chapter 15
Designing Resilience into Service Supply Chains: A Conceptual Methodology

Sigurd S. Pettersen, Bjørn E. Asbjørnslett and Stein O. Erikstad

Abstract This chapter presents a methodology for designing resilient service supply chains. The approach combines system design methods with methods from risk assessment. Service supply chains consist of multiple assets, cooperating to fulfill an operation. Each asset has functionality to perform a set of tasks in the operation, and the combined functionalities of the fleet of assets must cover the activities the service supply chain are to perform. When a module in one asset in the fleet experiences loss of functionality, it constitutes a disruption in the service supply chain, a failure mode. The objective of the proposed methodology is to give decision support reducing the vulnerabilities of the service supply chain through design actions that can increase overall service supply chain resilience. The methodology consists of four steps. The first step includes breakdown of operation and service supply chain, mapping of modules to tasks, and selection of service supply chain configuration based on costs and utility. In the second step, failure modes are identified and their criticality assessed. In the third step, we propose design changes to reduce the impact of disruptions. These are evaluated in Step 4, where decisions regarding redesign are made. The recommendations from this methodology can be used to plan for how to redesign in the case of contingencies, or be used as part of an iterative process where the new information is incorporated in the evaluation of initial service supply chain design.

15.1 Introduction

Resilience is an increasingly important system property to stakeholders in complex systems, as for instance in an extended supply chain context. Consider the propagation of delays throughout a logistics chain due to a disruption in one leg of the

---

S.S. Pettersen (✉) · B.E. Asbjørnslett · S.O. Erikstad
Department of Marine Technology, Norwegian University of Science and Technology, Trondheim, Norway
e-mail: sigurd.pettersen@ntnu.no

Y. Khojasteh (ed.), *Supply Chain Risk Management*,
DOI 10.1007/978-981-10-4106-8_15

transport mission. Like this, it is reasonable to expect that a disruption in a part of a complex operation, due to a failure of some specialized equipment, will have similar repercussions. Both in the case of failure in the logistics chain and the complex operation, the consequences may be far greater than the costs indicated by the initial disruption.

In this context, we define service supply chains as fleets of assets, which cooperate to fulfill an operation. The assets within the service supply chains contain different modules, units of equipment fulfilling specific functions. There may exist functional overlap between different modules and assets. In case of cost optimization, this functional overlap may be regarded as slack, driving costs. If this were the case, a designer would be tempted to down-size the service supply chain system to avoid such overlap, hence reducing initial costs. A result may be an increase in vulnerability as functional redundancy is lost.

The design methodology presented in this chapter outlines how designers can take advantage of functional couplings and increase service supply chain resilience, by addressing opportunities to use objects for tasks for which they were not originally intended. This can be accomplished either by actively redesigning the system, or by redeploying existing system components to new tasks.

The objective of the *design methodology for resilient service supply chains* is to give decision support for reducing supply chain vulnerabilities, by *proposal of design actions based on redundancy and flexibility* (Sheffi and Rice 2005; Rice and Caniato 2003) *to enhance overall supply chain resilience*. In the context of building the resilient service supply chain, the following design-related questions should be answered:

1. What functionality does an operation require?
2. What is the functional scope and number of assets required for covering the functional requirements of the operation?
3. To what extent does functional overlap exist among the assets?
4. What opportunities exist for using assets for activities, other than the activities for which the asset was originally assigned?

Further, the reader should note that the focus are the risks related to the functionality of the system components. A failure mode approach is used to assess the disruption risk that enables an understanding of which functionalities should be restored to ensure continuation of operations (Berle et al. 2011a).

15.2 Theoretical Foundations for the Methodology

The theoretical foundations for the design methodology is a synthesis of supply chain risk management, reliability theory and systems design. By combining these subjects, new insight is achieved about how we can design for resilience in service supply chains. The approach represents an example of risk-based design thinking in a supply chain context, as we build mitigation measures into the service supply chain design (Papanikolaou 2009).

Supply chain risk management has been developed in part as a response to the focus on efficiency and cost-reduction in logistics and production. Increased complexity in supply chains has forced us to consider concepts such as resilience. Frameworks for building resilience into supply chains were presented by Peck (2005), Peck et al. (2003) and Christopher and Peck (2004). Craighead et al. (2007) outlined the roots of disruption risks in supply chain design characteristics. Rice and Caniato (2003) suggested that flexibility and redundancy are key strategies for achieving resilience.

Drawing inspiration from reliability theory, specifically failure mode, effects, and criticality analysis (FMECA) (Rausand 2011), Berle et al. (2011a) used failure modes to address the criticality of lost functionality in a supply chain system. Vulnerability analyses (Asbjørnslett 2009; Asbjørnslett and Rausand 1999) provided another link between the understanding of supply chain disruption risks, and the mitigating measures that can help restore the system after an unwanted event. Vulnerability analysis is used in a methodology for reducing logistical disruption risks, and was combined with failure mode thinking in Berle et al. (2011b). Asbjørnslett et al. (2012) bridged the gap between vulnerability analyses and design by developing a simulation model combined with an optimization algorithm that re-optimizes fleet configuration after failure modes mature.

A generic framework for decision making under uncertainty was presented in McManus and Hastings (2006), focusing on enabling lifecycle properties like flexibility and reliability. To achieve new insights and generate knowledge about how the supply chain can be designed for resilience, we utilize methods based on this framework. We combine the tradespace paradigm for early stage system design (Wasson 2005; Ross and Hastings 2005) with usage of design structure matrices (Steward 1981; Eppinger and Browning 2012). The tradespace approach facilitates a broad search of the design space for better solutions in terms of the cost and utility balance. Design structure matrices are useful for delimiting the supply chain design space with respect to physical limitations and functional relationships. In the tradespace context, the ability to quantify changeability to identify and execute options for future design changes becomes important (Ross et al. 2008). When a failure mode matures and alters the utility or functional performance of a given supply chain, flexibility can be used to enhance the resilience of the supply chain.

15.3 Concepts and Definitions

The concept of resilience refers to the ability of a system, such as a supply chain, to recover from a disruption (Rice and Caniato 2003). Implicitly, we can assume that designing for resilience is about *building capabilities into the design to ease the recovery process*. Designers acknowledge that the number of failure scenarios is so large, that some disruption to the operation eventually will occur (Berle et al. 2011a).

It is thus necessary to design systems that can be restored after the occurrence of the disruption, hence minimizing the consequences of the undesired event.

The approach is mission oriented, and fulfilling the mission of the service supply chain is the objective. Figure 15.1 shows how the performance of a system deteriorates after a disruption, and how it can be restored, regaining a new stable performance level. Performance should be regarded as a function representing a mission-supporting or mission-enabling capability. Designing for resilience is in essence about designing into the system the capability to achieve a new level of operational performance, within a mission-feasible timeframe (short enough disruption time). That is the service supply chain's ability to fulfill its mission even if the initial attempt fails to succeed.

Some key concepts and definitions for supply chain vulnerability, risk and resilience from Asbjørnslett (2009) are shortly re-stated here. Vulnerability is a concept that may be used to characterize a supply chain system's lack of robustness or resilience with respect to various threats that originate both within and outside its system boundaries. The focus in this method is how the vulnerability of the service operation, based upon failures in functionality of the service supply chain, can be reduced through functional flexibility on the asset level, or even on the module level by redesigning the assets.

Opposite to vulnerability, we have robustness or resilience. A service supply chain can be said to be robust or resilient, with respect to a hazard or threat, if the hazard or threat is not able to produce any 'lethal' effect on the system. In our case, this means that the hazard or threat, or the resulting failure mode, does not reduce the functional performance level of the service supply chain below a level so that the service supply chain is no longer able to perform its mission. We define robustness as a system's ability to resist an accidental event, returning to do its intended mission and retaining the same stable situation as it had before the accidental event. Resilience may be defined as a system's ability to return to a new stable situation after an accidental event. As such, robust systems have the ability to

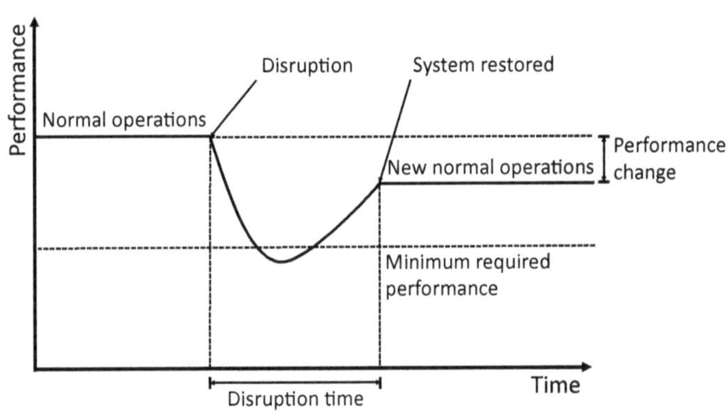

Fig. 15.1 Performance levels during normal operations and disruptions, based on Asbjørnslett and Rausand (1999)

resist, while resilient systems have the ability to adapt. In this approach, we seek to design service supply chains, consisting of assets that have the ability to adapt, given failure modes leading to loss of functionality.

For developing the methodology, we define the central building blocks of the service supply chain. Hierarchically, we can look at the service supply chain as built up by assets that cooperate to complete the mission. The assets are further built up by modules, which represent units of equipment performing the required functions. Function can in this respect be defined as "the actions for which a thing is fitted or used" (de Weck et al. 2011). Thus, each module has functionality, letting them perform specific tasks. In principle, every module can have several functions, so that it is possible for redundancies to exist without the initial intention of the designer.

15.4 A Methodology for Resilient Service Supply Chain Design

15.4.1 Overview of the Conceptual Methodology

The design methodology for resilient service supply chains is an iterative process. Starting from an initial supply chain design, it goes through a process in which failure modes are assessed, and design actions to increase resilience are proposed, and evaluated. The insights from the analysis enables the designer to establish a more resilient basis for design. Improved insight into the resilient properties of the

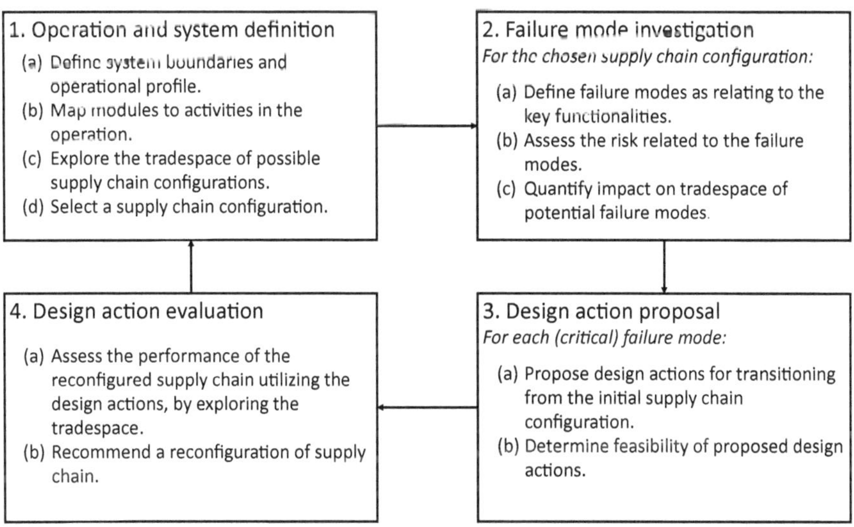

Fig. 15.2 Flowchart for the resilient service supply chain design methodology

service supply chain design can also support formulation of contingency plans for the supply chain. A flowchart for the design methodology is shown in Fig. 15.2.

To make the methodology easier to follow, we present it as applied on a case. The case we present comes from marine operations. More specifically, we consider a group of vessels as a service supply chain cooperating to perform an offshore construction mission. The case is illustrative, and serves as an explanatory parallel for the methodology.

15.4.2 Step 1: Operation and System Definition

In Step 1, we need to select a service supply chain configuration that fulfills the scope of operation. This step is an example of solving a fleet size and mix problem using tradespace exploration and design structure matrices by simultaneously exploring alternative service supply chains.

The tradespace of service supply chains to be explored is defined in terms of assets included in the service supply chain. These assets are heterogeneous, each being defined by the modules included in their design. In this case, assets are possible vessel designs, and modules represent equipment that serve a purpose towards fulfillment of the operational profile. Alternative vessel designs are defined based on what cranes and winches are included in the design. Based on this we completely enumerate the design space of alternative vessel configurations. Finally, we specify the architecture of possible service supply chains by combining vessels that together cover the functional requirements for all tasks in the operation. The system boundaries are thus set around the vessels that constitute the service supply chain.

The offshore construction operation is decomposed into individual tasks, so an operational profile for the service supply chain can be established. This allows us to select a service supply chain configuration according to the current operation context. In this case, the tasks to be performed are a small lift, a large lift, and a towing task.

As the structure of the operation and the system structure of the service supply chain now have been established, we can now map the modules in each asset to each task in the operation using design structure matrices. This mapping between modules and tasks is shown in Fig. 15.3. The numbering in the mapping matrix refers to the goodness of fit between module and task, where 2 indicates better performance than 1.

The service supply chain needs to be able to perform all tasks that are part of the marine operation. From Fig. 15.3 we can see that modules included in the proposed service supply chain offer functional redundancy. Several modules can perform the same task. For example, the large winch can perform small lifts in addition to towing, albeit at a lower capability level.

By establishing a cost-utility tradespace, we explore alternative service supply chain configurations. In this case, we estimate the cost for the service supply chain

Generic mapping between activities and modules

		Large crane	Small crane	Large winch	Small winch
Marine operation	Small lift	2	2	1	0
	Large lift	2	0	1	0
	Towing	0	0	2	2

Mapping for a specific service supply chain configuration

		Vessel 7		Vessel 12
		Large crane	Small winch	Large winch
Marine operation	Small lift	2	0	1
	Large lift	2	0	1
	Towing	0	2	2

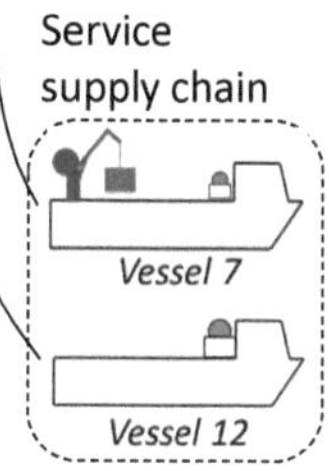

Fig. 15.3 Design structure matrix mapping between tasks in the operation and the modules in service supply chains

configuration from the number of vessels and the modules installed on each vessel. A multi-attribute utility function is established from several value attributes combined into a single, normalized metric (Ross and Hastings 2005). The value attributes measure objectives that to some extent are in conflict, and must be weighed against each other (Keeney and Raiffa 1993). In the case presented, the following value attributes are important:

- The number of vessels in the service supply chain.
- The overall service supply chain capability level.
- The amount of functional redundancy in the service supply chain.

The objectives that correspond to the attributes are to minimize the number of vessels in the service supply chain, and to maximize the capability level and the amount of functional redundancy. We assume a linear relationship between single-objective utilities and corresponding attributes. For simplicity, each of the value attributes are seen as equally important, and are assigned equal weights in the multi-attribute utility function.

Figure 15.4 shows the resulting tradespace representation of alternative service supply chains, after calculating costs and utility. All points in the plot refer to alternative service supply chain configurations. Three of these configurations are highlighted. The most interesting architectures to explore further are those close to the Pareto front, which are the designs that maximize the utility, for each possible budgetary constraint. Pareto optimal service supply chain give the most value (utility) for money spent.

The outcome of Step 1 of the methodology is the selection of one specific service supply chain configuration. In Fig. 15.4, we see that Service Supply Chain no. 146 is Pareto efficient. Hence, we select this as the initial configuration.

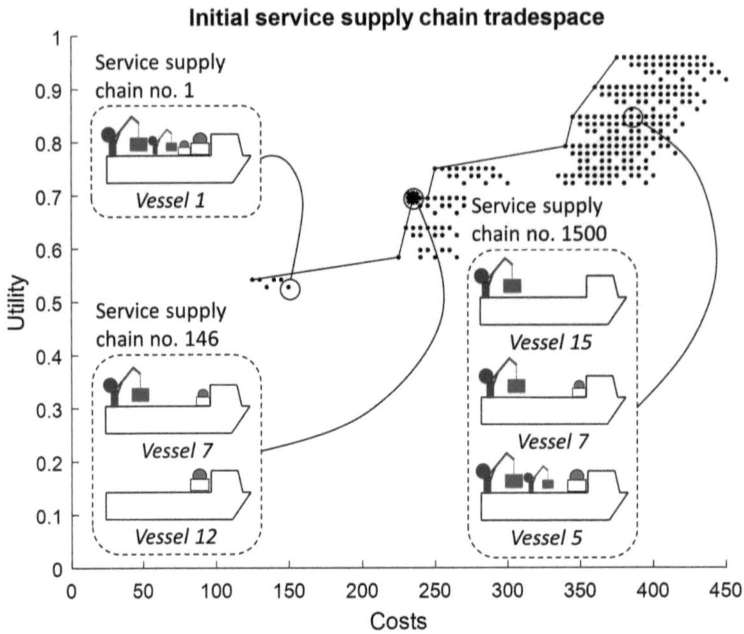

Fig. 15.4 Tradespace of alternative service supply chain configurations

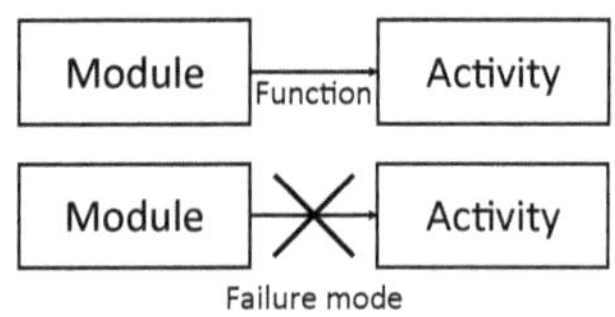

Fig. 15.5 Failure modes defined as loss of functionality, severing the link between a system module and a task

15.4.3 Step 2: Failure Mode Investigation

After selecting the initial service supply chain configuration, we need to account for possible failures in the marine assets included. Many failure modes can disrupt the offshore construction operation, and their effect on the operational performance must therefore be understood. Starting from the lowest level of indenture in the system decomposition in Step 1, the module level, we now must identify the failure modes from the related modules. We see how the functionality of a module allows it to complete a task in Fig. 15.5. The failure mode makes the module unfit for completing the task. The failure modes are thus related to the set of functionalities for each module in an asset, and loss of functional performance required in a task. Through decomposition of the service supply chain to the module level, we thus become able to identify failure modes easily.

To assess the importance of alternative disruption scenarios, we quantify the risk of each identified failure mode. Risk is defined as the product of likelihood and

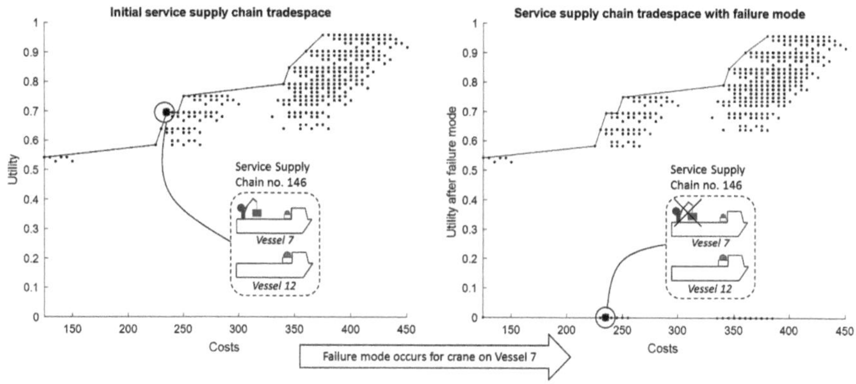

Fig. 15.6 Changes in tradespace due to the failure of the large crane module

consequence for failure. Likelihood estimates for functional failures in components can be found from existing handbooks of failure rate data, from experiments or simulation models. The consequence is found from the change in overall utility for the service supply chain due to the failure. At this stage, failure mode, effects, and criticality analyses can be used for assessing the risks of each failure mode (Rausand 2011). Risk priority numbers can then represent the risk. These risk priority numbers are tied to the negative impact on the utility of the service supply chain. Ideally, one should perform an extensive FMECA for the service supply chain in Step 2.

For illustrating the methodology, we show the effect of one crane failure aboard Vessel 7 on overall performance of the service supply chain. Note that this is only one of numerous scenarios that must be considered in Step 2. Figure 15.6 shows the tradespaces before and after the crane failure. We see that the chosen service supply chain configuration drops from the Pareto front, and becomes unable to fulfill its mission. Thus, utility is set to 0.

15.4.4 Step 3: Design Action Proposal

When the effects of alternative failure modes on the tradespace have been assessed, we can start looking for solutions that may restore normal operation of the service supply chain, for every failure mode. If possible, one would prefer to restore the service supply chain system to Pareto optimality. By taking advantage of current functional redundancy or exercising flexibility in the supply chain system, we seek to restore its performance. Using redundancy, we could take advantage of functional overlaps in the service supply chain. The modules included in assets in the service supply chain may not be at full utilization, and these modules can be reassigned to perform disrupted tasks. In the case of redundant functionality available, the service supply chain would drop from the Pareto front, while the configuration would remain feasible. For the failure shown in Fig. 15.6, this is not possible, as the large lift is a task that no existing module installed on either asset, Vessel 7 and Vessel 12, can perform. This renders the service supply chain infeasible. This means that a design action based on flexibility in the service supply chain design must be sought.

Exercising flexibility to mitigate the consequences of the failure mode thus implies some redesign of the service supply chain. Changing the configuration of the supply chain means that a transition occurs in the tradespace where all supply chain designs are plotted (Ross et al. 2008). The redesigned service supply chain will no longer be the initial point design we selected in Step 1 that was negatively affected by the failure mode introduced in Step 2. We separate between exercise of flexibility through adding modules to existing assets in the service supply chain, and exercise of flexibility through adding new assets to the service supply chain. In Fig. 15.7 we show how flexibility is exercised in the offshore construction case. All feasible transitions away from the supply chain experiencing functional failure are shown with circles. Two possible transitions are highlighted in Fig. 15.7, from Service Supply Chain no. 146 to Service Supply Chain no. 1725 and Service Supply Chain no. 3485, as these are Pareto optimal transition. These highlighted alternative transitions will add either Vessel 7 or Vessel 15 to the service supply chain, while keeping the other existing assets. In this case, all transitions to new service supply chain configurations indicate addition of assets, rather than redesigning assets by adding new modules.

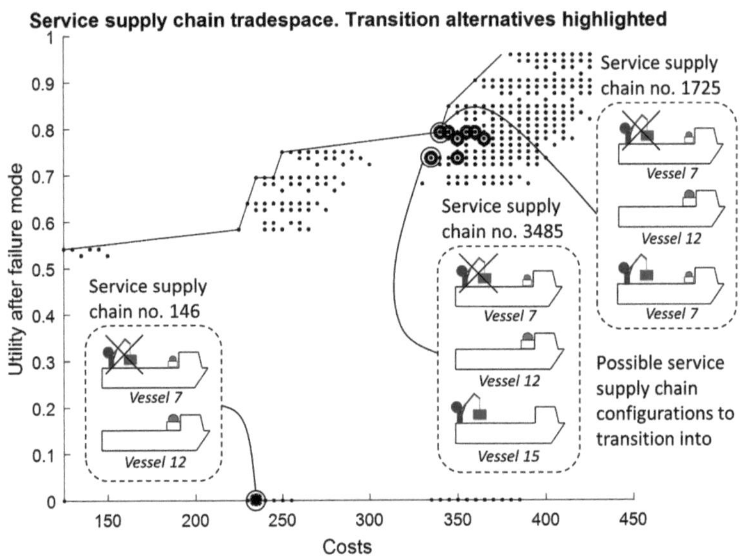

Fig. 15.7 Tradespace showing transition alternatives for the service supply chain after failure mode

To define whether a specific transition path representing a potential design action is feasible, we need to implement some rules. First, it is reasonable to consider only transitions that involve changing the assets by adding modules, or adding assets to the service supply chain. These transitions should ensure that the affected activities get a new functional module assigned to them. This corresponds to identifying possible transition paths.

Second, during an operation that is being disrupted due to a system failure, time will be a critical factor. Hence, the response must be agile, meaning that reconfiguring or adding new modules to the assets in the service supply chain should be simple and time-effective. Thus, depending on the time-horizon of the operation, larger retrofits of the assets involved in the operation may not be considered feasible transitions. As we saw from the explanatory case, adding wholly new assets to the service supply chain may be a better alternative. The highlighted transition paths in Fig. 15.7 are both based on addition of assets to cover the lost functionality.

To conclude Step 3, we point to the need for an appropriate cost threshold for the expense associated with implementation of a design action proposition (Ross et al. 2008). The cost threshold should represent the upper bound for expenditures, time and other resources that can be spent for restoring the service supply chain, through a design action proposal represented by a tradespace transition. This way we ensure that the measures taken through redesign of the service supply chain will serve their purpose and help restore the performance of the system without excessive cost slips. Ross et al. (2008) uses the term filtered outdegree to specify the number of transition paths falling within the cost threshold.

15.4.5 Step 4: Design Action Evaluation

In Step 4, the redesign opportunities found in Step 3 are evaluated. These redesign opportunities are the possible transitions in the tradespace. The cost of adding new assets or installing new modules on assets in the service supply chain, and the corresponding utility of the new service supply chain configuration, is information that can be obtained from the cost and utility calculations in Step 1.

While unacceptable transitions were filtered out in Step 3, there are still several tradeoffs to account for, before selecting a final transition path to a new service supply chain configuration. A possible tradeoff that the decision-makers face at this stage, are the expenditure associated with a transition, versus the timeliness of the transition. At the same time, one would prefer to transition back to the Pareto front, if possible. For further discussion of redesign using tradespace exploration, see Ross et al. (2008) and Fitzgerald and Ross (2012a, b).

Figure 15.7 highlighted a set of possible transitions away from Service Supply Chain no. 146, to amongst others Service Supply Chain no. 1725 and Service Supply Chain no. 3485. Observing all the service supply chains that are highlighted as possibilities for redesign, we see that only Service Supply Chain no. 1725 is

Pareto efficient. This alternative is perhaps the most reasonable choice for redesign based on the existing information.

15.5 Summary

The logic of the design methodology is summarized in Fig. 15.8. The original situation upon which we select the initial service supply chain design is shown as normal operations to the far left in the figure. This represents Step 1. In Step 2, as a failure mode occurs, the performance and hence value of each configuration in the tradespace will decrease. This is illustrated in the second illustration from the left. The third tradespace from the left represents Step 3, and shows some possible transition paths, in which the initial service supply chain will be redesigned by adding an asset, or by adding a new module to one of the assets. Finally, when we select among the alternative transitions in Step 4, we restore the service supply chain to a new stable level of normal operations. In the tradespaces, the selected service supply chain is highlighted by a triangle.

The link between Step 1 and Step 2 are summarized on a more detailed level in the design structure matrices in Fig. 15.9, showing the effect of two possible failure modes on three possible service supply chain architectures, where Service Supply Chain 1 has been selected as an initial configuration. Failure Mode 1 is defined as loss of functionality of Module 2 in Asset 1, while Failure Mode 2 is defined as loss of functionality of Module 4 in Asset 2. To the left, we show the original situation, while the effects of two alternative failure modes are shown to the right.

Figure 15.10 illustrates the tradespace representations corresponding to the design structure matrices shown in Fig. 15.9. As we see, the utility of all possible configurations declines due to the failure modes that may occur.

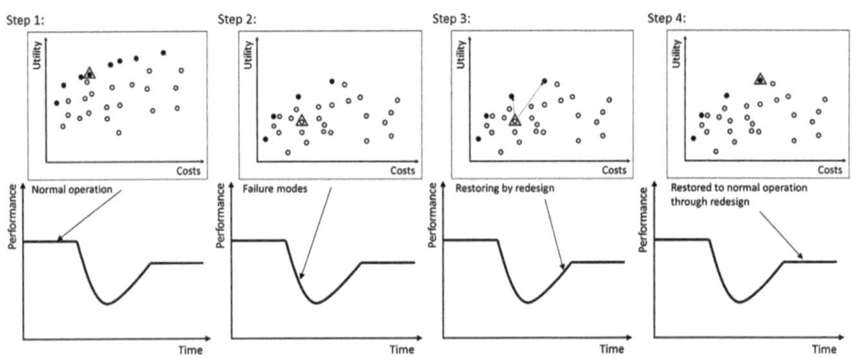

Fig. 15.8 Tradespace exploration connected to the resilience concept

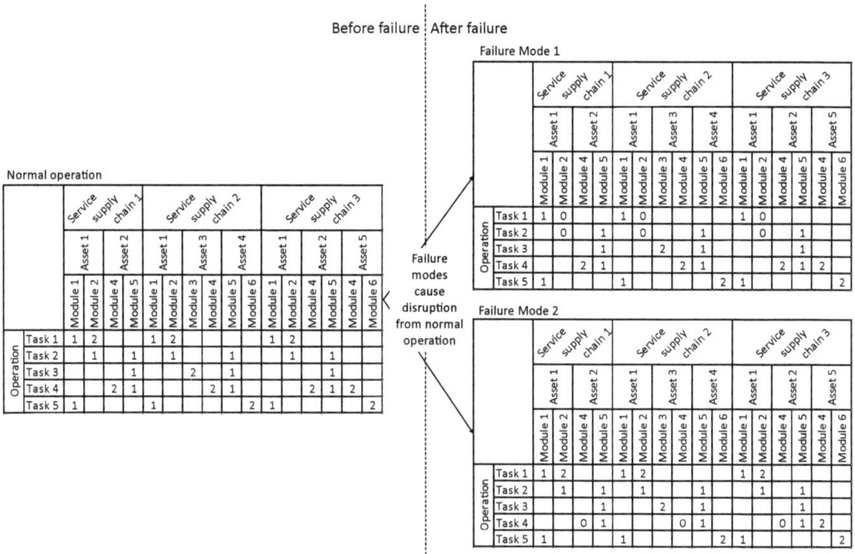

Fig. 15.9 Design structure matrices mapping modules to tasks during normal operation and two alternative failure modes

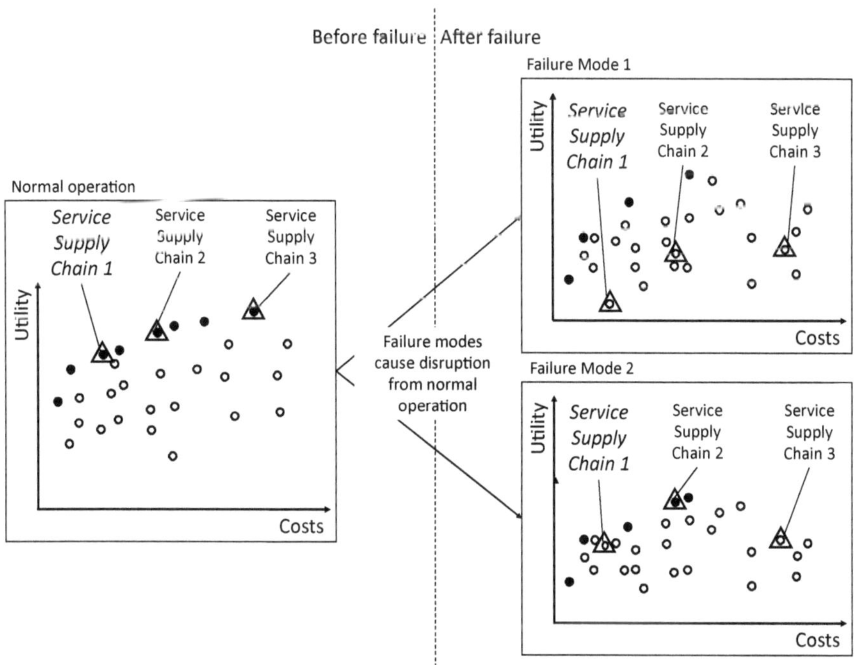

Fig. 15.10 Tradespace illustrating performance during normal operation and two alternative failure modes

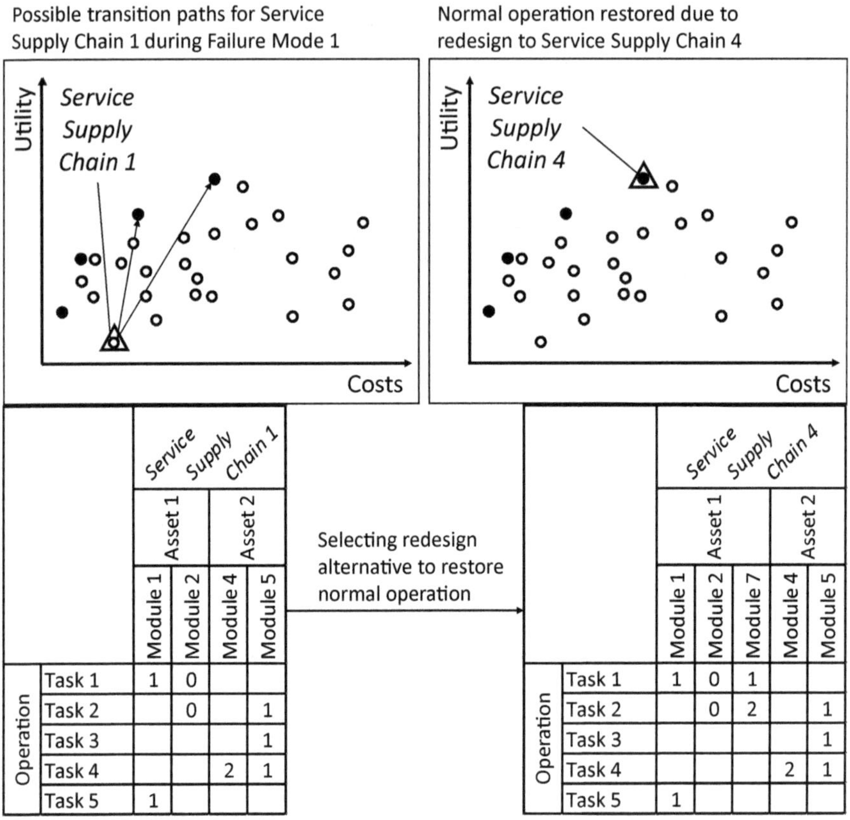

Fig. 15.11 Design structure matrix and tradespace illustrating the redesign of the service supply chain

Figure 15.11 illustrates the design structure matrix for the disrupted Service Supply Chain 1, and corresponding tradespace with two possible transition paths, to the left. When we identify transition paths for the redesign of the service supply chain, we go through Step 3 of the methodology. To the right, Fig. 15.11 shows the design structure matrix for Service Supply Chain 4, which is the resulting configuration after redesign by selecting one transition path. The location of Service Supply Chain 4 in the tradespace is also shown. The selection of this transition path corresponds to adding Module 7 to Asset 1. This redesign process fulfills Step 4 of the methodology.

Overall, the methodology offers a novel approach to designing more resilient supply chains for service operations. By combining proven concepts from engineering design and reliability theory, supply chain managers, designers and decision-makers get a new tool for increasing resilience in supply chains.

References

Asbjørnslett, B. E. (2009). Assessing the vulnerability of supply chains. In G. A. Zsidisin & B. Ritchie (Eds.), *Supply chain risk—A handbook of assessment, management, and performance* (pp. 15–33). New York, NY: Springer Science+Business Media.
Asbjørnslett, B. E., Norstad, I., & Berle, Ø. (2012). Risk-based design of maritime transport systems. In P. Hokstad, I. B. Utne, & J. Vatn (Eds.), *Risk and interdependencies in critical infrastructures* (pp. 161–174). London, UK: Springer.
Asbjørnslett, B. E., & Rausand, M. (1999). Assess the vulnerability of your production system. *Production Planning & Control, 10*(3), 219–229.
Berle, Ø., Asbjørnslett, B. E., & Rice, J. B., Jr. (2011a). Formal vulnerability assessment of a maritime transportation system. *Reliability Engineering and System Safety, 96*(6), 696–705.
Berle, Ø., Rice, J. B., Jr., & Asbjørnslett, B. E. (2011b). Failure modes in the maritime transportation system: A functional approach to throughput vulnerability. *Maritime Policy & Management, 38*(6), 605–632.
Christopher, M., & Peck, H. (2004). Building the resilient supply chain. *The International Journal of Logistics Management, 15*(2), 1–14.
Craighead, C. W., Blackhurst, J., Rungtusanatham, M. J., & Handfield, R. B. (2007). The severity of supply chain disruptions: Design characteristics and mitigation capabilities. *Decision Sciences, 38*(1), 131–156.
de Weck, O. L., Roos, D., & Magee, C. L. (2011). *Engineering systems: Meeting human needs in a complex technological world*. Cambridge, MA: The MIT Press.
Eppinger, S. D., & Browning, T. R. (2012). *Design structure matrix: Methods and applications*. Cambridge, MA: The MIT Press.
Fitzgerald, M. E. & Ross, A. M. (2012a). Mitigating contextual uncertainties with valuable changeability analysis in the multi-epoch domain. In *6th Annual IEEE Systems Conference* (pp. 281–288).
Fitzgerald, M. E. & Ross, A. M. (2012b). Sustaining lifecycle value: Valuable changeability analysis with era simulation. In *6th Annual IEEE Systems Conference* (pp. 202–208).
Keeney, R. L., & Raiffa, H. (1993). *Decisions with multiple objectives: Preferences and value tradeoffs*. Cambridge, UK: Cambridge University Press.
McManus, H. L., & Hastings, D. E. (2006). A framework for understanding uncertainty and its mitigation and exploitation in complex systems. *IEEE Engineering Management Review, 34* (3), 81–94.
Papanikolaou, A. D. (2009). *Risk-based ship design*. In: A. D. Papanikolaou (Ed.), Springer: Berlin, Germany.
Peck, H. (2005). Drivers of supply chain vulnerability: An integrated framework. *International Journal of Physical Distribution & Logistics Management, 35*(3/4), 210–232.
Peck, H., Abley, M., Christopher, M., Hayford, M., Saw, R., Rutherford, C., et al. (2003). *Creating resilient supply chains: A practical guide*. Cranfield, UK. Available at http://dspace.lib.cranfield.ac.uk/handle/1826/4374
Rausand, M. (2011). *Risk assessment: Theory, methods, and applications* (1st ed.). Hoboken, NJ: John Wiley & Sons Inc.
Rice, J. B., Jr., & Caniato, F. (2003). Building a secure and resilient supply network. *Supply Chain Management Review, 7*(5), 22–30.
Ross, A. M., & Hastings, D. E. (2005). The tradespace exploration paradigm. In *INCOSE International Symposium 2005*.
Ross, A. M., Rhodes, D. H., & Hastings, D. E. (2008). Defining changeability: Reconciling flexibility, adaptability, scalability, modifiability, and robustness for maintaining system lifecycle value. *Systems Engineering, 11*(3), 246–262.

Sheffi, Y., & Rice, J. B., Jr. (2005). A supply chain view of the resilient enterprise. *MIT Sloan Management Review, 47*(1), 41–48.

Steward, D. V. (1981). The design structure system: A method for managing the design of complex systems. *IEEE Transactions on Engineering Management, EM-28*(3), 71–74.

Wasson, C. S. (2005). *System analysis, design, and development: Concepts, principles, and practices*. Hoboken, NJ: John Wiley & Sons Inc.

Chapter 16
Resiliency in Supply Chain Systems: A Triadic Framework Using Family Resilience Model

Arash Azadegan and Jayanth Jayaram

Abstract Although the significance of supply chain resilience has been well explored, there is much to be explained about its formation and composition. Using systems theory and the Family Resilience model, this chapter offers a series of organizational characteristics that combine to form supply chain resilience. These subsets of supply chain resilience are categorized into three. The first, *inherent resilience*, comes from the strength of resources that are already possessed, are permanent and inseparable from the supply chain itself. The second, *anticipative resilience*, are ones developed purposefully to face crises and disruptions. These are preparatory resources that come in the form of excess resources, business continuity plans, or insurance policies. The third type is *adaptive resilience*, which can come in the form of collaborative capabilities, collective decision-making, and leadership that combines care and concern with the ability to make on the spot decisions. The chapter explains how supply chains, as organizational systems, leverage these three sub-sets to face disruptions.

16.1 Introduction

In today's global, dynamic and highly competitive business environment, success requires a sound approach to preparation and response to supply chain risks and disruptions. As of late, the frequency and extent of potential threats to supply chains for many companies have sharpened. Potentially as a result of the global reach of supply chains, and increased inter-dependence among supply chain members,

A. Azadegan (✉)
Rutgers Business School, New Brunswick, Newark, NJ, USA
e-mail: aazadegan@business.rutgers.edu

J. Jayaram
University of South Carolina, Columbia, SC, USA

Y. Khojasteh (ed.), *Supply Chain Risk Management*,
DOI 10.1007/978-981-10-4106-8_16

companies have become ever more concerned about their ability to manage risks and respond to disruptions (Blackhurst et al. 2011).

Supply chain resilience is a company's ability to rebound from adverse events, possibly more resourcefully and with more strength. Since resilience can help improve response and recovery in the face of disruptions better than one's competitors, a resilient supply chain can be a source of competitive advantage. It is not a surprise to see continually rising interest in better defining and explaining the concept during the recent past (Chopra and Sodhi 2014; Bode et al. 2011). While the significance of supply chain resilience has been well-explored, much remains to be explained about its composition and formation. Researchers have often relied on a tabulation of factors that could strengthen mitigation and response efforts in their explanations of supply chain resilience (Pettit et al. 2010). For instance, some suggest for flexibility, redundancy and innovativeness to be indicative of resilience in supply chains (Tang 2006; Sheffi 2015). Others suggest that collaborative efforts and human capital help with resilience (Blackhurst et al. 2011).

As research on supply chain resilience matures, it is becoming apparent that registering a handful of interesting variables may not adequately explain the concept of supply chain resilience. To date, minimal emphasis has been placed on a rigorous and theory-based explanation of supply chain resilience. Indeed, assuming that firms can fuse these elements together, how to combine and apply them so as to best manage disruptions is not explained. The interplay between factors that build supply chain resilience is rarely the topic of discussion. Moreover, many of the common factors considered in supply chain resilience are multifaceted. Flexibility, for instance, can come in the form of capacity flexibility, scheduling flexibility, material flexibility, sourcing flexibility and several others (Skipper and Hanna 2009). Similarly, innovativeness can be in the form of innovative ability in products or processes or even organizational structure (Azadegan and Dooley 2010). Missing from the literature is a theoretically sound explanation of the "how" and "why" of the effects of supply chain resilience.

In this chapter, we combine two theoretical explanations to help detail the nuances associated with supply chain resilience. We combine how systems theory characterizes resilient systems (Holling 1973; Ashby 1962) with how sociologists and psychologists studying military families characterize resilient families (Mccubbin and Patterson 1982). When faced with adversity and crises caused by deployment, injury or death of the service-person, some military families show much stronger response and recovery capabilities. The Family Resiliency (FR) model offers categories of resilience characteristics and explains the interaction among these categories (McCubbin and McCubbin 1996). In line with systems theory and the FR model, we define supply chains as interacting and interdependent group of companies making an effort to survive and succeed in their immediate environment.

According to systems theory, resiliency in living systems is enhanced when particular characteristics are present. The first characteristic is the ability of the system to maintain "fit" with its environment. Systems that can sense, respond, adjust and adapt faster than changes in their environment are more fit. Maintaining "fit" becomes harder as systems become more complex. In complex systems, not only is there a need for fit between internal operations and the external environment, but also a fit between operations of members with one another. Balancing the internal needs while addressing changes initiated outside the company can become difficult as the system grows larger and more complex. Because of the larger number of organizational members, complex supply chains carry more connections between companies, more layers of connections and more connections between individual agents. Naturally, these require careful orchestration of how the fit with the environment is implemented.

Another characteristic of resilient systems is the notion of *requisite variety* (Ashby 1962). To maintain stability, the number of conditions that a system can adjust to and accommodate needs to be greater than or equal to the number of conditions that the environment can throw at the system. As Ashby (1962) noted, "only variety can destroy variety". For example, a winning chess player might be said to have more variety of moves than his losing opponent. For supply chains, *requisite variety* implies that the combination of capabilities that a company provides should be prepared for handling more than what is emergent in the environment.

The third characteristic of resilient systems is the notion of *multi-stability* (Ashby 1960). Living systems have a preference toward a particular equilibrium point between them and the external environment (Cariani 2009). For instance, the human body operates best at 98.6 °F. Reverting to this preferred equilibrium point implies that our bodies return to an optimal pattern of operation. However, resilient systems are ones that can operate well under a multitude of alternative equilibria. These are called *metastable systems* (Holling 1973; Ashby 1956). While the human body best operates at 98.6 °F, humans are able to operate in temperatures fluctuating lower and above any place on earth, simply because of their ability to adjust and adapt through clothing, coolers/ACs, and other climate technologies.

How systems theory explains resilience has been applied extensively in families. Psychologists and sociologists have offered overwhelming support in how members of resilient families can face adversity and crisis more successfully than others (Walsh 1996; Patterson 2002). A popular model is the Resiliency Model of Family Stress, Adjustment, and Adaptation (RM Model hereafter) (McCubbin and McCubbin 1996).

According to the RM model, certain categories of family functioning are critical to family recovery in the face of a crisis (McCubbin and McCubbin 1996). These include the family's (1) *Family resources*, (2) *Patterns of functioning, and stressor appraisal*, and (3) *Problem-solving and coping* (Fig. 16.1). Families with weak finances, or health issues are more vulnerable to potential crises. Those with established patterns of bonding and cohesiveness are shown to be more successful in facing unfortunate events (McCubbin and McCubbin 1996). The FR model offers

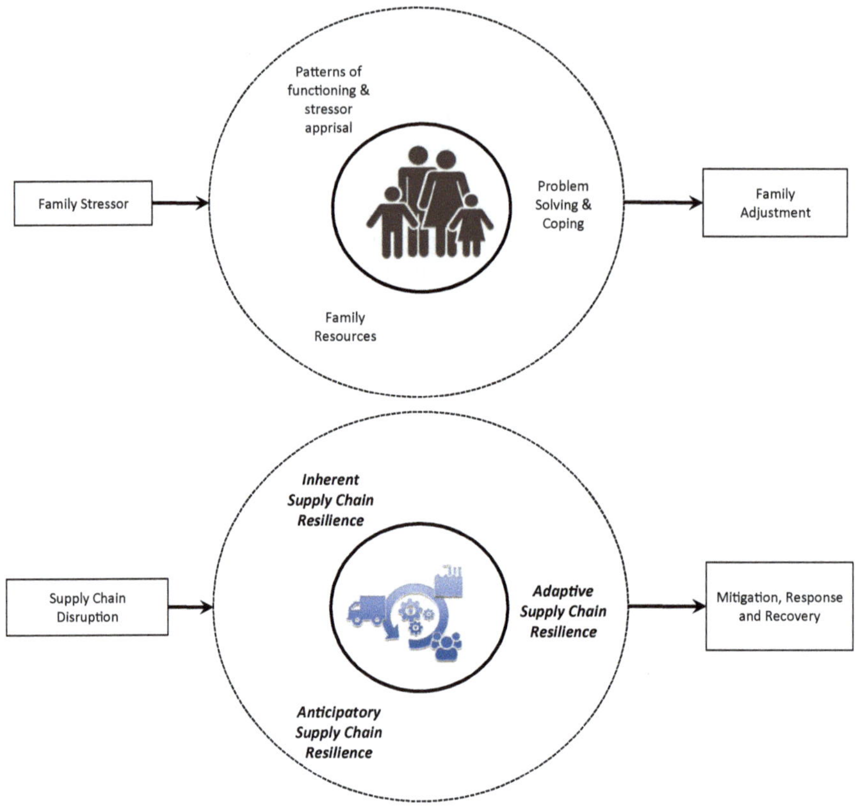

Fig. 16.1 Family resilience model and applicability to supply chains (adapted from McCubbin and McCubbin 1996)

two key insights to the study of resilience in supply chains. First, it offers a categorization of factors that lead to resilience based on how living systems operate. Second, it explains how these categories interact so as to mutually reinforce the system's abilities.

In this chapter, we relate explanations provided by systems theorists and the FR model to develop a conceptual model for resilience in supply chains. To start, using theoretical explanations and based on the OM/SCM literature, we categorize organizational characteristics that lead to resilience into three: (1) *inherent resilience*, (2) *anticipatory resilience* and (3) *adaptive resilience* (Fig. 16.1). We then go on to provide further specifics about the model to offer more explicit propositions. The result is a new conceptual model on the building blocks of supply chain resilience and how, when combined, they can enhance response and recovery in the face of supply chain disruptions (Fig. 16.2).

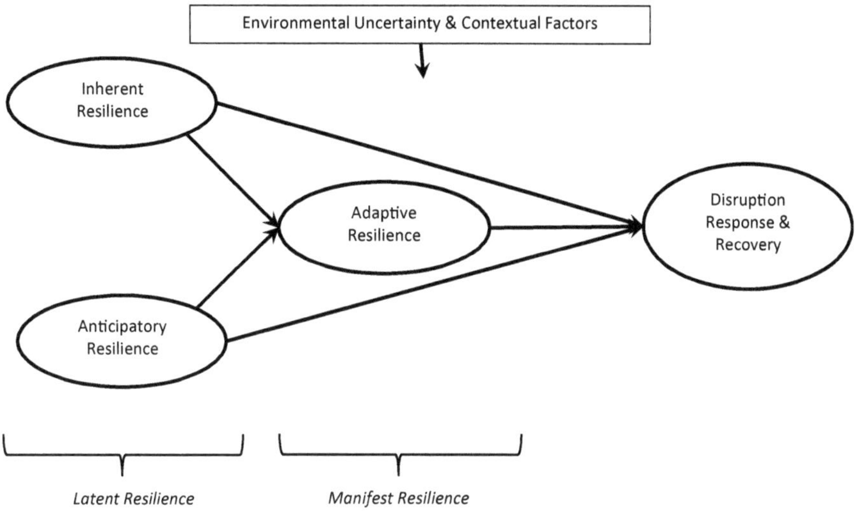

Fig. 16.2 Supply chain resilience model

16.2 Resilience, Systems Theory and Family Resilience Model

Resiliency in an everyday dialogue refers to the ability to "recover from or adjust easily to change." The source of this definition is from engineering science; derived primarily from how simple mechanical/industrial devices function. For instance, a resilient screwdriver is one that can maintain a relatively tight engagement of its blade with the slot of the screw, which makes it versatile when working in relatively inaccessible places, or "tight spots". This engineering definition for resilience may not adequately explain resilience in complex social systems (Holling 1973). Organizational resilience also requires positive adjustment during challenging conditions. Preserving the functioning within the system despite the presence of adversity (e.g. internal adversity, rapid change, or lousy leadership) is also important. As Weick noted, "What happens during the recovery can be crucial for the subsequent fate of the system" (Weick 1993).

Family resilience emerged as scholars combined ideas from general systems theory on families (Danielson et al. 1993). Particularly important to family resiliency researchers was the effect of stress on military families. The stress associated with having a career in the military, including deployment, spousal absence, health-related matters and potential combat injuries, all can make family lives challenging. Grounding their efforts with earlier work on family coping in wartime stress, McCubbin and McCubbin (1988) carried exhaustive studies on vulnerability and regenerative power of military families facing crises to develop the Family Resiliency (FR) model. To develop the FR model, they used observations from a longitudinal investigation of families facing prolonged war-induced stressor events (for instance, having a husband/father held captive or unaccounted for in the Vietnam War).

The basic premise of the FR model is that serious crises can derail the functioning of a family system, with ripple effects for all members and their relationships. The model highlights several major interacting groups of components that shape the family process and outcomes critical to family recovery in the face of a crisis (McCubbin and McCubbin 1988). It is the combination and interaction of these that enable the family system to rally in times of crisis, to buffer stress, reduce the risk of dysfunction, and support eventual adaptation (Walsh 2003). Moving beyond listing the elements of a resilient system, the FR model offers explanation on how groups of elements interact with one another, to enhance, redirect and align the family's efforts.

In the next section, we explore the parallels between families and supply chains, in order to set the stage on how a resilience model for supply chain management can be developed.

16.2.1 Parallels Between Families and Supply Chains?

There are notable similarities in the dynamics of family systems and supply chains. First, both systems are composed of members and a whole, with patterns of connections among members and between each member and the whole. Each member may be in a stronger or weaker relationship with others, but everyone is interconnected and interdependent. In families, it can be difficult to predict the behavior of individuals by merely considering them in isolation; one needs to know about the context of the individuals in the family (Cowan and Cowan 2006). The same can be said about supply chains. For instance, it is nearly impossible to understand why an exhaust manifold parts manufacturer adjusts the tolerance on a particular part, unless a broader view of the supplier's role in the automotive supply chain is considered. With regards to change and disruption, changes in one family member (e.g., job loss), a subsystem (e.g., the couple relationship), or the overall system (e.g., home destroyed by a tornado) reverberate across the family system (Whitchurch and Constantine 1993). Similarly, changes in one supply chain member (e.g., financial loss), a subsystem (e.g., buyer-supplier relationship), or the overall system (e.g., the entire supply chain over run by new technology) reverberate across the system.

A second parallel is the notion of boundaries. Systems theorists consider each member to have an invisible enclosure that separates it from the outside (Wagner and Reiss 1995). An important property of a system is the extent to which member boundaries are permeable. Non-permeable (or rigid) member boundaries denote disengaged members. For instance, rigid boundaries may cause the father to have difficulty in becoming included in the mother-son relationship. The same can be said about supply chains; a retailer may be excluded from a new product development strategy that is arranged between an original equipment manufacturer

(OEM) and supplier. At the other end of the permeability continuum, member boundaries can be so diffuse that they become overly enmeshed. For example, in some families children occupy the attention of their parents so constantly that there is no separation between the life of the couple and the life of the children (Cowan and Cowan 2006). Extending the examples to supply chains; retailers can be so involved in production planning of an OEM, such that there is no opportunity to develop strategies for other products or customers.

A third parallel is related with the notion of homeostasis and multi-stability. Homeostasis requires coordination between actions internal to the organization with activities in the external environment. Crises change the "fit" with the external environment and are thus likely to change the nature of internal relationship between members of the system as well. Multi-stable families and supply chains manage to ward off a diverse and wide-ranging type of disruptions because their members are able to accommodate and adjust to a multitude of operating optimality.

16.2.2 Supply Chain Resilience—A Review

Literature on supply chain resilience is at its nascence stages. To the best of our knowledge, the term "supply chain resilience" has only been referred to in the academic arena since 2004 (Christopher and Peck 2004). In this short period of time, copious articles have explored the concept to offer further explanations. While commonly mentioned characteristics of supply chain resilience are flexibility, redundancy and organizational culture, there are other factors identified as well. For instance, Christopher and Peck (2004) highlighted a culture focused on risk management awareness and comprehension of the supply chain risks (bottlenecks and critical paths) and collaboration as other important factors.

To date, beyond the aggregate level, literature has come short in explaining the effects of these factors on building supply chain resilience. For instance, factors that are often related to resilience (e.g. flexibility, redundancy and culture) can take various forms. Whether each of these forms is helpful in facing risk and disruptions has not been investigated. Tang and Tomlin (2008b) offered a detailed assessment of how different forms of flexibility relate to risk and disruption management. Whereas demand flexibility shifts production quantities across different products, production flexibility shifts production quantities across internal resources (plants or machines). Supply flexibility may imply the ability to shift order quantities across suppliers, shift order quantities across time, use multiple suppliers or use flexible supply contracts. Each of these variations may be effective or ineffective in the facing certain risks and disruptions.

Moving beyond flexibility and redundancy, Ponomarov and Holcomb (2009) note the importance of connectedness and risk sharing among supply chain members as traits that enhance resilience. Pettit et al. (2010) note financial strength and visibility among capabilities that enhance resilience. Blackhurst et al. (2011) highlight the importance of human capital (education and training) and organizational capital resources (contingency planning and risk management teams). However, missing from much of the findings so far is how different aspects of resilience relate and potentially enhance one another. In the next section, we detail how systems and family resilience theory offer explanations to help in this regard.

16.3 Family Resilience Model and Supply Chains

16.3.1 Inherent Resilience (System Strengths)

Every living system carries a certain degree of resilience inherently built into it. This allows the system to naturally flex, bend, and mold around its ever-changing environmental conditions. These built-in properties are a central building block around which organizational resilience can be structured around (Horne and Orr 1998). In military families, inherent resilience manifests in members' natural coping skills, spouse's self-reliance, or the father and mother's self-confidence in managing young children alone. At the family level, emotional and esteem support for each family member, and level of cohesion among members are part of the family's inherent strengths. Families that are open to change, can better reorganize and adapt to fit new challenges tend to be more resilient.

Inherent resilience for supply chains comes from the strength of resources that are already possessed. These capabilities are often permanent and inseparable qualities of the supply chain. For instance, agile (rapidly flexible) supply chain networks are advocated because they can be a competitive advantage (Lee 2004). However, agile supply chains are also capable of responding quickly to changing conditions can be a competitive advantage even when there are no immediate crisis in the horizon (Juttner and Maklan 2011). Flexibility, when built into the system rather than for purposes of risk and crisis management can be another form of inherent resilience. For instance, companies often leverage sourcing flexibility to quickly change inputs. However, the purpose is often far from what is needed for crisis response. Flexible sourcing may be for price reasons, or for strategic purposes or because the ability to change sources simply make good business sense. This type of flexibility is often inseparable from the fundamental structure of the supply chain.

Another form of flexibility that can be categorized as inherent resilience is that of design flexibility. During the product design process at SeaMicro, the microchip manufacturer, engineers take their design modifications to contract manufacturers and have them tested immediately. Deign flexibility saves weeks or even months when compared to more formal arrangements in design testing and validation. Yet another inherent resilience is that of product configuration. In a recent year, Deere built almost 8,000 variations of its popular 8R tractor line. The company's flexibility in product configuration allows Deere to serve the needs of diverse farm markets using a single product platform (Schlegel and Trent 2014). Finally, we note that flexibility-based inherent resilience takes several other forms; such as logistics, material, and lead time flexibility.

Inherent resilience can come in other forms. Families with a nest egg, inheritance or other forms of financial resources often handle crises better since economic resources help buffer the bitter experience of up-rootedness (Dyk and Schvaneveldt 1987). Similarly, supply chains operating in high-margin industries or those associated with an OEM or supplier that is financially strong tend to leverage these resources to mitigate disasters more easily. The extent of financial resources can be useful, although it was not developed for specific purpose of handling crises.

Information sharing is another form of inherent resilience worth noting. In supply chains, information comes in many forms. Information sharing regarding demand, supply, inventory, production schedules, and purchasing schedules enables firms to generate higher levels of supply intelligence and greater visibility of risk profiles (Christopher and Peck 2004).

16.3.2 Anticipative Resilience (Preparatory Capabilities)

Resilient systems develop resources dedicated to warding off and managing disruptions. For families, this type of resource helps resist and better appraise the effects of disruptions. For instance, those that have mapped and planned potential mishaps have a better chance of success. Similarly, families with better interpretive and forecasting abilities are considered to be more resilient. We categorize these capabilities under the term *anticipative resilience*. Anticipative resilience includes uniquely developed competencies that are designed to protect the system from unexpected or non-normative stressors and strains.

The most common form of anticipative resilience in supply chains is that of excess resources. Organizational reserves, such as redundancies in inventory, safety stock, operational capacity and suppliers are commonly used in anticipation of unfortunate events. Unlike inherent resilience, *anticipative resilience* entails resources that are specifically maintained for addressing disruptions. The strength of anticipative resilience comes from its dedicated form. For instance, safety stocks are essentially kept to handle demand fluctuations. Instead, substitutable parts can be used for multiple purposes, which means that they may not be available when a dire situation arises. Similarly, redundant processes are readily available. Similarly, adjustable processes may be preoccupied with other production priorities. Here again, further distinction in the type of flexibility is necessary. Flexibility in order fulfillment allows for the firm to quickly change outputs when there are raw materials shortages. Flexibility in modes of delivery using alternate distribution channels may be designed into supply chains to proactively mitigate logistical issues. If these capabilities are developed and incorporated for the primary reason of mitigating and responding to risks of disruption, then they can be categorized as anticipative resilience.

Carrying anticipative resilience can prove to be contentious. For instance, because redundancy involves the duplication of capabilities, some consider it as an unnecessary cost burden. Barring potential crises, redundant resources may lead to unutilized capacity, idle inventory, increased costs and potentially lower quality. For those less concerned with supply chain disruptions, there is a minimal need for redundancies. Nevertheless, with a rise in concerns over disruptions, the need for redundancies in the form of anticipative resilience does rise. Empirical research advocates for this. Hendricks and Singhal (2005) report how operational slack in the supply chain, lowers the likelihood that a negative stock market reaction will occur. Azadegan et al. (2012) note how operational slack, the form related to the firm's production processes operational slack lowers the likelihood of venture failure with an increase in environmental uncertainty.

Beyond redundancies, *anticipative* resilience can take several other forms. Insurance policies are among common ones (Alcantara 2015). Supply chain visibility for risk minimization efforts is yet another form (Christopher and Peck 2004). Many researchers have recommended sharing information as a preferred way to diminish supply chain risk. As compared to information sharing in operations, this type of information sharing is primarily meant to minimize large-scale risks. An example of these initiatives is the use of control towers, which can help in effectively responding to disruptions through, for example, identifying vulnerable suppliers, thereby allowing enough time to develop countermeasures against potential failures. Another means to enhance anticipative resilience is through Business Continuity Management (BCM) programs. BCM programs encompass the collection of risk mitigation, risk management, continuity planning and emergency response activities (Cerullo and Cerullo 2004).

16.3.3 Adaptive Resilience (Adaptation and Coping)

The third type of resilience highlighted by McCubbin and McCubbin (1996) is that of the family's problem-solving and coping strategies. The process by which families restore balance once faced with a stressor is often referred to as regenerative power (Patterson 2002). Problem solving is a regenerative power because it helps organize stressors and hardships into manageable components, to identify alternative courses of action, and to initiate steps to resolve interpersonal issues. Coping helps maintain the emotional stability and well-being of the family members.

We label these as "*Adaptive resilience.*" Adapting is the process of recalibrating one's expectations on the spot, with the surprise at hand, and acting exactly and speedily to mitigate, improvise, or innovate out of a failure. Several traits characterize adaptive resilience. To start, adaptive resilience relies upon the quality of decisions made in the face of disruptions. Supply chain disruptions are often fast-moving, high-stakes events that can be unforgiving to mistakes (Lee 2004). Decisions that are made collaboratively among informed and participative members, often evade glaring omissions. Collaboration helps unite supply chain members during disruptions. A focal firm is often unable to detect the root cause of disruptions, mitigate the effect of actual problems, or resume business operations by reconfiguring supply chain resources alone. To that note, adaptive resilience implies collective decision making to important solutions. Solutions created quickly and collectively in response to disruptions. Specific to leadership, adaptive resilience combines care and concern through situational awareness, with the agility to make expeditious and on-the-spot decisions. Indeed, how effectively the decisions made are executed is also important. Adaptive resilience carries the ability to maintain function on the basis of ingenuity or extra effort in crisis situations. This is also related to the leadership's ability to handle "tough choices" in the field quickly and responsibly as part of an adaptively resilient organization (Patterson 2002).

Proposition 16.1 *Resiliency can be accomplished through a combination of three components: (a) Inherent, (b) Anticipative, (c) Adaptive.*

16.4 Differentiating the Three Forms of Resilience and Significance of Adaptive Resilience

Inherent, adaptive and anticipative resilience are unique in many regards. Because inherent resilience is developed for purposes beyond risk management and more related to competitive and business advantage, inherent resilience rarely creates a cost burden that is directly accounted to risk management. Anticipatory resilience is likely to be accompanied with added operating costs. Maintaining slack inventory of raw materials, redundancy capacity in production or labor force all are bound to raise costs. As we noted above, anticipative resilience comes in the form of dedicated, idiosyncratic investments that are ready-to-use when a disruption occurs. In essence, anticipatory resilience comes with a more reliable assurance on its usefulness. For instance, emergency stock piles are bound to be there when needed.

Both inherent and anticipatory resilience can be considered as latent forms of resilience. Yet the issue with latent forms of resilience is in their "liquidity." These are reserve capabilities that are held to be used when disruptions occur. There rarely is an immediate payoff in developing or enhancing them; nor a complete guarantee on whether they will be useful when the disaster strikes. Nevertheless, time is on one's side in developing and refining them. In contrast, adaptive resilience offers the ability to develop response solutions that are customized to the disruption at hand. A summary of the three forms is given in Table 16.1.

We noted the works of Tukamuhabwa et al. (2015) and McCubbin and McCubbin (1988) identify both protective and recovery factors that work synergistically and interchangeably to respond successfully to crises and challenges. Protective factors facilitate adjustment, or the ability to maintain integrity and

Table 16.1 The three forms of supply chain resilience

	Definition and explanation	Examples	Sources (selective)
Inherent resilience			
SC flexibility			
– Sourcing flexibility	Ability to adjust the source and amount of raw material or parts	Part commonality, modular product design	Christopher and Peck (2004), Pettit et al. (2010), Rice and Caniato (2003), Sheffi and Rice (2005)
– Order fulfillment flexibility	Ability to adjust production to time and volume based changes to orders	Alternate distribution channels	
– Capacity flexibility	Ability to adjust production to changes in volume increase and decrease	Alternative suppliers and manufacturing sites	
SC integration	Order/inventory/distribution integration to improve operations performance	ERP systems, business intelligence	
SC efficiency	Production of output without waste	Labor productivity, asset utilization	
Postponement	Delayed differentiation; delay investment in product until last possible moment	Time, place and form postponement	
Financial strength	Capacity to absorb damage to cash and financial profitability	Profitability, Margins and product portfolio	
Market strength	Capacity to absorb injury to reputational and customer impressions	Customer loyalty, relationship and brand equity	
Anticipatory resilience			
SC redundancy			
– Safety stock	Surplus material primarily kept for risk management	Raw material and finished goods inventory	Azadegan (2014), Chopra and Sodhi (2014), Kildow (2011), Kleindorfer and Saad (2005), Pettit et al. (2010), Tomlin (2006), Zsidisin et al. (2005)
– Slack capacity	Alternative manufacturing, service and equipment maintained for risk management	Reserve capacity, reserve workforce	
– Supply redundancy	Reserve and redundant suppliers available for purposes of disruption management	Multiple sourcing	
SC flexibility	Ability to adjust sourcing, order and capacity with risk management as prime purpose	Supplier contract flexibility	

(continued)

Table 16.1 (continued)

	Definition and explanation	Examples	Sources (selective)
SC visibility	Physical and informational transparency to improve operations for risk management	Control towers	
Business continuity plans			
– Risk reduction activities	Activities meant to eliminate or reduce the chances of potential disruptions	Insurance policies, outsourcing	
– Risk mitigation activities	Activities meant to reduce the impact of potential disruptions	Business impact analysis, monitoring systems	
– Contingency planning	Activities developed in advance for various situations that might impact business	Playbooks, policy manuals and protocols	
– BCP in supplier selection	Activities meant to minimize risk and continuity issues in suppliers during selection	Listing and auditing critical suppliers	
Financial reserves	Liquid assets available to sustain an organization in the face of disruptions	Insurance, emergency reserves, marketable securities	
Security measures/Compliance	Procedures, and technology to protect supply chain assets from attack	Layered defenses. access restrictions	
Awareness	Ability to discern potential future events or situations	Near-miss analysis, early warning monitoring	
Adaptive resilience			
Situational awareness	Detailed situational understanding in the face of a disruption	Clear mental model, recognizing changes to situation	Craighead et al. (2007), Pettit et al. (2010)
Decisiveness	Ability to make decisions on operational adjustment in the face of challenges	Quickly deciding among choices, not delaying decisions	
Responsiveness	Ability to modify operations in the face of challenges	Fast re-routing and response to customer demands	
Recovery execution	Ability to focus on returning to normalcy	Resource mobilization, consequence mitigation	

functioning. But when the family (or supply chain) is challenged, recovery factors are called upon to promote the ability to adapt, or rebound to the crisis.

The significance of adaptive resilience at the "moment of truth" (or when disruptions actually happen) cannot be overestimated. Arguably, much of the investment and effort placed in developing resources in anticipatory resilience can prove ineffective if adaptive resilience is not there to correctly apply them. In many cases, years of preparation and planning can go to waste, simply because the leader did not make the right decision, or the systems in place did not respond the way they were intended to. This is particularly important when facing many of today's larger-scale supply chain disruptions that show unique characteristics that companies may not be familiar with. The Tsunami-nuclear disaster in Japan and Super-storm Sandy are examples of large-scale disruptions that were difficult to fully anticipate and prepare for. Facing these types of disruptions is particularly dependent on how adaptive resilience. Adaptive resilience helps counteract the restrictive tendencies through situational awareness. Awareness improves organizational confidence, which reinforces the capability for broad information processing. Jointly believing that an organization has capacity and that this capacity helps with accepting the confusion and ambiguity of the crisis at hand and to handle the matter more effectively.

Several considerations highlight the significance of anticipatory resilience. First, when faced with crises, systems are challenged to their extreme performance levels. To recover, systems often need an extensive, broad and immediate array of resources. To make matters worse, the array of needs can quickly change as the disruption unfolds. Adaptive resilience helps the system reconfigure and adjust itself quickly in the environment.

Second, it is natural for systems to behave overly rigid in threatening situations. Threatening situations lead to restriction of information processing and narrowing of one's field of attention (Staw et al. 1981). In the face of overpowering threat, organizations often respond by constricting control, such that power and influence become concentrated in the hand of a few executives, leading to a "command and control" model of crisis management. Therefore, we posit:

Proposition 16.2 *Adaptive resilience positively mediates the effects of inherent resilience and anticipatory resilience in facing supply chain disruptions.*

16.5 System Balance and Trade-off Among Forms of Resilience

Earlier, in Sect. 16.2.1, we noted the importance of maintaining balance (fit) between the system and its operating environment. At the same time, systems (families or supply chains) need to maintain a functional fit between their challenges and resources and in the interaction among various members. A disruption that unsettles the fit with external environment is likely to unsettle the internal balance of the system as well.

Systems theory suggests that multi-stability at the system level relies on multi-stability at the member level. For instance, multi-stable families that can modify their responsibilities to permit the transitioning parent to invest in work-for-pay, can better handle the change of a stay-at-home mother take on a new job. Similarly, supply chain members that can adjust in order to accommodate one another's production, delivery and scheduling plans, can better address a disruption. Here is one example: A pair of suppliers that are prepared to make parts usually produced by the other, while staying profitable helps the entire supply chain maintain its balance despite variations and disruptions. Similarly, a logistics provider that can ramp up its delivery capacity or ramp it down quickly can help the entire system maintain its balance despite weather and other natural disasters.

The above details suggest that improved resiliency in one system member may compensate for weaker resilience in others. In essence, as it relates to the supply chain, resilience may be transferrable among members. By extension, specific forms of resilience forms can also be compensatory. When a supplier comes short in anticipatory resilience (finished goods), manufacturer's anticipatory resilience (raw material from the supplier) can work to compensate (Fig. 16.3). Similarly, when a manufacturer had limited inherent resilience (weak profit margins), a distributor's inherent resilience (strong margins) can work to compensate.

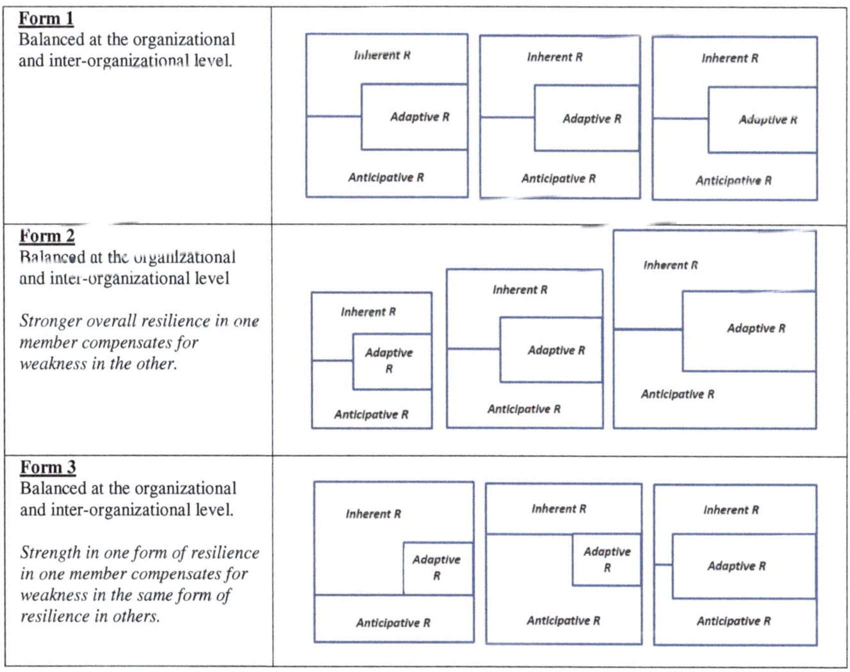

Fig. 16.3 Balanced resiliency across the supply chain

Proposition 16.3 *Increases in resilience among supply chain members helps compensate for weaknesses by others.*

16.6 Operating Context and System Boundaries

Earlier, in Sect. 16.2.1, we noted the significance of permeability in member and system boundaries as a key distinction. More perturbations means that there are more varieties of unexpected situations thrown at the organization. With a rise in uncertainty, be it in the form of dynamism, complexity or munificence, we anticipate higher permeability in the system. Faced with increased hazard, a system will need to place further emphasis on its resiliency capabilities. Building on explanations from the law of requisite variety, we suggest that more perturbations in the environment will require the system to carry a more robust arsenal of capabilities handle these variations. In short, the need for enhancing firm resilience becomes more necessary with a rise in uncertainty.

Proposition 16.4 *Uncertainty in the operating environment carries a detrimental effect on how supply chain resilience improves firm ability in facing supply chain disruptions.*

16.7 Discussion

This chapter dives deeper into the important topic of supply chain resilience to provide a theoretically grounded explanation of supply chain resilience. It groups various forms by which supply chain resilience can be developed into three forms and explains how they can complement one another. The chapter offers explanations based on how resilient systems (such as families or supply chains) are ones that are resourceful, robust, and adaptive in such a way that they fight through crises rather than succumb to them. Using well established research on systems theory and family resilience. The results is a model that shows the inter-relationship among the building blocks of organizational resilience.

Often, the simplest and most widespread strategy for mitigating the impact of supply chain disruptions is through redundancies, particularly in the form of inventory buffers. But for many, this strategy is synonymous with accepting system inefficiencies; a direct antithesis to what is advocated for a supply chain optimization (Tang and Tomlin 2008a). Despite its downside, resilience in an anticipatory form is popular because it can be easy to use and carry a high guarantee of usefulness in the face of disruption.

We highlight the nuances associated with flexibility as a form of resilience. To start, depending on its form and intended reason for developing flexibility can be categorized as either inherent or anticipatory resilience. Second, since flexibility has multiple uses, it may require more effort to develop and implement takes more time and requires the coordinated effort of the entire organization along with its partners. For instance, setting up technologies and systems for information sharing, adopting the build-to-order method, and observing international security compliance and procedures may require more time.

Another important matter worth noting is that related to inter-dependence of agents in a system. We often blame system interdependence as the cause for rising risks in the supply chain. It is no surprise to see supply chain disruptions in one corner of the world affect supply chain members operation at the other corner. Process improvements, such as Just-in-time manufacturing, and technological enhancements that help reduce delivery times, have reduced physical inventory and time buffers between supply chain members. These and other factors have helped raise the dependence and inter-dependence of members of the supply chains on one another.

In this chapter, we suggest that although inter-dependence may be an outcome of today's efficient supply chains, it may not necessarily have to be a deterrence. In fact, most people would consider inter-dependence in their family group as a positive enhancement to managing personal disruptions. Family inter-dependence can be the source of comfort, protection, assistance, and recognition; all when a member deems it necessary. The same can be noted about supply chains. When inter-dependence leads to increased concern and willingness to compensate for others' shortcomings, interdependence can be a positive attribute.

16.8 Future Research

There are several means by which the conceptual development offered here can be empirically tested and extended. To start, large-scale cross-section surveys that combine archival firm performance can be a viable means to test the validity of the proposed model here. Similarly, multiple case studies of how various firms have faced small and large-scale disruptions can be help determine the effectiveness of various forms of resilience.

Literature suggests that supply chain disruptions can take many forms: severity, unfamiliarity, and complicatedness to name a few. With the rise of any of these characteristics, the disruption becomes more challenging. For instance, disruption severity can determine the level of involvement of individuals at different levels of the organization and the extent of resources necessary as countermeasures (Hannah et al. 2009). Our work did not distinguish types of supply chain disruption nor the potential effects of inherent, anticipative and adaptive resilience in the face of disruptions. Future conceptual and empirical studies can address the nuances associated with the type of disruption.

Family resilience labels disruptions as a "stressor." An important factor alongside the perceived severity of stressors, a "pile-up" of stressors can tax the ability to recover. This is of particular significance in supply chain research, since the level of "stress" and pressure that a firm's operating environment causes can hinder the firm's ability to best recognize and respond to unexpected events.

References

Alcantara, P. (2015). Measuring the influence of industry sector membership on supply chain disruption reporting. *Journal of Business Continuity & Emergency Planning, 8,* 299–306.

Ashby, W. R. (1956). *An introduction to cybernetics.* London: Chapman and Hall.

Ashby, W. R. (1960). Adaptation in the multistable system. In W. R. Ashby (Ed.), *Design for a brain: The origin of adaptive behavior.* London: Chapman and Hall.

Ashby, W. R. (1962). Principles of the self-organizing system. In H. V. Foerster & G. Zopf (Eds.), *Principles of self-organization.* New York: Pergamon Press.

Azadegan, A. (2014). Supply chain disruptions, latent and manifest resilience. *Rutgers supply chain management—Thought Leader Series, 1*(3), 1–2.

Azadegan, A., & Dooley, K. J. (2010). Supplier innovativeness, organizational learning styles and manufacturer performance: An empirical assessment. *Journal of Operations Management, 28,* 488–505.

Azadegan, A., Patel, P. C., & Parida, V. (2012). Operational slack and venture survival. *Production and Operations Management, 22,* 1–18.

Blackhurst, J., Dunn, K. S., & Craighead, C. W. (2011). An empirically derived framework of global supply resiliency. *Journal of Business Logistics, 32,* 374–391.

Bode, C., Wagner, S. M., Petersen, K. J., & Ellram, L. M. (2011). Understanding responses to supply chain disruptions: Insights from information processing and resource dependence perspectives. *Academy of Management Journal, 54,* 833–856.

Cariani, P. A. (2009). The homeostat as embodiment of adaptive control. *International Journal of General Systems, 38,* 139–154.

Cerullo, V., & Cerullo, M. J. (2004). Business continuity planning: A comprehensive approach. *Information Systems Management, 21,* 70–78.

Chopra, S., & Sodhi, M. S. (2014). Reducing the risk of supply chain disruptions. *MIT Sloan Management Review, 55*(3), 73–81.

Christopher, M., & Peck, H. (2004). Building the resilient supply chain. *The International Journal of Logistics Management, 15,* 1–14.

Cowan, P. A., & Cowan, C. P. (2006). Developmental psychopathology from family systems and family risk factors perspectives: Implications for family research, practice, and policy. In D. Cicchetti & D. J. Cohen (Eds.), *Developmental psychopathology.* New York: John Wiley.

Craighead, C. W., Blackhurst, J., Rungtusanatham, M. J., & Handfield, R. B. (2007). The severity of supply chain disruptions: Design characteristics and mitigation capabilities. *Decision Sciences, 38,* 131–156.

Danielson, C. B., Hamel-Bissel, B. P., & Winstead-Fry, P. (1993). *Families, health and illness: Perspectives on coping and interventions.* United Kingdom: Mosby.

Dyk, P. A. H., & Schvaneveldt, J. D. (1987). Coping as a concept in family theory. *Family Science Review, 1,* 23–40.

Hannah, S. T., Uhl-Bien, M., Avolio, B. J., & Cavarretta, F. L. (2009). A framework for examining leadership in extreme contexts. *The Leadership Quarterly, 20,* 897–919.

Hendricks, K., & Singhal, V. (2005). An empirical analysis of the effect of supply chain disruptions on long run stock price performance and equity risk of the firm. *Production and Operations Management Journal, 14,* 35–52.

Holling, C. S. (1973). Resilience and stability of ecological systems. *Annual Review of Ecology and Systematics, 4,* 1–23.

Horne, J. F., & Orr, J. E. (1998). Assessing behaviors that create resilient organizations. *Employment Relations Today, 24,* 29–39.

Juttner, U., & Maklan, S. (2011). Supply chain resilience in the global financial crisis: An empirical study. *Supply Chain Management—An International Journal, 16,* 246–259.

Kildow, B. A. (2011). *A supply chain management guide to business continuity*. New York: AMACOM.

Kleindorfer, P., & Saad, G. (2005). Managing disruption risks in supply chains. *Production and Operations Management, 14,* 53–68.

Lee, H. L. (2004). The triple—A supply chain. *Harvard Business Review, 82,* 102–112.

McCubbin, H. I., & McCubbin, M. A. (1988). Typologies of resilient families - emerging roles of social-class and ethnicity. *Family Relations, 37,* 247–254.

Mccubbin, H. I., & Patterson, J. M. (1982). Family adaptation to crises. In H. I. Mccubbin, A. E. Cauble, & J. M. Patterson (Eds.), *Family stress, coping, and social support*. Springfield, IL: Charles C Thomas.

Mccubbin, M. A., & Mccubbin, H. I. (1996). Resiliency in families: a conceptual model of family adjustment and adaptation in response to stress and crises. In H. I. Mccubbin, A. I. Thompson, & M. A. Mccubbin (eds.) *Family assessment: Resiliency, coping and adaptation–Inventories for research and practice*. Madison, WI: University of Wisconsin System.

Patterson, J. M. (2002). Understanding family resilience. *Journal of Clinical Psychology, 58,* 233–246.

Pettit, T. J., Fiksel, J., & Croxton, K. L. (2010). Ensuring supply chain resilience: Development of a conceptual framework. *Journal of Business Logistics, 31,* 1–21.

Ponomarov, S. Y., & Holcomb, M. C. (2009). Understanding the concept of supply chain resilience. *International Journal of Logistics Management, 20,* 124–143.

Rice, J. B., & Caniato, F. (2003). Building a secure and resilient supply network. *Supply Chain Management Review, 7,* 22–30.

Schlegel, G. L., & Trent, R. J. (2014). *Supply chain risk management: An emerging discipline*. United Kingdom: CRC Press.

Sheffi, Y. (2015). *The power of resilience: How the best companies manage the unexpected*. Cambridge: MA, The MIT Press.

Sheffi, Y., & Rice, J. B. (2005). A supply chain view of the resilient enterprise. *MIT Sloan Management Review, 47,* 41–48.

Skipper, J. B., & Hanna, J. B. (2009). Minimizing supply chain disruption risk through enhanced flexibility. *International Journal of Physical Distribution & Logistics Management, 39,* 404–427.

Staw, B. M., Sandelands, L. E., & Dutton, J. E. (1981). Threat-rigidity effects in organizational-behavior—A multilevel analysis. *Administrative Science Quarterly, 26,* 501–524.

Tang, C. (2006). Robust strategies for mitigating supply chain disruptions. *International Journal of Logistics, 9,* 33–45.

Tang, C., & Tomlin, B. (2008a). How much flexibility does it take to mitigate supply chain risks? In G. A. Zsidisin & B. Ritchie (Eds.), *Supply chain risk: A handbook of assessment, management, and performance*. New York: Springer.

Tang, C., & Tomlin, B. (2008b). The power of flexibility for mitigating supply chain risks. *International Journal of Production Economics, 116,* 12–27.

Tomlin, B. (2006). On the value of mitigation and contingency strategies for managing supply chain disruption risks. *Management Science, 52*(5), 639–657.

Tukamuhabwa, B. R., Stevenson, M., Busby, J., & Zorzini, M. (2015). Supply chain resilience: definition, review and theoretical foundations for further study. *International Journal of Production Research, 53,* 5592–5623.

Wagner, B. M., & Reiss, D. (1995). Family systems and developmental psychopathology: Courtship, marriage, or divorce? In D. Cicchetti & D. J. Cohen (Eds.), *Developmental psychopathology*. New York: John Wiley & Sons.

Walsh, F. (1996). The concept of family resilience: Crisis and challenge. *Family Process, 35,* 261–281.
Walsh, F. (2003). Family resilience: A framework for clinical practice. *Family Process, 42,* 1–18.
Weick, K. E. (1993). The collapse of sensemaking in organizations—The Mann Gulch disaster. *Administrative Science Quarterly, 38,* 628–652.
Whitchurch, G., & Constantine, L. (1993). Systems theory. In P. Boss, W. J. Doherty, & R. Larossa (Eds.), *Sourcebook of family theories and methods: A contextual approach.* New York: Plenum Publishing Company.
Zsidisin, G. A., Melnyk, S. A., & Ragatz, G. L. (2005). An institutional theory perspective of business continuity planning for purchasing and supply management. *International Journal of Production Research, 43,* 3401–3420.

Chapter 17
Cultivating Supply Chain Agility: Managerial Actions Derived from Established Antecedents

Michael J. Braunscheidel and Nallan C. Suresh

Abstract Today's marketplace is characterized by intense competitive pressures as well as high levels of turbulence and uncertainty. Organizations require agility in their supply chains to provide superior value and also manage disruption risks and ensure uninterrupted service to customers. The cultivation of agility can be approached as a risk management initiative that enables a firm to anticipate as well as respond rapidly to marketplace changes and disruptions in the supply chain. Agility is thus of value for both risk mitigation and response. This chapter provides an updated perspective of an emerging body of literature devoted to supply chain agility. Next, based on our own research stream on this topic, we propose a set of supply chain initiatives as antecedents for cultivation of agility. These include internal integration measures, external integration with suppliers and customers, cultivation of external flexibility, and lean practices. We also provide more fundamental, cultural drivers for cultivating agility, which include market orientation, learning orientation and organizational culture types that are conducive for agility. These antecedents were established through empirical research, and we translate them into a set of managerial practices to address the cultivation of agility for both mitigation and response.

17.1 Introduction

In order to cope with the challenges of more competitive market places, a significant amount of research has been conducted on supply chain practices to improve the performance of supply chains. In addition to increasing competitive pressures, in recent years global markets have also been characterized by growing levels of

M.J. Braunscheidel (✉)
Department of Management, Canisius College, Buffalo, NY, USA
e-mail: braunscm@canisius.edu

N.C. Suresh
Department of Operations Management and Strategy, School of Management, State University of New York, Buffalo, NY, USA

Y. Khojasteh (ed.), *Supply Chain Risk Management*,
DOI 10.1007/978-981-10-4106-8_17

turbulence and unpredictability. Thus it has been stressed that organizations must consciously develop agility to provide value as well as manage disruption risk and ensure uninterrupted service to customers (Christopher 2000; Christopher and Towill 2001; Swafford et al. 2006).

The management of supply chain disruption risk is subject to increasing attention among both researchers and practitioners. Chopra and Sodhi (2004) classified supply chain risks into different categories, along with the drivers of these risks. Kleindorfer and Saad (2005) categorized supply chain risks into two types: (1) risks related to supply and demand coordination and uncertainty, and, (2) disruption risks that are caused by such events as natural disasters, terrorism and labor strikes. They outlined a list of 10 principles developed from the industrial risk management and supply chain literatures. Along these lines, there have been many prescriptive articles that have identified different types of risks and different types of actions to both anticipate such risks (mitigation) and different ways by which firms can recover quickly to such disruptions if and when they do occur (responsiveness).

In this chapter, we make the following contributions:

1. We provide an updated, parsimonious perspective of this emerging body of literature.
2. Based on our prior empirical research stream on this topic, we discuss a set of supply chain initiatives as antecedents for cultivation of agility. We also provide more fundamental, cultural antecedents towards cultivation of agility.
3. Since both construct and predictive validity of these models have been established, we translate the findings into a set of managerial practices that serve to address the cultivation of agility for mitigation and response.

Unlike the prescriptive literature of the past, the managerial actions advanced in this chapter are derived from actually established empirical relationships. This chapter is organized as follows. In Sect. 17.2, we provide an updated perspective, based on a representative set of studies on supply chain agility. In Sect. 17.3 we discuss the direct and indirect antecedents for supply chain agility based on our own research stream on this topic. In Sect. 17.4, we provide direction and guidance as to what managers can do to enhance supply chain agility, both to mitigate and respond to disruptions. Section 17.5 presents the conclusions from this set of studies.

17.2 Literature Review and Updated Perspectives

In today's complex, and turbulent market places, organizations and the supply chains in which they operate need to be responsive to the volatilities of demand, supplies and numerous other factors. While this basic notion of agility continues to dominate, the definitions of agility has also been evolving in recent years. Table 17.1 provides a summary of evolving definitions of agility amongst representative research studies, covering the breadth and range of concepts that have been included so far as part of supply chain agility.

Table 17.1 Evolving definitions of agility amongst representative studies

Study		Definition of agility and variables studies
Fliedner and Vokurka (1997)	E	Ability to offer low-cost, high quality products with short lead times and varying volumes. IVs: Internal initiatives e.g. process re-engineering and external initiatives like inter-firm cooperation
Naylor et al. (1999)	C	Using market knowledge and a virtual corporation to exploit profitable opportunities in a volatile market place. Placement of decoupling point
Christopher (2000)	CN	Ability to respond rapidly to changes in demand, both in terms of volume and variety
Mason-Jones et al. (2000)	E	Using market knowledge and virtual corporation to exploit in a volatile market place. Comparison of lean and agile paradigms; appropriate use of the decoupling point
Prater et al. (2001)	E	Agility requires speed and flexibility. IVs: Sourcing flexibility and speed; Manufacturing flexibility and speed; Delivery flexibility and speed; External vulnerability
Christopher and Towill (2002)	CN	Ability of the supply chain to react quickly to changes in market demand: in volume, variety or mix
Agarwal et al. (2006, 2007)	E	Ability to respond rapidly to changes in demand volume and variety IVs: Customer satisfaction, quality, cost, delivery speed, new product introduction, and lead-time
Narasimhan et al. (2006)		Ability to efficiently change operating states in response to uncertain and changing market conditions
Swafford et al. (2006)	E	Capability to adapt or respond speedily to changing marketplace. IVs: Procurement/sourcing flexibility, manufacturing flexibility, distribution/logistics flexibility
Li et al. (2008, 2009)	C, E	Agility is integrating an alertness to changes (opportunities/challenges), internal and environmental—using resources to respond to changes in timely and flexible manner. Strategic alertness and response capability, Operational alertness and response capability, Episodic alertness and response capability
Swafford et al. (2008)	E	Supply chain agility represents speed of firm's internal supply chain functions to adapt to changes IVs: Information technology integration, supply chain flexibility
Braunscheidel and Suresh (2009)	E	Capability of firm, in conjunction with key suppliers and customers, to respond in speedy manner to changing marketplace. IVs: Market orientation, learning orientation, internal integration, external integration, external flexibility
Vickery et al. (2010)	E	Responsiveness to needs and wants of customers. IVs: SC IT, and SC organizational initiatives
Chiang et al. (2012)	E	Capability of the firm and in conjunction with its key suppliers and customers, to respond in speedy manner to a changing marketplace. IVs: Strategic sourcing; Firm's strategic flexibility

(continued)

Table 17.1 (continued)

Study		Definition of agility and variables studies
Gligor and Holcomb (2012)	E	SC coordination, cooperation, communication on SC agility, operational and relational performance
Gligor et al. (2013)	E	Alertness, Accessibility, Decisiveness; Swiftness, Flexibility on firm's SC agility
Shao (2013)	E	Geographic dispersion; SC agility; SC integration; SC visibility on Disruption warning capability and disruption recovery capability

E Empirical study, *CN* Conceptual; *C* Case study

In the early work of Fliedner and Vokurka (1997), the authors contended that firms can no longer gain competitive advantage by positioning themselves at a particular point on the product-process matrix. Instead, due to the presence of dynamic markets, shorter product life cycles, faster pace of innovation, firms will need to become agile and simultaneously deliver on the basis of cost, quality, dependability and flexibility. Naylor et al. (1999) contended that a merging of lean and agile paradigms need to take place in supply chains, separated by a decoupling point. Mason-Jones et al. (2000) found that organizations first need to identify and understand the requirements of the market place before embarking on re-engineering programs. Christopher (2000) presented conceptual arguments to define agility as a business-wide capability that embraces organizational structures, information systems and mind sets, along with four characteristics that are vital to an agile supply chain: market sensitivity, information-based (vs. inventory based) posture, becoming a fully linked network, and collaboration among partners. Prater et al. (2001), using five case studies, maintained that the term agility inherently contains two concepts: speed and flexibility.

Agarwal et al. (2006) attempted to show that supply chain performance is improved if it is able to respond quickly to changing customer demand, while reducing costs. In a later work, Agarwal et al. (2007) found that supply chain agility also depends on customer satisfaction, quality and cost improvements, delivery speed, new product introduction, and service level improvement.

Given overlapping operating elements between agility and lean paradigms, Narasimhan et al. (2006) attempted to disentangle the elements between lean and agility. Swafford et al. (2006) made theoretical arguments that agility is an externally facing *capability*, drawing from many elements of flexibility that constitute internal *competences*. They found that an organization's supply chain agility is directly influenced by the degree of flexibility in manufacturing and procurement/sourcing and is indirectly influenced by distribution/logistics.

Li et al. (2008) presented a conceptual model consisting of strategic, operational and episodic design agility. Each of these consists of alertness and response capabilities, for six dimensions of supply chain agility. In a survey of North American firms, Gligor and Holcomb (2012) found that supply chain coordination, cooperation and communication had a strong influence on supply chain agility.

In turn, supply chain agility was found to significantly affect operational and relational performances. Gligor et al. (2013) identified five dimensions of agility: alertness, accessibility of relevant data, decisiveness, swiftness and flexibility. In an empirical study of Chinese manufacturers, Shao (2013) studied the relationship of supply chain characteristics and disruption mitigation capabilities.

As seen from this updated, but parsimonious summary of the literature, a wide range of concepts are being encompassed within agility, and much work remains to be done on supply chain agility. There is also a critical need at this juncture for summarizing the substantive body of research that has been done to date, and translate them into managerial actions, which forms the principal objective of this chapter.

17.3 Direct and Indirect Antecedents of Supply Chain Agility

In this section, we summarize the findings from an empirical research stream pertaining to supply chain agility among manufacturing firms in USA (Braunscheidel and Suresh 2009; Braunscheidel et al. 2010). The studies covered a wide range of firms spanning SIC codes 20–39, and the respondents were high-level supply chain management professionals. Details of the survey and demographic data of the respondents are provided in Braunscheidel and Suresh (2009). The constructs investigated in these studies are synthesized in Fig. 17.1. There were two sets of antecedents to supply chain agility: direct antecedents involving supply chain initiatives, and indirect, cultural antecedents. The direct antecedents are covered first in this section, followed by the cultural drivers.

17.3.1 Direct Antecedents

Much research has been done in the past on the impact of these constructs on operational and business *performance* of supply chains, but the focus of interest here is the impact of these factors on supply chain *agility*. It was shown that, in addition to performance, supply chain agility is impacted by four set of practices: (1) internal integration, (2) external integration with key suppliers and key customers, (3) external flexibility and (4) lean practices.

Internal integration, the first of these four direct antecedents, represents activities and practices that allow functions within an organization to coordinate and cooperate with one another (Braunscheidel et al. 2010). Internal integration involves use of cross-functional teams, internal communication regarding goals and priorities, openness and teamwork, routine formal meetings and informal, face-to-face meetings. Internal integration has been studied extensively in past research on supply chain management (e.g., Flynn et al. 2010; Droge et al. 2004). Several studies have suggested that internal integration is also a necessary first step

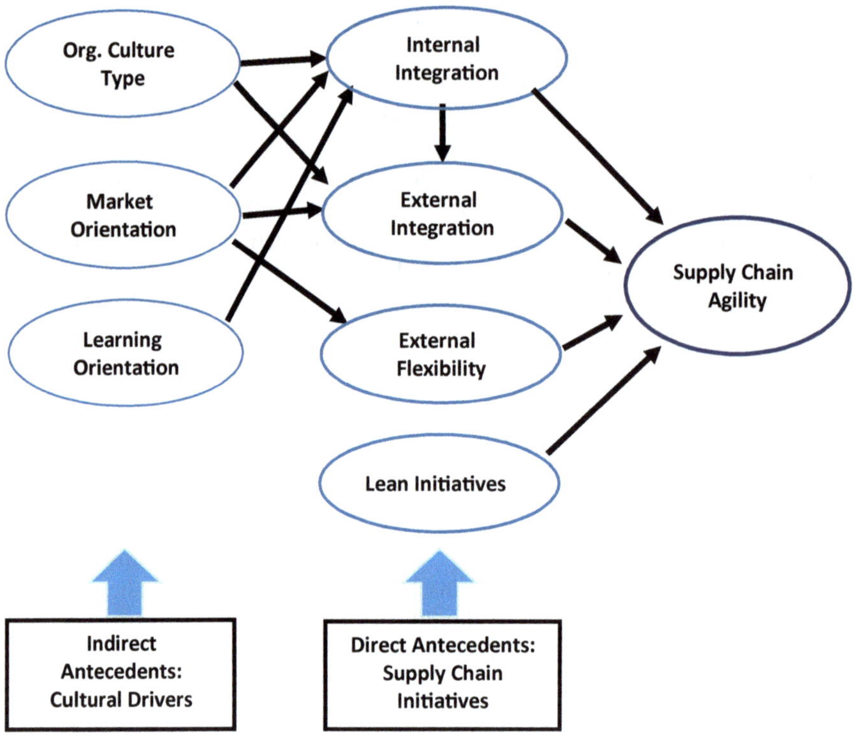

Fig. 17.1 Indirect and direct antecedents of supply chain agility

before integrating with both key suppliers and customers (e.g. Koufteros et al. 2005; Pagell 2004; Vickery et al. 2003). However, there has been a dearth of research on the impact of internal integration on supply chain *agility*.

The second important supply chain initiative, *external integration*, represents activities and practices that coordinate the flow of information and goods with upstream and downstream members of the supply chain (Braunscheidel et al. 2010). Again, there has been a significant amount of research on integration with customers and suppliers, and its impact on supply chain *performance*, but not enough on *agility*. Paulraj and Chen (2007) found the impact of external logistics integration with suppliers has a significant impact on agility. A study of German multi-national firms by Blome et al. (2013) concluded that there is a direct relationship between supply-side competence and demand-side competence with supply chain agility. Gligor and Holcomb (2012) found that the behavioral/relational elements of supply chain coordination and supply chain communication have a direct effect on a firm's supply chain agility. Braunscheidel and Suresh (2009), employing a second-order construct of external integration, found a highly significant pathway from this construct to supply chain agility.

Thirdly, many types of *flexibility* have been studied in the literature (D'Souza and Williams 2000; Koste and Malhotra 1999; Upton 1995; Zhang et al. 2003).

However, the two outward facing flexible manufacturing capabilities of *mix and volume flexibility* were shown to have a direct impact on agility in Braunscheidel and Suresh (2009). Mix flexibility is the ability of the organization to produce different combinations of products economically and effectively given certain capacity (Zhang et al. 2003). Mix flexibility is measured on the ability to produce a wide variety of products, different product types without major changeovers, different products in the same plant at the same time and quick changeovers. Volume flexibility is defined as the ability of an organization to operate at a variety of different output levels without compromising the performance of the system with regards to cost, quality or service (Zhang et al. 2003). It enables the firm to operate profitably at different levels of production, and to change production quantities easily, swiftly and cost effectively.

A fourth initiative, widely adopted in practice is *lean manufacturing* (Womack et al. 1990). Lean is associated with the elimination of waste from all processes within a firm and in the extended supply chain. Lean supply chains often operate with tightly coupled systems with very little slack. This comes at the expense of agility, rendering them vulnerable to disruptions in the supply chain. Despite this, it should also be noted that many elements of lean, such as reduction in setup times, quick changeovers, cross-trained workforce, dynamic scheduling, etc. also serve to contribute to agility in other ways.

The pathways shown in Fig. 17.1 are the antecedents that have been empirically established (Braunscheidel and Suresh 2009; Braunscheidel et al. 2010). It is seen that all four of the above direct antecedents were shown to contribute to agility. We next consider the indirect, cultural antecedents.

17.3.2 Indirect Antecedents: The Cultural Drivers

In this section, the impact of *organizational culture* and two cultural characteristics, *market and learning orientation* on agility are summarized. It is well known that supply chain efforts involve major cultural changes such as establishment of trust, a shift from adversarial relationships to collaboration and partnership among buyers and sellers in the supply chain, etc. These aspects are being researched extensively.

The first major cultural driver considered is the *organizational culture type*. Organizational culture refers to widely shared and strongly held values (O'Reilly 1989; Chatman and Jehn 1994). This definition of culture was adopted for three reasons. First, values are the defining elements of a culture (Enz 1988). Second, our definition is at the organizational level and we wish to study agility at the organizational level and employ values that are held by the members of the organization. Third, the values must be strongly held. That is, people in the organization must truly believe in the values of the organization.

To operationalize organizational culture, the competing values framework (CVF) of Quinn and Rohrbaugh (1983) was utilized. This scheme enables a systematic comparison across levels, organizations and national cultures and countries

(Howard 1998), and it has been widely applied in a variety of settings (e.g. Gregory et al. 2009). This framework involves two dimensions. The first dimension is related to an internal versus an external focus. The second is a continuum with one end being flexibility and the other end stability and control. This results in four distinct quadrants that identify four organizational culture types: *adhocracy, clan, hierarchy and market.*

The adhocracy culture is flexible in its approach but has an external focus. This culture type aims to grow and acquire resources through flexibility and readiness. The second, clan culture has an internal focus and is also flexible in its approach. This cultural type is characterized by cohesion and morale as the means, and human resource development as its end. The third, hierarchy culture, is typified by an internal focus and a structure of stability and control. Through effective information management and communication, firms with this culture type seek to establish stability and control. The fourth, market culture, also has an external focus, but its structural focus is on stability and control. Through planning and goal setting, this culture type aims to achieve productivity and efficiency (Quinn and Rohrbaugh 1983). The CVF permits the study of the dominant organizational culture while acknowledging the possibility that subcultures may exist within an organization (Deshpande et al. 1993).

One might expect that Clan and Hierarchy cultures will have a strong influence on internal integration due to their internal focus. On the other hand, Adhocracy and Market cultures may have an effect on external integration. But the results were found to be intriguing. It was found that a firm's Clan cultural score had no effect on any of the integration practices. A firm's Adhocracy score strongly affected its external integration practices while the firm's Market characteristic had a mild influence on these same practices. Interestingly, the firm's Hierarchy score strongly influenced both internal and external integration practices but in a negative way. That is, the more a firm exhibited a Hierarchical culture, the less it would integrate with key customers and key suppliers and internally integrate. None of these other three cultural scores had an impact on internal integration (Braunscheidel et al. 2010). We now turn to the other two cultural antecedents, market orientation and learning orientation.

Following organization culture type, the cultural characteristic *of market orientation* is considered. It has been defined as the organizational culture that creates the behaviors necessary for creation of superior value for customers. It entails having a sufficient understanding of one's target buyers to create superior value for them continuously, an understanding of short-term strengths and weaknesses as well as long-term strategies of current and potential competitors and coordinated utilization of company resources in creating superior value for target customers through the collective efforts of design, production, distribution and promotion (Narver and Slater 1990). Firms that possess high market orientation may be more knowledgeable about competitors' actions, and what customers demand and desire. In order to be better aligned with customer needs, better inter-departmental alignment and coordination could be effected within the firm. Likewise, externally, a firm can be better integrated with its supply-side and demand-side partners. It was found that market orientation was found to have a significant influence on both internal integration and external integration with key customers and key suppliers. In addition, market orientation exhibited a moderate influence on external flexibility (Braunscheidel and Suresh 2009).

Learning orientation is the third important cultural driver considered. In order to survive in dynamic and turbulent markets, firms must continue to seek the processes of learning, behavior change and performance improvements (Slater and Narver 1995). Sinkula et al. (1997) conceptualized learning orientation as an organizational value that influences the tendency of an organization to create and use knowledge, and hence, to learn and adapt. A learning organization is skilled at challenging the underlying assumptions that its business is based upon (Baker and Sinkula 1999). An organization with a learning orientation is committed to learning which refers to the relative value that a firm places on learning. It is open-minded, which relates to the concept of unlearning and to the emphasis that firms place on questioning the assumptions that govern. Cohen and Levinthal (1990) argued that a critical ingredient to a firm's innovative capabilities is the ability to recognize, assimilate and apply new, external information. Such studies, emphasizing the importance of being able to learn and adapt in dynamic markets, suggest learning orientation as a major cultural driver for agility.

The results with learning orientation have been somewhat counterintuitive. Learning orientation had a significant impact on internal integration only. There was no influence on either external integration or external flexibility, suggesting that the results of learning orientation of firms have so far been predominantly within the firm, and insufficiently at the supply chain level. However, learning orientation was seen to strongly influence internal integration, which in turn was seen to affect supply chain agility significantly.

17.4 Managerial Actions Required for Enhancing Agility

Based on the above empirically established research relationships, we next summarize the managerial implications as a comprehensive set of actions needed to ensure supply chain agility. We categorize them under the heads of: (1) supply chain initiatives, and, (2) more fundamental, cultural changes needed to enhance agility. The latter, cultural changes needed are generally accomplished over a longer time frame than the more tangible supply chain actions. Hence the supply chain initiatives can be viewed as short- and medium-term actions, and the cultural dimension as a more medium- and long-term transformation of the organization and its supply chain partners. We also characterize the numerous actions steps as either contributing to mitigation and/or response. To facilitate discussion, these managerial actions are summarized in Table 17.2a, b.

Table 17.2 (a) Supply chain initiatives to augment agility and flexibility, (b) Cultural transformation initiatives to augment agility

	Mitigation	Response
(a) **Initiatives**		
Supply chain configuration initiatives for agility		
Creation of the supply chain map	X	X
Examination of the supply chain map for vulnerable elements	X	
Creation of a SC vulnerability map to identify risks	X	X
Active information sharing with supply chain partners	X	X
Selective creation of capacity buffers to cope with potential disruptions	X	X
Selective creation of inventory buffers to cope with supply disruptions, demand surges, and to ensure fast response	X	X
Contingency plans for supply-side uncertainties and disruptions	X	X
Contingency plans for operational and demand-side uncertainties and disruptions	X	X
Ensuring flexibility in supply network, operations and distribution networks through alternate routing capabilities	X	X
Utilization of delayed differentiation (form postponement) and logistics postponement to enable customization and responsiveness	X	X
Use of rapid response initiatives like continuous replenishment (CR), vendor managed inventory (VMI), collaborative planning, forecasting and replenishment (CPFR), etc.	X	X
Inventory levels are visible throughout the supply chain	X	X
Demand levels are visible throughout the supply chain	X	X
Internal integration		
Formal meetings are routinely scheduled among various departments	X	X
Extensive use of cross functional teams to solve problems	X	X
Frequent internal communication across departments of goals and priorities by management	X	X
Encouragement of openness and teamwork	X	X
When problems or opportunities arise there is a preference for informal, face-to-face meetings across departments	X	X
External integration with suppliers and upstream partners		
Sharing of inventory levels with suppliers	X	X
Feedback on quality and delivery performance for suppliers	X	X
Striving to establish long term relationships with suppliers	X	X
Key suppliers deliver to plants on a JIT basis	X	X
High corporate level of communication on issues with suppliers	X	X
Sharing of information via Internet	X	X
Working with suppliers to seamlessly integrate inter-firm processes	X	X
Joint development of new products/services with suppliers	X	X
	X	X

(continued)

Table 17.2 (continued)

	Mitigation	Response
Joint planning with suppliers as an important element of purchasing		
Information integration with suppliers is given importance	X	X
Joint planning with suppliers is given importance in production	X	X
External integration with customers and downstream partners		
Feedback elicited from customers on quality and delivery performance	X	X
Customers actively involved in new product development process	X	X
Frequent sharing of demand information from customers	X	X
Sharing of production plans with customers	X	X
Sharing of inventory levels with customers	X	X
Joint planning with customers as an important element in logistics	X	X
Information integration with customers is given importance	X	X
Information integration with logistics service providers given importance	X	X
Cultivation of mix and volume flexibility		
Being able to operate efficiently at different levels of output		X
Being able to operate profitably at different production volumes		X
Ability to quickly change the quantities for our products produced		X
Ability to easily change the production volume of a process		X
Ability to produce a wide variety of products in our plant(s)		X
Ability to produce different product types without major changeover		X
Ability to build different products in the same plants at the same time		X
Ability to changeover quickly from one product to another		X
Implementation of lean manufacturing principles		
Production is 'pulled' by the shipment of finished goods		X
Use of a 'pull' production systems		X
Use of Kanbans, squares or containers of signals for production		X
Classification of products based on similar processing requirements		X
Equipment grouped to produce continuous flow of families of products		X
Factory layout based on families of products (cells)		X
Pace of production directly linked with rate of customer demand		X
Working systematically to lower setup time in the plant		X
Ensuring low set up times of equipment in the plant		X
Bringing equipment/processes under statistical process control		X
Extensive use of statistical techniques to reduce process variability		X
Charts showing defect rates used as tools on the shop floor		X
Use of fishbone diagrams to identify causes of quality problems		X
Use of process capability studies before product launch		X

(continued)

Table 17.2 (continued)

	Mitigation	Response
(b) **Cultural orientations**		
Cultivation of market orientation		
The business objectives are driven by customer satisfaction	X	X
Monitoring commitment and orientation to serving customers' needs	X	X
Strategy for competitive advantage is based on understanding of customer needs	X	X
Business strategies driven by beliefs on how to create greater value for customers	X	X
Customer satisfaction systematically and frequently measured	X	X
Close attention is paid to after-sales service	X	X
Salespeople share information within business concerning competitors' strategies	X	X
We respond actively to competitive actions that threaten the firm		X
Top management team regularly discusses competitors' strengths and strategies	X	X
Senior managers from every function visit current and prospective customers	X	
Information on successful and unsuccessful customer experiences shared across all business functions	X	X
All functions are integrated in serving needs of target markets	X	X
All managers understand how everyone in the firm contributes to value creation for customers	X	X
Cultivation of learning orientation		
Managerial view that firm's ability to learn is key to competitive advantage	X	X
Employee learning viewed as an investment, not an expense	X	X
The collective wisdom that once we quit learning, we endanger our future	X	X
All employees committed to the goals of this organization	X	X
A well-defined vision for the organization	X	X
Not afraid to reflect critically on assumptions on the way to conduct business	X	X
Managers encourage employees to "think outside of the box"	X	X
Managers accept that their "view of the world" can be questioned	X	X
Cultivation of organizational culture: positive attributes		
Organization a dynamic and entrepreneurial place where people are willing to take risks	X	X
Leadership in the organization generally exemplifies entrepreneurship, innovation and risk-taking?	X	X
Commitment to innovation and development is the glue that holds the organization together, along with an emphasis on being on the cutting edge	X	X

(continued)

Table 17.2 (continued)

	Mitigation	Response
The organization emphasizes acquisition of new resources and the creation of new challenges; Trying new things and prospecting for opportunities valued	X	X
Cultivation of organizational culture: negative attributes		
The organization is very controlled and structured place where established procedures generally govern what people do	−X	−X
The leadership generally exemplifies coordination, organization or smooth-running, efficiency	−X	−X
Formal rules and policies are the glue that holds the organization together. Maintaining a smooth running institution is important.	−X	−X
The organization emphasizes permanence and stability, with efficiency, control and smooth operations deemed important	−X	−X

Note−X indicates that this works counter to augmenting agility in an organization

17.4.1 *Supply Chain Initiatives for Agility*

Supply chain initiatives aimed at enhancing agility can be further grouped under the categories of: (a) reconfiguring the overall supply chain for greater agility; (b) internal integration; (c) integration with suppliers; (d) integration with customers and downstream partners; (e) the cultivation of various types of flexibility which contribute to supply chain agility; and (f) the implementation of lean manufacturing practices. These are elaborated in the following sections.

17.4.1.1 Supply Chain Configuration Initiatives for Agility

Consistent with supply chain management principles developed over the last two decades, firms are expected to actively share information with upstream and downstream partners, maintain visibility of demand forecasts, inventory information, production plans, etc. with suppliers and distributors. The supply chain map is examined critically to identify "pain points" i.e. points of vulnerability in terms of supply and distribution. Overdependence on one supplier, distributor or any other partner may prove economical but may also increase risks of disruption. After the creation of the supply chain map, it is examined carefully and redundancies in capacity and inventory buffers are established at critical positions to prevent possible disruptions. The sources of uncertainty must be examined systematically in all segments of the supply chain and their root causes must be addressed for mitigation, prior to developing contingency plans to react after disruptions occur at such positions.

A useful tool to identify potential risks, estimate the probability of occurrence and their consequences is a supply chain vulnerability map or a subjective risk map. Typically risk probabilities (low to high) are plotted on one axis and consequences (low to high) are plotted on the other. By employing inter-functional (internal integration) and inter-organizational (integration with customers and suppliers) teams, a comprehensive vulnerability map can be constructed. This enables the supply chain to not only identify potential risks but also enables the preparation of contingency plans that can be implemented in advance of a disruption. The identification of potential risks enables the prioritization of risks, the identification of controllable and non-controllable risks and the ability to assess the cost of mitigating risk exposure with the benefits of reduced risk exposure (Kouvelis et al. 2012; Van Mieghem 2012). That is, top management can make conscious decisions with respect to potential risks.

Supply chain initiatives such as form postponement (delayed differentiation) and logistics postponement are also aimed at ensuring agility and fast response to changing customer demands. Postponement strategies, by virtue of delaying product differentiation as close to the customer as possible, help to reduce the supply-demand mismatch that many global supply chains struggle with. Under normal circumstances postponement improves the capability to manage supply while during a disruption event, it enables a firm to change the configuration of different products quickly (Tang 2006). Systematic sharing of information, as part of initiatives such as vendor managed inventory (VMI), collaborative planning, forecasting and replenishment (CPFR) systems, etc. also involve sharing of demand forecasts and operating plans with other supply chain partners and they contribute to mitigation as well as coordinated response on the part of the supply chain members. In many situations the integration and synchronization of planning and execution of production plans via VMI, CPFR or similar initiatives can minimize and/or eliminate disruptions caused by demand-supply mismatches. In the same way the uses of such initiatives can also lead to increased forecast accuracy, reduced forecast variability and reduced lead times and lead time variability. Such supply chain configuration actions are listed in the first part of Table 17.2a.

17.4.1.2 Internal Integration

A next set of managerial actions pertains to internal integration, i.e. inter-functional and interdepartmental integration, which lead to a connected and more coordinated response to marketplaces changes and disruptions. In addition to economic performance of a supply chain, the above research stream has established that the agility of the supply chain is also improved by higher levels of supply chain integration. Essentially, internal integration results in a more coordinated and connected response on the part of firms in a supply chain. Internal integration has often been mentioned as a necessary first step in supply chain integration process (Stevens 1989; Rosenzweig et al. 2003; Vickery et al. 2003). Stevens (1989) identified four stages that a firm must go through to achieve supply chain integration. The first stage is characterized by functional silos with little synchronization while the second stage emphasizes the inbound flow of goods. Stage-three integration is called internal integration where an organization recognizes that it must effectively and efficiently manage the flow of goods into and out of the organization. The fourth stage is external integration with suppliers and customers.

Vickery et al. (2003), in a study of the automotive supply industry, found that there is a positive, causal relationship between integrative information technologies and supply chain integration, which comprised both horizontal integration (within a firm) and vertical integration (with suppliers and customers). It has also been shown that the joint application of external and internal integration practices has a synergistic effect on firm performance (Droge et al. 2004). Rosenzweig et al. (2003) employed the use of an integration intensity measure (consisting of both internal and external measures of integration) to demonstrate its impact on competitive capabilities and business performance.

In addition to its relationship with agility, internal integration is also one of the keys for the identification and assessment of potential risks. Firms with high levels of internal integration have cross-functional teams that include members of operations, marketing, procurement and logistics, to name a few. These functions are aware of real and potential risks in the supply chain (Hendricks and Singhal 2012). In addition to being knowledgeable of real and potential risks, these functions must coordinate with one another to ensure a smooth flow of product to their customers in normal times as well as when disruptions occur. Thus internal integration is beneficial during normal operations as well as when disruptive events occur. Table 17.2a lists some of the key action steps required on the part of management to foster internal integration.

17.4.1.3 External Integration with Suppliers and Upstream Partners

In order to ensure connected response on the part of suppliers, to potential and actual supply chain disruption, many supply-side integration measures are undertaken. These are normally the same set of measures needed to ensure better supply network performance: frequent sharing of information with suppliers, greater transparency, sharing of inventory information, providing frequent, constructive feedback on quality and delivery performance, striving to establish long term relationships with suppliers, working with suppliers to seamlessly integrate inter-firm processes, joint development of new products/services, joint operational planning, etc. One of the potential benefits of providing quality improvement feedback and integration of inter-firm processes is the identification and elimination of problems before they arise. Elimination of potential problems through process improvement is better than mitigating the impact of these problems (Van Mieghem 2012).

17.4.1.4 External Integration for Customers and Downstream Partners

As for integration with upstream partners, integration with downstream partners also involve information sharing, and frequent inputs on demand trends and marketplace changes from downstream partners. A well-developed sensing mechanisms geared towards elicit early market signals serve to prepare upstream partners to anticipate changes and be prepared for changes. These measures also include the conventional demand-side integration tactics such as feedbacks elicited from customers on quality and delivery performance, frequent elicitation on market signals, downstream partners actively involved in new product development process, frequent sharing of demand information from customers, sharing of production plans and inventory levels with downstream partners, joint production planning with downstream partners as an important element in logistics planning, information integration with downstream organizations, etc.

17.4.1.5 Cultivation of Mix, Volume and Other Types of Flexibility

Having established empirically that agility may also be affected by the extent of externally focused, mix and volume flexibilities, the constituent elements of these need to be systematically cultivated. These involve the ability to operate efficiently at different levels of output, being able to operate profitably at different production volumes, the ability to quickly change the quantities for our products produced, to easily change the production volume of a process, the ability to produce a wide variety of products in our plant(s), the ability to produce different product types without major changeover, etc. These flexibilities are customarily created through several constituent elements of lean production systems such as reduction of setup times, single minute exchange of dies (SMED) principles, cross-training of workforce, designing versatile tools which facilitate their applicability to a wider range of parts and machine operations, etc.

In addition to supporting agility, flexibility offers a two pronged approach and investment in flexibility reaps benefits during normal operations as well as in a disruption situation (Sheffi and Rice 2005; Rice and Caniato 2003). Firms do not need to justify investment in flexibility solely as a means to mitigate or respond to a disruption. Investment in flexibility enables a supply chain to better serve its customers during normal conditions as well as when disruptions strike.

17.4.1.6 Implementation of Lean Manufacturing

Even though lean manufacturing is generally identified with steady-state manufacturing systems, the underlying tools and techniques involved in lean are aimed at flexible manufacturing practices that are oriented towards coping with demand fluctuations and demand-side uncertainties. One of the hallmark characteristics of lean production systems is the adoption of statistical process control (SPC). Through the use of SPC, problems in the production system are continuously corrected and eliminated. As previously mentioned, eliminating problems is preferable to mitigating them. Another characteristic of lean systems is the use of a 'pull' system. That is, production rates are determined by customer demand as materials are pulled through the manufacturing system. Thus as customer demand changes, as will often happen in a disruption event, the pace of production can change as well. It is also worth reiterating that the journey to become agile is predicated on their ability to become lean (Van Hoek 2000; Womack and Jones 1996; Yusuf et al. 2004). As mentioned previously, lean entails the process of continuous improvement. This involves the elimination of waste in a process. By eliminating waste, the stage is set for a process to become agile. These lean practices are well known, and widely implemented.

17.4.2 Cultural Initiatives for Agility

Finally, the cultural orientations of market orientation, learning orientation and culture type of adhocracy are desirable firm characteristics to adopt in terms of agility. Cultural transformations, in general, do not happen overnight, and may thus be seen as long term initiatives. In some studies, organizational culture has been mentioned as key to establishing the ability to respond to disruptions in the supply chain (Sheffi and Rice 2005; Christopher and Peck 2004; Rice and Caniato 2003). However, definitive recommendations have not been made. We submit that in order to become and remain agile, firms must consciously examine the cultural orientations of their supply chain organizations.

In addition to having a direct relationship on internal integration, external integration and flexibility (Braunscheidel and Suresh 2009), market orientation also impacts visibility in the supply chain by virtue of its emphasis on customers and competitors. Firms with a high market orientation pay close attention to the needs of their customers so that superior value can be delivered. In a similar manner, close attention is also paid to the competitive landscape in terms of the strengths and weaknesses of current and potential competitors.

A firm's learning orientation has a direct effect on internal integration. That is, firms must learn to work in a cross-functional manner. As previously discussed, internal integration is a necessary step in becoming integrated with your customers and suppliers in addition to having a direct effect on agility. Another advantage of possessing a learning orientation is the ability for an organization and supply chain to learn from disruption events. When a disruption occurs, after it has been dealt with, an analysis should be conducted to determine what went right, what could be improved and what went wrong. That is, organizations with a learning orientation will incorporate this new information into how they contend with future disruption events.

When a disruption occurs in a supply chain, it is often the case that a specific contingency plan either was not put into place or despite the best planning efforts, the specific scenario at hand was not considered. It is suggested, therefore, that firms that have the listed positive attributes of organizational culture (Adhocracy) are better suited to handle the situation than those with the negative attributes (Hierarchy). When highly uncertain, low probability events occur employees may need to 'operate on the fly' with real time, updated information of the particulars of the event (Kouvelis et al. 2012). Situations such as these, demand that employees take risks as they try to respond to the disruption in real time. If an organization is highly structured with many formal rules and policies, employees who are first responders to the disruption will defer to higher levels for guidance as to how to handle the disruption. Valuable time may be lost in the implementation of a response. This may enable the disruption to become worse and have a greater impact on the firm and supply chain.

Additionally, research has empirically demonstrated that an adhocracy organizational culture has a positive effect on both internal and external integration practices. Those organizations with high levels of a Hierarchical culture have a negative impact on internal and external integration. Given that these integration practices are critical to the development of agility, it is evident that paying attention to a firm's organizational culture has an impact on its ability to respond to disruptive events in the supply chain.

The cultural drivers of market orientation and learning orientation represent somewhat actionable elements, whose elements are summarized in Table 17.2b. The positive (adhocracy) and negative (hierarchy) attributes of culture, based on the competing values framework, can also be seen in Table 17.2b. Admittedly, these elements are the most long-term in nature but they may hold the key to the development and sustainability of agility, and hence, the ability to mitigate and/or respond to supply chain disruptions.

17.5 Conclusions

In this chapter, the cultivation of supply chain agility was approached as a risk management initiative that enables a firm to anticipate as well as respond rapidly to marketplace changes and disruptions in the supply chain. Disruptions may have numerous impacts on supply chain performance. The scope and magnitude of the consequences of these disruptions requires intra- and inter-functional, as well as inter-organizational coordination and communication. This chapter has provided an updated perspective of an emerging body of literature devoted to supply chain agility. Based on our own research stream on this topic, a set of supply chain initiatives were discussed as antecedents for the cultivation of agility. These included internal and external integration measures, cultivation of external flexibility, and lean practices. Following this, more fundamental, cultural antecedents towards cultivation of agility were discussed, which included the constructs of organizational culture type, market orientation and learning orientation. Since the validity of these models has been established through empirical research, we have translated these findings into a set of managerial practices for the cultivation of agility for both mitigation and response.

Unlike the purely prescriptive literature of the past, the prescriptive summary of managerial actions provided in this chapter has been based on actually established empirical research results. Thus this chapter has attempted to develop an enhanced framework and provide guidance for managers and practitioners for agility in supply chains. Much work still remains to be done on supply chain agility, and it is hoped that this chapter has served to enhance our understanding of some of the major antecedents of agility.

References

Agarwal, A., Shankar, R., & Tiwari, M. K. (2006). Modeling the metrics of lean, agile and leagile supply chain: An ANP-based approach. *European Journal of Operational Research, 173*(1), 211–225.

Agarwal, A., Shankar, R., & Tiwari, M. K. (2007). Modeling agility of supply chain. *Industrial Marketing Management, 36*(4), 443–457.

Baker, W. E., & Sinkula, J. M. (1999). The synergistic effect of market orientation and learning orientation on organizational performance. *Journal of the Academy of Marketing Science, 27*(4), 411–427.

Blome, C., Schoenherr, T., & Rexhausen, D. (2013). Antecedents and enablers of supply chain agility and its effect on performance: A dynamic capabilities perspective. *International Journal of Production Research, 51*(4), 1295–1318.

Braunscheidel, M. J., & Suresh, N. C. (2009). The organizational antecedents of a firm's supply chain agility for risk mitigation and response. *Journal of Operations Management, 27*(2), 119–140.

Braunscheidel, M. J., Suresh, N. C., & Boisnier, A. D. (2010). Investigating the impact of organizational culture on supply chain integration. *Human Resource Management, 49*(5), 883–911.

Chatman, J. A., & Jehn, K. A. (1994). Assessing the relationship between industry characteristics and organizational culture: How different can you be? *Academy of Management Journal, 37*(3), 522–553.

Chiang, C., Kocabasoglu-Hillmer, C., & Suresh, N. C. (2012). An empirical investigation of the impact of strategic sourcing and flexibility on firm's supply chain agility. *International Journal of Operations & Production Management, 32*(1), 49–78.

Chopra, S., & Sodhi, M. S. (2004). Managing risk to avoid supply-chain breakdown. *MIT Sloan Management Review, 46*(1), 53–61.

Christopher, M. (2000). The agile supply chain: Competing in volatile markets. *Industrial Marketing Management, 29*(1), 37–44.

Christopher, M., & Peck, H. (2004). Building the resilient supply chain. *International Journal of Logistics Management, 15*(2), 1–13.

Christopher, M., & Towill, D. R. (2001). An integrated model for the design of agile supply chains. *International Journal of Physical Distribution & Logistics Management, 31*(4), 235–246.

Christopher, M., & Towill, D. R. (2002). Developing market specific supply chain strategies. *International Journal of Logistics Management, 13*(1), 1–14.

Cohen, W. M., & Levinthal, D. A. (1990). Absorptive capacity: A new perspective on learning and innovation. *Administrative Science Quarterly, 35*(1), 128–152.

Deshpandé, R., Farley, J. U., & Webster, F. E., Jr. (1993). Corporate culture customer orientation, and innovativeness in japanese firms: A quadrad analysis. *Journal of Marketing, 57*(1), 23–37.

Droge, C., Jayaram, J., & Vickery, S. K. (2004). The effects of internal versus external integration practices on time-based performance and overall firm performance. *Journal of Operations Management, 22*(6), 557–573.

D'Souza, D. E., & Williams, F. P. (2000). Toward a taxonomy of manufacturing flexibility dimensions. *Journal of Operations Management, 18*(5), 577–593.

Enz, C. A. (1988). The role of value congruity in intraorganizational power. *Administrative Science Quarterly, 33*(2), 284–304.

Fliedner, G., & Vokurka, R. J. (1997). Agility: Competitive weapon of the 1990s and beyond? *Production & Inventory Management Journal, 38*(3), 19–24.

Flynn, B. B., Huo, B., & Zhao, X. (2010). The impact of supply chain integration on performance: A contingency and configuration approach. *Journal of Operations Management, 28*(1), 58–71.

Gligor, D. M., & Holcomb, M. C. (2012). Antecedents and consequences of supply chain agility: Establishing the link to firm performance. *Journal of Business Logistics, 33*(4), 295–308.

Gligor, D. M., Holcomb, M. C., & Stank, T. P. (2013). A multidisciplinary approach to supply chain agility: Conceptualization and scale development. *Journal of Business Logistics, 34*(2), 94–108.

Gregory, B. T., Harris, S. G., Armenakis, A. A., & Shook, C. L. (2009). Organizational culture and effectiveness: A study of values, attitudes, and organizational outcomes. *Journal of Business Research, 62*(7), 673–679.

Hendricks, K. B., & Singhal, V. R. (2012). The effect of supply chain disruptions on corporate performance. In *Handbook of integrated risk management in global supply chains* (pp. 51–78). Wiley handbooks in operations research and management science. Hoboken NJ: John Wiley & Sons.

Howard, L. W. (1998). Validating the competing values model as a representation of organizational cultures. *International Journal of Organizational Analysis (1993–2002), 6*(3), 231–250.

Kleindorfer, P. R., & Saad, G. H. (2005). Managing disruption risks in supply chains. *Production and Operations Management, 14*(1), 53–68.

Koste, L. L., & Malhotra, M. K. (1999). A theoretical framework for analyzing the dimensions of manufacturing flexibility. *Journal of Operations Management, 18*(1), 75–93.

Koufteros, X., Vonderembse, M., & Jayaram, J. (2005). Internal and external integration for product development: The contingency effects of uncertainty, equivocality, and platform strategy. *Decision Sciences, 36*(1), 97–133.

Kouvelis, P., Dong, L., Boyabatli, O., & Li, R. (2012). Integrated risk management: A conceptual framework with research overview and applications in practice. In *Handbook of integrated risk management in global supply chains* (pp. 3–12). Wiley handbooks in operations research and management science. Hoboken NJ: John Wiley & Sons.

Li, X., Chen, C., Goldsby, T. J., & Holsapple, C. W. (2008). A unified model of supply chain agility: The work-design perspective. *International Journal of Logistics Management, 19*(3), 408–435.

Li, X., Goldsby, T. J., & Holsapple, C. W. (2009). Supply chain agility: Scale development. *International Journal of Logistics Management, 20*(3), 408–424.

Mason-Jones, R., Naylor, B., & Towill, D. R. (2000). Engineering the leagile supply chain. *International Journal of Agile Management Systems, 2*(1), 54–61.

Narasimhan, R., Swink, M., & Kim, S. W. (2006). Disentangling leanness and agility: An empirical investigation. *Journal of Operations Management, 24*(5), 440–457.

Narver, J. C., & Slater, S. F. (1990). The effect of a market orientation on business profitability. *Journal of Marketing, 54*(4), 20–35.

Naylor, B., Naim, M. M., & Berry, D. (1999). Leagility: Integrating the lean and agile manufacturing paradigms in the total supply chain. *International Journal of Production Economics, 62*(1), 107–118.

O'Reilly, C. (1989). Corporations, culture, and commitment: motivation and social control in organizations. *California Management Review, 31*(4), 9–25.

Pagell, M. (2004). Understanding the factors that enable and inhibit the integration of operations, purchasing and logistics. *Journal of Operations Management, 22*(5), 459–487.

Paulraj, A., & Chen, I. J. (2007). Strategic buyer-supplier relationships, information technology and external logistics integration. *Journal of Supply Chain Management, 43*(2), 2–14.

Prater, E., Biehl, M., & Smith, M. A. (2001). International supply chain agility. *International Journal of Operations & Production Management, 21*(5/6), 823–839.
Quinn, R. E., & Rohrbaugh, J. (1983). A spatial model of effectiveness criteria: towards a competing values approach to organizational analysis. *Management Science, 29*(3), 363–377.
Rice, J. B., & Caniato, F. (2003). Building a secure and resilient supply network. *Supply Chain Management Review, 7*(5), 22–30.
Rosenzweig, E. D., Roth, A. V., & Dean, J. W. (2003). the influence of an integration strategy on competitive capabilities and business performance: An exploratory study of consumer products manufacturers. *Journal of Operations Management, 21*(4), 437–456.
Shao, X. (2013). Supply chain characteristics and disruption mitigation capability: An empirical investigation in China. *International Journal of Logistics: Research & Applications, 16*(4), 277–295.
Sheffi, Y., & Rice, J. B. (2005). A supply chain view of the resilient enterprise. *MIT Sloan Management Review, 47*(1), 41–48.
Sinkula, J. M., Baker, W. E., & Noordewier, T. (1997). A framework for market-based organizational learning: Linking values, knowledge, and behavior. *Journal of the Academy of Marketing Science, 25*(4), 305–318.
Slater, S. F., & Narver, J. C. (1995). Market orientation and the learning organization. *Journal of Marketing, 59*(3), 63–74.
Stevens, G. C. (1989). Integrating the supply chain. *International Journal of Physical Distribution & Materials Management, 19*(8), 3–8.
Swafford, P. M., Ghosh, S., & Murthy, N. (2006). The antecedents of supply chain agility of a firm: Scale development and model testing. *Journal of Operations Management, 24*(2), 170–188.
Swafford, P. M., Ghosh, S., & Murthy, N. (2008). Achieving supply chain agility through IT integration and flexibility. *International Journal of Production Economics, 116*(2), 288–297.
Tang, C. S. (2006). Robust strategies for mitigating supply chain disruptions. *International Journal of Logistics: Research & Applications, 9*(1), 33–45.
Upton, D. M. (1995). What really makes factories flexible? *Harvard Business Review, 73*(4), 74–84.
Van Hoek, R. I. (2000). The thesis of leagility revisited. *International Journal of Agile Management Systems, 2*(3), 196–201.
Van Mieghem, J. A. (2012). Risk management and operational hedging: an overview. In *Handbook of integrated risk management in global supply chains* (pp. 13–49). Wiley Handbooks in operations research and management science. Hoboken NJ: John Wiley & Sons.
Vickery, S. K., Droge, C., Setia, P., & Sambamurthy, V. (2010). Supply chain information technologies and organisational initiatives: Complementary versus independent effects on agility and firm performance. *International Journal of Production Research, 48*(23), 7025–7042.
Vickery, S. K., Jayaram, J., Droge, C., & Calantone, R. (2003). The effects of an integrative supply chain strategy on customer service and financial performance: an analysis of direct versus indirect relationships. *Journal of Operations Management, 21*(5), 523–539.
Womack, J. P., & Jones, D. T. (1996). *Lean thinking: Banish waste and create wealth in your corporation* (First Free Press edition, Revised and updated). New York, NY: Simon & Schuster.
Womack, J. P., Jones, D. T., & Roos, D. (1990). *The machine that changed the world*. New York, NY: Macmillan.
Yusuf, Y. Y., Gunasekaran, A., Adeleye, E. O., & Sivayoganathan, K. (2004). Agile supply chain capabilities: Determinants of competitive objectives. *European Journal of Operational Research, 159*(2), 379–392.
Zhang, Q., Vonderembse, M. A., & Lim, J. (2003). Manufacturing flexibility: Defining and analyzing relationships among competence, capability, and customer satisfaction. *Journal of Operations Management, 21*(2), 173–191.

Chapter 18
Assessing Supply Chain Resilience upon Critical Infrastructure Disruptions: A Multilevel Simulation Modelling Approach

Paolo Trucco, Boris Petrenj and Seyoum Eshetu Birkie

Abstract Supply chain risk management (SCRM) approaches suggest that actors in a supply chain network should consider different risk scenarios to address and mitigate supply chain risks in a better way. Overall performance of a supply chain could be severely affected by disruptions that are triggered by failures or service disruptions in the critical infrastructure (CI) systems that the supply chain relies on. Interdependencies among the CI systems and supply chains, particularly the so-called Key Resources Supply Chains (KRSC) such as food, worsen the effects as disruption and consequences propagate in the network. In order to understand such interdependencies and enhance SCRM approaches with a more holistic view, this chapter introduces a multilevel modelling approach. The economic loss impact of disruptions in CI systems and the potential effectiveness of different strategies to improve resilience in KRSC are modelled and assessed. A combination of Discrete Event Simulation and System Dynamics is used at the different levels of the simulation model. The proposed approach is demonstrated with an application case addressing the vulnerability and resilience analysis of a fast moving consumer goods supply chain against disruptions in underlying CI systems. Results of the multilevel simulation offered relevant insights toward a better understanding of the strength and dynamics of the interdependence between KRSC and CI, and consequently on resilience improvement efforts. Results help supply chain managers to prioritise resilience strategies, according to their expected benefits, when making decisions on the amount and location of resilience capabilities within a supply chain. The results strongly support the implementation of collaborative and coordinated resilience strategies among supply chain actors to direct efforts where they can be most effective.

P. Trucco · B. Petrenj · S.E. Birkie (✉)
School of Management, Politecnico di Milano, Milan, Italy
e-mail: seyoumeshetu.birkie@polimi.it

S.E. Birkie
EiT-M, Mekelle University, Mekelle, Ethiopia

Y. Khojasteh (ed.), *Supply Chain Risk Management*,
DOI 10.1007/978-981-10-4106-8_18

18.1 Introduction

Chile is the number one copper producer in the world. Supply of copper from Chile was disrupted in April 2014 after the earthquake and ensuing tsunami at an epicentre far from the major copper mines (e.g. Clarke and MacDonald 2014). The disruption was, however, mainly due to the ruined roads, power outages, and closed ports, rather than direct damage to production facilities or capacity. This real-life example demonstrates that in any supply chain the flows of materials, information and money can easily be disrupted due not only to supply or demand problems but also due to affected critical infrastructure systems that the supply chains depend on. Similarly, a recent news on Wall Street Journal also indicated that the future prices of copper was threatened by water shortage in a small town due to drought (Patterson 2015).

Managing supply chain risks involves decision making under uncertainty on multiple parameters. Actors in a supply chain network are often required to consider multiple levels of decision to better address and mitigate supply chain risks as much proactively as possible. Such a detailed and multilevel consideration of disruption risk interactions is important because it is not sure where the sources of disruption affecting a supply chain might emanate from. As indicated in the aforementioned example, a supply chain could be severely affected by disruption in the critical infrastructure (CI) used by the supply chain. These effects are magnified due to the (inter)dependencies between CI systems and disruption propagation to Key Resources Supply Chains (KRSC), i.e. supply chains of some industries marked as critical (such as food or pharmaceuticals) which are heavily dependent on other CI.

Supply chain risk and disruption of CI are complex phenomena that are difficult to understand in real life circumstances. To evaluate resilience strategies, consequences (losses) of CI disruptions need to be quantified; this requires an adequate understanding of all the possible cascading effects within the CI and to the supply chain network level as well. Simulation modelling approaches provide a relatively simple and cheap way of representing, experimenting and designing for such phenomena. However, simulation approaches to supply chain risk management (SCRM) or critical infrastructure protection and resilience (CIP-R) which focus on just one level provide limited support for such understanding; the complex interdependences of disruptions in CI systems and on supply chains is not given enough attention in literature.

This chapter focuses on assessing the impact of CI disruptions on KRSC, the economic losses caused and the potential effectiveness of different strategies to improve resilience in KRSC. A few recent disruption incidents are used as cases for a qualitative discussion to demonstrate the relevance of the issue. After having briefly discussed the state-of-the-art on simulation modelling approaches in SCRM and CIP-R, a multilevel simulation modelling approach is then introduced. The proposed approach is finally demonstrated with a practical application case addressing the vulnerability and resilience analysis of a fast moving consumer goods (FMCG) supply chain under different disruption scenarios of interdependent CI systems.

18.2 Mutual Dependencies Between SC and CI Systems

18.2.1 Critical Infrastructure Disruption and Supply Chain Risk

Critical Infrastructure can be defined as those assets and systems that, if disrupted, would threaten national security, economy, public health and safety, and way of life (McNally et al. 2007). Contemporary societies are increasingly dependent on availability, reliability, correctness, safety and security of CI (The Council of the European Union 2008). The vital functions and services of CIs are supplied through networks and assets including electricity grids, roads and communication networks.

CI systems have interdependence among each other; that is, a bidirectional or unidirectional relationship exists between the states of any given pair of CI systems (Rinaldi et al. 2001). These interdependencies can be described in terms of physical, cyber, logical, and geographic types. Physical interdependency exists when an input of one CI is dependent on material/energy output of another (e.g. a rail network depends on power supply). Cyber interdependency describes the dependence of CI on information infrastructure. When elements of multiple infrastructure are in close spatial proximity, geographical interdependence occurs (e.g. joint exposure to the same natural phenomena). When an interdependence between CIs exists and is not any one of the aforementioned three classes, it is classified as logical (e.g. increased highway usage by commuters due to railway strikes and service interruptions).

A disruption of CI or SC can be described as an unplanned and unanticipated event which prevents or limits flow of material, information or money in a system (Craighead et al. 2007). Kim et al. (2015) argued that disruptions may occur at node (i.e. facility), arc (e.g. transportation), or network (both node and arcs) level of a supply chain. Disruptions that occur at network level are much more important than the other two as they may cause severe consequences on supply chains. By focusing on disruptions at CI, this chapter discusses how resilience strategies minimise the effect of disruptions that can affect multiple actors, i.e. nodes and arcs, in a supply chain–KRSC in our case. Disruptions in a CI include information and communication disruptions, transportation, power, and other infrastructure failures, which is the main concern in this chapter. Disruptions of these CI have a significant impact not only on other interdependent CI but also on supply chains that utilise the CI (Ouyang 2014; Rinaldi et al. 2001). In fact, the consequences can ripple along different CI systems and multiple supply chain levels. Societal life can be severely affected by disruptions in CI directly or indirectly as supply chains that provide inputs for human day-to-day activities depend on them. For example, in the aftermath of Hurricane Katrina, oil pipes and telecommunications systems failed due to power outages (Santella et al. 2009). Folgers coffee plants (back then owned by Procter and Gamble) in the area were hit hard by the hurricane, affecting coffee supply. Even worse was the lack of access for the recovery effort in the area due to damaged roads, which forced them to use helicopters.

18.2.2 Supply Chain Resilience

Tang (2006) describes different robust SC strategies that aim to improve a firm's capability to manage supply and/or demand better under normal circumstances and to enhance the firm's capability to sustain its operations when a major disruption hits. The majority of these strategies rely on the availability of infrastructure systems that serve the supply chain, either as primary subject of intervention or as subsequent objective associated to other categories of risks. We can say that disruptions of such infrastructure represent one of the most important risk category and their improvements enable to protect SC from either CI disruptions or all the other risk categories closely linked to them.

In general, resilience can be understood as the ability of a global supply chain to anticipate, reorganise and deliver its core function continually, despite the impact of external and internal shocks to the system (Birkie et al. 2014; Ponomarov and Holcomb 2009; Tang 2006). Sheffi (2007) describes resilience as the capacity to be better positioned than competitors to deal with and to gain advantage from disruptions. These definitions essentially focus on capabilities that a supply chain has in mitigating disruptions happening somewhere in the network (Kamalahmadi and Parast 2016) and possibly turn them into an opportunity to gain competitive advantage. At supply chain network level, resilience can be seen as an attribute to withstand such disruptions triggered at a node (facility) or an arc (transportation) (Kim et al. 2015) as the consequences of a disruption at one point can ripple along the supply chain (Ivanov et al. 2014).

Rice and Caniato (2003) identified flexibility and redundancy as two broad strategies for SC resilience. Flexibility entails creating capabilities within the organization to redeploy some existing and previously committed capacities from one area to another (to make up for lost or delayed capacity). Redundancy, by contrast, is the additional capacity that would be used to replace the capacity loss caused by a disruption (Rice and Caniato 2003). Both approaches require investments in infrastructure and resources prior to the point of need.

When evaluating effectiveness of resilience strategies applied to specific parts of the SC, we also consider different levels of resilience capacity, achievable through either flexibility or redundancy, or most typically a mix of the two.

18.2.3 Review of Relevant SC Risk and CI Disruption Cases

The Chile copper supply disruption situation mentioned earlier is one demonstration of how supply chain disruptions are caused or worsened by failure in the CI systems that the supply chain depends on. Similar cases that reveal how supply chains are vulnerable to disruptions in CI systems and cascading effects are reported in Table 18.1.

Table 18.1 A few supply chain disruptions and their dependence on CI failures

Supply chain disruption	Related/underlying CI interdependences	Disrupted CI	Consequences of the disruption
1. Copper supply shortage in Chile (2014)	Supplies could not be transported due to damages to roads and power interruptions because of earthquake; employees of mines went to families	Road transport Power supply Rail transport Manpower Ports	Copper prices showed increases up to as high as 1% on London Metal Exchange and New York Mercantile Exchange in speculation of shortages (Clarke and MacDonald 2014)
2. Delay of essential goods including medical supplies in the EU due to migration crisis (2015)	Border closures and tighter controls to deal with chaos due to stowaways meant that the supplies were severely disrupted, especially those urgently needed	Road transport Rail transport	Great Britain alone lost an estimate of at least 1 billion USD a year due to the crisis (BSI 2015)
3. Auto and electronics parts shortage following the triple disaster in Japan (2011)	The damaged power and transportation infrastructures had greatly influenced recovery from the disruption	Airfreight Power supply Water supply Road transport Ports Manpower Gas and fuel supply	The direct economic impact of the disruption is estimated to be more than 22 billion USD excluding damages to damaged buildings and infrastructure (e.g. World Economic Forum 2012)
4. Import items to US stranded at ports (2002)	Workers' strike caused the blockage; airfreights (as alternative routes) became more expensive than they usually are as few fast companies already leased the capacity	Ports Airfreight Manpower	Retrospective analysis estimated more than 1 billion USD per day for economic loss to US economy for each day of strike that went for 11 days (Hall 2004)

To start by reciting the Chile earthquake situation, the main cause of copper supply shortage was not damage at the copper mines. The epic centre of the earthquake was not very close to copper mines, which are mainly located in Northern Chile. In fact, the major mining companies have announced shortly after the quake that the mines and smelting plants were intact. It was, however, difficult to transport the produced copper due to the damaged roads and power interruption. Some of the mines have also stopped production for a while because employees were sent to join and support families affected by the earthquake and the subsequent tsunami.

Large amount of mostly perishable items have been stranded at the US West Coast ports during the 2002 dock workers strike. Items supposed to be delivered for Christmas sales season were delayed, and partly spoiled. The US economy as well as large retailers had to bear enormous consequences (Hall 2004).

During the Great Japan Earthquake in 2011, automotive and electronics manufacturers felt the pain of the natural disaster. Even those companies with no physically damaged facilities or whose Japanese suppliers could still produce parts had to deal with shortages due to power outages, failed roads, sea ports and airports (e.g. MacKenzie et al. 2012; World Economic Forum 2012).

The 2015 migration crisis in Europe, which has exacerbated since late 2015, has caused severe disruptions to logistics and custom services to several European centred supply chains. It has caused enormous disruption to the medical and other essential supplies. Some European countries blocked or tightened security at their borders, which, together with the influx of migrants, caused extremely long traffic jams. The United Kingdom alone incurred 1 billion USD a year due to the supply chain disruption because of the crisis (BSI 2015).

The aforementioned cases show how much modern global supply chains are vulnerable to failures or unavailability of CIs, such as road transport, ports, electrical power, water supply, fuel and gas supply. The vulnerability and the associated consequences becomes much more severe when we consider key resource supply chains, such as food or pharmaceutical products. We will get back to that in later sections when we discuss the simulation model. Before that, let us briefly look at modelling and simulation approaches used in SCRM and CIP-R research.

18.3 Simulation Modelling Approaches in SCRM and CI

Inheriting from the broader supply chain management domain, three main simulation modelling approaches are used in SCRM and resilience. These are: Discrete Event Simulation, System Dynamics and Agent Based Modelling (Fahimnia et al. 2015; Owen et al. 2010; Tako and Robinson 2012; Wu et al. 2013). We conducted a literature search and reviewed the use of the three approaches depending on the nature, goal and aggregation level of phenomena modelled. Discrete Event Simulation (DES) is process-centric (mid-low abstraction level) and facilitates the simulation of interdependent systems through occurrence of time-dependent discrete events that approximate real-world processes. System Dynamics (SD) is a rigorous top-down approach, with high abstraction level, used for modelling the behaviour of a complex system over time (Sterman 2000). Stocks (the accumulation of resources in a system), flows (the rates of change that alter those resources), and feedback are the central concepts in this approach. Agent Based Modelling (ABM) approach allows for emulating emerging behaviours resulting from the interaction of autonomous agents (bottom-up approach) (e.g. Wu et al. 2013).

We extended the literature search to review the use of the same or compatible approaches for simulation modelling of CI systems, identifying their main advantages and drawbacks. This is described in the following sub-sections.

18.3.1 Simulation Modelling in SCRM

Tako and Robinson (2012) analysed simulation modelling approaches used in 127 journal articles published between 1996 and 2006. Their work was based on the belief that SD was mostly used to model problems at a strategic level, whereas DES was used at an operational/tactical level. The aim of the review was to test if this hypothesis was true. The paper explored the frequency of application of DES and SD as modelling tools for decision support systems in the domain of SC Management by looking at the nature and level of issues modelled. The findings suggest that DES has been used more frequently to model SC, with the exception of the bull-whip effect which is mostly modelled using SD. The study concluded that in terms of the level of decision making (strategic or operational/tactical) there is no difference in the use of either DES or SD.

Owen et al. (2010) did similar literature review referring to the three approaches (DES, SD and ABM) used in the papers reviewed. A total of 439 peer-reviewed papers were identified and then a sample of 100 papers was selected, reviewed and classified (Owen et al. 2010). This review revealed that both SD and ABM have been equally used to address strategic issues. DES, on contrary, was more heavily weighted towards planning problem types and was also the only approach to address operational problems.

It can be observed how the SC modelling applications in the period 2007–2010 influenced the picture as a whole. In addition, the results of our search showed examples underlining how the use of SD in the last years mostly focused on the strategic view (e.g. Ivanov and Sokolov 2013; Kumar and Nigmatullin 2011). An increase of using quantitative and analytical modelling approaches, including simulation in risk management is observed particularly after 2005 as evidenced by relatively large number of SCRM papers with modelling methodologies (Fahimnia et al. 2015).

The bibliography dealing with simulation approaches applied to SCRM theme is generally sparse. We did a literature search on the simulation approaches applied to model and analyse supply chain risk and resilience using the keyword combinations shown in Table 18.2a and we found very limited number of publications. Based on our last search with the keyword combinations on Scopus, (dated 14 February 2016), only 19 journal articles and 16 conference papers were found to be relevant after filtering for duplicates and relevance of content. Of the three simulation modelling approaches in SCRM, ABM seems to be relatively limited. We identified only 5 journal articles and 3 conference papers implementing this approach. Many of the publications discussed risk at supply chain network level, even though some had analysis at shop floor or inside a supply chain facility. For example, Wu et al.

Table 18.2 Literature search on the three simulation modelling approaches (a) in SCRM, and (b) in CIP-R

Simulation modelling approach in SCRM	Articles in journals	Conference papers	Total	*(a)*
DES	8	7	15	
ABM	5	3	8	
SD	6	6	12	
Total	19	16	35	
Search keywords: *{"supply chain risk" OR "supply chain disruption"} AND {"discrete event simulation" OR "agent based model*" OR ("system dynamics" AND "Simulation")}*				
Simulation modelling approach in CIP-R	**Articles in journals**	**Conference papers**	**Total**	*(b)*
DES	1	6	7	
ABM	8	11	19	
SD	13	9	22	
Total	22	26	48	
Search keywords: *"critical infrastructure" AND {"discrete event simulation" OR ("agent based model*" AND simulation) OR ("system dynamics" AND "Simulation")}*				

(2013) model risk of stockout at retailers to model the individual behaviour of competing manufacturers using ABM, it considers the customers as autonomous entities making their own decision towards the purchase of competing products. The supply chain risks discussed in the different studies are often assumed to have been "externally triggered" and not deliberate acts of the autonomous supply chain actors. Perhaps this could be a reason why ABM was limited in the papers.

18.3.2 Modelling Approaches in CIP-R Literature

When it comes to CIP-R, Ouyang's (2014) review on modelling and simulation of interdependent infrastructure systems provides the dominant approaches in research publications, including ABM, SD, and DES, as well as some other variants. In this domain, we found a relatively higher number of publications that applied one of the three simulation techniques (see Table 18.2b) compared to that of SCRM. Especially SD seems to be used more dominantly. All of the abovementioned papers focus on simulation modelling and analyses at supply chain network level mainly, or consider only the failures of CI systems. Some papers discuss different simulation approaches for SC risk modelling and analysis due to failure in CI (e.g. Wu and Olson 2008; Yang and Wu 2007). However, most of them tend to assume the CI failure simply as the given trigger that has a single point disruption impact on the supply chain. Therefore, there is a clear lack of studies implementing simulation modelling approaches to better represent the real complexity and dynamics of interdependencies between CI and supply chain.

18.4 A Multilevel Modelling Approach

The different simulation approaches have differences in their underlying assumptions, strengths and implementation frameworks. It has been however recognised that many management decision making problems may require more than one possible viewpoint, even at the same level of abstraction, to accommodate different frames of reference and reduce risk of missing some relevant aspects (Brailsford et al. 2014; Pidd 2003).

For example, most modelling approaches to CIP-R are motivated by decision making for better protecting CI systems that the dependency with KRSC are not well addressed (Conrad et al. 2006; Santella et al. 2009). Creating a multilevel (hybrid) model that combines different approaches in a uniform framework enables to better represent and understand complex systems (Brailsford et al. 2014; Ouyang 2014) such as interdependent CI and KRSC. In the context of this chapter, by multilevel modelling we are referring to what is described as multiscale and multimethod modelling in Brailsford et al. (2014).

Being cautious about the differences, experts in the field have recognised the benefit of having multimethod, multilevel simulation modelling for managerial decision making. In fact, the different chapters in Brailsford et al. (2014) provide empirical evidence of how different modelling approaches could be used complementarily or as alternatives. Recent developments in multimodel simulation software packages, such as Anylogic®, appear to support efforts in this direction.

The conceptual model proposed in this chapter seeks to represent three levels (see Fig. 18.1): the physical interdependencies between different CI systems, the relationship between possible CI service disruptions and the availability of critical resources and services for the different actors of the SC, and finally the dynamic behaviour of the KRSC as a whole. In Fig. 18.1, the arrows indicate directional dependence/interdependence of different CI and KRSC components. The output variable represents the performance of the KRSC in generating turnover, given the abovementioned dependencies and the resilience capabilities of the SC actors.

The model applies the hierarchical method wherein the lower level model runs and generates data which is used by a higher level model, which again informs the lower level.

In our model, we have chosen DES and SD simulation approaches. DES was chosen as it is very appropriate to represent phenomena which are event based involving queues, lead times, etc. The third level (KRSC) has these features, making DES appropriate. We primarily assume that the behaviour of the overall interdependent system involving the CI can be explained by the feedback nature of causal relationships that characterise the structure of the system (Brailsford et al. 2014). In SD "agents" can be homogenously mixed and aggregated to the higher level. Thus, to model the first and second levels in our study, SD is preferred over ABM which models individual agent behaviour that may evolve heterogeneously.

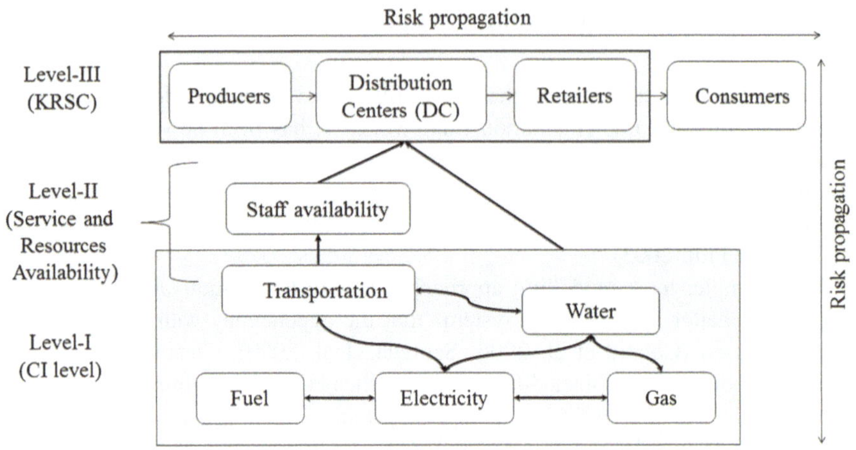

Fig. 18.1 Multilevel simulation modelling framework

18.4.1 The First Level: Critical Infrastructure

In the first level, we can find the different CI systems and their sub-models of supply. The level was built using System Dynamics methodology (Fig. 18.2a) and is composed by the following sub-models:

- Sub-model of fuel supply through pipeline;
- Sub-model of fuel supply through road and rail;
- Sub-model of gas supply through pipeline;
- Sub-model of water supply through pipeline;
- Sub-model of power supply.

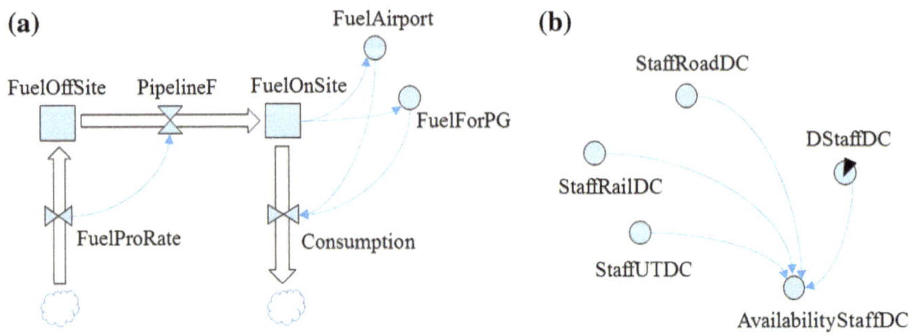

Fig. 18.2 An example sub-model of **a** fuel supply through pipeline; **b** staff availability at distribution centres

18.4.2 The Second Level: Service and Resource Availability

The second level models the availability of services supplied by CI and of other resources used either for the KRSC or for the first level needs. This level was built with SD methodology as well. As example, Fig. 18.2b shows the computation of the total staff availability at the distribution centres, taking into account the staff which uses railway (StaffRailDC), road (StaffRoadDC), or the urban train (StaffUTDC) transportation systems to reach the workplace.

18.4.3 The Third Level: KRSC Model

The third level represents the KRSC model. It embodies the internal production and logistic phases, the import SC and the connection between distribution centres (DC) and Retailers. This level was built with a multimethod approach. Indeed, the initial part of the SC, in which we can find the flows of the internal and external productions (import rate), implements a SD approach. The part of the SC between the DC and retailers was modelled with DES instead. The rationale for adopting a multimethod approach is that, on one hand it assures a continuous systemic view of the dependencies from the upper levels, while, on the other hand, DES better models the capacity and lead times involved in the distribution and delivery processes.

18.4.4 Multilevel Model Assumptions

There are some key assumptions at the basis of the overall modelling approach:

- The model is isolated from outer environment, which means it can only be affected by inner entities (concepts);
- The physical dependencies between CI systems and other services is linear. For example, if 100 ton per day [t/d] of fuel is required to support 100% of generation capacity of a power plant, then 80 t/d of fuel supports 80% of the same capacity;
- The amount of KRSC demand is constant (i.e. an average day is simulated).

Coherent with the abovementioned assumptions, the multilevel model is able to implement inter-dependencies between CI systems. In our specific application, power generation plants and airports need fuel and/or natural gas. Furthermore, fuel is also used by road transportation. On the other side, power is used for fuel and gas production, urban transport service, water supply, road, railway, and air transportation. Staff availability is influenced by the status of urban transport: road and railway systems. As for the FMCG sector, the production rate is influenced by power and fuel, while the distribution process is affected by staff availability and three kinds of transportation: road, railway and air. Finally, the purchasing rate is influenced by staff availability and power.

18.5 Pilot Application: The Italian Fast Moving Consumer Goods Supply Chain

FMCG supply chain deals with the delivery of non-durable goods, such as drinks and grocery items. At the consumer side, the main characteristics of these products are: high frequency purchase, low prices and low involvement. Looking from the producers and distributors side, the main characteristics of these products are low contribution margin, extensive distribution network and high stock turnover. A key issue in managing this type of supply chains is the perishability of the products and thus the lead-time that these goods can undergo.

The model of the FMCG supply chain consists of the following actors (Fig. 18.1, level III):

- Producers (P)—can be classified considering both the firm dimensions (Big vs. Small and Medium producers) and the typology of products (Food vs. Health & Care);
- Distribution Centres (DC)—retailers' facilities for temporary storage with the main function of receiving daily orders from the retailers and deliver them to the purchasing organization that will buy the products required (e.g. warehouse or other specialised buildings);
- Retailers (R)—subjects who receive goods in large quantities from the DC, and then sell smaller quantities to the consumer for a profit (e.g. Supermarket);
- Consumers (C)—persons who pay for the products intended for private consumption.

The model of FMCG Supply Chain as it was implemented in Anylogic® is partially presented in Fig. 18.3. In part (a) of the figure, an implementation of SD is shown, representing flow of imported and locally produced FMCGs to the DC using different modes of transportation (rail, road, air). Part (b) of the figure shows DES implementation to model the flow of goods from distribution centres to retailers.

In our analysis, we considered that the lead-times between the distribution centre and the final retailers for different product categories vary between 7 and 12 days (these figures represent the expected mean lead-time values assured by logistics service providers for the Italian FMCG sector).

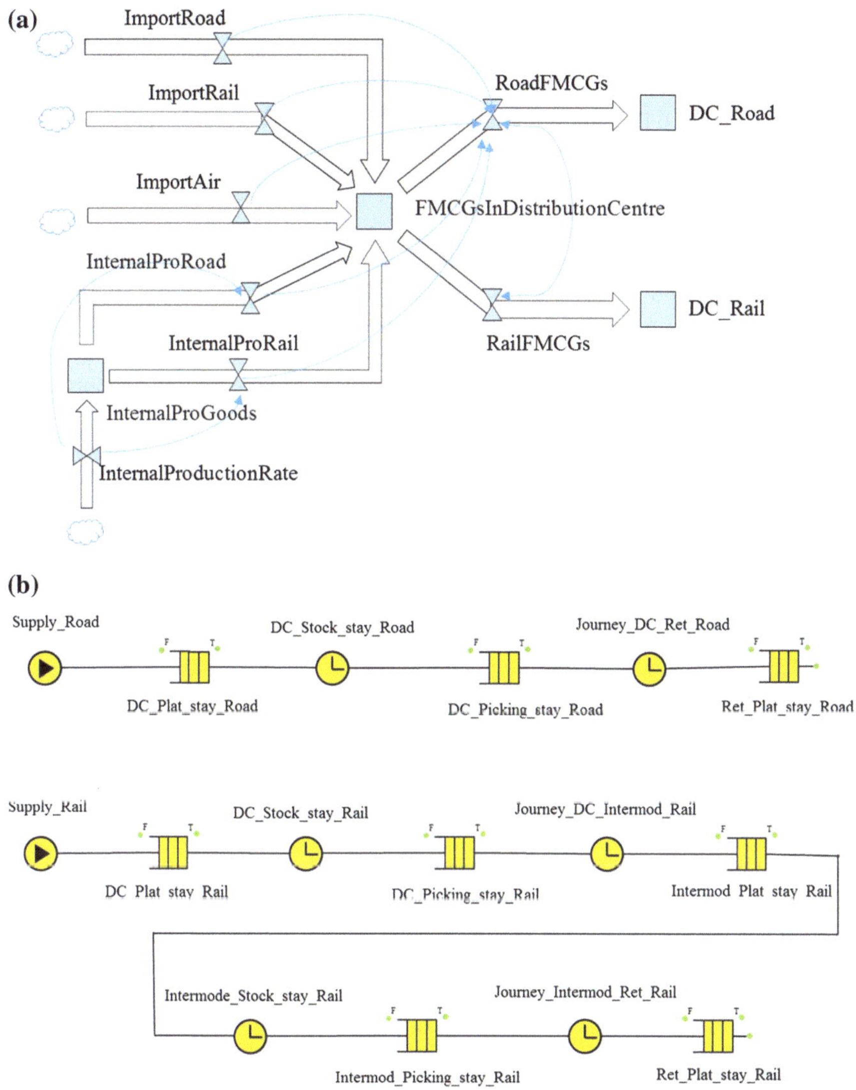

Fig. 18.3 FMCG supply chain model implementation in Anylogic® **a** SD model, **b** DES model

18.5.1 Resilience Strategies and Capacities

In face of a disruption, resilience capabilities to mitigate disruptions at the first level CI—namely, gas, fuel, power generated and water—can be exploited at the three segments of the SC. The downstream segment, which includes the part of SC between DC and Retailers, the midstream segment dealing with the logistics from Producers to DC, and the upstream segment, dealing with production planning and management within the Producers. We assume that the part of the SC dealing with import is not modifiable in the short range, thus its contribution to SC resilience is negligible.

The strategies represent the package of actions that SC managers and other company managers can actuate in order to sustain the business continuity of a specific segment of the SC. In particular, four basic strategies were identified and investigated:

- Strategy 1—Exploiting resilience capabilities within just one of the supply chain members located in the upstream or downstream segments of the supply chain (e.g. resilience capabilities of retailers only);
- Strategy 2—Extends resilience capabilities of strategy 1 to a pair of supply chain members located in the upstream or downstream segments of the supply chain (resilience capabilities of both retailers and producers);
- Strategy 3—Exploiting resilience capabilities of triple supply chain members in the network by extending strategy 2;
- Strategy 3 *plus water*—This strategy adds a resilience capability of restoring some level of water supply disrupted at the producer. The justification to include this element is that restoring disrupted water supply is relatively low investment compared to the other CI services (e.g. water tanks installed at production site). We intend to observe the marginal effect of having this additional capability on recovered turnover. Hence, this strategy applies to scenarios where resilience capability of a producer is invoked.

A further dimension covered in the simulation deals with the capacity level (or strength) of the resilience capabilities activated under different strategies. In particular, three levels of resilience capacity were considered for each strategy:

- Resilience capacity of 20%—i.e. a capacity able to mitigate up to 20% reduction of critical services due to some CI disruption;
- Resilience capacity of 50%—i.e. a capacity able to mitigate up to 50% reduction of critical services due to some CI disruption;
- Resilience capacity of 90%—i.e. a capacity able to mitigate up to 90% reduction of critical services due to some CI disruption.

Consequently, a 20% reduction of critical services at some point of the FMCG SC is the minimum “trigger level” for the activation of the available strategies and capacities along the entire SC.

18.5.2 Data Specification and Collection

The initial set of data was collected from Eurostat (Directorate-General of the European Commission), namely:

- European shares of electricity, gas and water supply;
- European shares of railway, road and pipeline transportation;
- Input-output data related to:
  - Manufacture of coke, refined petroleum products and nuclear fuels;
  - Electricity, gas, steam and hot water supply;
  - Land transport and transport via pipelines;
  - Air transport;
- Total turnover per single infrastructure sectors in Italy;
- Input value of single infrastructure sectors to the FMCG supply chain in Italy;
- Consumption (per year) of electricity, fuel, gas and water by DC, retailers and transport infrastructures;
- Flow rates (per year) of fuel, gas, water and goods through pipelines and/or roads, rails and air;
- Production and procurement rates (per year) in FMCG supply chain in Italy;
- Desired staff at different segments of the FMCG supply chain.

From Eurostat data, the conversion factors for each CI were also estimated, i.e. coefficients to transform physical units, such as litres gas per year, kilograms of fuel per year, kilowatt-hours of electricity per year, litres of water per year, into a common unit of euros per year. This computational approach enabled the merging of sub-models and the definition of a unique economic indicator to measure the performance of the entire system-of-systems in terms of annual turnover.

18.5.3 Simulation Plan

Four simple crisis scenarios were defined, dealing with the disruption of each one of the CIs at the first level: (1) 50% gas disruption for 5 days; (2) 50% fuel disruption for 5 days; (3) 50% power generation disruption for 5 days; and (4) 50% water disruption for 5 days.

For each disruption scenario the four strategies were applied independently at different resilience capability levels (20%, 50%, and 90%), thus generating 48 different crisis scenarios to be simulated. The reference scenario (baseline), corresponding to the full availability of all the critical services, was finally added to complete the list of planned experiments. Due to the presence of stochastic processes in the FMCG SC, introduced by triangular distributions of lead-times, 20 replications covering a time window of 100 days (after 10 days of warmup run) were used to estimate the average performance values of each scenario.

18.6 Results of Numerical Experiments

18.6.1 Reference Scenario (No Disruption)

Under standard demand and nominal operational conditions, the Italian FMCG supply chain generates an average daily turnover of 37,673 million euros (M€), according to our model (baseline). If referred to the contribution of FMCG sector to the Italian GDP in the years 2008–2012 (INIS 2015), the absolute percentage error of our model ranges from −2.3 to +2.9%, with a mean absolute percentage error (MAPE) of −0.2%.

18.6.2 Full Disruption (Worst Case) Scenarios

The aim of the second scenario simulated is to assess the impact on the FMCG supply chain of a disruption occurring to each of the CI systems belonging to the first level, where 50% of service is lost for 5 consecutive days. Results are shown in Table 18.3. The change (Δ) in turnover and recovered turnover percentage are based on the reference scenario of no disruption (baseline turnover = 37673 M€).

It can be seen that the CI with the heaviest impact on the FMCG SC was gas, causing the major amount of turnover loss (4.6 billion Euros or 12.2% of baseline scenario in the course of 100 days). On the contrary, power generation (PG) presented the least severe consequences among the four. Fuel and water unavailability had almost similar impacts on the economic performance of the FMCG SC.

18.6.3 Disruption of CI with Different Levels of Resilience Capacity

This final step is intended to estimate the expected benefits from the application of the four strategies, in their multiple configurations, with different resilience capacity levels (20, 50 and 90%). As stated earlier, each simulation run had warm-up time of 10 days, and lasted 100 days with a 50% unavailability of a single critical service during 5 consecutive days. Results related to the disruption of the four CI systems

Table 18.3 Worst case scenarios with 5 days of CI disruptions

Disrupted CI	Fuel	Gas	PG	Water
Average turnover for 100 days [M€]	33518	33073	34373	33504
Average Δ in turnover [M€]	4155	4600	3300	4169
Average turnover loss [%]	11.0	12.2	8.8	11.1

are depicted in Figs. 18.4, 18.5, 18.6 and 18.7. The available resilience options are reported in decreasing order of effectiveness (i.e. increase in the total turnover loss in reference to the baseline). The notions used in the figures are described in the notes of Table 18.4 where a summary of the simulation results is given.

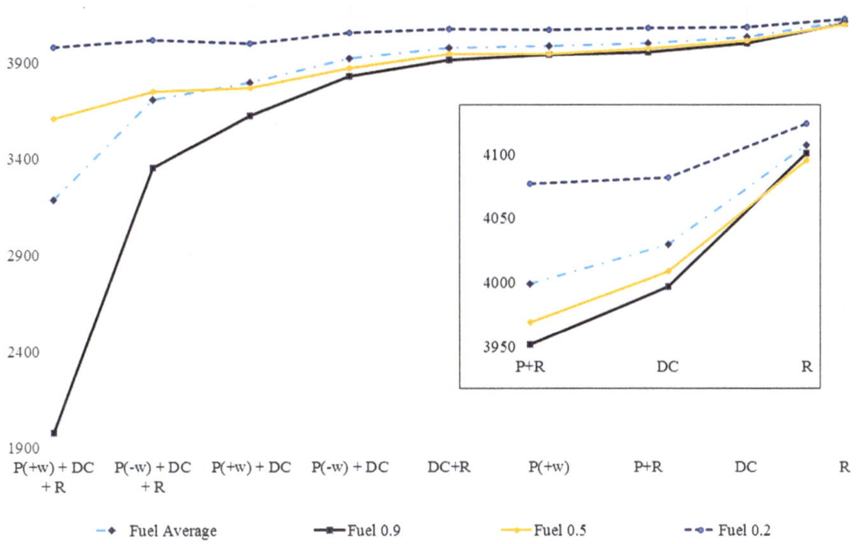

Fig. 18.4 Average change in turnover with 5-day fuel disruption at different resilience levels

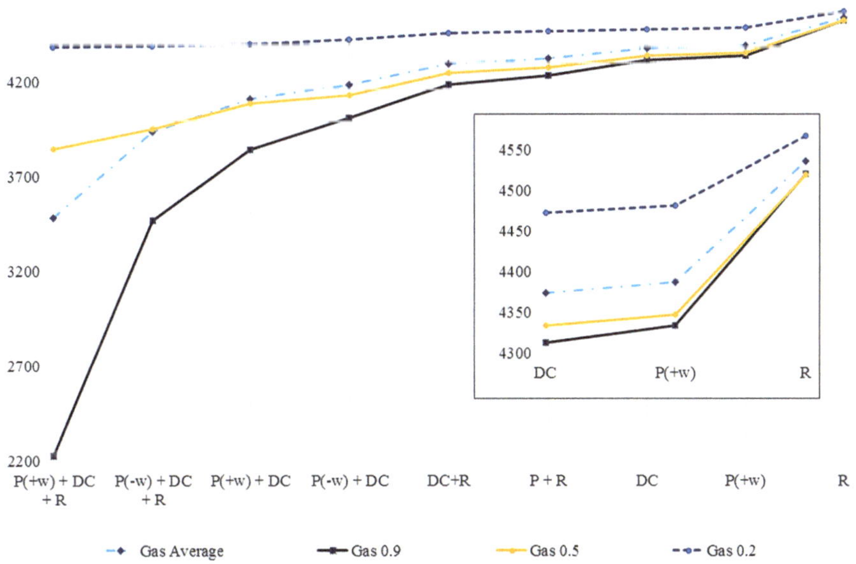

Fig. 18.5 Average change in turnover with 5-day gas disruption at different resilience levels

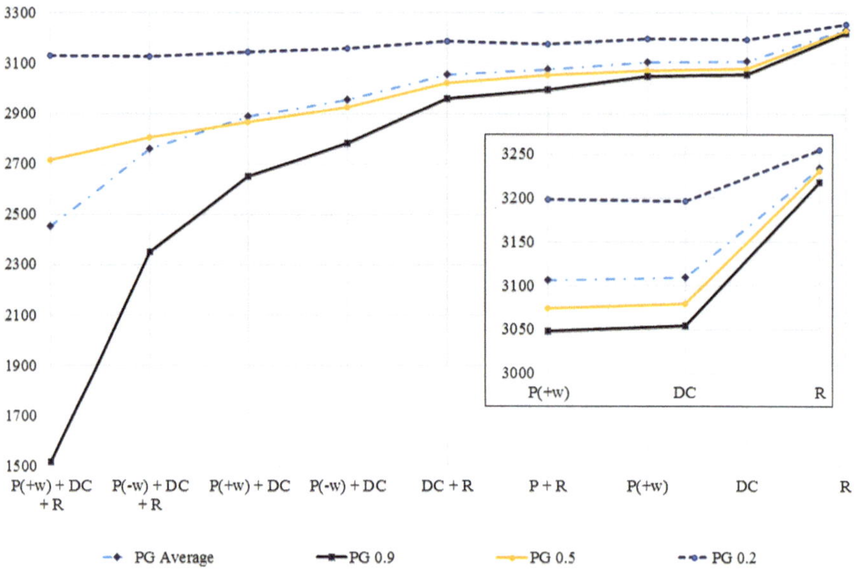

Fig. 18.6 Average change in turnover with 5-day power disruption at different resilience levels

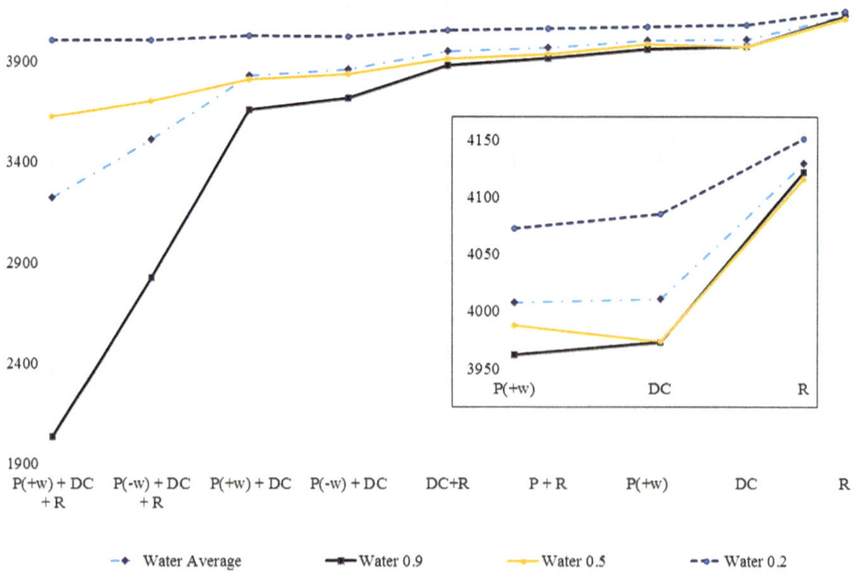

Fig. 18.7 Average change in turnover with 5-day water disruption at different resilience levels

Table 18.4 Summary of the simulation results—5 days of 50% service loss from different CIs

Actor(s) with resilience capabilities[a]	Average Δ turnover from the baseline, at different resilience capability levels (ResLev) [M €]												Average recovered turnover [%] at different resilience capability levels[b]		
	Fuel			Gas			PG			Water					
	0.9	0.5	0.2	0.9	0.5	0.2	0.9	0.5	0.2	0.9	0.5	0.2	0.9	0.5	0.2
P(+w) + DC + R	1977	3605	3976	2226	3842	4384	1514	2715	3131	2032	3630	4005	52.2%	15.0%	4.5%
P(-w) + DC + R	3352	3744	4017	3470	3950	4388	2348	2806	3126	2823	3704	4008	26.1%	12.5%	4.2%
P(+w) + DC	3619	3764	3998	3840	4084	4399	2648	2866	3145	3660	3811	4028	15.1%	10.5%	4.0%
P(-w) + DC	3826	3868	4054	4006	4127	4420	2780	2927	3157	3718	3838	4025	11.7%	9.0%	3.5%
P + R	3951	3969	4077	4230	4275	4462	2995	3056	3177	3915	3938	4064	7.0%	6.1%	2.7%
DC + R	3907	3939	4069	4183	4244	4452	2960	3023	3187	3879	3917	4057	8.0%	6.8%	2.8%
P(+w)	3936	3943	4068	4334	4347	4481	3048	3074	3198	3962	3988	4073	5.8%	5.4%	2.5%
DC	3997	4009	4082	4313	4334	4473	3054	3079	3196	3973	3974	4085	5.5%	5.1%	2.4%
R	4101	4095	4124	4520	4519	4567	3218	3231	3255	4122	4116	4151	1.6%	1.6%	0.8%

Note [a]P(+w) = Producer (with water included in the strategy); P(-w) = producer (with water not included in the strategy); *DC* Distribution Centres; *R* Retailers

[b]Percentage values calculated as the ratio of the difference between average turnover at some ResLev and worst case scenario, and difference between baseline turnover and turnover at the same ResLev

18.7 Discussion

Resilience capacity of recovering 20% does not seem to be making a big difference when applied across the different combination of actors. The recovered turnover compared to the worst situation is very small except for the power generation which showed marginally better values (compare Fig. 18.6 with Figs. 18.4, 18.5 and 18.7). The specific location of this resilience capacity level in the supply chain does not seem to bring much difference as well; it is not much different if a supply chain actor or multiple actors, upstream or downstream the supply chain, had little resilience capacity. The maximum possible turnover recovered from the worst case with ResLev = 20% (by multiple actors upstream the supply chain) on average across the disruptions in the different CI systems is only 4.5%; the lowest is 0.8% (see Table 18.4). It is to be noted that this resilience capacity equals the minimum trigger level of disruption.

When it comes to a higher level of resilience capacity (ResLev = 50%), the benefit of all the strategies are far more significant compared to the previous scenario. Multiple supply chain members upstream the supply chain with this level of resilience can recover up to an average of 15% turnover compared to the worst case. The minimum value of recovered turnover is 1.6%, when the corresponding resilience capacity is located only at the retailer.

In the best resilience scenario, involving the highest level of resilience capacity (ResLev = 90%), improvements in turnover from the worst case range from a minimum of around 1.6%, when the resilience capacity is concentrated at the retailer, to a maximum of 52% granted by a mixed allocation of the resilience capacity throughout all the three SC members, included the capacity to overcome the water shortage.

In general, the results of the study show a very high vulnerability of the FMCG SC when it is hit by the unavailability of some critical services; even with the highest (90%) resilience strategies implemented and the capacities mobilised to offset for a disruption in CI systems, the average recoverable turnover is about 52% of the potential losses. It appears that there is a structural rigidity of the FMCG SC, mainly due to the strong dependence of all transport systems on energy. The results reveal that there is only limited room for making supply chains, and KRSC in particular, more resilient against electrical blackouts and energy disruptions in general.

As expected, the average turnover loss due to CI disruptions, compared to the baseline (no disrupted scenario), is lower for higher value of resilience compared to the lower values, under all disruption scenarios and resilience strategies. This result is however limited to the benefits of resilience capacities in face of unavailable work force at a respective supply chain actor.

Resilience strategies at multiple number of actors perform better than strategies with a similar capacity level allocated at fewer or one supply chain actor only (compare Figs. 18.4, 18.5, 18.6 and 18.7). Furthermore, resilience capacities at the upstream of the supply chain (i.e. producer) are able to recover more turnover compared to a similar level of resilience capacity in the downstream. This result has at least two implications. First, SC resilience depends on a coordinated effort between different actors independently from the level of available capacity. Second, this collaborative approach to improve the SC resilience may lead to a rebalance in the value chain, since under widespread CI disruptions, retailers benefit from turnover recovery thanks to resilience capacities primarily implemented by producers and distribution centres.

Another observation is that multiple forms of resilience capacities perform better than a single type of resilience capacity at a higher level. In our case, the capacity to offset water disruption in addition to other resilience capacities gave rise to recovery almost the same turnover compared to a much higher resilience capacity without mitigation strategies against water shortage; e.g. P(+w) + DC at ResLev = 0.5 is estimated to recover 11% of turnover loss, whereas P(-w) + DC at ResLev = 0.9 is expected to recover only 12% (see Table 18.4). This observation seems further strengthening the role of interdependence relationships in a system-of-systems resilience, not only those existing between CI systems and related services, but also those influencing the effectiveness of resources allocation within the supply chain.

18.8 Conclusions

The results achieved with the present study are of relevance for both science and practice. As for the scientific contribution, the study offers original results at both methodological and content levels. Research on the analysis and modelling of the dependencies between KRSC and CI is still limited, mostly if we consider the resilience research stream. The majority of modelling techniques require a large amount of detailed data that are difficult to collect; alternative solutions, demand less data but model the non-linear dynamics of CI disruptions and the consequent spread of cascading effects in a poorly detailed way. In the present study, we tested a multimethod approach that uses a combination of SD and DES; based on the achieved results, it is possible to conclude that it represents a good trade-off and a better choice to support high-level system design or strategic decisions on resource allocation and coordination towards better system resilience. In this regard, the proposed multimethod approach expands the extant literature on system-of-systems modelling, with the aim of better supporting the vulnerability and resilience analysis of global supply chains against their multifaceted dependence on a wide set of CI systems. From a methodological point of view, further research is encouraged to offer a broader set of test cases and a systematic comparison of different modelling strategies and combinations of methods, including ABM also. Indeed, the modelling approach implemented in the present study still suffers for some limitations:

- the contribution of tactical decisions made by different actors during the disruption event, and their direct influence on the evolution of the event are not taken into consideration;

- similarly, the impact of geographical interdependencies is not accounted for, since the current model is not able to address issues related to the topology of CI systems, and the location of different supply chain facilities as well.

When these elements are the most relevant for the specific study, then ABM simulation should be adopted to model actors' behaviours at both CI and KRSC levels, so as to account for the former; network-based and flow-based approaches to CI modelling should be used to accommodate for the latter (Ouyang 2014).

Further developments at methodological level could also address:

- the extension of the simulation model to incorporate a cost index for different strategies and resilience capacities;
- the integration of a set of resilience indicators enabling a more comprehensive and detailed comparison of disruption scenarios and response strategies.

Indeed, just looking at the specific case application, there is wide room for further in-depth investigation of cascading effects between CI and the FMCG SC, to achieve a better understanding of the dynamics of bottlenecks within the FMCG SC under different scenarios and response strategies.

As for the specific application domain, with reference to the FMCG supply chain, the study offers some relevant and original insights toward a better understanding of the strength and dynamics of the coupling between KRSC and CI, and consequently on resilience improvement efforts. Firstly, the study made it clear that supply chains react in completely different ways under distributed or localised disruptions. Cascading effects within the CI layer, activated by existing interdependencies, clearly result into a dispersed impact at supply chain level despite the location and the possible limited extension of the triggering event. Consequently, the attempts to achieve higher supply chain resilience cannot concentrate on a limited number of nodes, neither on a set of isolated investments and actions. The nature and dynamics of supply chain disruptions induced by CI interdependencies call for more coordinated and collaborative resilience strategies, involving all the relevant actors of modern global supply chains. In this line, the study also gives justification and support to future research on organisational capabilities and operational coordination in the context of supply chain resilience. More specifically, further research is needed to better understand the specific roles and contributions that different actors may cover, as well as the type of support they should be granted of, within a collaborative response and recovery set up. Resilience capabilities of organisational nature, both intra- and inter-organisational, need to be better investigated and understood. Finally, larger studies are encouraged in future to overcome some of the limitations that affect the present study when it comes with modelling and quantifying the key processes and factors shaping the behaviour of CI. Indeed:

- some of the hypotheses at the basis of the CI model we adopted in the study are still simplistic, such as neglecting staff factor in power, water and gas facilities, so the assessment of critical service unavailability and the consequent turnover loss in the FMCG supply chain may not be accurate (underestimated);

- the quantification of the FMCG model was based on secondary and sector related data; to achieve better precision and reliability of results, more detailed data of confidential nature should be collected (e.g., actual stock location and product coverage, switch time and quantity between different mode of transports);

Supply chain managers may also benefit of the suggested prioritisation of resilience strategies, according to their estimated benefits, when making decisions on the amount and location of resilience capacities within KRSC, and the FMCG supply chain in particular. Again, the results of the present study strongly support managers' commitment and decisions in favour of collaborative or coordinated resilience practices among supply chain actors; as well as the adoption of advanced tools and solutions to get higher visibility of risks coming from vital services and related infrastructure.

References

Birkie, S. E., Trucco, P., & Kaulio, M. (2014). Disentangling core functions of operational resilience: A critical review of extant literature. *International Journal of Supply Chain and Operations Resilience, 1*(1), 76–103.

Brailsford, S., Churilov, L., & Dangerfield, B. (Eds.). (2014). *Discrete-event simulation and system dynamics for management decision making*. New York: Wiley.

BSI (British Standards Institute). (2015). *Security risk index*. London: BSI Supply Chain Solutions. 2015.

Clarke, L., & MacDonald, A. (2014). Copper ends slightly higher after jolt from Chile earthquake, *Wall Street Journal*, 2 April. Available at: http://www.wsj.com/articles/SB10001424052702304157204579476440226661758

Conrad, S. H., LeClaire, R. J., O'Reilly, G. P., & Uzunalioglu, H. (2006). Critical national infrastructure reliability modeling and analysis. *Bell Labs Technical Journal, 11*(3), 57–71.

Craighead, C. W., Blackhurst, J., Rungtusanatham, M. J., & Handfield, R. B. (2007). The severity of supply chain disruptions: Design characteristics and mitigation capabilities. *Decision Sciences, 38*(1), 131–156.

Fahimnia, B., Tang, C. S., Davarzani, H., & Sarkis, J. (2015). Quantitative models for managing supply chain risks: A review. *European Journal of Operational Research, 247*(1), 1–15.

Hall, P. V. (2004). 'We'd have to sink the ships': Impact studies and the 2002 West Coast port lockout. *Economic Development Quarterly, 18*(4), 354–367.

INIS (Italian National Institute of Statistics). (2015). "I.Stat", *National Accounts Data*. Available at: www.dati.istat.it

Ivanov, D., & Sokolov, B. (2013). Control and system-theoretic identification of the supply chain dynamics domain for planning, analysis and adaptation of performance under uncertainty. *European Journal of Operational Research, 224*(2), 313–323.

Ivanov, D., Sokolov, B., & Dolgui, A. (2014). The Ripple effect in supply chains: Trade-off 'efficiency-flexibility-resilience' in disruption management. *International Journal of Production Research, 52*(7), 2154–2172.

Kamalahmadi, M., & Parast, M. M. (2016). A review of the literature on the principles of enterprise and supply chain resilience: Major findings and directions for future research. *International Journal of Production Economics, 171*(1), 116–133.

Kim, Y., Chen, Y., & Linderman, K. (2015). Supply network disruption and resilience: A network structural perspective. *Journal of Operations Management, 33–34*, 43–59.

Kumar, S., & Nigmatullin, A. (2011). A system dynamics analysis of food supply chains—case study with non-perishable products. *Simulation Modelling Practice and Theory, 19*(10), 2151–2168.

MacKenzie, C. A., Santos, J. R., & Barker, K. (2012). Measuring changes in international production from a disruption: Case study of the Japanese earthquake and tsunami. *International Journal of Production Economics, 138*(2), 293–302.

McNally, R. K., Lee, S.-W., Yavagal, D., & Xiang, W.-N. (2007). Learning the critical infrastructure interdependencies through an ontology-based information system. *Environment and Planning B: Planning and Design, 34*(6), 1103–1124.

Ouyang, M. (2014). Review on modeling and simulation of interdependent critical infrastructure systems. *Reliability Engineering and System Safety, 121*, 43–60.

Owen, C., Albores, P., Greasley, A., & Love, D. (2010). Simulation in the supply chain context: Matching the simulation tool to the problem. In *Proceedings of the 2010 Operational Research Society Simulation Workshop*, pp. 229–242.

Patterson, S. (2015). Water troubles in tiny Chilean town threaten global copper supply. *Wall Street Journal*, 26 November. Available at: http://www.wsj.com/articles/scarcity-of-water-poses-challenge-for-copper-miners-1448549196

Pidd, M. (2003). *Tools for thinking: Modelling in management science* (2nd ed.). New York: Wiley.

Ponomarov, S. Y., & Holcomb, M. C. (2009). Understanding the concept of supply chain resilience. *The International Journal of Logistics Management, 20*(1), 124–143.

Rice, J. B., & Caniato, F. (2003). Building a secure and resilient supply network. *Supply Chain Management Review, 7*(5), 22–30.

Rinaldi, S. M., Peerenboom, J. P., & Kelly, T. K. (2001). Identifying, understanding, and analyzing critical infrastructure interdependencies. *IEEE Control Systems Magazine, 21*(6), 11–25.

Santella, N., Steinberg, L. J., & Parks, K. (2009). Decision making for extreme events: Modeling critical infrastructure interdependencies to aid mitigation and response planning. *Review of Policy Research, 26*(4), 409–422.

Sheffi, Y. (2007). *The resilient enterprise: Overcoming vulnerability for competitive advantage*. Cambridge, MA: MIT Press.

Sterman, J. (2000), *Business dynamics: Systems thinking and modeling for a complex world*. New York: McGraw-Hill.

Tako, A. A., & Robinson, S. (2012). The application of discrete event simulation and system dynamics in the logistics and supply chain context. *Decision Support Systems, 52*(4), 802–815.

Tang, C. S. (2006). Robust strategies for mitigating supply chain disruptions. *International Journal of Logistics Research and Applications, 9*(1), 33–45.

The Council of the European Union. (2008). Council Directive 2008/114/EC of 8 December 2008 on the indentification and designation of European critical infrastructures and the assessment of the need to improve their protection. *Official Journal of the European Union*, pp. 75–82.

World Economic Forum. (2012). *New models for addressing supply chain and transport risk*. World Economic Forum: Industry Agenda.

Wu, D., & Olson, D. L. (2008). Supply chain risk, simulation, and vendor selection. *International Journal of Production Economics, 114*(2), 646–655.

Wu, T., Huang, S., Blackhurst, J., Zhang, X., & Wang, S. (2013). Supply chain risk management: An agent-based simulation to study the impact of retail stockouts. *IEEE Transactions on Engineering Management, 60*(4), 676–686.

Yang, T., & Wu, J. (2007). The impact of transportation disruptions on performance of e-Collaboration supply chain. In L. Xu, A. Tjoa & S. Chaudhry (Eds.), *IFIP International Federation for Information Processing, Research and Practical Issues of Enterprise Information Systems II Vol. I* (Vol. 256, pp. 663–667). Boston: Springer.

MIX
Papier aus verantwortungsvollen Quellen
Paper from responsible sources
FSC® C105338

If you have any concerns about our products,
you can contact us on
ProductSafety@springernature.com

In case Publisher is established outside the EU,
the EU authorized representative is:
Springer Nature Customer Service Center GmbH
Europaplatz 3, 69115 Heidelberg, Germany

Printed by Libri Plureos GmbH
in Hamburg, Germany